The Social Origins
of Human Rights

Critical Human Rights

Series Editors
Steve J. Stern ❦ Scott Straus

Books in the series **Critical Human Rights** emphasize research that opens new ways to think about and understand human rights. The series values in particular empirically grounded and intellectually open research that eschews simplified accounts of human rights events and processes.

Is the current age of human rights activism a historical rupture? Is it the story of a vision of rights that took off in law, politics, and social action since the 1970s, and *displaced* an earlier politics of social justice? Or is human rights activism a new chapter within a longer and more continuous story of organizing for social justice? In this compelling study of front-line human rights activists and their adversaries in Barrancabermeja, Colombia's oil capital and a zone of intense dirty war conflicts, Luis van Isschot shows that the human rights movement emerged organically from a century-long experience of struggle against socioeconomic exclusion and repression. This book offers a profoundly original history of human rights in Colombia, and a critical complement and challenge to global histories that emphasize short timelines, transnational actors, and legal developments as keys to understanding human rights.

The Social Origins of Human Rights

Protesting Political Violence in Colombia's Oil Capital, 1919–2010

Luis van Isschot

The University of Wisconsin Press

The University of Wisconsin Press
1930 Monroe Street, 3rd Floor
Madison, Wisconsin 53711-2059
uwpress.wisc.edu

3 Henrietta Street, Covent Garden
London WC2E 8LU, United Kingdom
eurospanbookstore.com

Printed in the United States of America

Library of Congress Cataloging-in-Publication Data

Van Isschot, Luis, author.
The social origins of human rights: protesting political violence in Colombia's oil capital, 1919–2010 /
    Luis van Isschot.
        pages   cm — (Critical human rights)
        Includes bibliographical references and index.
        ISBN 978-0-299-29984-2 (pbk.: alk. paper)
        ISBN 978-0-299-29983-5 (e-book)
    1. Human rights—Colombia—Barrancabermeja.   2. Barrancabermeja (Colombia)—
    Social conditions.   3. Human rights movements—Colombia.   4. Colombia—
    Social conditions—1970-.   I. Title.   II. Series: Critical human rights.
JC599.C72B37   2015
332.409861'25—dc23
2014035662

To
Jordi
and
Nicolasa

Contents

Illustrations

Maps

Photos

Illustrations

Preface

Every day thousands of people travel to and from Barranca-bermeja by boat. Most come from the countryside to look for work, to sell produce and fish, or in search of safety. Water taxis known as *chalupas* and low-slung motorized canoes known as *johnsons* buzz and skip across the Magdalena River in the shadow of Colombia's largest oil refinery. Concrete ramparts extend for two kilometers along the shore. Before reaching the city, vessels originating from Puerto Wilches, Cantagallo, Puerto Berrío, Simití, or other small towns may be subject to searches by Colombian security forces, paramilitaries, or guerrillas. Barrancabermeja is the unofficial capital of a vast, resource-rich and war-torn region known as the Magdalena Medio. The Magdalena Medio is a hot and humid lowland territory that extends over an estimated thirty thousand square kilometers and includes parts of seven Colombian provinces, or *departamentos*.[1] Despite the fact that much wealth is produced in the Magdalena Medio, it has been estimated that up to 70 percent of the area's one million residents live in poverty, nearly double the national average.[2] Since the middle of the twentieth century the Magdalena Medio has also been the staging ground for insurgency and counterinsurgency operations. Economic hardship and violence have led tens of thousands of people to permanently abandon rural areas.

At a navy checkpoint just north of the refinery, travelers are questioned and registered by young conscripts. From here, it is a short journey to the municipal waterfront. Migrants then make their way up from the port area, through the congested commercial center of the city, past modest rows of apartments. Along the way they might catch a glimpse of el Cristo Petrolero (see fig. 1), Christ the oil worker, a 26-meter-high ironwork sculpture of Christ, his hands raised to the sky, erected in 1995 in the Ciénega Miramar, the marsh that separates the refinery from downtown Barranca. City buses

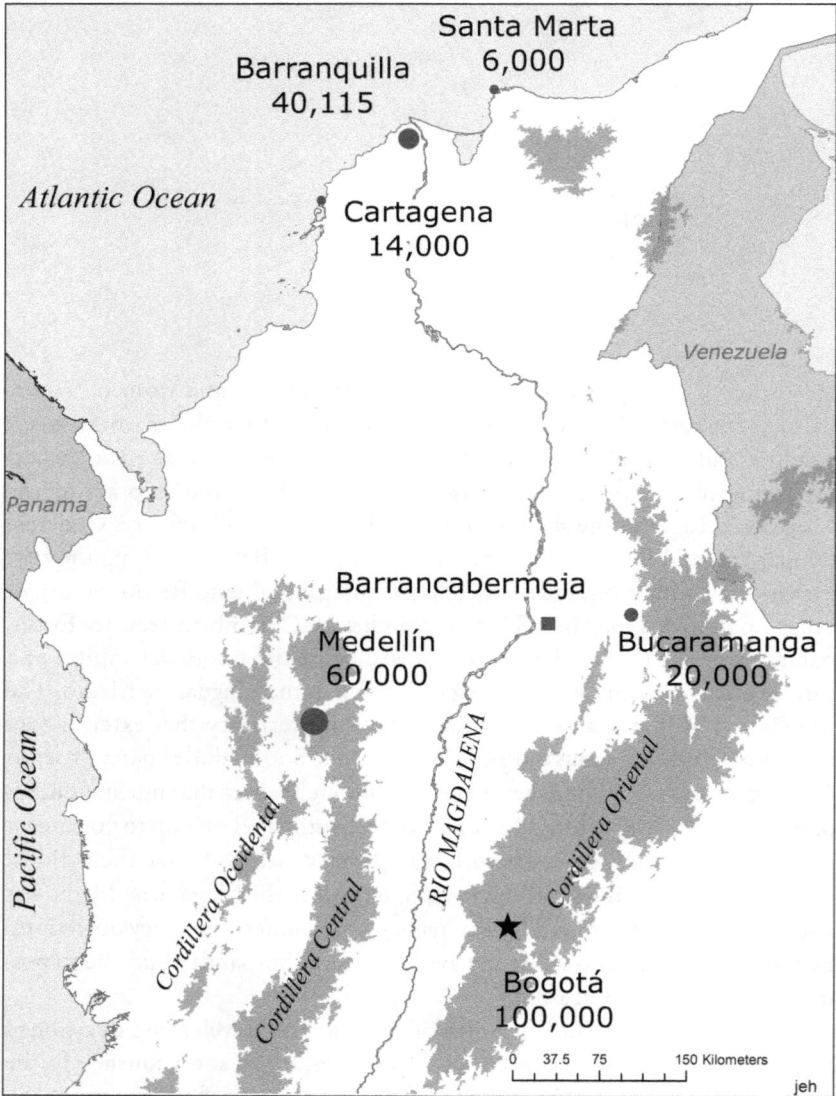

Map 1. Northern Colombia, with population figures for main urban areas, circa 1905. Source for population data: Frederick Martin, Sir John Scott Keltie, Isaac Parker Anderson Renwick, Mortimer Epstein, Sigfrid Henry Steinberg, and John Paxton, *The Statesman's Year-book*, vol. 45 (London: Macmillan and Co., 1905), 868. Map by John Harmon.

Figure 1. Christ the oil worker, el Cristo Petrolero, symbol of Barrancabermeja. Photo by the author.

and scooters rumble and grind past the oil workers' union headquarters, eventually crossing the tracks into the city's ever-expanding popular neighborhoods. The *barrios orientales* that a majority of *barranqueños* call home consist mainly of small concrete cottages, with clusters of newer wooden shacks assembled at the edges. The land on the other side of the railway overpass known as the *puente elevado* is surprisingly verdant yet physically isolated from the more prosperous city built with the proceeds of the oil industry.

Since the early twentieth century, Barranca has also been connected to Bogotá and the outside world by air. When you arrive by plane, the first thing that hits you is the heat. Humidity fills the cabin of the Avianca Airlines twin propeller Fokker 50 as you descend toward the lush valley below. Barranca has an average temperature of 30 degrees Celsius (86 degrees Fahrenheit), but the mercury often exceeds 45 degrees by midday. Unlike the coastal areas of Colombia, Barranca is bathed in thick wet air. It is located five hundred kilometers (311 miles) from the sea. There is scarcely any breeze, and the leaves hang motionless on the trees. The groaning, silt-laden Magdalena River affords little respite. Managers and engineers working for the oil industry have been coming from the capital, and beyond, since Jersey Standard arrived in 1919. Under central government control since 1961, Barranca has remained the country's most important industrial center. Through the last decades of the twentieth century the city became a major site of armed conflict, and of the official repression of social activism. Since that time, oil company personnel have been joined on flights to Barranca by small groups of human rights workers.

I lived in Barrancabermeja from January through December 1998. At the time I was working as a volunteer with Peace Brigades International (PBI), a human rights organization founded on the principles of nonviolence that has worked in support of threatened Latin American popular movements since 1981. We were sometimes described as "unarmed bodyguards," and our work largely consisted of accompanying human rights defenders in their daily rounds.[3] We spent many hours in the offices of local civil society organizations. When an activist received direct individual death threats, we would spend twenty-four hours a day at his or her side. We also undertook regular fact-finding trips to towns along the Magdalena River. Everywhere we went there were ordinary citizens, priests, trade unionists, peasant organizers, attorneys, municipal councillors, and schoolteachers who formed a regional network of human rights activists.

While in Colombia I met frequently with National Police, army, and navy officials engaged in counterinsurgency work. Some of these encounters took place in small villages, in bunkers pitted by machine gun fire. Young soldiers told us that they had to travel in pairs, fully armed, to make the short trip across town to call their families and girlfriends from the local Telecom office. I also met with high-ranking officers, such as General Fernando Millán, the once-indicted paramilitary organizer who was commander of the Fifth Brigade of the Colombian army in the city of Bucaramanga. As he spoke angrily about human rights activists from Barranca, denouncing individuals by name as bandits and subversives, I studied what appeared to be a photo of him posing with the Chilean dictator Augusto Pinochet on the wall behind his desk. It was moments like these that made the dangers of human rights work clear.

On the evening of May 16, 1998, in Barrancabermeja, a large group of armed men wearing military fatigues killed seven people and abducted another twenty-five. Miguel, a PBI volunteer from Spain, called to tell us the news. At the time he was accompanying Osiris Bayter, then president of the Regional Corporation for the Defense of Human Rights (CREDHOS). The details were not yet clear, and nobody knew exactly how many people had been killed. Our fears and disbelief were fed by rumors and misinformation. The list of dead young men and women was updated by word of mouth. Over the next week Barranca was gripped by the largest protests in a generation. We spent five days and nights accompanying activists from different local groups as they stood vigil by the barricades that had been set up at strategic points around town. Taking turns at the Peace Brigades office, we wrote reports about everything that was happening and sent them to human rights groups around the world, including Amnesty International, Human Rights Watch, the Washington Office on Latin America, and the Inter-Church Committee for Human Rights in Latin America.

The 16 de mayo massacre and ensuing civic strike took place at a time when Colombian human rights activists were increasing their international profile as critics of the United States' revived war on drugs. Prior to the attacks on the World Trade Center on September 11, 2001, Colombia was a leading foreign policy concern of the U.S. government. In June 2000 a $1.3 billion U.S. military aid package was signed into law by President Bill Clinton following more than a year of public debate. Barranca was poised to become a focal point of international concern. Human rights groups sought to forestall the so-called Plan Colombia by exposing links between the Colombian armed forces and paramilitary death squads. To do so, many drew upon the history of Barranca as a cautionary tale.[4] Longtime Colombia observer Adam Isaacson wrote following a visit to the area in 2001: "Barrancabermeja is hard to pronounce, and very little of last year's billion-dollar package of U.S. military aid for Colombia will end up anywhere near this city. But as Washington edges closer to Colombia's long, bloody conflict, 'Barranca' offers a preview of the nightmare to come."[5] As Plan Colombia was being discussed in the U.S. Congress, dozens of Colombian human rights activists made trips to Washington, DC, to convince lawmakers not to approve what amounted to a thinly veiled counterinsurgency plan. Liberal-minded Democrats insisted on humanitarian assistance for the thousands of people certain to be displaced by the Plan Colombia–funded military push into the rebel-controlled south.[6] Opportunists jostled for arms contracts. The number of international organizations present in the Magdalena Medio would increase visibly during those months.

Despite the attention being paid to Barrancabermeja, human rights workers would face terrible new challenges. As Plan Colombia went into effect, peace talks between the government of Andrés Pastrana and the Revolutionary Armed Forces of Colombia faltered, and political violence in the Magdalena Medio escalated. I left Barrancabermeja in December 1998, but continued to work for PBI's Colombia Project until 2003. During my tenure with the organization, I traveled regularly between Washington, DC, Ottawa, and Bogotá to help rally civil society groups, diplomats, lawmakers, and ordinary citizens to the defense of human rights workers. I was able to return to Barranca a number of times during the final months of the eventual paramilitary conquest of the city in 2001. Along the way, I learned that long before Barranca became known as one of the most violent cities in one of the most violent countries in the world, it had been a model of social movement organizing. When I returned to conduct the research for this book in 2005, I found Barranca transformed. The paramilitaries now exerted near hegemonic control over the politics and economy of the city. Frustrated by the setbacks that they had suffered, yet determined to neutralize the ongoing threat of violence, many of the activists with whom I spoke were in a reflective mood. During our conversations I learned extraordinary things about the city's popular movements, and their relation to the recent context of guerrillas, paramilitaries, and state security forces. The multiple threads of a long history of social activism unspooled as we explored personal journeys through hope, disillusionment, and survival.[7]

One of the people I interviewed while conducting research for this book was CREDHOS's president David Ravelo, who was arrested and imprisoned on September 14, 2010. On December 7, 2012, David Ravelo was sentenced to eighteen years and three months for aggravated homicide. Margaret Sekaggya, former United Nations Special Rapporteur on the Situation of Human Rights Defenders (2008–2014), has stated that the case against Ravelo was part of a pattern of legal harassment of human rights advocates in Colombia.[8] Dozens of Colombian and international human rights organizations and experts have denounced irregularities in the judicial process to which Ravelo was subjected. Many observers have pointed out that the case against Ravelo, like those against other social activists, hinged on the declarations of demobilized paramilitaries who traded their testimony for reduced sentences under the terms of the controversial 2005 Justice and Peace law. The key witness against Ravelo was the paramilitary commander Mario Jaimes Mejía, alias El Panadero, who is currently serving time for his part in the massacre of thirty-two people in Barrancabermeja on May 16, 1998.[9] In 2014, investigations were announced against El Panadero on charges of fraud and false testimony, in relation to the case of David Ravelo, and kidnapping, torture, and sexual assault, in relation to the case of the journalist Jineth Bedoya. Since his arrest, David Ravelo has been the subject of death threats and intimidation.

The experiences of the many activists with whom I spoke, and the questions they raised, were the inspiration for this book. I have been very fortunate to have had the opportunity to research, write, and teach about the roots of human rights movements in Latin America. This book was developed out of the creative tension between scholarship and practice.

As I write, most of the people I interviewed and consulted continue to work for social change in Barranca, such as the women of the Organización Femenina Popular, shown on the front cover in a march in Bogotá in 2002.

Acknowledgments

I would like to thank everyone in Colombia who shared their stories and expertise with me, many whose names appear in the pages that follow, and many others as well. Very special thanks to CREDHOS for generously allowing me into their archive.

I also thank Miguel Fernández, Glenis Pérez, Mirjam Koppe, Elena Rey, Camilo Castellanos, Eleanor Douglas, Katia Urteaga, and Peace Brigades International for their hospitality and support, in Bogotá and Barrancabermeja. Thank you as well to all of my Colombian friends, teachers, and mentors, especially Rosa Pinzón, Amanda Romero, Francisco Campos, Régulo Madero, Yolanda Becerra, Luisa Serrano, Leila Celis, Matilde Vargas, Pedro Galindo, Alfonso Torres Duarte, and Mauricio Archila. Thanks to Barrancabermeja's extraordinary community of scholars, especially Rafael Velásquez, who has brought to light the story of the Yareguíes indigenous people. Thanks as well to the local historians Jorge Nuñez, Fernando Acuña, and Germán Plata. My gratitude is also due to William Mancera for his assistance conducting research in the libraries of Bogotá.

Thank you to Catherine LeGrand for her energy and wisdom. When I lived in Colombia in 1998, several years before I began my PhD, a friend of mine who taught history at the Universidad de la Paz in Barrancabermeja told me about Catherine LeGrand. He had never met her, but said she had written a *clásico* of Colombian history, and that I absolutely had to look her up when I got back home to Montreal. I could never have imagined just how significant his advice would prove.

Thanks to Winifred Tate and Mary Roldán for their in-depth feedback and support. Also thank you to Nancy Appelbaum for her immensely generous comments on the manuscript. Thank you to Aviva Chomsky for her feedback and encouragement.

At the University of Wisconsin Press I want to thank Gwen Walker, Sheila McMahon, and Steve J. Stern. It has been an immense pleasure working with UW Press, and I am deeply indebted to everyone who provided me with advice, editorial support, and encouragement. Thanks as well to Matthew Cosby, Carla Marolt, and all of the other individuals who have worked with me toward the culmination of this project.

Throughout much of the writing process I was closely accompanied and supported by John Jairo Bedoya, who provided in-depth comments on the manuscript. John Jairo is a great friend, a formidable academic, and a tireless activist.

At the University of Connecticut I have many people to thank for their support of this project and their friendship, especially Jason Chang and Mark Overmyer-Velázquez, and many other colleagues at the Department of History, the Human Rights Institute, and El Instituto: Institute of Latina/o, Caribbean, and Latin American Studies. Special thanks to Orlando Deavila for his research assistance and professionalism. Jason Chang has been a great source of energy for me these past two years, and I am hugely appreciative of his comments on draft chapters. I am also indebted to John E. Harmon, emeritus professor at Central Connecticut State University, for creating original maps for this book.

Thank you to my parents, Joyce Canfield and Carlos van Isschot, my sister Andina van Isschot, and Bernard Pelletier. Also thanks to my sister Isabel van Isschot. My mother's love, intellect, and strength are quite simply boundless. I think that my father must know, but it bears repeating here, that he has inspired me with his love of Latin American history and his rebellious spirit. In this book I have tried to honor a vision of social and political justice in Latin America that I first learned at home. Thanks as well to the late Christopher Conway. Our many conversations about his experiences as a member of a Scottish tank crew in World War II and an advocate for prisoners' rights in the Canadian penal system have had a big impact on my thinking about the politics of remembrance, the costs of war, and human dignity. Thank you for being a wonderful storyteller and an incorrigible nonconformist.

In Washington, DC, thanks to Michael Evans and Carlos Osorio at the National Security Archive at George Washington University, and Viviana Kristicevic and Michael Camilleri at the Center for Justice and International Law (CEJIL). At McGill University, special thanks to Daviken Studnicki-Gizbert and Stephen J. Toope for their generosity and support. Thank you as well to the inimitable Samuel J. Noumoff. Thank you to all of the staff at McGill's Department of History. At Concordia University I would like to thank everyone with whom I worked on the Montreal Life Stories Project, particularly my fellow staff members Anna Sheftel and Sandra Gasana, as well as Stacey Zembrzycki and Steven High. Steven High and the Life Stories teams of community researchers helped me to see my work through a critical lens.

This project was made possible through the support of the Fonds québécois de recherche sur la société et la culture (FQRSC), the McGill Centre for Developing Area Studies (now the Institute for the Study of International Development), the McGill University Department of History, and the Social Science and Humanities Research Council (SSHRC) through Cristina Rojas at Carleton University.

Thank you to Jesús Abad Colorado for the beautiful cover image.

My many friends and colleagues at Peace Brigades International deserve recognition, and this project would have been inconceivable without them. If there are any insights in this book that ring true, it is because the clearest arguments are those that have already passed the test of consensus. This history therefore belongs to the dozens of Peace Brigades members who have spent time in Barrancabermeja over the years. On a research visit in 2006 I participated in an exercise of historical memory during which more than a dozen Peace Brigades members shared stories of this most extraordinary of Colombian cities. I hope that I have captured a small part of this collective wisdom in the pages that follow.

This book could never have been completed without the love and support I receive from Stephanie Conway. She has shared my passion for this work. Above all else, Stephanie and I have shared the joys of parenting our two beautiful children, Jordi and Nicolasa, to whom I have dedicated this book.

Abbreviations

AAA	Alianza Americana Anticomunista (American Anti-communist Alliance)
ACCU	Autodefensas Unidas de Córdoba and Urabá (United Self-Defense Forces of Córdoba and Urabá)
ACDEGAM	Asociación Campesina de Agricultores y Ganaderos del Magdalena Medio (Association of Peasant Farmers and Ranchers of the Middle Magdalena)
ACMM	Autodefensas Campesinas del Magdalena Medio (Peasant Self Defense Forces of the Middle Magdalena)
ACVC	Asociación Campesina del Valle Cimitarra (Peasant Association of the Cimitarra Valley)
AGN	Archivo General de la Nación (Colombian National Archive)
ANUC	Asociación Nacional de Usuarios Campesinos (National Association of Peasant Users)
ASFADDES	Asociación de Familiares de Desaparcidos-Detenidos (Association of Families of the Detained-Disappeared)
ASODESAMUBA	Asociación de Desplazados del Municipio de Barranca-bermeja (Association of the Displaced in the Municipality of Barrancabermeja)
ASORVIN	Asociación Regional Victimas de la Violencia en el Magdalena Medio (Regional Association of the Victims of Violence of the Middle Magdalena)
AUC	Autodefensas Unidas de Colombia (United Self-Defense Forces of Colombia)
AUSAC	Autodefensas Unidas de Santander y Sur de Cesar (United Self-Defense Forces of Santander and Sur de Cesar)

CAJAR	Corporación Colectivo de Abogados José Alvear Restrepo (José Alvear Restrepo Lawyers' Collective)
CEJIL	Centro para la Justicia y el Derecho Internacional (Center for International Justice and Law)
CINEP	Centro de Investigación y Educación Popular (Center for Research and Popular Education)
CNRR	Comisión Nacional de Reparación y Reconciliación (National Reparation and Reconciliation Commission)
CODHES	La Consultoría para los Derechos Humanos y el Desplazamiento (Consultancy on Human Rights and Displacement)
CONVIVIR	Cooperativas de Vigilancia y Seguridad Privada (Private Security Cooperatives)
CREDHOS	Corporación Regional para la Defensa de los Derechos Humanos (Regional Corporation for the Defense of Human Rights, formerly the Regional Committee for the Defense of Human Rights)
CSTC	Confederación Sindical de Trabajadores de Colombia (National Union Federation of Colombia)
CUT	Central Unitaria de Trabajadores (Central Union of Workers)
DANE	Departamento Administrativo Nacional de Estadística (National Administrative Department of Statistics)
DAS	Departamento Administrativo de Seguridad (Administrative Security Department)
DIJIN	Dirección de Instrucción Criminal (Central Directorate of the Judicial Police and Intelligence)
Ecopetrol	Empresa Colombiana de Petróleos (Colombian Petroleum Company)
ELN	Ejército de Liberación Nacional (National Liberation Army)
EPL	Ejército Popular de Liberación (Popular Liberation Army)
FAM	Frente Amplio del Magdalena Medio (Middle Magdalena Broad Front)
FARC-EP	Fuerzas Armadas Revolucionarias de Colombia-Ejército Popular (Popular Revolutionary Armed Forces of Colombia-People's Army)
FEDEPETROL	Federación de Trabajadores del Petróleo (Federation of Petroleum Workers)

FILA	Frente de Izquierda Liberal Auténtico (Authentic Liberal Leftist Front)
FUNPROCEP	Fundación para la Promoción de la Cultura y la Educación Popular (Foundation for the Promotion of Popular Education and Culture)
ILSA	Instituto de Servicios Legales Alternativos (Institute for Alternative Legal Services)
IPC	Instituto Popular de Capacitación (Institute for Popular Training)
IPS	Institute for Policy Studies
JACs	Juntas de Acción Comunal (Community Action Councils)
JUCO	Juventud Comunista Colombiana (Colombian Communist Youth)
M-19	Movimiento 19 de Abril (April 19 Movement)
MAS	Muerte a Secuestradores (Death to Kidnappers)
MRL	Movimiento Revolucionario Liberal (Liberal Revolutionary Movement)
OAS	Organization of American States
OFP	Organización Femenina Popular (Popular Women's Organization)
PBI	Peace Brigades International
PCC	Partido Comunista de Colombia (Communist Party of Colombia)
PSR	Partido Socialista Revolucionario (Socialist Revolutionary Party)
SIJIN	Seccional de Policía Judicial e Investigación (Local Branch of the Judicial and Investigative Police)
UIS	Universidad Industrial de Santander (Industrial University of Santander)
UP	Union Patriótica (Patriotic Union)
USAID	United States Agency for International Development
USO	Unión Sindical Obrera (United Workers Union)
WOLA	Washington Office on Latin America

Chronology
of Barrancabermeja History

1905	Roberto De Mares gains rights to Barranca oil concession
1916	Drilling begins by Tropical Oil Company
1919	Tropical Oil Company sold to Standard Oil of New Jersey
1921	Refinery built at Barranca
1922	Incorporation of Municipality of Barrancabermeja
1924	First major oil strike
	Strike leaders arrested and prosecuted by military tribunal
1926	Barranca-Cartagena pipeline completed
1927	Second major oil strike
1929	"Bolchevique" uprising in Santander and Tolima
1935	Third major oil strike
1938	Fourth major oil strike
1948	Fifth major oil strike
	Uprising following murder of Jorge Eliécer Gaitán: *La comuna de Barranca*
1950	Strike for nationalization of Colombian oil production
1951	Drilling operations nationalized
1958	Declaration of Sitges: end of La Violencia and start of National Front
1960	Unión Sindical Obrera "solidarity strike" with oil workers in other regions
1961	Barranca refinery nationalized
1963	First major oil strike in thirteen years
	First *paro cívico* for social rights and local development
1964	Ejército de Liberación Nacional first military action in Magdalena Medio
1967	Establishment of the National Association of Peasant Users (ANUC)

1968	The FARC opens a front in the southern Magdalena Medio
1970	Conservative candidate Misael Pastrana Borero elected president
1971	Oil workers' strike and occupation of refinery
	Court martial of strike leaders
	Split in national peasant organization ANUC
1972	Organización Femenina Popular established
1973	Army carries out Operación Anorí against the Ejército de Liberación Nacional
1975	*Paro cívico* for public services and land for peasants
	Establishment of Barrio Primero de Mayo through land invasion
1976	Magdalena Medio declared a "war zone" by national government
1977	Series of short strikes by oil workers
	Oil workers' strike lasting forty-three days
	Military mayor named to Barranca
	National *paro cívico*
1978	Formation of "self-defense" group that would become the Autodefensas Campesinas del Magdalena Medio (ACMM)
	Liberal candidate Julio César Turbay Ayala elected president
1980	First evidence of human rights abuses by paramilitary groups
1981	Formation of Muerte a Secuestradores (MAS) in southern Magdalena Medio
1982	First human rights protests in the Magdalena Medio, organized out of Puerto Berrío
1983	*Paro cívico por el agua* (civil strike for potable water)
	Creation of Coordinadora Popular civil society coalition
1984	Massacre of Vuelta Acuña, followed by mass displacement to Barranca
1985	Assassination of ELN cofounder and social activist Ricardo Lara Parada
1986	Assassination of Patriotic Union party congressman Leonardo Posada
1987	Grenade attack on three members of Patriotic Union party
	Paro cívico to protest attacks against Patriotic Union party
	Murder of fourteen-year-old Sandra Rondón
	First major human rights protest (*Paro cívico por la vida*)
	Paro del noroirente regional peasant protests
	Creation of Regional Corporation for the Defense of Human Rights (CREDHOS)
	Organización Femenina Popular becomes independent from Catholic Church

1988	*Paro cívico* to protest murder of labor leader Manuel Gustavo Chacón
	Peasant march and protest marking first anniversary of *paro del nororiente*
	Massacre of peasants by Colombian army at Llana Caliente
	Paro cívico to protest murder of labor leader Hamet Consuegra
	I General Assembly of CREDHOS
1989	First Regional Human Rights Forum hosted by CREDHOS
	La Rochela massacre of twelve Colombian government judicial officials by military/paramilitary forces
	Paro cívico to protest murder of Patriotic Union city councillor Orlando Higuita
	Establishment of the Albergue Campesino shelter for displaced peasants
1990	Creation of Human Rights Committee of Sabana de Torres, Santander
	II General Assembly of CREDHOS
1991	Creation of the Colombian Naval Intelligence Network
	Oil workers' strike during collective bargaining
1992	III General Assembly of CREDHOS
	Six members of CREDHOS exiled
	Paro cívico to protest murder of city councillor and newspaper publisher Ismael Jaimes
1994	Peace Brigades International establishes permanent presence in Barranca
1997	Marcha Campesina peasant march from Magdalena Medio to Cartagena
1998	May 16 Massacre in *suroriente* (seven killed, twenty-five disappeared)
	Founding of Barranca branch of Association of Families of the Detained-Disappeared
	Conservative candidate Andrés Pastrana Arango elected president
	Occupation of major Barrancabermeja public buildings by thousands of peasants from war-torn rural Magdalena Medio during Marchas Campesinas
	Exile of CREDHOS president Osiris Bayter
1999	Funding for Plan Colombia approved by U.S. Congress
2001	Paramilitary siege of Barrancabermeja
2002	Election of Álvaro Uribe Vélez as president of Colombia

2003	Coordinadora Popular civil society coalition is dissolved
	Creation of NGO Corporación Región by former CREDHOS directors
	Establishment of the Espacio de trabajadoras y trabajadores de derechos humanos del Magdalena Medio
2005	Establishment of state-run National Commission for Reconciliation and Reparations
	Establishment of the Movimiento Nacional de Víctimas de Crímenes de Estado by a coalition of Colombian human rights groups, including CREDHOS
2010	Arrest of CREDHOS president David Ravelo

The Social Origins
of Human Rights

Introduction

"My basic training took place in the street"

CREDHOS's birth was not accidental. It was born in the heat of everything that was happening at the time, on the one hand the violence, and on the other hand the efforts to build an infrastructure worthy of Barrancabermeja. . . . Social movements were on the threshold of a very important struggle.

Rafael Gómez Serrano, human rights activist[1]

Paro Cívico por la Vida

The May 2, 1987, murder of fourteen-year-old Sandra Rondón by paramilitary gunmen in Barrancabermeja inspired the first general strike for human rights in Colombian history. Rondón was on her way to church on a quiet Sunday in the central neighborhood of Torcoroma when two men pulled up on a motorcycle. The man riding on the rear opened fire at close range with a 9 mm pistol. Struck multiple times, she died instantly.[2] Rondón had recently been identified by local media as a key witness to an attack on three left-wing political activists. Two weeks earlier, a hand grenade had been tossed into a crowded ice cream parlor, injuring eight people, including Rondón's younger brother.[3] Hers was not the first murder in the dirty war in Barranca.[4] But the killing of Sandra Rondón shocked local residents as only the death of an innocent child can, and she immediately became a symbol of the city's struggle for human rights. While local elected officials and social movements

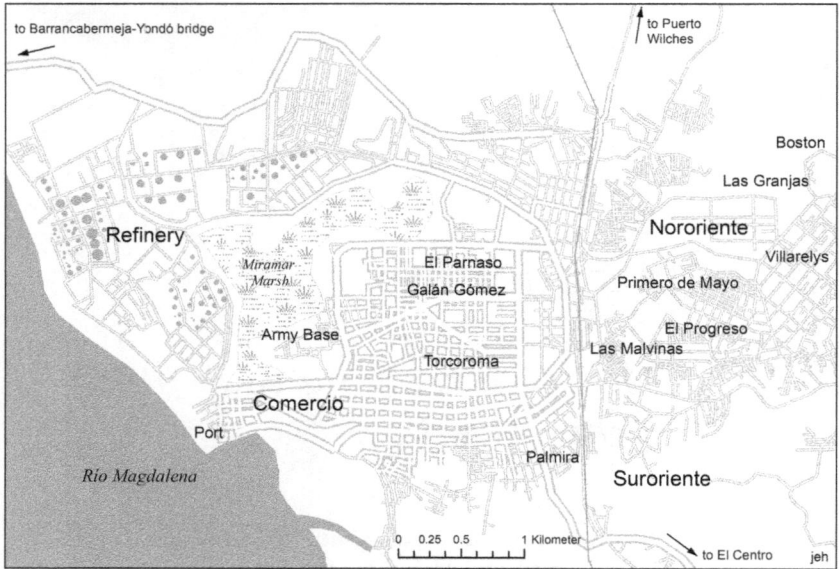

Map 2. Barrancabermeja, selected neighborhoods, refinery, downtown, and northeastern *barrios*, circa 1998. Map by John Harmon.

denounced Rondón's murder, there was no response from Bogotá. Catholics, Communists, Liberals, trade unionists, and community organizers in Barranca then staged a mass demonstration, as they had dozens of times before, to demand that the national government guarantee fair wages and public services such as water, education, and health care. This time, however, they called for the protection of civilians from violence.

The Barrancabermeja-based Regional Committee for the Defense of Human Rights (CREDHOS) was established at a time when military and paramilitary repression threatened to reverse hard-fought gains made by local popular organizations. In the city a civic-popular movement had brought together the forces of labor, progressive political parties, and community groups. Barranca activists' confidence that they were close to achieving genuine social and political change was buoyed by dynamics being played out at the national level. Through the mid-1980s a record number of Colombians took to the streets to claim a wide range of rights.[5] Colombians organized forty-seven citizen-led general strikes, or *paros cívicos*, in 1987. That was more than double the already impressive yearly average of *paros cívicos* during the previous decade.[6] The year CREDHOS was founded was also the cruelest in Colombia's history since the end of La Violencia.[7] Colombian authorities estimated that armed conflict had resulted in 2,500 deaths and 200 disappearances in what the national news media dubbed "The Year of the Dirty War."[8] There would be around 250 politically motivated homicides in Barranca alone in 1987.[9] As many of the city's most prominent social and labor leaders were killed, human rights activism emerged as the dominant paradigm of popular protest.

Historic struggles for social justice provided Barranca's human rights activists with the bases to muster large numbers of citizens. As historian Mauricio Archila writes: "Civic movements in the 1960s and 1970s demonstrated the radical implications of people taking an interest in their own municipality."[10] The *paro cívico* or "civic strike" as practiced by popular movements in Colombia was an intentional combination of the tactics used during industrial actions, urban land invasions, and peasant marches by workers, squatters, and poor rural farmers over previous decades. *Paros cívicos* entailed the stoppage of all commercial activity, the occupation of city streets, and the staging of mass rallies in public plazas. In this regard, *paros cívicos* were different from the strikes led by oil workers, which focused on conditions inside the refinery. Peasant movements were the first to regularly use what sociologist Leon Zamosc has termed "collective bargaining by disruption" for the purposes of forcing high-level talks between local communities and the national government.[11] Through *marchas campesinas* organized since the 1960s, which often culminated with the takeover of regional urban centers by thousands of protestors, peasant groups demonstrated that the mass mobilization of ordinary citizens could draw high-level officials into negotiations over land title, social services, and economic development. The influx of poor rural people into Barranca, notably politicized peasants fleeing war-affected areas, inspired new urban social movements along these same lines. The civic campaigns for social justice in Barranca in the 1970s would eventually become a model for the campaigns for human rights of the 1980s, and beyond.

Protestors took advantage of Barranca's unique urban topography. There was only one main road into the city and just a handful of routes linking the highly segregated central and eastern districts. A *paro cívico* would begin with groups of young people gathering simultaneously at two main strategic points within the city. One was an overpass spanning the railway line that divides Barranca. On the western side is the planned, formal Barrancabermeja. On the eastern side are the *barrios orientales*, or eastern neighborhoods, that since the early 1960s have been the site of organized land invasions by poor migrants. Known as the *puente elevado*, this bridge was the main road connecting these two halves. The other key strategic point was the As de Copas, an intersection situated at the top of a rise at the southern edge of the main urban area, named for a convenience store at this location. Also of strategic importance was the

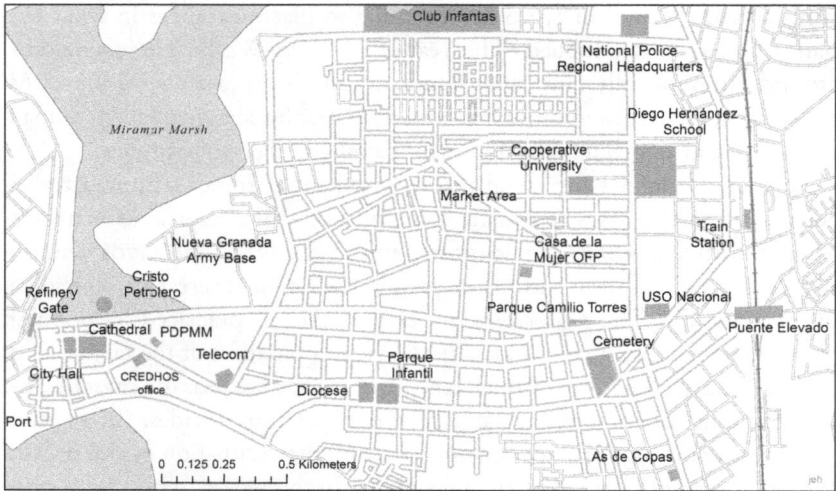

Map 3. Popular landmarks, social movement offices, and main streets in central Barrancabermeja, circa 1998. Map by John Harmon.

fork in the road leading out of town toward Bucaramanga, to the east, and Bogotá, to the south. This point is known as El Retén, for the old security forces' checkpoint located there, complete with a heavy boom gate. Though somewhat isolated, this position was narrow, and could be held by a small group of protestors. By setting fire to rubber tires and other debris at two or more of these points, *paro cívico* organizers could effectively contain all movement within the city until exhaustion set in, or the army showed up in large numbers.

The 1987 *paro cívico por la vida*, a protest against political violence staged in the wake of fourteen-year-old Sandra Rondón's murder, was exceptional because of its scale, its spontaneity, and its singular focus on human rights. The first large *paros cívicos* organized in Barranca during the 1970s often coincided with rounds of collective bargaining by oil workers, addressed long-standing grievances about public services, and required weeks of preparation. By contrast, the *paro cívico por la vida* and other human rights protests were carried out in direct response to specific repressive actions, and entailed relatively little notice. An organizing committee was convened by social movement leaders the morning after Rondón's murder. However, several hours before the *comité de paro* could send its members to blockade the city center, groups of young people had already proceeded to the usual meeting places.[12] Francisco Campos, a lifelong activist born and raised in Barrancabemeja, recalls the first *paros cívicos* for human rights in the late 1980s as exhilarating experiments in popular democracy. Campos, still a teenager at the time, was completely engrossed by the city's protest movement: "We all took risks. We were a bit irresponsible. We were still young, but totally convinced of what we were doing, nobody made us do anything, nobody manipulated us. We didn't sleep. We participated in the *paro cívico* from start to finish. We ended up exhausted, but it was happiness. This was the best training we had as young people. I was educated there, and afterward I went to university, and I got a degree in human rights. But my basic training took place in the street."[13] The *paro cívico* in response to Sandra Rondón's murder lasted three days and involved tens of thousands of people. The lack of constraints described by Campos, the shedding of inhibitions, was part of the ethos of *paros cívicos*, generally. The outpouring of the *paro cívico por la vida* was a harbinger of the permanent state of unrest into which many activists in the city were about to plunge.

Sandra Rondón's murder galvanized a broad cross-section of society in Barranca, and beyond. Local civic groups, the oil workers' union, and elected officials were all present at the barricades set up at strategic entry points to the city. So too were the guerrillas. And so Barranca's human rights movement was born: rife with divergent interests and contested meanings. Peasant organizations, which were actually the first to sound the alarm that massive violations were being carried out by security forces and their paramilitary allies, were also among the first to question whether taking to the streets to demand basic human rights offered a way forward. Were human rights too politically narrow? As Communist Party intellectual and head of the Bogotá-based Permanent Committee for the Defense of Human Rights, Hernando Hurtado, observed at the time: "Unlike previous protests, this one did not make economic or social demands, only a call for the right to life."[14] A historic mobilization of peasants, called the Paro del Nororiente, conceived as a mass exodus from rural areas around Barranca, was being planned at the time of Sandra Rondón's murder. Some peasant leaders were worried about exhausting their membership and testing the patience of the wider community, including the people living in towns and cities who would host thousands of peasants, in public parks, schools, and churches. In the end, both protests took place, and peasant groups were present at both. In the year following Sandra Rondón's murder, activists in Barranca would organize eight more *paros cívicos* in favor of human rights. In addition to peasant movements, which had been denouncing human rights violations for several years prior, the oil workers union, Catholic Church, Organización Femenina Popular women's organization, and others began organizing around human rights on their own terms, striking specialized human rights subcommittees and publishing urgent actions.

Human Rights as Social Protest

This book examines why, how, and with what impact people living in conflict areas organize collectively to assert human rights. Thousands of people have been killed in Barrancabermeja as a consequence of direct orders given and carried out by the Colombian armed forces and their paramilitary allies, on the one hand, and leftist rebels, on the other.[15] Barrancabermeja-based social activists rallied around the cause of human rights in the midst of an armed conflict in which the majority of victims were civilians. Paramilitary units working in collaboration with state security forces had been undertaking repressive actions against popular movements in the southern Magdalena Medio region since the early 1980s. At the same time, guerrilla groups expanded their influence and control over strategic territories. In response to paramilitary attacks against peasants living in areas under guerrilla influence, tens of thousands of people abandoned the war-torn countryside, seeking refuge in shantytowns on the outskirts of Barrancabermeja. By the middle of the decade, homicides and forced disappearances were being carried out on the streets of the city, targeting social and political leaders and activists. In the late 1980s CREDHOS brought together popular movements from Barranca and the surrounding Magdalena Medio region to expose the perpetrators of violence, advocate on behalf of victims and their families, call upon the Colombian state to protect human rights, and denounce the deeper socioeconomic inequalities they saw as sources of conflict.

Human rights movements have tended to emerge in places where the state is strong. This is evident across Latin America in the concentration of human rights organizations in large urban centers, particularly in capital cities where interaction with government is most direct. Although Barrancabermeja is distant from Bogotá, located in what is generally thought of as a frontier region, there is a robust state presence owing to oil. For decades Barranca has been home to the most important trade union movement in Colombian history. Throughout the twentieth century, Colombia's ruling Liberal and Conservative parties guaranteed the flow of oil through repressive actions against trade unionists and regular interruptions of the constitutional order known as declarations of "state of siege."[16] The entrenchment of two-party rule during the National Front governments of the 1960s and 1970s inspired the formation of new social movements, alongside armed insurgencies. For Barranca residents, national authorities represented a foil to popular radicalism. For Bogotá, Barranca represented a problem to be contained. Human rights activism in the 1980s was therefore a response to state-sponsored repression.

Figure 2. Barrancabermeja refinery. Photo by the author.

Barrancabermeja and the surrounding Magdalena Medio have long been associated with radical politics. The founders of the Ejército de Liberación Nacional initially took the name Brigada José Antonio Galán, after the *santandereano* leader of the late eighteenth-century Comuneros Revolt.[17] During the first decade of the twentieth century, popular Liberals fleeing Conservative repression established colonies in the area. In the 1920s, socialist Raúl Mahecha organized the first oil workers' strikes. In 1927 a self-described Bolshevik movement based out of a railroad station just a few kilometers from Barranca participated in the first Communist uprising in Latin American history, five years before Agustín Farabundo Martí took up arms in El Salvador. In 1948 *barranqueños* loyal to populist presidential candidate Jorge Eliécer Gaitán seized control of the city when their leader was assassinated. During the ensuing civil war, left-leaning Liberal guerrillas became a dominant force in the region. The midcentury conflagration known as La Violencia lasted from 1948 to 1958, during which 300,000 Colombians were killed. During this period, the oil workers' union was banned, and popular politics were driven underground. These events would directly inspire the guerrilla groups that formed in the region during the 1960s.

Armed insurgent movements, particularly the Ejército de Liberación Nacional (ELN) and the Fuerzas Armadas Revolucionarias de Colombia

(FARC), played critical roles in the recent history of Barrancabermeja. Urban guerrilla militia were established in the city during the 1980s. This was a major strategic shift for what had hitherto been rural-based movements. As we shall see, the guerrillas' early military actions in the city were mostly limited to attacks on security forces and oil infrastructure, as well as occasional political kidnappings. More disconcerting to the city's social movements were the guerrillas' attempts to opportunistically capture popular protest. The guerrillas were never as brutal as the military and paramilitaries, and local social movements were able to maintain a high degree of autonomy. Guerrilla members were mainly local, and they enjoyed broad sympathy. But the guerrillas' efforts to build mass movements entailed serious risks. When state repression came, the members of legal political movements associated with the FARC (Patriotic Union) and the ELN (¡A Luchar!) were among the first to be targeted. As counterinsurgency operations escalated through the 1990s, the guerrillas multiplied their armed actions within the city. During this decisive period of time, as paramilitary groups closed a circle around Barrancabermeja, the guerrillas unwittingly compromised the political gains being made by Colombia's oldest social movements.

Popular movements in Barrancabermeja had for decades been focused on interlaced questions of labor and social justice, as manifest in the refinery, the oilfields, and the city's poorest neighborhoods. As such, the turn to human rights as a form of resistance to political violence on the part of Barrancabermeja's popular movements entailed a significant discursive shift. The vocabulary of human rights was new to many veteran activists, even though their traditional concerns could have been construed as issues of social and economic rights. The concepts of torture, extrajudicial killing, enforced disappearance, arbitrary detention, and displacement would progressively become part of the language of protest in the city. As anthropologist Winifred Tate writes, "human rights violation" is itself a category for making violence socially legible and establishing accountability, and locating specific acts within broader histories.[18] For the embattled social movement activists in Barranca, the question of basic human rights was indivisible from the issues of social and economic justice, regional development, political recognition, and nationalism. It was not the fact of violence that united human rights activists in Barranca. It was the fact that violence had been directed against popular movements, as well as against ordinary citizens such as Sandra Rondón. The very legitimacy of human rights activists in Barranca was determined by the experiences they shared with the people for whom they spoke.

Barranca has been described as the "heart of activism" in Colombia.[19] While Colombia has long been dominated by the Liberal and Conservative parties, and extensive clientelist networks associated with each, Barranca developed a unique brand of nonconformism. The remarkable longevity and combativeness of the city's social movements is due to its history as an oil-refining enclave, and widespread identification among *barranqueños* with nationalist, working-class and anti-establishment politics.[20] Interviews conducted with popular leaders who experienced the shift to human rights in Barranca during the late 1980s demonstrate a direct relationship between social upheaval, political violence, and the renewal of popular protest. In the words of Irene Villamizar, who has worked for decades as a teacher and community activist in the city's poor southeastern *barrios*, "This town does not belong to the rich."[21]

Understanding Paramilitary Repression

My research examines the intersection of human rights activism, paramilitarism, and processes of state formation. The advent of human rights in the 1980s altered the political landscape of violence in the Magdalena Medio. Protests carried out by peasant movements in the region shed light on the abusive behavior of the Colombian armed forces. As activists' efforts to document and expose extrajudicial killings, arbitrary detentions, and torture multiplied, so too did threats against them. This backlash was part of a larger wave of counterinsurgency violence that swept through the countryside, reaching the city by the middle of the decade. In Barrancabermeja, the use of unmarked cars and motorcycles by assassins wearing civilian clothes substantiated activist claims that covert operations were being carried out by state security forces. The establishment of third party paramilitary death squads during this period further obfuscated state responsibility for human rights violations. Paramilitarism was a continuation of the politics of state of siege by other means, whereby the national government justified the suppression of civil liberties in the name of national security, as had been the case during the great oil workers' and civil strikes of the 1970s. The military remained concerned with public order in Barrancabermeja and the surrounding area, but through the end of the twentieth century the main business of killing was either concealed or devolved to paramilitaries. Human rights activists denounced these contradictions, and thus shed light on the everyday corruption of state sovereignty.

Paramilitarism refers to a multivariate set of phenomena, ranging from legally constituted organizations such as Hitlerjugend to illegal organizations such as the Serbian White Eagles. Scholars of Latin America have written extensively about paramilitary groups dedicated to counterinsurgency, from

Guatemala (*patrullas de autodefensa civil*) to Chiapas (*guardias blancas*). In Colombia, paramilitary groups refer to armed organizations that function as ancillary to regular army units. These include both autonomous and semi-autonomous groupings, as well as clandestine units organized directly by the different branches of the military. The first modern paramilitary groups were created by regional authorities in the 1950s during La Violencia. The second wave of Colombian paramilitary groups appeared in the late 1970s as clandestine "death squads" organized by the Colombian military out of Bogotá.[22] A third wave of paramilitary groups appeared in the early 1980s, funded by drug traffickers and rural elites in the southern Magdalena Medio. The Pablo Escobar–backed Muerte a Secuestradores and similar groups together comprised hundreds of men-at-arms. As recently as 1987 the Colombian military manual Regulations for Counterinsurgency Combat encouraged the organization of paramilitary units or "self-defense committees."[23] That same year the newspaper *El Tiempo* counted eight paramilitary groups with national coverage, as well as more than a hundred regional groupings. Among these were nine in the Magdalena Medio with names such as Rambo and Death to Revolutionaries.[24] Paramilitary groups would be declared illegal in 1989, but by then it was too late to reverse the proliferation of so-called private justice.[25] In 1994 the government of President César Gaviria used emergency powers to once again allow for the legal constitution of paramilitary groups to "protect citizen security."[26] These groups' status was revoked just three years later in response to human rights complaints, but many of the newly formed security cooperatives, or CONVIVIR, continued to function. By the late 1990s paramilitary networks of varied provenance, from different regions of the country, some tracing their origins to the late 1970s, had banded together under a national organization, known as the United Self-Defense Forces of Colombia, or AUC.

The case of Barrancabermeja demonstrates the importance of distinguishing between paramilitary groups, on the one hand, and paramilitary actions carried out by state security forces, on the other. In dozens of *denuncias* published by human rights groups in Barranca, the perpetrators of acts of violence and intimidation are referred to as *presuntos paramilitares*, or presumed paramilitaries. The reason for this is simple. In most cases, the perpetrators do not reveal themselves. Even when acts were committed or death threats were signed in the name of purported "self-defense" groups such as the AUC, human rights defenders were careful not to corroborate the alibi of paramilitarism. Paramilitarism in Colombia has been correctly associated with counterinsurgency operations in rural frontier zones, where the presence of the national

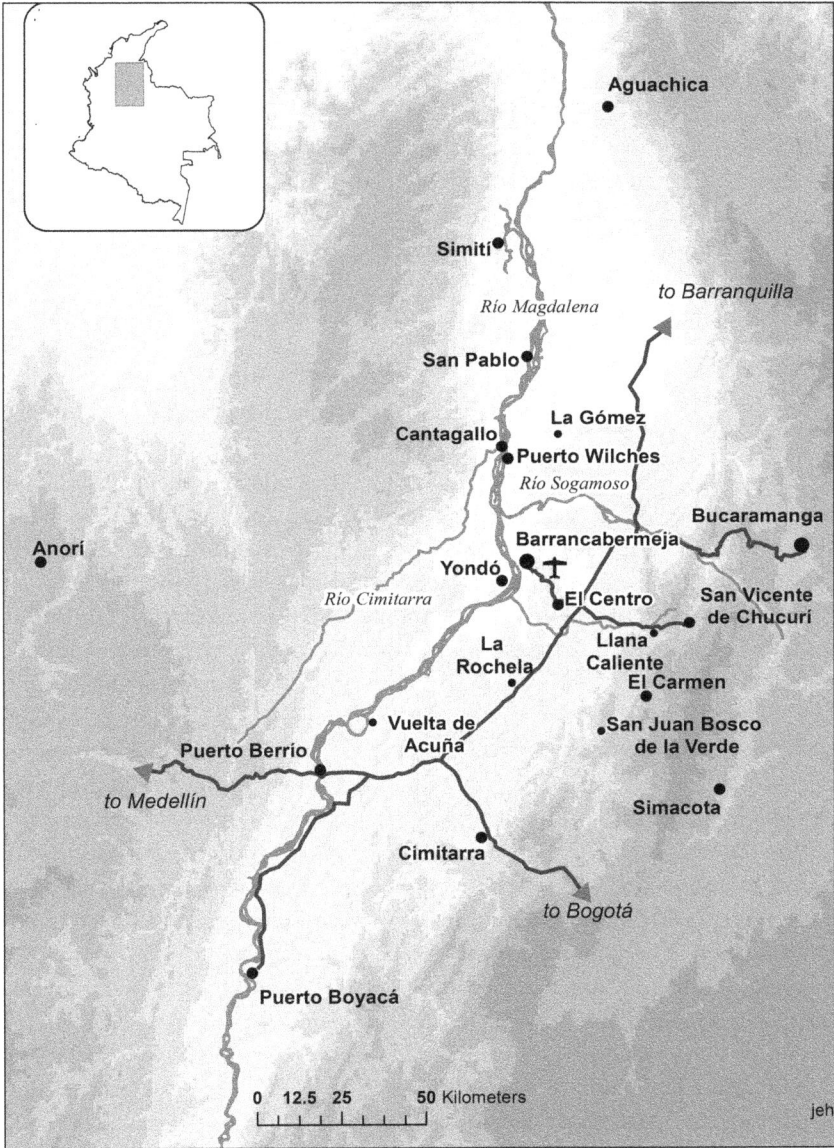

Map 4. Magdalena Medio region, including topography, important rivers, selected *municipios*, and sites of guerrilla and paramilitary activity, circa 1987. Map by John Harmon.

state and social movements was weak.[27] The early impetus for paramilitary organizing in the Magdalena Medio came from the counterinsurgency nexus of drug traffickers, landholders, and armed forces commanders in the country-side. These networks of actors were essential to the spread of paramilitarism into Barranca as well.[28] The most important point in terms of Barranca's distinctiveness is the extent to which national security forces directly carried out clandestine attacks on nonmilitary targets in an effort to suppress the city's strong grassroots social movements. National security forces used paramilitary tactics in Barranca more flagrantly than in regions of the country where AUC leaders proclaimed their autonomy. It was not until the end of 2001 that para-military organizations claimed to have a permanent presence in Barranca.

A New Paradigm of Social Protest

"Human rights" are contingent norms and practices, derived from lived experiences of authoritarianism, war, poverty, and exclusion. This study focuses on human rights first and foremost as a modality of protest. Opposition to political violence was a significant change in emphasis for Colombian popular movements that had coalesced around demands for social justice. The shift to human rights was pivotal, as local activists turned to the international community for solidarity. In this respect, the history of Barran-cabermeja is closely related to the global movement for human rights that came together around Latin America during the late Cold War. Yet the modus operandi of popular mobilization around local issues continued to dominate, challenging the notion that human rights activists are mainly transnational in orientation. Indeed, the people who became human rights activists in Ba-rranca, most often referred to as human rights defenders, were deeply engaged in local processes of transformation, including electoral politics and community-based economic development. Even as local activists distinguished themselves in national and transnational debates around the impact of the Colombian conflict on civilian populations, and the U.S.-sponsored War on Drugs, previous projects for social change continued. As we shall see, human rights activism in Barrancabermeja entailed a commitment to a multiscaled politics, an attempt to position the city's robust civic movement within broader processes. Human rights activists in Barranca in the 1980s were engrossed in a struggle to physically protect the civilian population. At the same time, attempts were made to link this urgent purpose to an analysis of the political economy of the city and the surrounding region.

This book presents a fine-grained study of a grassroots human rights movement. Building on the work of Colombian scholars that privilege local sources, I demonstrate the ways in which human rights are socially produced. Scholarly activism on human rights in Colombia dates back to the immediate post–La Violencia period. Generations of social scientists and historians have been called into service to help explain the country's devastating and extraordinarily complex cycles of social and political conflict. Published in 1962 by scholars affiliated with the National University, *La Violencia en Colombia* was the first comprehensive study of the phenomenon of violence and remains a foundational text for the Colombian human rights movement.[29] The parish-level details recorded in this study demonstrate the importance of local knowledge for understanding human rights movements. In the 1980s the many scholars who study violence in Colombia became known simply as *violentólogos*. The most significant work published in this era was the government-commissioned analysis of violence produced under the direction of historian Gonzalo Sánchez in 1987, titled *Colombia: Violencia y democracia*.[30] A third landmark study was published by a government-funded commission in 1992, titled *Pacificar la paz: Lo que no se ha negociado en los acuerdos de paz*.[31] Between 2005 and 2012, the Historical Memory Group of Colombia's National Commission for Reconciliation and Reparations published two dozen detailed case studies. The final report, titled simply *Enough!*, makes extensive use of the records created by grassroots human rights activists as well as oral historians. All of these are scholarly efforts to narrate and explain the Colombian conflict through the vector of human rights.

For more than twenty years, beginning in the late 1980s, the primary focus of trade union and social movement activists in Barrancabermeja and across Colombia was the defense of basic human rights, defined mainly in terms of freedom from the violence associated with dirty warfare.[32] Human rights activism was a direct response to the escalation of political repression, particularly abuses committed by state security agents and their paramilitary allies. The adoption of human rights discourse by activists in Barranca, and elsewhere in Colombia, set the tone for the next quarter century. Activists would learn to carry out field investigations, write reports, formulate "urgent action" appeals, and undertake transnational advocacy work. The mobilization of street protests in favor of human rights constituted a fundamental linkage to the longer history of popular protest in Barranca. Because of these efforts, human rights would become an important tool for understanding the Colombian conflict and the basis upon which political change would be contested. By 1988 human rights was the number one reason for social protest in Colombia.[33]

Between 1989 and 1994 the total number of human rights organizations in Colombia increased fourfold.[34]

When Colombian scholars began looking at the complexities of political violence in the early 1960s, they employed new research methods that challenged the official narrative of civil war pitting Conservatives against Liberals. The first academic monograph published on the rise of the movement for human rights in Colombia is the anthropologist Winifred Tate's *Counting the Dead: The Culture and Politics of Human Rights Activism in Colombia* (2007).[35] Tate's pathbreaking ethnographic research looks historically at the human rights discourses and tactics employed by activists, as well as by governments, judiciaries, and armed forces. As Tate writes, human rights first became part of the language of protest in Colombia in the 1980s as embattled social activists sought to name the sources, types, and impacts of political violence to which they were exposed. Tate's book is one of a handful of important studies produced on the politics and history of human rights organizing in Colombia.[36] Human rights activists, and their intellectual forbearers such as the group that compiled the aforementioned *La Violencia en Colombia*, sought to explain violence as a complex set of nested phenomena. Tate writes: "Confronted with the complex panorama of Colombian violence, activists began using the human rights framework to classify the violent homicides that years earlier had been considered partisan violence, or part of insurgent and counterinsurgency campaigns."[37]

The legal scholar Upendra Baxi reminds us that the history of contemporary human rights movements are "chronicles of contingency" that must be understood within their specific local contexts.[38] He argues that we need to develop a "social theory of human rights" that can account for the diversity of popular responses to repression and suffering. The anthropologist Richard A. Wilson has taken this imperative one step further in making a case for an ethnography of rights. He writes: "Studying the 'social life of human rights' would involve focusing on, inter alia, the performative dimensions of human rights, the dynamics of social mobilization, and the attitudinal changes of elite and non-elite social actors towards formulations of 'rights' and 'justice,' both inside and outside the legal process."[39] One way of undertaking this important project is to tell the history of human rights from the perspective of frontline activists who seek to confront violence through direct action, rather than from the perspective of the United Nations' functionaries, elected officials, and judges who are responsible for negotiating and enforcing legal norms. By seeking to better comprehend the circumstances that give rise to human rights movements at the local level, we can illuminate the specific ways in which human rights are constructed and utilized. This approach will also allow us to better observe the historical changes set in motion by the advancement of human rights.

The transnational activist networks that were the focus of Margaret Keck and Kathryn Sikkink's seminal work, *Activists beyond Borders: Advocacy Networks in International Politics*, are in fact composed of three levels of interaction between individual activists and groups.[40] At the transnational level, well-funded international NGOs work alongside community-based groups linked to progressive faith communities, committees comprising refugees from violence-affected regions, trade unions, governments, and international organizations such as the Organization of American States (OAS). Keck and Sikkink are primarily interested in human rights work that takes place at this level, focusing on the effectiveness of campaigns that aim to alter the behavior of abusive states. Shifting to the national level, Winifred Tate has examined the activities and cultures of Colombian human rights activist networks and their interactions with government and military authorities. Tate has significantly expanded the model proposed by Keck and Sikkink to look at the direct actions taken by national nongovernmental organizations to impact the Colombian government, state security forces, and nonstate armed groups. Moving to the third, previously unexamined level, this book aims to look at the scope and impact of actions undertaken by human rights activist networks at the local level. My social-historical approach both complements and challenges the work of scholars who recount the history of human rights mainly from the point of view of lawyers and lawmakers.

The main aim of this book is to better understand the social origins of human rights movements, with a focus on the outcomes of armed conflict in late twentieth-century Latin America. In writing the history of a specific human rights movement in a conflict area, I consider three sets of broad historical questions. The first set of questions hinges upon the social, political, and economic conditions that beget human rights movements in the first place. What is the relationship between historical struggles for social justice and contemporary struggles for human rights? The second set of questions revolves around the historical changes set in motion by the advancement of human rights. Do human rights movements create new channels of popular participation? Do they encourage solidarity within communities and among diverse social and political actors? Or do human rights movements narrow existing struggles for change? The third set of questions concerns the special problems facing human rights activists in conflict areas. How do governments, state security forces, and nonstate armed actors respond to human rights activism in contexts of internal armed conflict? Can human rights movements maintain their autonomy and effectiveness in the face of these pressures?

This book focuses on the history of Colombia's most important oil refinery town and center of social activism, which in the late 1980s gave birth to a combative and influential human rights movement. How did popular protest change in response to historical ruptures caused by political violence, from the colonization of a frontier region by the world's largest petrochemical company in the 1920s, the civil war known as La Violencia at midcentury, the emergence of guerrilla groups in the 1960s, the military suppression of the oil workers' union in the 1970s, the dirty war of the 1980s, the armed battle for control of the city in the 1990s, and the period of paramilitary hegemony in the twenty-first century? For more than five decades Colombia has been embroiled in what is now most commonly described simply as El Conflicto. It is somewhat misleading to speak of "The Violence" or "The Conflict" in the singular. Regional approaches to Colombian history reveal that multiple forms of social and political violence occur simultaneously, in different configurations. A regional approach allows us to look at the confluence of local, national, and international forces that shape the identities and behaviors of social actors. Barrancabermeja has been a crucible of Colombian history: a place of convergence of foreign capital, the national state, guerrilla groups, and military and paramilitary forces.

What emerges out of social movement organizing in Barrancabermeja is a heterodox approach to human rights that emphasizes the causal links between inequity and violence. In its legal incorporation papers, filed in 1989, CREDHOS defined its first objective as "the development and training of promoters of social rights and human rights through popular organizations" and its second objective as "undertaking appropriate legal action."[41] The ways in which human rights were talked about and operationalized reflect these twin goals and the group's diverse origins. At the height of social movement effervescence in the mid-1980s this diversity was seen very clearly. The cause of human rights was put into action by many sectors, including labor, peasants, students, women, political parties, and the Catholic Church. Amid a terrible wave of violence, these groups were to agree on basic human rights principles. As we shall see, the participation of each was fundamental to building a consensus around the claims they made.[42] Joint actions, from documenting human rights atrocities, to filing habeas corpus writs, to convening street protests, were facilitated by the fact that the popular movement had a long history of collaboration, and was deeply rooted in local communities. Does the language of human rights, particularly the standardized register utilized by transnational activist networks, flatten political differences? The arc of Barrancabermeja's recent history is indicative of wider trends in human rights across the Latin American region, where popular movements initiated similar processes of transformation in response to severe repression. While the diverse social bases of human rights movements are not reflected in the reports that circulate among international organizations, it is evident when we look at the full range and sophistication of their activities.

Overview

This book is organized chronologically. The first chapter focuses on the development of Barranca as a foreign-controlled enclave through to the end of La Violencia (1919–1961). The second chapter explores the nationalization of the oil industry and the emergence of new social movements against the backdrop of the Cold War and left-wing guerrilla insurgency (1961–1980). The next four chapters take an in-depth look at the advent of human rights activism in response to paramilitary violence (1980–1997). The final chapter examines the process of paramilitarization that Barranca endured beginning in 1998, taking pause to consider the possibilities and limitations of human rights organizing in a conflict zone from the point of view of frontline activists.

The history of the oil town of Barrancabermeja and the Magdalena Medio sheds light on the sources and outcomes of political violence in Colombia in the twentieth century and the relationship between different modes of popular social and political organizing. To understand how human rights activism emerged in Barranca, it is important to understand the circumstances that caused political violence in the surrounding region. The forms of violence that took shape in the Magdalena Medio reflected the special roles that the national state has played in Barrancabermeja. The history of Barranca is the history of a decades-long struggle for social justice, regional and national economic development, and human rights. Barranca has been the site of direct and protracted confrontation between the state and social movements. It has also been a site of national state intervention in the field of human rights. I situate the experiences of human rights defenders within the broader history of social movements and the Colombian armed conflict.

1

Oil Workers, *Colonos*, and the Roots of Popular Radicalism

Most cities have a symbol that represents them: Paris, the Eiffel Tower; Rome, Saint Peter's Basilica; Zipaquirá, the Salt Cathedral; Bogotá, Monserrate, and Barrancabermeja, the refinery. But for me, for those of us who have lived many years in Barrancabermeja, there is something even more singular: the factory siren. How do you paint the sound of a factory siren and create a symbol for a city like this? Maybe Picasso would have known how, but he is dead.

Aristóbulo Quiroga, oil worker[1]

Rebel City

Barrancabermeja has long suffered a bad reputation. It is known among Colombians as a place of moral transgression and danger. Yet the city has also represented hard work and economic opportunity. At the time of the oil boom in the 1920s, young men were lured to Barranca to make and spend money. If they did not succumb to illness or get run out of town for participating in a strike, employees of the Tropical Oil Company might stay long enough to tell their stories to the next generation of *tropeleros*, or rabble-rousers. Young women also went to Barranca, and many gained employment in the sex trade. In her novel *The Dark Bride*, Laura Restrepo writes: "Back then [Barranca] was distinguished in the great vastness of the outside world as the city of the three p's: that is *putas*, *plata* and *petróleo*, that is whores, money, and oil. *Petróleo*, *plata* and *putas*. Four p's really, if we remember that it was paradise in the middle of a land besieged by hunger."[2] According to an old joke, Barranca was little more than a brothel, presided over by a mayor and a priest: *un burdel, con alcalde y cura*.[3] Throughout its history, Barranca has also been stigmatized for its association with radical politics. Young conscripts from Barranca fulfilling their military service have been said to worry they will be accused of being *guerrilleros* and mistreated by their superiors. Pregnant women have been said to leave the city to give birth in nearby Bucaramanga, so that their children's national identity cards do not indicate they were born in Barranca. The mere mention of Barranca raises eyebrows across Colombia. As if in Barranca the untamed, the poor, and the Communists would eat you for lunch.

For many people, Barrancabermeja also holds a special mystique: *Barranca tiene mística*. Barranca is full of life. The city's popular movements occupy a key place in this mythology. The socialization of workers in Barranca took place in the refinery, but also in the spaces that eager migrants opened up all around it. In the poetry of Colombia's frontier zones, there is space for *tropel*, meaning turmoil and dissent.[4] In his essay based on oral histories recorded in Barrancabermeja in the 1970s, *Aquí nadie es forastero*, Mauricio Archila describes an open and welcoming place, whose citizens are deeply conscious of their place in Colombian history: "As soon as you set foot in Barranca, you feel a special atmosphere, maybe unique in Colombia. It is not the heat exactly, or the Magdalena River . . . or the relative proximity of the Atlantic Ocean, or the rarified air produced by the permanent combustion of gases derived from petroleum. It is more than that; it is the spirit of the people. It is the warm welcome that they give to visitors, it is the thirst for learning, the pride of living in the oil capital of Colombia."[5] In Barranca there are few traces of the customary deference to authority and the country club politics of the *sierra*, the conservative Catholic morality of Antioquia, the tight webs of economic and political clientelism of the *eje cafetero*, or the conspicuous racial divisions of the Pacific coast and Urabá.[6] Beyond the *noir* vision of Barranca, populated by so many prostitutes and ruffians, the city was also a place of personal freedom, of opportunity.

When the Tropical Oil Company, a subsidiary of Standard Oil of New Jersey, acquired the drilling rights for the area around Barrancabermeja in 1919, it set in motion powerful processes of economic, social, and political innovation. During this period *barranqueños* from different walks of life came to identify as members of an imagined community of independent-minded and progressive working-class Colombians.[7] In this chapter I discuss four linked historical processes: the colonization of the Magdalena Medio region leading up to the oil boom of the 1920s, the invention of the city of Barrancabermeja, the conflicts that pitted oil workers and other residents against the Tropical Oil Company, and the transition to state control over Tropical Oil holdings through the end of the 1950s.

Prior to the arrival of the Tropical Oil Company, the Magdalena River valley was an area of indigenous resistance, peasant struggles over land, and a refuge for Liberal fighters from the nineteenth-century civil wars. The development of an oil industry by foreign investors resulted in the formation of a new working class of migrant laborers, represented by a combative and fiercely nationalist union. From the 1920s through the 1940s a succession of strikes pitted oil workers against La Troco. Like other frontier areas, the Magdalena Medio region had no important local oligarchy and a relatively weak presence of the Catholic Church. Throughout this early history the presence of the Colombian state was manifest mainly in security concerns, including the deployment of National Police and army troops to safeguard the oil industry. Left-wing political organizing in the region culminated in 1948 with an armed uprising known as La Comuna de Barrancabermeja, the Barrancabermeja Commune.

Conquistadores, Colonos, and Capitalists

The early history of the riverine valley now known as the Magdalena Medio was one of dispersed indigenous populations and sparse Spanish settlement. In colonial-era chronicles, the region appears as little more than a footnote. The Magdalena Medio would be progressively shaped by the forces of both private and public investment. In the nineteenth century, *mestizo* laborers and homesteaders drawn to the area by export booms in forest products led to a growth in peasant farming, both along the Magdalena River and upland in the hills of Santander and Boyacá. A handful of small towns, including Barrancabermeja, emerged as trading posts. National and regional government authorities were increasingly called upon by settlers, investors, and the Catholic Church to adjudicate land disputes, enforce public order, and control the native population.[8] The Magdalena Medio would later provide refuge for popular Liberals following their loss of Colombia's deadliest nineteenth-century civil conflict, the Thousand Days' War (1899–1902). By the turn of the twentieth century, the area around Barrancabermeja remained a relatively isolated, yet highly contested, frontier.

In April 1536, Gonzalo Jiménez de Quesada, an Andalusian lawyer with no military experience, led an ambitious expedition up the Magdalena River. Inspired by Francisco Pizarro's recent conquest of the Inca capital of Cuzco, the governor of the Canary Islands, Pedro Fernández de Lugo, personally financed a plan to explore and claim new territory in what was then known as the Reino de la Nueva Granada. Jiménez de Quesada acted as lieutenant general of a large and well-equipped force that left Santa Cruz de Tenerife in November 1535. They arrived in the port city of Santa Marta on the Caribbean coast of Nueva Granada in January 1536. Three months later, Jiménez de Quesada would embark for the Río Grande de la Magdalena in search of gold, territory, and Indians to conquer.

Jiménez de Quesada's journey of conquest would prove costly. His expeditionary force consisted of eight hundred Spaniards and one hundred African and Indian slaves.[9] About five hundred men traveled overland by foot and horseback from Santa Marta. Another four hundred men sailed and rowed upriver in five custom-built brigantines. The ground troops departed first, laden with heavy weapons and supplies, followed two weeks later by the ships. Jiménez de Quesada's first attempt to sail up the Magdalena River was scuppered by a storm that struck just as his shallow-bottomed fleet approached the mouth of the river.[10] Two boats sank, three were damaged, and many of the survivors deserted. Jiménez de Quesada was forced to return to Santa Marta to regroup, acquire new ships, and recruit new men. Six months later he was ready to continue, and eventually he met up with the ground forces at a previously agreed location approximately fifty leagues upstream.[11] After two more months Jiménez de Quesada and his troops arrived at a small native settlement they came to refer to as Barrancas Bermejas, after the red earth that colored the shoreline.[12] Since first setting out from Santa Marta, about two hundred men had died, mostly due to illness, exhaustion, or drowning.

The Spaniards' goal was to make passage to the highland interior, where they hoped to find something worth claiming. While the majority of the surviving troops remained at Barrancas Bermejas to wait out heavy rains, Jiménez de Quesada sent small groups of men further upriver in search of passage to the mountains. Gonzalo Fernández de Oviedo y Valdéz, official historian of the Indies, would later give an account of the trials and triumphs of the voyage. In one passage he writes of a thick black tar that "boiled and flowed out of the earth" that the local indigenous people used for medicinal purposes, and the Spanish used to repair their boats.[13] The advance patrols that had been dispatched by Jiménez de Quesada returned after three months with a few bags of salt and a minor quantity of gold. More significantly, they brought back news that there were indeed prosperous Indian settlements to the south, located on a fertile and temperate plateau. This was sufficient to encourage continued exploration. Jiménez de Quesada abandoned Barrancas Bermejas in January 1537. By then there were just 179 men remaining out of 900. Jiménez de

Quesada persisted until April 27, 1537, when he reached the Muisca city that he named Santa Fé de Bogotá.[14] Rival expeditions led by the veterans of colonial campaigns in Venezuela and Peru rushed to compete with Jiménez de Quesada for the right to govern the new territory. Ultimately, the contenders would have to travel to Spain to plead their case before Carlos V of Spain. Wishing to avoid a civil war such as that which had broken out among the conquistadors in Peru, the Spanish crown settled the dispute in favor of the more experienced Sebastián de Benalcázar.[15] Conflicts between colonial officials would delay the settlement of the Colombian interior for decades to come.

The economic and political integration of Colombia from the colonial period to the present has depended on the conquest of remote areas by private actors. The Magdalena River was linked to the port city of Cartagena de Indias by means of the 118-kilometer Dique Canal in 1582. But a lack of resources for maintenance caused the publicly funded project to fall into disrepair.[16] The only Spanish outpost in the region was the quartz and gold mining center of Simití, located about 100 kilometers north of Barrancabermeja. The Magdalena Medio was gradually opened to the outside world as a result of the international trade in quina, tagua, rubber, wood-based dyes, and charcoal.[17] Interest in Colombia's natural resources grew on the heels of the successful development of similar economies in the equally remote Amazon River basin. Upon his return from Brazil, British plant collector John Weir explored the Magdalena River and its tributaries in January 1864. In a dispatch to members of the Royal Horticultural Society, Weir reflected on the exhausting trek he had undertaken into the hill country east of the Magdalena River in search of orchid samples to send back to Kew Gardens: "The navigation of the river Sogamoza is both difficult and dangerous. For about seventeen leagues from its junction with the Magdalena it flows through a comparatively flat and densely-wooded track and is navigable for canoes; but above this it flows in a deep and narrow mountain gorge, and is full of rapids and rocks. From this point to Bucaramanga is three days journey on mule-back."[18] From the perspective of the cash-strapped and isolated government in Bogotá, remote areas such as the Magdalena Medio were a dilemma: though rich in natural resources, and clearly attractive to outsiders, they were difficult to access and nearly impossible to govern. As Frank Safford writes, in an "undercapitalized, sparsely populated country" such as Colombia, the trade in forest products "made sense."[19]

The colonization of the Magdalena Medio would proceed gradually as the regional economy continued to grow and diversify in the later half of the nineteenth century. What is sometimes overlooked is the extent to which state authorities became indispensable to this process, especially in transportation.[20] The settlement of non-indigenous peoples along the length of the Magdalena

River was only enabled when the newly independent Colombian government granted a shipping monopoly to a German company in 1824.[21] The first permanent mule tracks connecting lowland and highland Santander were cleared by forest products traders in the mid-nineteenth century, with the financial backing of the sovereign state of Santander.[22]

The political incorporation of a few of the larger settlements that had been built up in the area would be initiated by regional authorities. However, Barranca itself remained undeveloped and unrecognized. A census taken by the Colombian government in 1864 counted just eighty-five residents in Barrancabermeja, most of them adult men working in transportation.[23] Though small in size, Barranca was an established hub for moving goods to the coast.[24] The village of Barranca comprised a small group of wooden and thatch homes perched on a muddy riverbank, behind which lay by an expanse of swamps, ditches, and gullies. The site was located at the confluence of two important navigable tributaries of the Magdalena River, the Sogamoso and the Opón. Barrancabermeja was renamed Puerto Santander in 1868. Two years later the regional government under the leadership of José Pacífico Solón Wilches began construction on a railway between Bucaramanga and the Bocas del Rosario port village, just north of Barranca. Trains began delivering lumber to Bocas del Rosario in 1882, and the *municipio* of Puerto Wilches was created in 1887. In the meanwhile, Barranca continued to grow, albeit slowly. The town's population increased with the development of coffee plantations in the nearby foothills. Barranca would be designated a *corregimiento* in 1881 under the jurisdiction of the booming agricultural *municipio* of San Vicente de Chucurí, where cacao, tobacco, and fruit were being produced for international and domestic markets.[25] Santander was the leading coffee region in Colombia in this period, producing upwards of 60 percent of the country's total exports through the turn of the century.[26]

As commerce along the Magdalena River steadied through the late nineteenth century, private investors called on government to provide for security.[27] Among the capitalists' most pressing concerns was protection against the threat of raids by Yareguíes warriors. Non-indigenous traders reported being ambushed along the paths linking Barranca and the highlands.[28] Although there was no reliable census data on the indigenous population, the total number of Carib-speaking Yareguíes living in the departments of Santander, Cundinamarca, and Boyacá at the time may have been higher than five thousand.[29] The Yareguíes were semi-nomadic hunters, divided into five *cacicazgos*, or chiefdoms. The story of a great Yareguíes chief named Pipatón said to have repelled early Spanish invaders endured, helping to animate colonists' anxieties. There had been periodic battles between Spanish forces based in highland

Santander and the Yareguíes through the end of the late colonial period.[30] Sporadic military engagement served to keep the indigenous at a distance from Spanish settlements along the spine of the central *cordillera*. Official policy toward the Yareguíes would change from relegation to "reduction and civilization" as the volume of goods being carried down to the Magdalena River increased.[31] Some travelers reporting on conditions in Yareguíes territory likened the indigenous to disease-spreading mosquitoes and wild animals.[32] Others emphasized the indigenous peoples' reputed ferocity, and accordingly justified their subjugation. Between 1866 and 1918 the government of Santander issued six different laws ordering the relocation of the Yareguíes into Catholic Church–run *reducciones*.

While the increase in tropical forest and agricultural exports shaped the demography and politics of Colombia's frontier zones, so too did armed conflict. The first waves of Colombians of European, *mestizo*, and *mulato* descent to colonize the countryside in the vicinity of Barranca were Liberal soldiers and their families displaced during the Thousand Days' War (1898–1902).[33] Many important battles in the last of Colombia's nineteenth-century partisan wars had been fought in Santander.[34] The single most infamous incident of the war was the Battle of Palonegro, which took place on the western outskirts of the city of Bucaramanga in May 1900. The battle between Liberals and Conservatives lasted two weeks and claimed an estimated 2,500 to 4,000 lives. Palonegro marked the defeat of the unified Liberal army, leading to a period of guerrilla warfare carried out by small bands of independent fighters in the region. Internal refugees were drawn to the Magdalena Medio by the availability of unclaimed arable land and the natural protection afforded by mountains and ravines. Their outlook on politics was stubbornly anti-authoritarian. They were the inheritors of a progressive brand of Liberalism with roots in Santander. The persistence of an ethic of self-defense among the colonists earned the region a reputation as a "red zone," or an area inhabited by political radicals.[35] These new *colonos* understood that their interests were threatened by the presence of absentee investors.

The people who came to live along Colombia's most important navigable river between Puerto Boyacá to the south and Morales to the north experienced processes of social and political conflict related to the competition for resources.[36] While some settlers were armed for the purposes of self-defense, they also pursued legal strategies to claim land rights. Outside interests had been present in the region since the days of the tagua boom, but there had hitherto been few permanent settlements, no incentive to acquire formal title, and little conflict. In the area around Barrancabermeja in the first decade of the twentieth century, *colonos* reported being forced to sign contracts with the powerful Barranquilla-registered Ogliastri and Martínez Lumber Company, or face eviction or imprisonment.[37] The *colonos* fought a prolonged and bitter legal battle against company representative and Bucaramanga businessman Victor Manuel Ogliastri. In 1911 the national government initially resolved the Ogliastri and Martínez dispute in the settlers' favor. The *colonos* celebrated the decision in their favor by stoning company offices and threatening a local manager. It was a pyrrhic victory. In 1913 the Magdalena Commercial Company, a U.S.-owned export conglomerate, purchased an extensive tract of land from Ogliastri and Martínez that included the disputed parcel, establishing the first modern multinational corporate presence in the area.[38]

The Magdalena Medio region was not a tabula rasa prior to the oil bonanza of the 1920s. Economic activity in the region in the nineteenth century was brisk at times, if uneven. The government in Bucaramanga helped finance the expansion of transportation routes. The Catholic Church led efforts to pacify the Yareguíes indigenous peoples. National authorities intervened to resolve *colonos'* disputes with investors in coffee, lumber, and cacao. There was no permanent state presence to speak of in the lowlands. But the Magdalena Medio was nonetheless being transformed. By the beginning of the twentieth century, a majority of Yareguíes had been assimilated or killed.[39] While the region remained thinly settled, it was a well-known sanctuary for homesteaders, internal refugees, and other nonconformists. Many of the processes of social and political conflict underway at the turn of the twentieth century would intensify during the Tropical Oil Company era. With the arrival of La Troco, national economic concerns came into focus, and the central state became a leading political player in Santander, alongside their regional counterparts. Demands for Bogotá to defend investors' claims, on the one hand, and to defend workers' rights, on the other, increased as scores of migrants came to the area in search of work and new beginnings.

Arrival of the Oilmen

In 1905 French-born Colombian engineer Roberto De Mares ventured into the Magdalena Medio region in search of rubber.[40] While the international markets for quina and tagua had long since lapsed, the rubber business was booming, stimulated by the mass production of the pneumatic tire. Uncultivated *hevea brasiliensis* was already being exploited on a large scale in the Putumayo in Colombia's disputed southeastern jungles and on a small scale in the Magdalena River valley. While in the area, De Mares met local entrepreneur José Joaquín Bohórquez, who explained that while rubber trees were scarce, oil was in such abundance that it literally seeped up out of the earth and formed large black pools.[41] Oil had remained untouched since Jimenez de Quesda's men first remarked on it four hundred years earlier. Along with Bohórquez and a Barranquilla-based investment firm, Roberto De Mares purchased the rights from the national government to exploit oil resources within a 1.5 million acre tract of land for a thirty-year period.[42]

Oil has ensured Barrancabermeja's prominent place in Colombian history. The oil industry provided a framework for private economic expansion across a large and remote frontier region, with Barrancabermeja as its *capital natural.*[43] Oil also fueled mutually constitutive processes of social and state formation. The development of the Magdalena Medio, with Barrancabermeja as its center, bound together diverse populations, including industrial laborers, peasant farmers, merchants, provincial elites, and political activists. Many residents of Barrancabermeja, including both those who worked in the oil industry and those who worked in service sectors, would come to view the foreign company as antagonistic to their interests. Area residents were untrusting of politicians from Bogotá, although they demanded state intercession to protect labor rights. The country's first industrial trade union was formed in Barranca during a series of strikes that linked issues of labor and social justice to economic nationalism. Meanwhile, Tropical Oil officials saw themselves as battling ungrateful workers, as well as an unforgiving natural environment, hostile natives, and a capricious state. The development of Barrancabermeja was celebrated in Jersey Standard's reports to shareholders as nothing less than the conquest of a savage land.[44]

Bogotá was eager to recognize the potential of oil. De Mares's friend the Conservative president general Rafael Reyes approved the deal by decree, invoking emergency measures to sidestep the usual congressional consultation processes.[45] From 1904 to 1909 President Reyes presided over a politically divided and economically ruined Colombia. Reyes had risen through the ranks of the Conservative Party during the Thousand Days' War, which had devastated the country between 1898 and 1902. The loss of Panama in 1903 following the United States–backed mutiny of disgruntled elites in Colombia's northern territory deepened the crisis.[46] President Reyes, who believed that the state should play a larger role in fostering the development of export industries, was nicknamed El Modernizador by his admirers.[47] He undertook fiscal reforms that increased state revenues, serviced Colombia's foreign debt, subsidized new industries, built railways, and encouraged foreign investment.[48] Colombia was experiencing a long boom in coffee exports, but the benefits were not evenly distributed across the national territory, nor were the revenues being effectively captured by the central state. More needed to be done. Colombia lagged behind most Latin American countries in terms of per capita economic output and infrastructural development. President Reyes was intent on taking advantage of Colombia's natural resources.

The first global oil rush that began during World War I, combined with a desire to secure new sources of production beyond revolutionary Mexico, drove British and U.S. companies to vie for opportunities in South America.[49] Standard Oil of New Jersey began exploring their options in Colombia, as did English industrialist Weetman Pearson. A staunch ally of Mexico's recently ousted President Porfírio Díaz, Pearson made a bid to buy the rights to prospect for oil in an area encompassing half of Colombia. In response, Jersey Standard sent representatives of one of their subsidiaries to persuade the Colombian government against the proposal.[50] Meanwhile, Roberto De Mares needed capital to demonstrate the potential of his property. De Mares's first international partners were J. S. Weller and John W. Leonard, experienced oil developers based in the thriving steel-producing city of Pittsburgh, Pennsylvania. Together with De Mares they raised $2 million U.S. toward the creation of the Tropical Oil Company, incorporated in 1916. By 1917 the government of Mexico had proclaimed all subsoil the property of the Mexican state, and Jersey Standard shifted its attention decisively to Colombia.

Competition over oil in the Magdalena Medio aggravated a pattern of conflict over land between local settlers and outside investors, and gradually pulled the national state deeper into regional affairs. Local *colonos* sent written petitions to government authorities in Bogotá to protest the usurpation of their claims by speculators. Following the purchase of the De Mares Concession, dozens of applications were made by Colombian and foreign companies seeking the rights to survey the Magdalena River valley. The Ministry of Mines and Energy received bids covering the adjoining *municipios* of Simití, Puerto Wilches, Lebrija, El Carmen, Simacota, Puerto Berrio, Casabe, and others.[51] While some bids were being made on land in the even more remote regions of Urabá and Casanare, the majority of interest was concentrated in the vicinity of the De Mares Concession. During this same period, the Ministry of Mines and Energy received dozens of reports of unauthorized oil exploration from local residents.[52] In 1918 a group of *colonos* registered complaints about *terrenos baldíos* being unlawfully fenced off by speculators seeking to rent public lands to Tropical Oil. *Colonos* living near the De Mares Concession also registered grievances with the Minister of Agriculture, accusing Tropical Oil of sending thugs to raze settlers' homes.

Setting up an oil-drilling infrastructure was arduous and expensive work, requiring spectacular feats of engineering and human endurance. The equipment used by Tropical Oil to build the derricks that soon dotted the countryside was all imported, yet in order to deliver, run, and maintain them, the company relied on local labor. Though navigable for nearly a thousand kilometers from Honda, in the department of Huila, to the Caribbean Sea at Bocas de Ceniza, the Magdalena River is shallow, and subject to constantly shifting channels, overgrowth of vegetation, and flooding. Standard Oil historians George S. Gibb and Evelyn H. Knowlton write of Tropical Oil's early travails in terms reminiscent of Jiménez de Quesada's journey of conquest several centuries earlier: "The search constituted one of the great epics of the oil industry. The De Mares concession itself was a wilderness—a land of steaming temperatures, unbelievable rainfalls, and none-too-friendly native tribes. Transportation facilities consisted of river boats and canoes, and the caprices of the Magdalena made navigation difficult."[53] Heavy-duty road-building and drilling equipment was transported from North America to Barranca, and then to oilfields that lay inland, by cargo ship, train, river barge, and brute force. The mouth of the Magdalena River near the port city of Barranquilla was impassable by ocean vessel due to the occurrence of large sandbars formed by silt brought down hundreds of kilometers from the Andes. Once delivered to Colombia's Caribbean coast, equipment had to be disassembled, transported across winding, uneven terrain by a short-gauge railroad, and then unloaded onto slow-moving flat-bottomed rafts that ploughed their way up river. After arriving at Barranca, the equipment had to be dragged across shallow streams and swamps.

The fledgling Tropical Oil Company exhausted its capital demonstrating the viability of the property. Oil was soon flowing out of the Magdalena Medio in great profusion. Three wells drilled in 1919 proved immediately productive.[54] International Petroleum, a Canadian-based subsidiary of Standard Oil of New Jersey, agreed to buy Tropical Oil in August 1920 for $33 million U.S.[55] By the mid-1920s Tropical Oil owned the largest modern shipping fleet in Colombia, including six steamers and a dozen barges. The company established six bulk stations and four distribution centers for delivering oil to major domestic markets. Annual production jumped from 66,750 barrels in 1921 to 322,786 barrels in 1922. As the Colombian Ministry of Industry boasted, by 1924 Barranca's output was equivalent to about half of that produced in the oil-rich U.S. state of California.[56] Tropical Oil continued to grow apace, and by 1925 production exceeded 6 million barrels. A 560-kilometer pipeline between Barranca and Cartagena was completed by 1926. Before the end of the 1920s annual profits from oil in Colombia surpassed those of precious metals and bananas. By 1930 annual oil production exceeded 20 million barrels.[57] Barranca was Jersey Standard's largest overseas venture.[58]

The early success of the Tropical Oil Company would inspire an ongoing surge of applications for exploration and drilling rights. It was an opportunity for the national government in Bogotá to extend its influence to other frontier zones. By 1923 Colombia had received 674 applications for oil contracts from national and international investors.[59] Most of the proposals covered large uncharted tracks of land where the Colombian state had little or no presence. The most significant of these, in terms of its impact on the Magdalena Medio region, would be the concessions granted in the area south of Barranca, known as the Territiorio Vásquez. In 1926 these would be unified under the control of the Texas Petroleum Company and serve as an important secondary pole of economic development and popular organizing in the area. Within the next decade Royal Dutch Shell of the Netherlands would strike oil across the river from Barranca in an unsettled corner of the Department of Antioquia. The drive to increase drilling in the vicinity of Barrancabermeja's established oil-fields motivated the Industry Ministry to map the Magdalena River. Mapping projects were undertaken by Bogotá in direct response to applications for oil rights in the department of Bolívar, the border zone near Panama known as Urabá, and the eastern plains of Putumayo and Caquetá.[60]

Sensitized to nationalist concerns from the outset, Standard Oil of New Jersey took measures to conceal the fact that it alone controlled all aspects of a transcontinental business that connected Barrancabermeja to the Caribbean coast, the United States, and Canada.[61] The first international shipment of crude oil from Barranca arrived in Montréal by tanker on August 8, 1926. The Tropical Oil Company was in charge of drilling. The Andian National Corporation was in charge of transportation by pipeline to the Caribbean coast and beyond. The refinery in Montréal's industrial east end, which had been built in 1917, was owned and operated by Imperial Oil.[62] Imperial Oil, Andian National, and Tropical Oil were all owned by Standard Oil of New Jersey, but registered in Canada. It was a convenient way for the petrochemical giant to dodge accusations of U.S. imperialism.[63] On August 9, 1926, the *Globe and Mail* newspaper of Toronto declared, "Canadians Conquer Tropical Obstacles to Secure Crude Oil."[64] Sir Herbert Holt, chairman of Andian National and president of the Royal Bank of Canada, was on hand to open the valve emptying a container carrying 90,000 barrels of Colombian oil. He remarked that the flow of oil from Colombia "under all-Canadian control" would make "the Dominion [of Canada] independent of foreign supplies of oil."[65]

International oil sales proved to be of major importance to Colombia's economic development in the twentieth century. Public investments in roads and railways, the concomitant expansion of coffee production, as well as booming small- and medium-scale manufacturing required capital and fuel.[66] The Colombian state drew a 10 percent royalty from the wells exploited at Barranca. While Tropical Oil and other international companies generally considered Colombian oil legislation to be unfavorable because of "high taxes" and the thirty-year limit placed on concessions, profits far outweighed these concerns.[67] In the 1930s foreign investments in the oil sector continued to multiply. By the start of World War II, Colombia was the world's eighth largest petroleum-producing nation.[68]

Life and Work in a Boomtown

Barrancabermeja stood out as one of the strangest contradictions on the Colombian landscape. The city was poor and isolated, yet wealthy in many ways. It boasted a golf course for its North America personnel, while most of the Colombian workers paid exorbitant rents for space in cramped rooming houses. Barrancabermeja was built by the Tropical Oil Company as a protected base of operations for the extraction, refining, and distribution of oil. Unlike Henry Ford's Brazilian rubber utopia of Fordlandia, built "to wrench the Amazon into modernity," scant attention was paid to the accommodation, health, education, or recreation of the Colombian workforce at Barranca.[69] The many people employed in service, building, transportation, and other related industries fared even worse. As the historian Jacques Aprile-Gniset writes: "Since its beginnings, Barranca has been a city with no mules, but with trucks; with no blacksmiths or lawyers, but where soldiers and laundries proliferate; and thousands of peasants who would become the first proletariat in the country."[70]

As was typical of foreign-run enclaves in Latin America, Barranca was segregated along the lines of national origin, ethnicity, and class. In the earliest years, a majority of Colombian workers slept in wooden shacks and tents, or in hammocks on boats moored in Barranca's port. In 1910 there were three hundred people living in Barranca. By 1922 Tropical Oil employed four thousand people.[71] Despite this relatively large population, the municipality registered only 226 houses.[72] Meanwhile, most foreign managers lived in the comfortable Tropical Oil camp at El Centro, located about thirty kilometers inland. El Centro consisted of a large compound of ranch-style homes and tidy apartments, as well as a medical clinic, commissary, meeting rooms, administrative offices, golf course, and a firing range, surrounded by fences and patrolled by a private security force. There was also housing for a small group of foreign personnel at Barranca itself, located in the heart of the city center, but this area was off-limits to Colombian workers and other residents, except by special authorization. Workers of Anglo Caribbean origin also came, and Tropical Oil built accommodation specifically for them. Known to Colombians as *yumecas*, a derivation of the word Jamaican, these men spoke English and had worked on industrial projects before, including the digging of the Panama Canal.[73] The preferential treatment of North American managers and the separate status of Jamaican laborers engendered resentment on the part of many Colombian migrants to the area.

Conditions in the enclave were precarious, even for those employed by Tropical Oil. In the 1920s reports in the national press described systematic problems, including poor health care, unreliable pay, arbitrary discipline, and a general lack of transparency on the part of the company.[74] Tropical diseases were rampant, and on some days 50 percent of the labor force would be stricken with malaria or hookworm.[75] Tropical Oil paid its Colombian workers on average one peso per day, equivalent to about a dollar U.S. per day.[76] While this was a significantly higher wage than the average Colombian laborer would have made at the time, the money did not go far. Housing prices in Barranca were determined by landlords who owned multiple buildings and rented beds to single men at a premium. Workers found ways of sharing the burden, even taking turns sleeping in the same bed, in shifts. According to the Conservative newspaper *El Porvenir*, the food served by Tropical Oil cost workers as much as 60 percent of their daily earnings.[77] The schedule was ten to twelve hours a day, six days a week. Much of the early work in road building, drilling, and hauling equipment was temporary. These factors contributed to a high desertion rate, which forced Tropical Oil to continuously replenish their labor force. Recruiters known as *enganchadores* traveled to Antioquia, Santander, and the Caribbean coast to enlist workers on behalf of Tropical Oil.[78]

Barrancabermeja was subject to extraordinary security measures commensurate with its special status as a foreign enclave. In 1922 a National Police base was set up in Barranca, reinforcing the municipal and private police forces already present in the area.[79] Aprile-Gniset observes: "Barranca may be the first and only [Colombian] city to be born under a premature state of siege and periodically governed by a dual civil and military administration."[80] The Colombian army also had a base in Barranca, and navy ships patrolled the Magdalena River.[81] In 1928, there were 298 people employed by public institutions in Barrancabermeja, 65 percent of whom worked for armed security forces. Created in 1891, the National Police force was originally intended to replace local police forces across the country. However, Colombia's strong regionalism and the recurrence of bipartisan violence prevented any national security policies from being implemented until the 1960s. In the meantime, the National Police were deployed very selectively. In the early twentieth century, the ruling Conservative Party established National Police garrisons in a few traditional Liberal Party strongholds, such as the department of Santander.[82] Special deployments were also made to areas where export products and foreign interests were present, including the Santa Marta banana zone, the Shell oil camp in Casabe, and Barrancabermeja.

The next step in the development of Barrancabermeja was for Tropical Oil to secure its claim in political terms and make certain that the company would not be subject to the interests of local political officials. In 1922 Barranca was designated a *municipio*. This meant that Barranca would no longer fall within the jurisdiction of the agricultural center of San Vicente de Chucurí. It was not clear whether Barrancabermeja fulfilled the legal requirements to be named a *municipio*, but Tropical Oil Company executives urged the Colombian government in Bogotá to expedite the change. The decision to create the *municipio* of Barrancabermeja included an agreement that 5 percent of oil royalties earned by the Colombian state from the Tropical Oil Company's activities at Barranca would be used to provide services and infrastructure for local residents, as well as pay salaries of municipal functionaries.[83] In principle, this was a major benefit to the citizens of Barranca, who rightly expected greater attention would be paid to local issues. In practice, Tropical Oil simply asserted its dominion over the lives of local residents with little concern for public services. It was a license to continue to implement highly exclusionary labor and social policies.

In the early years, the culture of Barranca was rough and ready. The prevalence of single men in the city contributed to the development of a thriving sex trade. Prostitutes from Colombia and Europe demanded a premium for their services, equivalent to an oil worker's daily wage. The memoir of Texas oilman W. O. Durham, who spent two stints in Barranca in the 1920s and 1930s, provides a firsthand account of life in the early years of the Tropical Oil Company. Like dozens of other drillers from the United States and Canada, Durham went to Barranca to make money and find adventure. He traveled from Texas to New Orleans by train and then to Santa Marta by United Fruit Company steamer before making the long trek up the Magdalena River to Barranca. Durham was an experienced wildcatter who set up small appraisal rigs in order to find the best sources of oil. He describes a hard-drinking and rugged lifestyle. The foremen wore sidearms and spent their wages at the brothels in town. Many of these skilled foreign laborers took pride in their capacity to endure the hardships of life in the South American oilfields. They saw themselves as individualists and adventure seekers.[84]

By contrast, the North American managers and their families who lived in El Centro and Barranca remember few hardships, other than the heat.[85] That is because administrators lived inside gated enclaves built by Tropical Oil to separate them from the mass of Colombian laborers. Their experiences offer clues as to the sources of conflict between Colombians and foreigners at the time. Pauline Appelbaum, the daughter of Tropical Oil's chief purchasing agent, was born in Barranca. In a special contribution to the *New York Times* in 1973, she recalled in great detail the trip by paddle wheeler up the Magdalena River between the Caribbean port of Barranquilla and Barranca. Visiting Barranca nearly forty years after she lived there, Appelbaum observed that while the city had grown and seemed more "Americanized" with paved roads, cinemas, sports facilities, and shops, some things had remained the same: "We intuit a clue as to why Americans in foreign lands cause resentment. Even in death we see here caste and race distinction, with foreigners buried on higher ground, separate from the natives."[86] In similar terms, when Felipe Simanca, one of the protagonists of Gonzalo Buenahora's novel *Sangre y petróleo*, arrives in Barranca in the early 1920s in search of work, he immediately remarks on the way in which the town is divided: "It was a kind of border between Colombia and Gringolandia."[87]

The demanding lives of Barranca's *petroleros* have long been of interest to Colombian writers. The earliest fictional account of Barranca written from the perspective of Colombian oil workers was published in 1934.[88] Rafael Jaramillo Arango's *Barrancabermeja: Novela de proxenetas, rufianes, obreros y petroleros* tells the story of a young man from Bogotá who comes to the oil center to make his fortune.[89] He is overworked by his North American supervisor, falls in love with a prostitute, and is caught up in violent confrontations between workers and the Colombian army following a strike.[90] Jaramillo's *Barrancabermeja* was the first in a series of hardboiled, socially engaged novels that denounced U.S. imperialism in Barranca. Between 1938 and 1978 Gonzalo Buenahora published thirteen novels, poetry collections, and plays about life in Barranca. Born in nearby Piedecuesta, Santander, Buenahora was educated in Bogotá and worked as a physician among the oil workers of Barranca for four decades. Buenahora was deeply influenced by the Marxist worldview of friends and associates from the oil workers' union. In his most celebrated work, the social realist novel *Sangre y petróleo*, Buenahora tells the story of young men from the Colombian countryside who migrate to the enclave in search of work, come face to face with the power of the foreign oil company, and participate in protests and strikes.[91] Subsequent generations of writers, notably Laura Restrepo, would continue to publish novels set in Barrancabermeja that looked at the problems of labor and poverty through the eyes of marginal figures.

The decoupling of local development from the locomotive of industrialization is typical in oil enclaves the world over. Social and labor conflict is common because of the capital-intensive manner in which oil is exploited and the way in which revenues are dispersed, providing comparatively few benefits to surrounding communities.[92] Oil enclaves tend to attract many more people to a region than the industry can employ, greatly exacerbating tensions. People drawn to oil operations frequently find themselves at odds with large corporations over issues of economic justice. In the early phases of operations in Barrancabermeja, oil workers protested to improve working conditions and forestall layoffs, subcontracting, summary dismissals, and other strategies utilized by the company to bring down the cost of labor. In tropical regions, oil enclaves are poles of attraction for national and transnational workers, and they are often structured along ethnic lines. Typically, the most-skilled and best-paid positions are occupied by "white" North American or European personnel, and the least-skilled and worst-paid positions are occupied by third-world workers.[93] Discrepancies between the way foreign managers and national laborers are treated come into focus around wages, but also basic public services, especially health.

Relations between the local workers and the more experienced, more highly paid North American engineers and managers were fraught with bitterness and misunderstanding. There was little social mixing between national and expatriate personnel, as even the residences of higher-ranking Colombians were segregated from North American employees.[94] The company would later concede that the failure to provide adequate services for national workers might possibly have contributed to labor unrest.[95] As Gibb and Knowlton remark in their 1956 official history of Standard Oil: "Quite inadvertently, it seemed, the foreign companies in Colombia, as elsewhere in Latin America, were helping spark a revolution."[96] In the 1930s Tropical Oil would develop more and more services for workers and their families, including schools and housing. Colombian workers began to occupy higher-paid positions, and the need for *peones* to carry out road-building and other back-breaking tasks diminished. However, Colombian and foreign employees continued to live separate lives.[97] There were still few opportunities for advancement for Colombians, and the problem of mistrust grew.

The Roots of Radical Political Culture

Radical nationalist and anti-authoritarian political culture in Barrancabermeja has its roots in the structural, economic, and social inequalities that prevailed in the city during the Tropical Oil era. The presence of a foreign corporation in the Magdalena Medio region created economic opportunity for thousands of Colombian men, while maintaining a hierarchy that denied these workers the privileges reserved for foreign bosses. Life was centered around oil workers' associations and left-wing political movements. In the 1920s, strikes were organized by the Socialist Revolutionary Party (PSR), the forerunner of the Communist Party of Colombia (PCC).[98] Ideas about labor rights circulated among workers in Barranca and along the Magdalena River through public meetings, as well as through newspapers and pamphlets. The nationalist stance of the oil workers' first union, the Unión Obrera, echoed the concerns of the Liberal fighters who had helped to settle the region in the first decade of the twentieth century. Railroad and dock workers based out of Barranquilla and Puerto Wilches also helped to broadcast ideas about labor and social rights. These forces combined during oil strikes, many of which were carried out despite being declared illegal by the national government.

There are a number of turning points in the history of Barrancabermeja that help to chart the city's development as a center of social and political conflict. Major strikes by oil workers took place in 1924, 1927, 1935, 1938, and early 1948. Many of these ended in violence. During these events, two dynamics emerge that would inform the development of a common culture of protest among Colombian workers in Barranca. First, the national government in Bogotá remained mainly concerned with public order. Throughout this period, successive Colombian governments interceded to suppress strike actions and protests. Second, the fact that the foreign-owned Tropical Oil Company treated workers with such apparent disregard reinforced a militant brand of nationalism. The first two industrial actions, in 1924 and 1927, defied a general prohibition on union activity. Workers' demands for recognition were celebrated movements around the country and attracted well-known organizers such as María Cano and Raúl Mahecha.

The Colombian labor movement was very much in its infancy when Tropical Oil arrived in Barranca. During the early twentieth century, workers' aspirations kept pace with Colombia's export-led economic growth yet clashed with the interests of foreign investors.[99] The 1920s was a period of mobilization among workers across the rapidly developing Caribbean coast, extending from the Santa Marta banana export zone to Barranca. In February 1910 Barranquilla-based dock workers organized the first modern strike in Colombian history in response to allegations that the British-owned Compañías Aliadas was withholding wages.[100] The next major collective actions against an international corporation in Colombia were organized by United Fruit Company workers in 1918 and 1919, which resulted in significant wage increases and other concessions.[101] In 1920 there were an unprecedented thirty-two labor strikes across the country, including several in the Magdalena Medio region.[102] These workers set an example for others toiling in the export economy to follow.

The 1920s labor movement in Barranca was supported by a new generation of independent, left-wing, and nationalist political leaders. One of the most prominent organizers of the era was Raúl Eduardo Mahecha, who arrived in Barranca in 1922 from Medellín. Mahecha had fought in the Thousand Days' War, had been eyewitness to U.S. "gunboat diplomacy" in Panama, and had participated in a strike among railway workers in 1919 at La Dorada, Caldas, the most southern port town in the Magdalena Medio. Mahecha was thirty-eight years of age, and his reputation for strong anti-imperialist leanings was well known to Colombian authorities. Mahecha helped found the Unión Obrera on February 12, 1923. In Barranca, he organized rallies and published an influential newspaper called *Vanguardia Obrera*, which reported on workers' rights and local politics.[103] The grievances highlighted by the Unión Obrera at this time were very much centered on living conditions. Access to housing, health care, and quality food were at the top of the list. Mahecha also used the *Vanguardia Obrera* to denounce the fact that Colombian workers occupied the lowest positions in the company.[104] Integral to Mahecha's critique of Tropical Oil was a concern for all local residents, and for what Barrancabermeja could represent for all Colombians.

The Colombian government acknowledged workers' complaints but did not abide radical spokespeople such as Mahecha, nor did policymakers want to recognize the collective bargaining rights of the Unión Obrera. In March 1924 an agreement was signed between the Colombian Ministry of Industry and Tropical Oil that covered a wide range of issues, including remuneration, health care, food, housing, education, and vacation.[105] Tropical Oil officials also agreed to employ more Colombian workers in skilled jobs and to build an aqueduct for the provision of potable water. It was the first such arrangement made in the oil industry in Colombia. The government negotiator and spokesperson, Minister of Industry Diógenes Reyes, was quick to clarify that he did not believe that workers were being mistreated. Following a fact-finding visit to Barranca in March 1924, Reyes concluded that the Unión Obrera's mistrust of Tropical Oil was largely "baseless."[106] The minister praised the sanitary conditions established by Tropical Oil, while lamenting the fact that a number of bars and "houses of corruption" had been established in the area by former oil workers.[107] Reyes accepted the company's assurances that workers' basic needs were going to be met. In return, Reyes stated that the government would provide security for the company.[108]

Government attempts to simultaneously mollify workers and reassure the oil company would prove disastrous. Organized workers in Barranca were impatient to see improvements to conditions put into effect and were exasperated with what they perceived to be the arrogance of the Tropical Oil Company. They also sought legal recognition for the union. In October 1924 oil workers organized the first strike in Barrancabermeja history. The list of claims prepared by strike leaders underscored many of the points granted in the recently signed agreement between Tropical Oil and the government. The workers also denounced cases of arbitrary treatment and demanded that abusive supervisors be dismissed. Workers' appeals published in the *Vanguardia Obrera* garnered measured support in Bogotá, particularly among opposition Liberals. Some statements of sympathy were even made by a few Conservative government officials. Tropical Oil directors countered that the Colombian government, which received royalties from the oil industry, should be responsible for public services. One company representative in Barranca wrote to the U.S. ambassador in Bogotá to protest what he saw as nationalist posturing on the part of the Colombian government. He complained that the minister of industry echoed workers' claims merely to "score political points."[109] When push came to shove, Bogotá supported the oil company. Army troops were sent from Bucaramanga to Barranca to put an end to the 1924 strike after just ten days. The Colombian army carried out hundreds of arrests. Raúl Mahecha was sent to prison. More than 1,200 workers were sacked and banned from returning to Barranca.[110] In its official newspaper, the *Lamp*, Standard Oil barely made allusion to the strike, boasted to shareholders about the outstanding services it provided to local workers, and praised Colombia as "a progressive country" with a "stable and progressive government."[111]

The 1924 strike had put Barranca on the political map. The fate of Colombian oil workers garnered the attention of left-wing movements. Well-known progressive leaders from Antioquia such as María Cano, Ignacio Torres Giraldo, and the photographer Floro Piedrahita were among the first to join forces with Raúl Mahecha's organization in Barranca.[112] In 1925, the Communist writer and campaigner María Cano, known as the revolutionary Flower of Labor, gave a now-legendary speech in Barranca to protest the transfer of imprisoned oil workers from the oil enclave to the city of Medellín following the 1924 strike.[113] During her address she expressed personal anguish and spoke with a religious fervor about the injustices done to Barranca's workers: "This small group of brave souls, who yesterday cried out in rebellion in order to stop the terrible avalanche of foreign oppression, have received cruel imprisonment, humiliation and, worse still, indolence."[114] Cano would return to Barranca the next year as part of an organizing drive along the port towns of the Magdalena River. During her second visit, Cano was accompanied by Ignacio Torres Giraldo, the secretary general of the socialist trade union federation, the Confederación Obrera Nacional. Their 1926 stop in Barranca was timed to generate popular support for a planned second oil workers' strike. Cano and Torres left Barranca on January 1, 1927, and the strike was declared one week later.[115]

The 1927 strike was a high-stakes replay of the 1924 strike. Raúl Mahecha and other organizers had returned to Barranca. The level of conflict between workers, the company, and the state was increasing. Strike leaders were convinced that the workers' bargaining position was enhanced by the exponential increase in oil production achieved by Tropical Oil in the intervening three years. The national government's resident inspector called the 1927 strike a "ridiculous pantomime carried out by known exploiters of the workers in the region."[116] Between January 7 and January 12 the inspector, National Police based in Barranca, and Ministry of Industry officials in Bogotá exchanged multiple telegrams, many commenting on the dangerous "pseudostrike" led by "bolsheviks."[117] In point of fact, none of the issues raised by workers during the 1924 strike concerning housing, health, food, and the institution of eight-hour shifts had been resolved. The Unión Obrera also demanded that the organizers of the 1924 strike be exonerated. This time striking *petroleros* were joined by dockworkers employed in the shipment of oil and employees of the Andian National Corporation, the Standard Oil subsidiary that owned the recently inaugurated pipeline to Cartagena. Bogotá imposed military "state of siege" measures up and down the Magdalena River, including curfews and checkpoints, and once again the army was deployed to the city.[118] Several union members were killed when security forces opened fire on a demonstration at the gates to the refinery. Strike organizers were arrested on January 28, and the action was brought to an end. Mahecha and several other leaders were displayed in public stocks in small towns as they were transported to prison in the highlands in Tunja, in the department of Boyacá. Mahecha was released from prison six months later, after which he relocated to the Caribbean banana zone, accompanied by a number of displaced Tropical Oil workers. Once in Santa Marta they renewed their organizing efforts, now targeting the United Fruit Company.

Colombia's export zones attracted a broad spectrum of new political forces. The most prominent of the new progressive national leaders to emerge in the late 1920s was Jorge Eliécer Gaitán, an independent-minded, young, and charismatic lawyer from the Liberal Party, who made his name denouncing the December 1928 massacre of banana workers.[119] Gaitán, a dark-skinned lawyer from a modest Bogotá family, distinguished between what he called the *país político* and the *país nacional* to emphasize the breach between the exclusionary world of politics and ordinary citizens.[120] Outside of Gaitán's hometown of Bogotá, the labor bastions of Barranquilla and Barranca were the two major centers of support for the young leader.[121] In the 1920s the left wing of the Liberal Party increased its reach by courting workers' organizations, including the Unión Obrera in Barranca. Many peasants in the area who had fought for the Liberal Party in the Thousand Days' War also identified with emerging progressive forces. Gaitán's only visit to Barranca took place in July 1929 during a speaking tour he conducted en route back to Bogotá from Ciénaga, the site of the banana workers' massacre the previous year.[122] Seeing the populist *caudillo* for the first time, some in attendance were so moved that they jumped into the river to greet his boat.[123]

As the Colombian export economy grew in the late 1920s, workers increased demands on employers and on the state, and the state demonstrated its willingness to use force to ensure foreign investments. Strikes in the oil and banana sectors were emblematic of a rising tendency. On July 27, 1929, armed rebellions were launched concurrently from leftist strongholds in the departments of Tolima and Santander. The *bolcheviques* of Líbano (Tolima), San Vicente de Chucurí, and Puerto Wilches (Santander) led what has been described as the first Communist insurrectionary movement in Latin American history.[124] In Santander, the movement centered around La Gómez, a train station that serviced the lumber town of Puerto Wilches on the Magdalena River, twenty kilometers north of Barranca.[125] Many of the rebels were young men drawn to the Magdalena Medio from different parts of the department of Santander to clear land and lay tracks. The movement's leaders were descended from veterans of the Thousand Days' War who saw themselves as participating in a historical effort to bring down an oligarchic state.[126] Intrepid, yet isolated, the *bolcheviques* rebellion was swiftly crushed.[127] Some two hundred army troops were sent from Bucaramanga to Barranca to ensure the protection of Tropical Oil property. In Barranca, suspected rebel sympathizers were jailed. In nearby Puerto Berrío, workers were detained and locked up aboard a navy gunboat.[128] As a consequence, these strategically important areas were kept out of the fighting.[129]

Barrancabermeja's oil workers embraced a form of popular radicalism that incorporated aspects of Communism, Liberalism, and even anarcho-syndicalism. It was the outcome of how Barranca and the surrounding area were settled, incorporating migrants from different regions of Colombia, refugees from past wars, and new movements. These "Liberal leftists, anarchists, independent radicals and Communists" were inspired by the triumphs of the

Mexican Revolution of 1910 and the Bolshevik Revolution of 1917.[130] The people who came to Barranca in search of work were united by the harshness of their material circumstances and rising expectations commensurate with the wealth being produced by Tropical Oil. They participated in groundbreaking forms of trade union and social movement organization, despite official repression. The coarseness of life and labor in a foreign-run oil enclave was given voice through workers' organizations and meaning through rituals of public protest. Barranca became a city of counterhegemonic invented traditions, an important center of radical organizing and a symbol of resistance for Colombian working peoples.[131] Uninhibited by traditional social and economic structures, popular expressions of anti-authoritarianism mingled with Liberalism, Communism, and economic nationalism. Workers' organizations led strikes against Tropical Oil, challenged the Conservative Party government in Bogotá, rattled the Liberal Party establishment, and gave impetus to reformers and rebels.

The Barrancabermeja Commune Uprising

Popular radicalism in Barranca peaked in 1948 with an armed uprising during which anti-government forces seized control of the city. Organized in response to the April 9 murder of Jorge Eliécer Gaitán, the Comuna de Barrancabermeja demonstrated *barranqueños'* identification with a culture of defiance.[132] Building on a history of labor militancy at the local level and riding a tide of progressive populism at the national level, the Comuna de Barrancabermeja expressed the frustration of *barranqueños* from many walks of life. Because the city and environs were areas of recent colonization, Barranca's political culture was being shaped by migration and the continuous interplay between rural and urban communities. Notably, leaders of the Comuna de Barrancabermeja would go on to establish guerrilla groups in the surrounding countryside. Agitation by women domestic workers would likewise point to the creation of new channels of civic engagement. Similar uprisings took place in cities and towns across Colombia, with similar outcomes.[133] The repression of the Comuna de Barrancabermeja, and subsequent measures undertaken by the national government to ensure the flow of oil, resulted in a steep decline in trade union and social movement organizing over the next decade. The aspirations of those who participated in the Comuna would be have to wait.

The last major strikes against the Tropical Oil Company were carried out in late 1947 and early 1948 in the midst of a power struggle over oil nationalization. Tropical Oil had been pressuring Bogotá for an extension of its control over the De Mares Concession since the early 1940s. Both the government and the nationalist-oriented Unión Sindical Obrera (USO) opposed the plan.[134] The Tropical Oil Company and the Colombian government disagreed as to the exact date that the return should take place. The government argued that Tropical Oil's drilling rights expired in 1949. Tropical Oil maintained that the date should be 1951. Tropical Oil's claim was eventually vindicated by the Colombian Supreme Court in 1944.[135] The stakes in the dispute were high for both sides. By mid-decade Tropical Oil's activities in the Magdalena Medio accounted for more than 50 percent of Colombia's total oil output and employed more than five thousand people.[136] Tropical Oil continued to demand more time and warned that Colombia would have to increase gasoline imports if nationalization went ahead as planned. Workers' representatives accused the company of deliberately reducing the flow of oil in protest.[137] Output at Barranca decreased from 20.5 million barrels in 1941 to 12.3 million barrels in 1947.[138]

During this period of increasing tension and decreasing oil output, industrial workers were not alone in making demands on Tropical Oil. As the personal papers of Tropical Oil staff reveal, women domestic workers also acted collectively to seek improvements. The Canadian accountant John Edgar Hicks had lived and worked in the Tropical Oil camp at El Centro from March 1939 to March 1941. Following military service during World War II, Hicks returned to the area for another two years. Now serving as account paymaster, Hicks was joined by his twenty-seven-year-old wife, Catherine, and their two young children. A third child, daughter Virginia, was born in El Centro on May 8, 1946. John Hicks was the eldest son of an educated and affluent Toronto family. Catherine Hicks was a French national and the granddaughter of Ferdinand de Lesseps, the engineer and developer of the Suez Canal. In a letter addressed to his parents, dated March 21, 1946, Hicks describes the demands that domestic workers presented to Tropical Oil: "Our maids here presented the most amazing statement, not a strike, but their twenty points, ranging from a fifty percent increase, we pay ours twenty pesos for which she does all the baby laundry and a lot of other laundry, cleans the house (great exaggeration) cooks the meals. One of the ten clauses that really burnt us up was the request for prenatal and post natal care. As 25 percent of the maids are affected I can readily understand the inclusion of such a clause."[139] The rate of pay for the Hickses' domestic help would have been the equivalent of roughly twelve dollars per month, high by Colombian standards for similar work, but less than half of what the men who labored in the oilfields were earning and woefully insufficient to cover the high costs of living. By way of illustration, the Hickses' own home, owned by Tropical Oil, cost twenty dollars per month to rent. In subsequent letters, Hicks himself expressed feelings of resentment toward company directors for poor remuneration. In one case, he describes the problem of buying Christmas presents at privately run shops in Barranca, where a jigsaw puzzle for his children was selling for about five dollars.[140]

The prelude to the nationalization of Tropical Oil's drilling operations was marked by acrimony between unionized workers and the company. The strike that began November 3, 1947, included for the first time an explicit demand that the "reversion" process be expedited. John Hicks described the strike in a letter to his parents as events unfolded, remarking on the issues at stake and a change in tone among workers:

> The demands of the union (a very red flavoured affair) are extreme, they want a month holiday with pay and plane fare to any point in Colombia, all kinds of raises, hospital nationalized and also the Commissary, not to mention several staff members they want removed, and to top everything they want 2/3 rds pay for all the time they are on strike, the strike leaders are men with very negligible education and very little reasoning power, oh yes they also want the field expropriated by the government, that is a good joke as without foreign staff the field would run about a month. . . . The men walked out on Monday and joined a parade which was headed by a large Colombian flag, all the different departments had their own banners, all on a red background, the tone of the mob was little ugly compared to previous walkouts when most of the men seemed rather sheepish and ashamed, this time they shouted almost angrily. Apparently the routine for joining the parade is to wait for it with your group and dept. flag the[n] join as you join the mob you raise and clench your right fist and shout "Viva la huelga" to which the others in the parade reply, there these is a series of shouts, Viva Colombia, Colombia—Libre.[141]

Hicks, who knew the company well, expressed anxiety about the union's power. He also remained skeptical that the Colombian state would be capable of effectively managing the handover. On the final day of the strike, November 17, he wrote another letter, observing that "the company is in a very poor bargaining position as they cannot lockout the workers . . . since the Colombian government and economy is dependent on continued production."[142] A few days later Tropical Oil dismissed 107 workers, ostensibly due to declining productivity. The union, supported by the country's most important labor federation, as well as opposition Liberals, immediately demanded the company reinstate the workers.[143]

A longer strike was organized from January 7 through February 24 of 1948. The forty-nine-day work stoppage played out against the backdrop of an ever-deepening rift between progressive and reactionary political forces in the country. Conservative president Mariano Ospina Pérez eventually pressured Tropical Oil to sign a new labor agreement, but only after a series of repressive measures had been carried out against strike leaders, including the use of soldiers to secure pumping stations, mass arrests, and the dismissal of strike leaders. Rallies and solidarity actions in support of the USO were organized by unionized workers in Bogotá. In the middle of February, as the strike appeared to reach an impasse, the union agreed to binding arbitration. True to form, the oil company was unhappy with the intervention of the state. President Ospina was criticized by workers for supporting undemocratic actions yet lauded for his role in securing concessions from Tropical Oil. After the strike was over, Ospina ordered the reinstatement of the 107 dismissed workers.[144] Despite the resolution of the dispute, events in Barranca had revealed a sharp cleavage in Colombian politics.

By the late 1940s the politics of mutual tolerance between Liberal and Conservative leaders in Bogotá was over. The assassination of Jorge Eliécer Gaitán on April 9, 1948, led to the largest riot in Latin American history, known to historians as El Bogotazo. Gaitán was shot around 1:00 p.m. outside the front entrance of the building where his office was located in central Bogotá. The presumed assailant was attacked by an angry crowd and killed before he could be detained and questioned. Almost immediately, the Colombian capital was set ablaze. Nobody was ever detained for the murder of Colombia's president-in-waiting. However, the outrage of *gaitanistas* was intense, and they blamed the Conservative government. Hundreds died in the streets of Bogotá in the first couple of days and in similar outbursts in other smaller cities across the country. Even more severe was the backlash against Gaitán's supporters. Official armed forces and paramilitaries were mobilized against Liberal supporters, who organized militia in response. The civil war that ensued was most intense in contested zones, where neither party held hegemonic power. From there, the conflict engulfed frontier areas as well. La Violencia would end up claiming at least 200,000 lives between 1948 and 1958.[145] Popular fury at the assassination of Gaitán reached its apogee in the initial period. The year 1948 would be one of the most violent in Colombia's long history of internal warfare, with an estimated 43,557 violent deaths.[146]

The rebellion set off by the murder of Gaitán called the Comuna de Barrancabermeja involved the wider community more completely than any of the previous union-led strikes.[147] Its suppression similarly demonstrated a bipartisan consensus among the political elites in Bogotá around the importance of oil. The Comuna was the first instance in which a broad-based local movement composed of oil workers and other residents came together to challenge the authority of the Tropical Oil Company and the Colombian government. Although inspired by the murder of the leader of the Liberal Party, the Comuna was independent, and benefited from the cooperation of a majority of local residents, regardless of political affiliation. Even local security forces personnel joined the rebellion, providing much-needed weapons and expertise to hastily organized militia units. The rebels placed oil barrels on the airport runway to prevent planes from landing, blocked roads, and even used sections of oil pipeline to fabricate canons to guard against incursions from the national army.[148] They seized control of the refinery and threatened to sabotage it. Committees were organized by Comuna leaders to ensure the distribution of food and water, since the city was effectively cut off from the outside world. In the final analysis, the uprising was isolated and unsustainable. By April 19, 1948, the Comuna was the last of the *gaitanista* uprisings still standing. National Liberal Party officials concerned about the fate of the refinery helped to broker an agreement between the revolutionary junta and the national government. The spokespeople of the Comuna de Barrancabermeja negotiated an amnesty for themselves and put down their arms. However, the amnesty was violated the following day, and the army occupied the city. Comuna leaders were prosecuted by a military tribunal, *consejo verbal de guerra*, and a military mayor was installed.[149]

Early during La Violencia, the former commander of the Comuna de Barrancabermeja, Rafael Rangel Gómez, escaped to the countryside to continue fighting. Rangel was a police officer, and like many other officials in Liberal-controlled areas, he responded to Gaitán's death by rebelling against the government of the Conservative president Mariano Ospina Pérez.[150] After spending a few months in prison, Rangel began organizing a guerrilla force in the mountains outside of Barranca. On the day of general elections held on November 27, 1949, Rangel led an assault on the nearby town of San Vicente de Chucurí. Rangel and his supporters, most of whom were *gaitanistas* and Liberals, waged a campaign against Conservative-led forces across the department of Santander for the next few years.[151] Commerce along the Magdalena River was disrupted by Liberal and Conservative guerrillas, as well as by opportunistic bandits who raided shipping "in the shadow of Rangel."[152] Strategic towns to the south and north of Barranca were sites of brutal counterinsurgent violence. The area of Puerto Berrío recorded the highest number of violent deaths in the Department of Antioquia through 1951 and 1952. Rangel's forces demobilized in 1953 and received a warm but subdued reception in Barranca.

The period of La Violencia was calm in Barranca itself, due in substantial part to an unwritten agreement between warring factions to stay out of the oil capital. A large presence of the army and National Police helped contain local labor and social movements. A national state of siege was declared by President Mariano Ospina on May 31, 1948, that lasted for a decade.[153] Throughout that period, Barranca was subject to directives banning popular forms of social and political assembly. The USO lost its legal status in 1950 as part of national anti-union legislation, and it was not restored until 1961 when the Tropical Oil Company refinery reverted to state control. In the interim, the city of Barranca and the department of Santander were governed by military officers.[154]

The relative calm that prevailed in Barrancabermeja during La Violencia allowed for the peaceful handover of the De Mares Concession to the Colombian state in 1951. Barrancabermeja was the first major oil venture in Latin America ever to be surrendered to state control without recourse to expropriation. The Empresa Colombiana de Petróleos (Ecopetrol) was created in 1951 as the result of a largely top-down process. At a ceremony on August 26, 1951, attended by thousands of *barranqueños* and dignitaries from Bogotá, as well as Standard Oil and International Petroleum officials, the De Mares Concession was relinquished to the state. The official parlance of the day was that the oilfields were "reverting" to state control, which made the point that oil had been a matter of national patrimony from the outset. It was the first step in a two-phase process of nationalization of all of the Tropical Oil holdings in the Magdalena Medio. Tropical Oil retained a ten-year lease on the refinery at Barranca, which came to an end in 1961. Of the more than 5,000 workers in Barranca and the surrounding area, 1,500 of them now worked for Ecopetrol.[155] Fireworks and cheers greeted the official announcement made at midnight, followed by music and dancing until dawn.

The creation of Ecopetrol put into evidence what Mary Roldán has described as the emergence in the middle of the twentieth century of an increasingly interventionist, if diffuse and "morally weak," Colombian state.[156] In his influential study of La Violencia of the 1950s, the historian Paul Oquist describes how certain areas of "state coherence" were impervious to fighting, due either to the hegemony of a single political party or the relative harmony between the two parties.[157] The historian Alberto Flórez-Malagón writes that "the strength and the clarity of the system of power" in some regions helped to minimize competition between elites and sustain social order.[158] The presence of a large transnational corporation in Barranca encouraged stability, although, as Roldán has shown, political violence was carried out by rival Liberals and Conservatives across the river from Barranca in the Shell-owned oil camp in Casabe, Antioquia.[159] What accounted for the low level of conflict in Barranca during La Violencia was a consensus between the leaders of rival political factions in Bogotá about its exceptional strategic importance. And while the Liberals were certainly the more popular of the two main political parties in Barranca, the party's influence was not hegemonic. Moreover, it was the now leaderless left wing of the Liberal Party that had held sway in Barranca. The impact of La Violencia was much more direct in areas of the country where Liberals and Conservatives had a history of competition over land and resources.[160]

Differences between the Liberal and Conservative parties in Colombia, which had framed civil wars dating back to the early nineteenth century, were inflamed during La Violencia. However, the official antagonism between the two traditional political groupings cast a shadow over far more complex and deeper regional and class conflicts. While La Violencia was not strictly speaking a product of the Cold War, the outcomes of the conflict would dovetail into a period of open ideological struggle in subsequent decades. The calm that reigned in Barranca hinged on the capacity of both the Tropical Oil Company to discipline its workforce and the national government to ensure that trade unionists were kept quiet. This eerie silence was indicative of the simmering problems facing Colombia. As explored in the next chapter, the pact known as the National Front, a formal settling of differences between the Conservatives and the Liberals, attempted to shut out left-wing voices, with perverse consequences.

Conclusion

This chapter has explored the relationship between region and class in the development of social and political identity in Colombia's oil enclave.[161] Between 1919 and 1961, Barrancabermeja was transformed from a small frontier outpost into a state-of-the-art industrial enclave. Nowhere else in Colombia have there existed social and labor movements so densely knitted together and so durable. Barranca is home to the oldest and most powerful industrial trade union in Colombia, the USO. This is an extraordinary legacy by any standard and utterly unique in Colombia, where labor and social movements have remained modest in size when compared with other Latin American countries.[162] The uprising that took place on April 9, 1948, was the apogee of Barranca's radical popular movement during the Tropical Oil era.[163] Barranca allows us to view the national state as a constant presence in an area of special strategic and economic importance over a prolonged period of time.

To understand the role of the national state in the history of Barrancabermeja is to understand why the city's labor and social movements remained the most militant and energetic in all of Colombia in the twentieth century. While the tropical lowlands around present-day Barranca were sparsely settled, they were nonetheless contested by *colonos* and capitalists, including foreign investors. The arrival of Tropical Oil created new sources of tension, as thousands of people came to Barranca in search of work. The Colombian state defended Tropical Oil and subdued oil workers' strikes through a combination of emergency legal measures and military force. Union organizers viewed the state as mostly antagonistic to workers' interests. This dynamic of conflict between the state and the oil workers was particularly acute during the period leading up to the reversion of the De Mares Concession to state control. Competing claims made on Colombia's national oil industry by workers, Tropical Oil, and the state came to a violent climax in 1948. The departure of the Tropical Oil Company in 1961 would sharpen the conflict between *barranqueños* and Bogotá.

2

Oil and Water

New Social Movements Come Forward

> The "cosmopolitanism" of Barranca, along with the "weakness" of traditional forms of domination, has made *barranqueños* open to new things, in particular to all forms of discourse that are alternative to the dominant discourse. . . . The ties of solidarity are a product of the uprooting that immigrants to Barranca experienced . . . and especially the solidarity of labor.
>
> Mauricio Archila, historian[1]

New Forms of Protest

In a speech delivered live on national radio and television on August 15, 1971, Colombian President Misael Pastrana Borrero vowed to defeat terrorism and disorder.[2] He made no distinction between social movements and the guerrillas. In fact, he did not even mention Colombia's four main armed rebel groups.[3] President Pastrana spoke instead of the "subversive" threat posed by labor, students, and organized crime. A national student strike had recently been suppressed through military intervention, made possible by the declaration of a national state of siege.[4] Colombian elites were also coming to grips with a series of high-profile kidnappings for ransom, including that of the industrialist Diego Echavarría, whose murder one month later would be attributed to an ambitious twenty-two-year-old thug named Pablo Escobar. However, foremost in the president's mind was a strike in Barrancabermeja that had begun ten days earlier with unionized workers' occupation of the country's most important oil refinery. The takeover of the refinery lasted just two days, but the toll was devastating. Hundreds of striking oil workers were summarily dismissed by the state-owned oil company, Ecopetrol. Forty-six members of the Unión Sindical Obrera (USO) were prosecuted by a military court on a long list of charges, ranging from kidnapping to sabotage.

The departure of the Tropical Oil Company in 1961 had renewed, rather than laid to rest, social and political conflict in Barranca. Instead of being invited by the government at the time to play a part in the nationalization process, the oil workers were marginalized. This ensured the deepening of conflict between the state and the USO. To understand how and why this occurred, we need to bear in mind that the state oil company Ecopetrol was created at the height of a civil war during which organized labor had been all but extinguished at the national level. The oil workers' union was denied legal status for most of the first decade following nationalization. At the end of the conflict, Liberals and Conservatives signed an agreement that made it impossible for independent political parties to effectively contest elections. The upshot of this extended crackdown on civil and political rights was a reconfiguring of longstanding forms of participation. Barranca was at the center of this drama. The USO was reinstated in 1961 following a series of protests that involved thousands of workers in multiple sectors in Barranca and across the region. The nationalization of oil in Barranca underscored the failure of the state to provide for local citizens. The oil workers union became a venue for expressions of popular radicalism, now in concert with new social movements.

In the 1960s new modalities of public protest emerged that reflected the transformation of Barrancabermeja from oil enclave to cosmopolitan urban center. The most significant innovation of this period was the advent of a civic-popular movement, which brought together labor, student, peasant, and neighborhood groups. The shift to national control over the oil industry in Barranca in 1961, coupled with rapid population growth, persistent underdevelopment, and disenchantment with partisan politics, confirmed local residents' antagonistic relationship with the central state. The nationalization of the Barranca refinery was finalized by a National Front government, formed in 1958 as the result of a peace agreement between the leaders of the Liberal and Conservative Parties. Unionized oil workers, silenced during La Violencia, supported both the nationalization and the peace accord. But their optimism soon evaporated. The first National Front government of President Alberto Lleras Camargo passed legislation in 1959 banning strikes across many key sectors of the economy, from oil to banking.[5] The labor strongholds of Barranquilla, Puerto Berrio, and Barrancabermeja responded through a series of industrial actions in defiance of the law. The movement would crest in 1963 with the first major oil strike in more than a decade and the first *paro cívico* in Barranca's history. Oil workers and other local residents of Barranca concluded that they were no better off under the publicly run company, and that they had little recourse to bring about improvements through conventional political means.

Despite tremendous natural resource wealth, a skilled workforce, and apparent political stability, Barranca in the 1960s was beset by intractable social and political problems.[6] The crisis in Colombia's oil capital was made worse by brisk urbanization and an attendant rise in demands on the national government. The population of Barranca nearly doubled during the decade from 48,985 to 88,500.[7] The city administration was totally unprepared to respond to this major demographic change. Ordinary citizens in Barranca did not have access to the modern medical clinics, homes, social clubs, and well-stocked commissaries run by Ecopetrol.[8] Daily flights to Bogotá ensured that oil company managers and engineers could return to the capital to visit their families on weekends. While the flight to Bogotá took less than one hour, the journey by bus between Barranca and the departmental capital of Bucaramanga was a slow slog that took a full day. The road to Bogotá was much longer and susceptible to landslides. The city remained essentially poor, and its residents felt ignored. In the absence of effective political representation, the citizens of Barranca once again took to the streets.

Regional identity, more than social class or ethnic origin, was the most important basis of popular movement organizing in Colombia in the late twentieth century.[9] This dynamic achieved its most eloquent expression in the 1970s when pluralist civic movements emerged in smaller urban centers, including Barranca. One of the outcomes of political upheaval in 1960s Barranca was therefore the consolidation of a new civic identity, beyond the nexus of labor and capital. Moreover, a series of costly strikes by oil workers in the 1960s and 1970s undermined the binding power of organized labor. Open conflict with the national government had the impact of uniting *barranqueños* from many walks of life. In this context, opposition political parties, especially regional variants of left-wing and populist movements, became major players on the city's elected municipal council. So too did new social movements. The historian Alejo Vargas writes, "there seemed to be a process of coming together amongst the actors confronting the state and this allowed for the creation of bonds of solidarity and mutual legitimization among them."[10]

The most important events of this era in terms of the formation of a civic-popular movement were the staging of *paros cívicos*, or civil strikes that shut down the city for days at a time. *Paros cívicos* involved a combination of tactics, including the disruption of transportation and the physical occupation of public space. They also entailed intensive negotiations with state authorities and the organization of public meetings to debate the issues. As stated in the introduction to this book, the *paro cívico* is of critical importance to the history of Barrancabermeja as a means by which ideas about rights were animated. The right to clean water, and by extension other public services, was the rallying cry of *paros cívicos* from the 1960s forward. Such a claim could be made by anybody, regardless of whether they worked for the oil company or not. The citizen-led general strikes of the 1960s and 1970s constituted the largest acts of civil disobedience ever staged in the city and were precedent-setting models of collaboration between labor, civic, and peasant groups. *Paros cívicos* would account for nealy half of all protests in Colombia during the 1970s.[11]

The first half of this chapter examines the correlation between popular protest and its suppression, the escalation of political violence, and the emergence of new social actors in Barrancabermeja during the 1960s and 1970s. Landless squatters carried out the first major urban land occupations in Barranca in 1959, 1961, and 1963.[12] While squatters do not play a central role in the urban popular movement until the following decade, the growth of the city through informal means is a major shift that increases pressure on Barranca's already overextended infrastructure. This is also an illustration of the problems with categorical distinctions between "rural" and "urban." The influx of peasant populations into the city demonstrated unequivocally that urban areas were not isolated from the tumultuous events unfolding in the countryside. The first major oil strike in Barranca since nationalization was organized in 1963. The first *paro cívico* for improvements in public services was convened in 1963. Before the end of the decade, there were two insurgencies active in the Magdalena Medio, the National Liberation Army (ELN) and the Revolutionary Armed Forces of Colombia (FARC). Each of these developments is discussed in sequence, within the context of a narrowing of the space for political action and the deepening of the Cold War.

The second half of this chapter focuses on the interaction between labor, social activists, and the Colombian state during the 1970s in order to better understand the context out of which human rights activism would emerge in the 1980s. Even prior to nationalization there was a far more direct relationship between oil workers and the state than would have been the case in other important sectors of the economy, whether in coffee, textiles, or gold mining. This unique relationship was extended to all residents of Barranca as new social movements sought to draw the national state more directly into local affairs. The Colombian state had made frequent recourse to extraordinary legal measures for purposes of suppressing strikes during the Tropical Oil period. This tendency continued with the nationalization of oil, the establishment of the National Front, and the growth of armed insurgent movements. As political scientist Francisco Leal Buitrago writes, the Colombian state treated protest as "a matter of public order managed exclusively by the military and police."[13] Out of the turmoil provoked by strikes and street battles, there emerged during the 1970s a civic-popular movement in Barranca, led by the Catholic Church, and composed mainly of poor *barrio* residents. Through the organization of *paros cívicos*, new social movements became the carriers of Barranca's radical politics, interlocutors with government, and targets of military repression.

The Rebirth of Barranca's Popular Movements

The situation in Barranca in the early National Front period was illustrative of deep contradictions in Colombia. In April 1963 the director of the state oil company Ecopetrol traveled from El Centro to Bogotá to seek the advice of researchers at the newly established Department of Sociology at the National University.[14] He wanted to fund a study into the socioeconomic dynamics in Barranca, with an eye to formulating proposals for local development. The timing could not have been more apt. On May 20, 1963, the citizens of Barranca organized a massive *paro cívico*, or civil strike, to protest the lack of basic services and infrastructure. Researchers from the Land Tenure Center at the University of Wisconsin–Madison teamed up with National University faculty to undertake the study. The Land Tenure Center director and sociologist Eugene Havens and the Colombian anthropologist Michel Romieux made the trip together to Barranca in the wake of the *paro cívico*, with financing from the United States Agency for International Development (USAID).[15] Together they witnessed the deep divisions at the root of social unrest in Barranca: "In the case of the De Mares Concession there appears a strange organism in the country, the Oil Company, with all of its services, installations and personnel. When nationalization happens, fundamental changes take place. The struggle is now directed openly against the ruling classes in the country; ECOPETROL and the municipio of Barrancabermeja are a microcosm of the struggle developing in the rest of Colombia, the transformation of a semi feudal, semi colonial country into an industrialized and self-sufficient country."[16] Barranca in the 1960s was at a crossroads, as was Colombia. The National Front pact between Liberals and Conservatives that had put an end to partisan warfare in 1958 did not address the issues of inequality and poverty that had been among the root causes of La Violencia. The nationalization of Ecopetrol and the social mobilizing taking place in Barranca brought these problems into focus.

Nothing represented Barranca's woes more vividly that the problem of water. It was said that the quality of tap water in Barrancabermeja was so poor that it had to be boiled before you could use it to wash your floors.[17] Fouled by runoff from drilling and refining operations, the stuff literally reeked of oil. When the level of the Magdalena River was low, the city was obliged to draw its water from fetid swamps. In a city with average daytime temperatures in the high 30s Celsius (about 100 degrees Fahrenheit), and humidity often exceeding 70 percent, the provision of clean water was especially critical. Other pressing needs included paved roads, a new public hospital, and a municipal slaughterhouse.[18] Many of the city's main roads were unpaved and poorly maintained, the existing hospital was small and out of date, and there were concerns about the safety of the meat being sold in the city's markets. But none of these issues was as pressing as the question of potable water.

The organization of the May 1963 protest would provide a template for future movement building. The *paro cívico* was a site of encounter of labor and community, accomplished through the mobilization of networks that included trade unions, political parties, community-based organizations, and the Catholic Church. Individuals who were otherwise uninvolved in politics were moved to join the protests, and young people served key functions on the frontlines. Maintaining a *paro cívico* over the course of several days required a great deal of planning. Without popular support, *paros cívicos* would break under the stress caused by the suspension of work, schools, and the closing of food markets across the city. Organizers held public meetings, gave interviews to local news media, and went door-to-door to convince residents to participate or bear with the inconvenience. City councillors were also asked to take part, and many did. Cars fitted with loudspeakers drove through the backstreets of the city announcing when and where to gather. The first *paro cívico* in Barrancabermeja was successful in large part because it was organized around an urgent cause that united disparate social and political groups within the city. Concerns about civil liberties and official violence pertaining to the authorities' crackdown on the protest itself were also raised. These concerns would become central issues going forward.

Within twenty-four hours of the start of the *paro cívico* on May 20, 1963, the national government declared a state of siege for Barrancabermeja and the adjacent municipalities of Puerto Wilches, Lebrija, and San Vicente de Chucurí.[19] The *paro* ended three days later in street fighting between protestors and the army. On the last tumultuous afternoon, a young man by the name of

Figure 3. Labor march, early 1960s. Courtesy of Foto Estudios Joya.

Alfonso Sánchez was shot and killed by a soldier who fired into a crowd. Demonstrators had gathered around the entrance to the oil refinery, threw bricks, and were dispersed by water cannons, tear gas, and rounds of gunfire. Soldiers then hurried to recover Sánchez's body. This prompted an angry response from some of the protestors and encouraged a surge in rioting. There was talk of storming the army base over the course of the next few hours. Fearing further unrest, the army returned Sánchez's body to his family. Sánchez was buried in a public ceremony two days later, which was attended by thousands of mourners. The governor of Santander then replaced Barranca's civilian mayor with an army officer, and a curfew was enforced.

The *paro cívico* had ended tragically, yet it produced results in terms of official recognition of the basic needs of the population. Despite the imposition of military rule, work soon began on a modern public hospital and a new aqueduct.[20] The Colombian oil business was growing again, albeit at a slow rate. There was a steady national market, and several major international companies began to express interest in the development of new concessions. New drilling made up for a decline in productivity of old wells. At the same time, upgrades to the capacity of the refinery went online, resulting in modest increases in the production of motor oil and jet fuel, with the promise of further increases pending. Approximately 50 percent of the more than thirty million barrels of crude oil refined annually in Colombia was processed by Ecopetrol, mainly in Barranca.[21] State interest in Colombia's oil industry was 41.1 percent, significantly less than in neighboring Venezuela (67.3), in Great Britain (65.5), or in the Middle East (62.5).[22] Nonetheless, Ecopetrol was able to make gestures toward its workers and to the city in the form of infrastructural improvements. But the legacy of mistrust would prove hard to overcome.

The *paro cívico* had been organized amid rising tensions at the refinery. The USO began negotiating a new collective agreement with Ecopetrol in March 1963. There arose a series of seemingly minor disagreements that the union saw as signs of bad faith on the part of Ecopetrol. There had been fractious debates over the extension of benefits to workers' common-law spouses, and the suspension of a union member who had spent time in the Soviet Union.[23] When the threat of a strike surfaced one month later, the main point of contention was not around the collective agreement. Ecopetrol had suspended several workers at the company store, including the president of the union, whom the company accused of irregular accounting and theft.[24] The union immediately called a strike at the commissary, during which workers locked the manager inside.[25] They released the manager within two hours, and national police charged the workers with kidnapping. Two days later, as union leaders met with their legal team, the governor of Santander requested that soldiers be deployed on the streets of Barranca. The mayor declared a curfew and banned alcohol sales.[26] A war of recrimination ensued until July 20, when the union shut down the refinery.

"Communism to Blame for Events in Barranca," declared a headline in the *Vanguardia Liberal*, the main daily newspaper of Santander.[27] Barranca was once again at the center of a polemic pitting industrial trade unions against the state. Unionized workers at the Shell-owned oilfields in nearby Casabe declared the government "antipatriotic" and incapable of understanding the oil workers' nationalist philosophy.[28] Strikes were organized by workers at nearby drilling sites operated by Shell and Texas Petroleum in solidarity with the USO. Workers at the state-owned fertilizer plant in Barranca also threatened to walk out. Oil pipelines were bombed.[29] In response, Justice Minister Aurelio Camacho Rueda declared: "Communism has launched a challenge to the republic and its democratic institutions, which in response have no recourse except to accept this fact and contain it."[30]

The 1963 oil strike was born out of botched negotiations, descended into a war of words, and ended with violent clashes between protestors and the police. The national government quickly declared the strike illegal and threatened workers who refused to go back to work with "severe sanctions."[31] The

USO's legal status was revoked. Dozens of workers were fired, and the union president was arrested.[32] A few days following the detention of the union president, the Colombian army rounded up an additional fifteen strike leaders, including the entire union executive staff. In response, the USO organized a series of mass demonstrations in Barranca and in nearby Puerto Boyacá.[33] The army then raided the offices of the union. By the end of August 1963, following mediation in Bogotá by a commission of the House of Representatives, the strike finally came to an end.[34]

Despite the major setbacks endured by the union itself, the 1963 oil workers' strike produced tangible results. A new collective agreement was signed and the union's legal status restored. The mayor of Barranca lifted the alcohol ban and curfew, and Ecopetrol allowed workers back into the refinery. Mario Galán Gómez was named the president of Ecopetrol one week following the end of the strike, a position he would hold for the next eleven years. Galán was the scion of a prominent Liberal family from Socorro, Santander, grandson of a veteran of the Thousand Days' War, and a founder of the engineering school where many petroleum officials were trained. In his report to the Colombian Congress in 1964, Galán hailed the conclusion of the strike as a great success in the "perfection" of industrial relations in Colombia. A number of additional developments came out of the strike. One of these was the construction of a new campus for the Diego Hernández de Gallegos public high school, where oil workers sent their children. Soon afterward, a technical college was built next to the high school for the training of oil workers, including courses for electricians, pipefitters, foremen, and supervisors.[35] While the appointment of Galán to head Ecopetrol "seemed to offer hope" to oil workers, the Colombian military would continue to patrol the streets and occupy city hall. These contradictory circumstances reinforced the dynamic whereby *barranqueños* would undertake direct action to demand rights. The institutions created by Ecopetrol during this era would help to ensure a continuation of the city's radical workers' culture. The combined effect of the *paro cívico* and the strike was to reinforce a pattern of "bargaining by disruption" that would endure for the next half century.

Popular protest was renewed in Barranca during the 1960s. This occurred in the midst of ever more direct confrontation between the Colombian national state and local activists. The manner in which the 1963 *paro cívico* unfolded, with expressions of popular outrage met by official repression, would establish a standard for future protests. The initial resurgence of organized labor in Barrancabermeja was also a direct response to the failed promise of peace, democracy, and prosperity that had accompanied the end of La Violencia in 1958. Oil workers in Barranca had publicly lauded the National Front government as a means of moving beyond partisan politics.[36] It was a false promise. Through most of La Violencia, the USO was banned outright. The Sindicato Colombiano de la Empresa de Petróleos (Sincopetrol), a company union, was established in August 1951. However, attempts to domesticate the labor movement would eventually fail. The subsequent repression of the 1963 strike would occasion a sharp turn to the left on the part of the oil workers. During the 1960s the USO aligned itself with the Communist Party–dominated Confederación Sindical de Trabajadores de Colombia (CSTC). For the first time since the early days of the Partido Socialista Revolucionario (PSR), oil workers organized themselves under a banner other than that of the Liberal Party–dominated Confederación de Trabajadores Colombianos (CTC).[37] The USO would sign new collective agreements every other year through the 1960s and avoid going to strike until 1971. Mistrust of the national government and Ecopetrol remained high among oil workers and other area residents, and the feeling was mutual.

New Regional Identity

New social movements, including those of peasants, the Catholic Church, and left-wing political parties, emerged in the 1960s to challenge the Colombian state for dominion over the Magdalena Medio region. By 1963 Communism was being blamed for popular upheaval in the city of Barrancabermeja. Within the next couple of years, as Cold War repression continued apace, radical opposition movements had indeed gained a significant foothold in the region, expressing themselves through mass protest actions. The national government's negative response to popular mobilization in Barranca in 1963 set a tone of hostility between local activists and the central state. Diego Montaña Cuellar—Communist Party activist and legal counsel to the oil workers' union for two decades—would later observe that the repression of the 1963 strike convinced many oil workers of the need to support revolutionary options for change.[38] These events unfolded amid rising fears of international Communism expressed by U.S. and Colombian policymakers during the dénouement of La Violencia. The term "Magdalena Medio" was in fact first utilized in the 1960s by Colombian army officials who sought the pacification of the central Magdalena River valley.[39] The colonization of the territory by the Colombian military would serve to integrate and define the region. Simultaneously, new civil society groupings would establish a basis for an alternative regional politics, based on social justice claims.

Through the twentieth century, the Catholic Church was the only significant nongovernmental presence in Barranca besides that of the oil workers' union. Since the late nineteenth century the Magdalena River valley had been under the influence of the Jesuits. When the diocese of Barrancabermeja was created in late 1962 it helped give shape to the social and political idea of a Magdalena Medio region. The diocese included fourteen *municipios* in the departments of Santander, Bolívar, and Antioquia. The diocese of Barrancabermeja would provide the emerging civic-popular movement with solid political support. In 1963 there were just five priests working out of the old Municipal Cathedral that sits across from City Hall. That number would more than double by the end of the decade, with the arrival of a number of forward-thinking seminarians, led by its first bishop, Bernardo Arango. New recruits would be assigned to the city's growing squatter settlements, as well as to the impoverished towns built up along the Magdalena River. The first parish church in the city's impoverished northeastern *barrios* was Señor de los Milagros, established in 1965 in Barrio Versalles. While the parish was located four kilometers from the city center, it was an area of interest to Liberal and Conservative organizers, who initially resented the presence of progressive priests. Señor de los Milagros would soon become a hub of social organization, attracting Assumptionist Sisters and lay missionaries from Barranquilla, and later university students.[40] These men and women formed part of a wave of religious workers inspired by new trends in progressive Catholic teaching and practice.[41]

Priests in Barranca would rally people from across the city and region to the cause of social change. One of the most influential instructors at the University of Pamplona seminary in the department of Norte de Santander was a young priest named Eduardo Díaz. He was the son of an Ecopetrol manager and had lived with his family in Barranca while in his early twenties. Díaz was inspired by liberation theology, a radical Catholic movement that gained intellectual and political force with the reforms undertaken at the Vatican II Council in Rome in 1962–1965 and the inception of leftist guerrilla movements in Latin America. In September 1970 Díaz was expelled from the University of Pamplona, along with another professor and ten students. The students were eventually readmitted to school, but Díaz requested to be transferred to Barranca.[42] Díaz wanted an opportunity to develop new kinds of pastoral work that responded to both the spiritual and material needs of the local population: "When I arrived in Barrancabermeja, I met up with a team of young priests who had been recently ordained and were very enthusiastic. The openness to diversity expressed by Bishop Bernardo Arango gave us space to develop new initiatives and undertake new exploration in our pastoral and social work."[43] Municipalities to the north, south, and west of the city of Barranca were now part of the new diocese. All of these areas—including

Puerto Wilches, San Pablo, Yondó, Cimitarra, and Sabana de Torres—had hitherto been peripheral provinces of dioceses in distant Bucaramanga, San Gil, Medellín, and Tunja. New churches were being built, and the priests who led them benefited from their close connections to Bishop Arango and prominent newcomers like Eduardo Díaz. People who lived in the Magdalena Medio were increasingly pulled into the orbit of Barranca.

The settlement of the region around Barrancabermeja was dominated by peasant farmers and fishermen rather than agribusiness. These *campesinos'* livelihoods were directly impacted by the development of oilfields, by Ecopetrol, Shell, and Texas Petroleum. Pipelines cut through the countryside in every conceivable direction out of Barrancabermeja, and camps of oil workers were established in a half-dozen small towns. Opportunistic homesteaders, many of whom were refugees who had fled to Liberal-dominated areas during La Violencia, had established small farms along the Magdalena River before the oil boom. In 1961 a modest agrarian reform law was passed by the National Front government that promised to distribute land to small landholders. In the first few years, the reform was implemented unevenly and slowly, in part because of ongoing counterinsurgency efforts.[44] Colombia's National Front government worried about peasant radicalization. As a result, *campesino* organizations that emerged in the region during this period were subject to pressures from the armed forces based in Barranca.[45] In 1963, 1964, and 1965 local *campesino* associations denounced being subject to raids, intimidation, and arbitrary detentions. Among the most vocal of these groups was the Agricultural Union of the Petroleum Zone of Ecopetrol (Sinagrapetrol). At their 1964 general assembly in Barranca, members of Sinagrapetrol denounced the fact that Colombian armed forces personnel were carrying out spot checks and aggressively questioning *campesinos* throughout the region.[46]

Government efforts to contain peasant movements in the 1960s would backfire. Peasants accounted for about one third of the total population of Colombia in the 1960s and thus represented an important political force.[47] A national peasant organization known as the National Association of Peasant Users (ANUC) would be established by Liberal president Alberto Lleras Restrepo in 1967. ANUC was created by Presidential Decree as a way to mobilize extant farmers' cooperatives, local councils, and unions behind national agrarian policies.[48] In so doing, the government hoped to resolve tensions between peasants and the state that arose from chronic poverty in rural areas, as well as competition for land between small landholders and large investors. Within its first year, ANUC's membership exceeded six hundred thousand. By 1971 more than one million "users" or clients had signed up.[49] In short order, ANUC became a school of radical citizenship.[50] Peasant leaders within

ANUC educated themselves and their constituencies about Colombian law, and convened public protests to demand their rights. They also undertook land invasions, and petitioned Bogotá for title to undeveloped *terrenos baldíos*. In the Magdalena Medio, as elsewhere, central government authorities negotiated with peasant groupings affiliated with ANUC, and agreements around the reclamation of land were signed. This emboldened more peasants to undertake land invasions, leading to a split in ANUC in 1971. The newly independent "Línea Sincelejo" of ANUC would have a strong following in the Magdalena Medio. That same year, some 645 land invasions were carried out across Colombia, involving tens of thousands of peasants.[51]

The Magdalena Medio region was also an important area of support for left-wing and dissident political parties in the 1960s.[52] In congressional elections held in 1960 Alfonso López Michelsen—the son of the Liberal president and reformer Alfonso López Pumarejo (1934–1938)—had led the left-leaning Liberal Revolutionary Movement (MRL) to an impressive showing.[53] The MRL captured seventeen seats and included among its successful candidates Rafael Rangel, the former Liberal guerrilla and leader of the April 1948 uprising in Barranca.[54] In the 1962 presidential elections López Michelsen garnered 624,438 votes, or about 24 percent of the total votes cast at the national level.[55] In Barranca, López Michelsen earned more than twice as many votes as the Guillermo León Valencia, the Conservative candidate who would become president. At the local level, the left made tangible gains. The Communist Party of Colombia (PCC) held majorities in the municipal councils of Cimitarra and Florián.[56] The councils of Barrancabermeja and the neighboring *municipios* of Puerto Wilches and San Vicente de Chucurí were all dominated by the socialist current of the National Popular Alliance (ANAPO), an independent populist movement established under the leadership of former military president Gustavo Rojas Pinilla.[57]

The Magdalena Medio would also become synonymous with guerrilla insurgency, first and foremost with the homegrown Ejército de Liberación Nacional (ELN). Founded in 1964 by students at Santander's engineering school, the ELN was the first guerrilla movement in Colombia to seek to overthrow the state.[58] Most of the founding members of the ELN had previously been associated with radical movements for political change in the Magdalena Medio. José Solano Sepúlveda had been a Rangelista guerrilla fighter. Martha González was the niece of the Liberal guerrilla leader Gustavo González, who had also fought during La Violencia in the 1950s. Nicolás "Gabino" Rodríguez Bautista was the son of Pedro Rodríguez, who had participated in the 1929 *bolchevique* uprising.[59] The ELN focused its early efforts on areas with a tradition of rebel politics, such as the town of Simacota, where their first armed action took place on January 7, 1965. The largest public university in the departmental capital of Bucaramanga, the Universidad Industrial de Santander (UIS) was a hotbed of student radicalism in the early 1960s. The UIS had been training petroleum engineers since 1954, many of whom went on to work for Ecopetrol. It is where oil workers would send their own children to study, if they could afford it. Several founding members of the ELN—including Ricardo Lara Parada, the Barrancabermeja-born son of an oil worker—had been activists with the Asociación Universitaria de Santander (AUDESA) during the student strikes of 1964.[60] In that year, the army occupied the university and prosecuted student leaders in military courts on charges of sedition.[61] The student activists' message of revolutionary change resonated with Barranca residents, just as there had been broad support for the messages put forward by María Cano and Raúl Mahecha during the early years of the Tropical Oil Company.

Colombia's two main guerrilla groups were present in and around Barranca in the mid-1960s. The ELN guerrillas emerged out of Liberal, Communist, and other political movements with strong roots in Barranca. From these shared histories developed a sometimes ambiguous relationship between the guerrillas and local civil society, including trade unions and the Catholic Church. The history of the FARC is similar in many respects, and it too had strong roots in the region. The FARC established itself early in the Magdalena Medio, with peasant "self-defense" forces allied with the Communist Party in the area around Puerto Boyacá. As the historian Alejo Vargas writes, the FARC designated the Magdalena Medio as one of three strategic areas for further growth during their II Conference held in 1966.[62] The FARC established its Fourth Front in the *municipio* of Cimitarra in 1968. At the time, the FARC grew mainly through political and social activism, with the Communist Party as the legal expression of the movement, rather than offensive military actions. This was the context in which the citizens of Barranca organized collectively for social change in the 1960s.

Bases of a Civic-Popular Movement

During the 1970s the focus of popular protest in Barranca shifted definitively from the refinery to the street. While the first *paro cívico* organized in 1963 engaged a broad cross-section of society, there was no grassroots organizational structure in the poorest neighborhoods at the time. This all changed with the dramatic growth of squatter settlements and the consolidation of new community-based processes led by Pastoral Social, the social service arm of the Catholic Diocese of Barranca led by Father Eduardo Díaz.

Relationships between neighborhood groups, trade unions, and municipal councillors would form the bases of the city's new civic-popular movement. Events in Barranca mirrored developments taking place at the national level, as social movements surged in all of Colombia's major urban areas.

In early 1971 a series of university student strikes gripped the country.[63] The Conservative president Misael Pastrana declared a national state of siege and dispatched the army to disperse rallies and protests in major cities from Barranquilla on the Atlantic coast, to Cali in the southwest, to Bucaramanga in the highland interior. Fifteen protestors were killed in confrontations with the army on the streets of Cali, Colombia's third largest city and capital of the department of Valle de Cauca, on February 26, 1971.[64] But the most prominent and radical student activists in Colombia were based at the Universidad Industrial de Santander in Bucaramanga.[65] Between February and August of 1971, the student union at the UIS organized strikes demanding increased student participation in the governance of Colombia's public universities and an end to U.S. involvement in higher education reform.[66] General Álvaro Valencia Tovar—then commander of the Second Division of the Colombian army in Bucaramanga—said that allowing students to "take control" of the country's universities would lead to the downfall of the government.[67] General Valencia, a Korean War veteran who had commanded counterinsurgency troops in Bucaramanga since the mid-1960s, warned of the influence that the ELN continued to have at the UIS. The student union itself had never engaged in violent actions. Nonetheless, the historic association between student groups at the UIS and the guerrillas provided the army with grounds to intervene.

The student leader Juan de Dios Castilla was part of a new generation of social activists in Barranca who, over the course of the next decade, would claim a prominent place alongside the oil workers' union. During the first military occupation of the UIS campus in April 1971, the Colombian army detained dozens of students in the name of combating subversion. Castilla was expelled from the UIS and returned home to Barranca, emboldened.[68] His worldview, like that of many other people coming of age in Barranca in the 1970s, was influenced by Marxism and liberation theology. Camilo Torres Restrepo, a radical priest and sociology professor from Bogotá who died in combat in 1966 fighting with the ELN guerrillas near Barranca, had inspired a generation of Catholic progressives. Castilla explains:

> When I graduated from secondary school in 1967, I went to study at the Universidad Industrial de Santander. When I was at university, it was a hotbed of revolutionary theories. . . . It was during this time that I was first exposed to Marxism and to the practices of activist Christians, activist

Catholics. I was a member of Catholic Student Youth and became active with the student movement at the UIS. Then I was expelled in 1971. I returned to Barrancabermeja defeated, but having made a heroic gesture on behalf of the popular and social cause. It was the time of great influence of Camilo Torres, of the theory of liberation, of the influence of the Golconda Group.[69] It was a time of great political and social reflection within the Catholic Church.[70]

Not long after returning to Barranca, Castilla moved out of his parents' home and into the popular neighborhood of Las Granjas. He spent the next twelve years working in the *nororiente* as a lay community organizer on behalf of the recently established Pastoral Social. He married into a local family and never looked back. Living among the hard-working migrants who had settled Las Granjas, Castilla's political convictions were strengthened.[71]

Barranca's population continued to grow over the next few years, and by 1978 nearly three-quarters of the population was composed of people born outside of the *municipio*. The growth of squatter settlements amplified social and economic disparities within the city, drawing attention to the gaps between the city's small business class, unionized oil workers, and the vast majority of residents. The transfer of the principal functions of Ecopetrol from El Centro to Barranca proper in 1969 had entailed the relocation of hundreds of workers and their families. Ecopetrol established a public corporation dedicated to the development of housing for oil workers, which oversaw the planning and construction of workers' housing in two neighborhoods, Galán Gómez and El Parnaso. Ecopetrol thus helped to build dozens of small but modern attached homes, some with patios or gardens. They were constructed a few blocks away from the municipal baseball stadium and the Club Infantas, a recreational center for workers and their families. Barranca was one of the wealthiest cities in Colombia, and these neighborhoods stood for the relative prosperity of oil workers. Nationally, Barranca ranked twenty-second in terms of total population and seventh in economic output.[72] The city was home to a modern refinery and distribution system that delivered gasoline to every region of Colombia. But there were few other sources of steady employment. Even accounting for the transfer of many oil workers' families to the city, only a tiny minority of area residents worked directly for *la empresa*. Oil accounted for more than 90 percent of Barranca's economy, yet just 2 percent of city residents were employed by Ecopetrol.

The outcomes of growing inequality in Barranca included the isolation and stigmatization of the majority of *barranqueños*. The two main areas of the low-income outer city were connected to one another by a single dirt road, making transportation difficult. Traffic between the eastern and central city was limited to just three railway crossings. The northeast and southeast neighborhoods of the city were often referred to collectively as the *barrios orientales*, although the area was in fact heterogeneous. Some sections had been constructed in the 1950s, while others remained mostly unoccupied. In the newest areas of settlement, *campesino*-style wood, straw, and bamboo *ranchos* were common. Many low-income areas lacked electricity, telephones, water, indoor plumbing, paved roads, and decent housing. What did flourish in the unregulated poor suburbs were open-air bars, dance clubs, and brothels. These thriving vice industries reminded residents of the poor *barrios* of their status in the city. Juan de Dios Castilla recounts: "It was total marginalization. At the entrance to the *nororiente*, there was a tolerance sector. The only contact that people from the rest of the city had with the *nororiente* was with the whores who worked in the neighborhood. Beyond was unknown territory, absolute poverty."[73] Many residents feared to venture beyond the bridge that separated the two cities.

The Pastoral Social, under the leadership of the dynamic Eduardo Díaz, crossed the *puente elevado* more frequently and engaged a broader network than any other organization or movement. Díaz's influence among the organizers of *paros cívicos* in the 1970s had four significant impacts that reflected changes taking place in Barranca at a broader level. First, Díaz helped smooth over differences between members of the city's diverse activist communities, including differences between the members of different political parties. Liberals, Communists, ANAPO, and even Conservatives were all present at city council meetings and *paro cívico* organizing sessions. Second, Díaz facilitated communication across social and economic differences, notably between poor *barrio* residents and the oil workers' union. Some oil workers mingled easily among the city's squatters, thanks to family connections, but there were still big differences to overcome. Third, Díaz enjoyed the support of the bishop. As director of Pastoral Social, Díaz spoke on behalf of the diocese of Barranca. And finally, Díaz had the moral and political credibility to negotiate directly with government officials. As a priest, Díaz proved an effective spokesperson in direct conversations with officials in Bogotá, or locally.

The new activism led by priests and peasants put pressure on Ecopetrol and the national government to increase public investments in the city. While the central state retained direct control over major projects, including the construction of workers' housing, the municipal government was gaining influence. In 1968 Ecopetrol and the *municipio* of Barrancabermeja signed a deal that guaranteed an annual investment of 100 million pesos in oil royalties toward the city's development, including improvements to public services. A study completed by the Centre for Urban Planning at the Universidad de los Andes in Bogotá in 1970 described Barranca's infrastructure and administration as woefully inadequate: "The environment in the city does not offer acceptable conditions for social progress in terms of health, education and public amenities. The local administration has no instruments for coordinating or making objective decisions that would permit it to be an agent of the change that is desired and sought by leaders from all sectors [of society]."[74] In the report, the legacy of Barranca's enclave economy is highlighted as the main impediment to development. Moreover, the study predicted that Barranca's population would double within a twelve-year period, seriously exacerbating the situation. With mayors appointed by the departmental government in Bucaramanga, the citizens of Barranca had limited power over the decisions affecting their social and economic welfare.[75] Yet the city council managed contracts for water, road building, and other public services, and was an important site of political struggle.

Of all of the public figures to have emerged from Barranca, none is as well known as Horacio Serpa Uribe. An ambitious lawyer from Bucaramanga, Horacio Serpa had a major impact on Barranca's politics for the better part of two decades. He began his career as a judge in Barranca but quickly moved into the political sphere. The governor of Santander named Serpa the mayor of Barranca in 1969.[76] Serpa then served multiple terms as a member of the House of Representatives and Senate, before being appointed attorney general and minister of the interior. He ran for president of Colombia three times, before retiring from the national scene to run for governor of Santander in 2008. Horacio Serpa's term in municipal office lasted just ten months. The man who replaced him as mayor of Barranca, Luis Pinilla, recalls the advice that Serpa gave him prior to the handover of power: "Luis, there is very little to be done here, because there is no money. Try to maintain the roads in good condition. That should be enough to satisfy the constant demands that you address the needs of the population."[77] Serpa established a left-leaning populist movement within the Liberal Party known as the Authentic Liberal Leftist Front, or Frente de Izquierda Liberal Auténtico (FILA). He understood that in order to stay in power in Barranca the Liberal councillors needed to speak to the poor majority and evoke the radical traditions for which Santander and Barranca were famous.[78] As we shall see, Serpa's FILA movement would remain a major force in Barranca politics long after he had left for Bogotá.

One of the striking features of Barranca's municipal politics in this era is the near total absence of conservative voices. Although dominated by the Liberal Party, Barranca's municipal council included a strong contingent of activists from left-wing movements who approached their work in much the same way that social movement leaders did. In 1969 the council declared its solidarity with the recently elected socialist president of Chile, Salvador Allende. It also passed a motion demanding that the remains of the rebel priest Camilo Torres Restrepo be returned to his family (his body had been disposed of by the Colombian army in a secret location not long after he was killed in 1966).[79] Another case in point was the council's combative response to the controversial election of the Conservative president Misael Pastrana in 1970. Within days of the elections, Barranca's municipal councillors passed a motion denouncing Pastrana's victory as fraudulent.[80] Moving beyond the realm of the symbolic, city councillors proposed that Barranca host a dialogue for peace and reconciliation with the FARC and ELN guerrillas. City councillors were directly involved in the planning of popular protests as well. Council meetings were often packed to capacity as Barranca lurched from one crisis to the next, and civil society leaders attended the meeting to air their views. Municipal politics were thus mainly contested between the left wing of the Liberal Party and a chorus of more radical voices, represented by the PCC, ANAPO, and social movements themselves.

Activists from the community-based Pastoral Social projects had a greater impact on the mobilization of poor *barranqueños* than any political party. The municipal council was influential as well. Ten urban land invasions were carried out in the eastern *barrios* of Barranca between 1970 and 1980.[81] These were large-scale seizures of private and public property by *campesinos*, fishermen, and casual laborers and their extended families, sometimes involving thousands of individuals. The municipal branches of traditional political parties supported many of these invasions, often in an obvious attempt to capture votes.[82] But the Pastoral Social was the only institution with a permanent presence in the *barrios orientales*, providing residents with in situ support during confrontations with the military, as well as lobbying for the provision of essential services. Some elected officials were participants in the civic-popular movement, and moved easily between City Hall and the street. As the national government clamped down even more tightly on trade unionism in the coming years, Barranca's experiment in community-based organizing would prove more important than anyone anticipated.

The 1971 Oil Strike

The prosecution of union leaders by court-martial following the 1971 strike set a belligerent tone between organized labor and the state in Barranca during the 1970s. The broader outcome was a regrouping of the popular movement in Barranca that increased the power of community-based social movements in the low income *barrios orientales*. Traditionally, the USO was the heart of Barranca's popular radical culture. Despite the fact that very few *barranqueños* were employed by Ecopetrol, the oil workers' union supported the interests of the broader community. Pedro Galindo, former president of the national Federation of Oil Workers, observes: "The function of the USO in Barranca was not just to oversee collective agreements. That was a task. But the purpose of the USO was the organization of society."[83] In the wake of the 1971 strike, the standing of the union declined, making room for the advance of new social movements. The repression of the oil workers' union would also inspire the establishment of the first human rights group in Colombian history, focused on the rights of political prisoners.

Oil was at the very heart of national debate on economic development in the 1970s. Following a 1971 general strike by Colombia's major trade union federations, a special commission was convened by the Colombian House of Representatives to propose solutions to Colombia's fiscal problems.[84] Oil, the report concluded, was the most viable hope for rescuing state finances. In 1970 national petroleum production was nearly eighty million barrels per year, the third highest in South America.[85] Yet there had been no increase in total output in nearly twenty years. Despite demonstrable interest on the part of foreign companies in terms of new applications for drilling rights and calls for deregulation by Ecopetrol executives, production remained static.[86] It was at the time estimated that the Ecopetrol-controlled oilfields of the Magdalena Medio represented more than 50 percent of the country's total unexploited petroleum reserves. If these reserves were not tapped, and demand continued to increase, Colombia would deepen its dependence on imported oil.

Disappointed by the outcome of the 1971 national general strike and increasingly aware of its unique bargaining power, the USO went on the offensive. It began by organizing a series of short actions that revealed deep mistrust between the union and the national government. On July 26, 1971, workers at the Barranca refinery organized a sit-down strike to protest the rescheduling of lunch breaks by management. Ecopetrol accused the USO of disrupting oil production on a trivial pretext.[87] The union countered that Ecopetrol had violated the collective agreement by making arbitrary changes to the workday.[88] Ecopetrol president Mario Galán Gómez then accused the strikers of threatening to sabotage the refinery.[89] Ecopetrol fired union president Ricardo Mantilla and secretary general Heriberto Bautista Gómez.[90] The company suspended six workers for participating in the strike and sent letters of warning to another forty-six workers.[91] The USO responded by organizing a second sit-down strike on August 4, 1971. This time it involved all seventeen hundred workers at the refinery in Barranca. More than a hundred workers at a pumping station located a thousand kilometers away in Puerto Salgar, Cundinamarca, walked off the job in solidarity.[92]

On August 5, 1971, the USO commenced one of the most costly labor actions in Colombian history. Union members in Barranca stopped working at 6:00 a.m. and began to concentrate in strategic locations inside and around the refinery. In response, President Pastrana Borrero issued Decree 1518, extending the definition of crimes under the jurisdiction of military justice to include damages done to "public services."[93] There were 680 soldiers stationed at the Bogotá Battalion in Barranca at the time, whose main purpose was the defense of the Ecopetrol refinery. By contrast, the police force responsible for all other aspects of public security within the city numbered just thirty-six officers.[94] Workers employed water hoses and stones against soldiers at the entrance to the refinery. Soldiers fired rounds in the direction of the workers. At 10:00 a.m. a twenty-five-year-old worker named Fermín Amaya was shot dead. Workers held sixteen Ecopetrol managers inside the refinery. Soldiers detained workers who had been sent to get provisions for the strikers inside the refinery.[95] On the second day of the strike, the municipal council denounced the military response and recognized workers' demands.[96] Cut off from food and water supplies, the strikers' resolve was exhausted.[97] On August 7, 1971, the Ministry of Labor suspended the union, and the strike officially ended.

The national government and news media depicted the strikers as criminals. Ecopetrol estimated losses in the range of 100 million pesos due to lost work hours and sabotage.[98] According to company directors, workers had deliberately wrecked valuable equipment.[99] Army investigators accused union members of having taunted captive Ecopetrol managers with a hangman's noose.[100] Further allegations were made that workers had used carbolic acid as a weapon against soldiers during confrontations at the refinery gate. The national newspaper *El Espectador* published a photograph of a bus that had been painted by oil workers with the words "we don't want blood," cropped to read "we want blood." Above the photo appeared the headline "Threat of the Gallows in Barranca."[101] Santander's Liberal governor Jaime Trillos Novoa flew to Bogotá on August 9, 1971, to speak directly with President Pastrana. He described the situation in Barranca as "terrifying," adding, "You cannot imagine how people who call themselves Colombian could attack our most important national company and the country."[102] Some forty-six unionized workers were charged with sabotage and kidnapping. The case against the strikers was brought before a military court, or *consejo verbal de guerra*.

Legal proceedings in the wake of the 1971 strike were held inside an army base across the river from Barranca in the former Shell-run oil enclave of Casabe, Antioquia. Despite the fact that news media were not allowed inside the courtroom, the case captured the attention of the entire country. From reports that appeared daily in regional and national newspapers, based on interviews with people in attendance, we know that both sides couched their arguments in nationalist rhetoric.[103] The presiding judge, General Ramón Arturo Rincón Quiñones, commander of the Fifth Brigade in Bucaramanga, set a stern tone the morning the trial began. As reported in the *Vanguardia Liberal*: "General Rincón Quiñones emphatically declared that he would apply 'severe sanctions and inflexible justice' against anyone implicated in crimes of kidnapping, personal injury, damages and attacks against the national economy."[104] On the first day, union activist Ubadel Puentes spoke in his own defense for nearly eight hours.[105] The president of the refinery workers' local, Gilberto Chinome, denounced Ecopetrol and the shortcomings of Colombia's energy policy, and accused the company of pandering to foreign investors keen to exploit Colombia's vast oil wealth.[106]

The USO paid dearly for its occupation of the refinery. The *consejo verbal de guerra* lasted thirty-five consecutive days, ending on September 24, 1971. Sentencing came one month later. Forty-one people received sentences ranging from two months to fourteen years. The longest sentences were reserved for USO leaders.[107] Five people were acquitted. Hundreds lost their jobs. Dozens of workers were forced to leave Barranca and ordered never to return.[108] Of the accused, only seventeen were in custody and present at the tribunal. The rest, including the president of the USO, Ricardo Mantilla, had gone into hiding and had to be tried in absentia.[109] Friends and family responded to the reading of the sentences with screams and declarations of disbelief.[110] Barranca residents marched through the streets of the city in silent protest, and a handful of workers at El Centro staged a hunger strike. The Conservative Party took advantage of the political vacuum created by the dismissal of so many strike leaders to take provisional control over the union. Whether due to fear or because they were vexed by the strike leaders' obstinacy, Barranca's political establishment, small business owners, and a good number of poor residents turned away from the union. As veteran activist Jairo Chaparro observed: "The strike was like a divorce, of separate beds for the union and the people. They organized it by themselves with the rest of Barranca simply watching. Do you know what I mean? The USO was married to Barranca. But like all marriages, there are honeymoons and there is divorce."[111] After 1971, the Catholic Church, as well as left-wing and traditional political parties, recognized that new bases of support for social change would have to be built in what had hitherto been considered the margins of society.

The oil workers' strike in 1971 represented the culmination of a long season of popular protest that had engulfed the entire country. State responses to political dissent, including the suppression of student demonstrations and the court-martial of union leaders, directly inspired Colombian social activists to take up the cause of human rights for the very first time. The *consejo verbal de guerra* in Barranca represented one of the most egregious attacks on civil rights of the National Front era. While it was held behind closed doors, the 1971 trial of the oil workers received extensive media coverage. One of the effects was to raise concerns at the national level around the use of military tribunals to prosecute civilian activists. In August 1973 Justice Minister Jaime Castro asked the Colombian Congress to commute the sentences of the fifteen oil workers who remained in prison.[112] But concerns about the use of military justice did not go away. Colombia's first nongovernmental human rights organization, the Committee for Solidarity with Political Prisoners (CSPP), was established in 1973 in Bogotá in response to the detention of USO leaders. It was joined by peasant and other social movements whose members had been victims of arbitrary detentions. The CSPP's first public meeting was held immediately following the announcement that a group of oil strikers was to be released.[113] Among the organization's founding members were delegates from Barranca-bermeja, representing the USO and the ANUC.

Defeat of the Guerrillas: Operación Anorí

The repression of the USO in 1971 was carried out in the context of sweeping anti-Communist and counterinsurgency efforts by the Colombian military in the Magdalena Medio region in the early 1970s. Guerrilla actions targeting national oil infrastructure was a particular concern at the time. In October 1971 the ELN dynamited oil pipelines on the outskirts of Barranca and another in the poor neighborhood of El Cerro.[114] Military sweeps of the city were conducted immediately afterward, and the army detained more than three hundred people for not carrying proper identification.[115] Pressure on social movement activists accused of supporting the ELN continued through 1972, culminating in numerous arrests in Bogotá, Bucaramanga, Medellín, and Barrancabermeja. More than one hundred alleged guerrillas, including students and trade unionists, were arrested in the first week of July 1972 in one of the largest urban counterinsurgency operations in Colombian history. Of the total, eighty were arrested in Barranca.[116] The national press described these arrests as a victory over the urban support network of the ELN. More arrests were carried out over the next weeks. In August 1972 a *consejo verbal de guerra* was convened in Casabe, Antioquia, to process detainees. The legal defense team was comprised of two military officials, as well as labor lawyer Ángel Ramiro Aponte, who had served as legal counsel to striking oil workers the previous year.[117] As per the regulations of military law, the proceedings were held in camera.

The 1970s proved especially disastrous for the ELN, which suffered a crushing defeat in 1973 at the hands of the Colombian army. In and around Barranca, the guerrillas were well ensconced. In 1973 the ELN consisted of just 250 fighters divided into five columns, which were in turn divided into smaller fronts and commissions, some of which consisted of as few as six individuals. Mostly local to the region, the guerrillas' founding members had garnered support among progressive clergy, students, as well as some union activists and peasant leaders. Conceived as a *foquista* rebel force, they set out to lead by moral example rather than control of territory. The ELN's historical ties within the region allowed them to operate with relative agility, undertaking minor offensive actions against military positions and oil lines, going underground when necessary. In Barrancabermeja, Remedios, and San Vicente de Chucurí, the ELN organized channels for supplying rural operations.[118] Venturing outside of this local comfort zone would prove a formidable challenge. Even so, in 1972 they began concentrating their forces in unknown territory in Antioquia. They did not expect that the Colombian army would mobilize thousands of troops in response.

In January 1973 the Colombian army undertook an offensive to annihilate the ELN. To accomplish their objective, Defense Minister Hernando Currea approved the creation of a new mobile counterinsurgency unit, the Comando Operativo No. 10, based out of Bucaramanga, drawing on the resources of five different battalions, including air and naval support.[119] Located about 150 kilometers east of Barranca in northeastern Antioquia, Anorí was *terra nova* for the ELN. It was a *municipio* with a strong Conservative Party tradition, and army commanders believed its population could be persuaded to collaborate against the guerrillas. By the end of ten months of fighting, the ELN was reduced to 10 percent of its total force. The literal decimation of the ELN during Operación Anorí was a major turning point in the history of Colombia's guerrilla conflict and in the history of Barranca. In conversation with the Chilean sociologist Marta Harnecker in Havana in 1988, ELN commander Felipe Martínez observed, "Those were years when we paid for the sin of vanguardism, of *caudillismo* in terms of our leadership."[120]

The ELN leadership had overestimated its capacities. Fabio Vásquez Castaño, who served as the commander-in-chief of the ELN from 1964 through 1974, would ultimately be blamed for the defeat. Vásquez was a feared leader who led internal purges that shook the movement at its very foundation. It is estimated that he personally ordered or approved the execution of two hundred ELN members and supporters during his tenure with the guerrillas. Among the most notorious of his actions was the assassination of the former student leader Jaime Arenas in March 1971.[121] Arenas had been one of a generation of idealistic young Colombians who followed in the footsteps of Camilo Torres Restrepo. He left the guerrilla embittered by what he saw as an authoritarianism that betrayed the values of the revolution. Arenas then wrote about his experiences. Arenas's murder was committed in the context of a clandestine war on the state. But it could also be read as evidence of Vásquez's obsession with revolutionary discipline. The ensuing leadership crisis, compounded by mass arrests and military catastrophe, combined to threaten the guerrillas' existence. In any event, Fabio Vásquez fled to Cuba in November 1974, and the ELN began to rebuild.[122]

The men who emerged as leaders of the ELN following this period—the Spanish priest Manuel Pérez, alias "El Cura," and Nicolas Rodríguez Bautista, alias "Gabino"—would define the organization's political and military directions for the next twenty-five years. These men were more pragmatic and broadminded, if not always lenient. As we shall see, this new generation of guerrilla leaders would prove far more successful in building a mass movement. They would later describe the crisis of the early 1970s in terms that put the blame squarely on their own shortcomings as an organization: "It was obvious that the ELN, preoccupied with resolving its own internal issues, would not be able to keep up with the popular movement or respond to the political demands of the era."[123]

Popular Claims on Social Rights

In a period of crisis for the oil workers' union, and backlash against the guerrillas, new social movements burst forth to speak on behalf of the poor urban squatters who constituted the vast majority of Barranca residents. Neither the union nor the guerrillas disappeared from the scene altogether. The guerrillas would restructure over the course of the next decade, riding a national wave of new social movement organizing, as frustration with traditional politics persisted. The union also rebounded from the debacle of 1971 to organize another desperate battle against the state in 1977. But for the time being, a new civic-popular movement seized the momentum. In January 1975 a broad coalition of social groups organized a *paro cívico* around the issue of clean water that would demonstrate an unprecedented level of social engagement on the part of poor *barrio* residents. As one activist priest observed, "In 1975 we turned a corner, because that is when the civic-popular movement was born."[124] The trade union leader and CREDHOS cofounder Rafael Gómez moved to Barranca in 1975 in the midst of the upheaval at the time: "I arrived during the *paro cívico grande por el agua*. . . . It was big, huge! I think that it was the biggest *paro cívico* Barranca had ever had."[125]

The 1975 *paro cívico por el agua* was actually much broader than a fight for clean water. There were many issues related to public services at stake, including improvement to roads, sewers, schools, and health care. Questions around civil rights were also explicitly on the agenda, particularly in light of restrictions on commerce and travel in rural areas enforced under the terms of another declared "state of siege." Among members of the coalition who planned the protest were groups representing peasants, students, small business owners, and professionals. Liberals, Conservatives, Communists, and others all participated in the committee that drew up a list of ten demands to the national government. These demands included a new aqueduct, hospital upgrades, and the withdrawal of armed forces from the countryside. The Organización Femenina Popular, a women's organization working under the auspices of the Catholic Church, was pivotal in rallying people from the poor *barrios* to participate in the protest.[126] The *paro cívico por el agua* of 1975 seemed to demonstrate the possibilities of new lines of social solidarity in the city.

For a full month in early 1975 Barrancabermeja was transformed. The intention to convene a *paro cívico* was announced by the city's mayor on January 14. Government Minister Cornelio Reyes was quick to recognize that the lack of potable water in Barranca constituted "an emergency," and he pledged 67 million pesos toward the immediate construction of a new system to transport water to the city's poorest residents. Two days later the governor of Santander traveled to Barranca to meet with *paro cívico* organizers. But the protest committee remained unconvinced of the sincerity of government promises. Church, labor, and other groups convened nightly planning sessions in the city's poor neighborhoods. On the evening of Monday, January 20, a rally of five thousand people was held at the Parque Infantil in central Barranca.[127] An estimated five hundred police were deployed to surround the rally, while soldiers patrolled the streets. By a show of hands it was agreed that the protest would be sustained for at least twenty-four hours. The city was shut down that night, and there were no incidents of violence reported. Negotiations continued afterward, but both sides dug in their heels, and little progress was made.

As tensions mounted, divisions among the *paro cívico* organizers began to show. Small business owners were among the first to withdraw their support for the protests. It was during the trying second week of the protest campaign that Catholic Church leaders distinguished themselves. Led by the Pastoral Social, protest preparations continued, as did negotiations with Bogotá. On January 28, the national government declared that the movement was being led by "a few agitators."[128] In a public statement signed by President Alfonso López Michelsen, the government reiterated their pledge to improve the water infrastructure, as well as complete the highway between Barranca and Bucaramanga, expand public schools, and build a new courthouse. Meanwhile, large daily assemblies continued to be held in the Parque Infantil, which had been rebaptized the Parque del Pueblo, or the People's Park. These were opportunities for leaders of the Comité Cívico to assess the energy, patience, and agreement of the crowd. Unconvinced by the promises, and frustrated by the labeling of the *paro cívico* as "subversive," Bishop Bernardo Arango of Barranca convened a large rally on January 30. Another round of protest began that night. Thousands of people participated, despite the presence of police tanks armed with water cannons.

By the third week of the campaign, there were few signs that a resolution was near. Bishop Arango demanded that the national government desist from stigmatizing the protesters. Civic-popular movement organizers then received official support from the archbishop of Bucaramanga, Héctor Rueda. This prompted the governor of Santander to cautiously restate the government offer.[129] But this failed to convince the movement leaders in Barranca. Yet another *paro cívico* began on February 10, 1975, at 3:00 a.m. with tremendous enthusiasm. As one journalist described the events: "The announced 72-hour *paro cívico* began amidst sirens, the sound of drums, trumpets, firecrackers and empty pots . . . applause and shouts."[130] That same night, army reinforcements were sent from Bucaramanga to Barranca to take control of the city. Soldiers used tear gas to clear the barricades and enter the city. In a tersely worded letter to Barranca's mayor, Minister Cornelio Reyes said that *paro* organizers had purposefully created confusion by making demands that had "nothing to do" with the reality in Barranca, such as repealing security measures being enforced by the Colombian army in the rural Magdalena Medio.[131] The protestors grew weary. By the second day of what would prove to be the final round, food and water were running low, and the *paro cívico* came to an end.

The 1975 *paro cívico por el agua* was a pivotal moment in the formation of Barranca's civic-popular movement. After this point, popular sectors led by the Catholic Church would definitively take on the leadership of the push for social change. By 1975 the oil workers were in a process of rebuilding. And the guerrillas were nearly destroyed. United States Embassy staff were following events in Barranca as they unfolded, and in one cable to the Department of State, they summarize what occurred. The author's appreciation for the protestors is evident:

> Dirty water or holy water? A 24-hour civic strike in Barrancabermeja January 21 was followed by a peaceful demonstration January 30 in which another strike was declared this time for three days beginning February 10. The civic unrest is primarily based on the scarcity and uncleanliness of water in that city and the alleged refusal of the GOC [Government of Colombia] to take corrective action. The civic action has widespread support in the community including that of the Bishop of Barrancabermeja. . . . Several priests are among the leaders of the citizen activities. Bishop Arango's support for the January 21 strike prompted GOC Minister of Government to accuse Bishop of "trying to foment a revolution with holy water," to which the Bishop replied: "We cannot cause a revolution here with holy water because the water is so bad that it cannot even bear a blessing." Demonstrations and even disturbances in Barranca are not unusual. . . . The added twist to the current demonstration is the prominent role of the Catholic clergy, which in the past has been reluctant to assume a leadership role.[132]

Toward the end of February 1975 a delegation of civil society groups from Barranca met with President López in Bogotá.[133] The government signed a commitment to improve water services, invest in the public hospital, and even hear *campesinos'* concerns around land tenure. But *barranqueños* had every reason to distrust the government's intentions. Over the next few months, urban squatters clashed with police during land invasions, rumors of labor conflict at Ecopetrol circulated, high school students staged walkouts, and elementary school teachers went on strike. In June 1975 the Santander governor named Colonel Óscar Burbano as mayor of Barranca. Burbano immediately effected restrictions on freedom of movement and assembly, including a curfew and a ban on public meetings.[134] The imposition of strict security measures in Barranca would encourage the organizers of the 1975 *paro cívico* to establish a permanent basis for collective organizing.

The Militarization of Barranca

The tendency toward conflict between social movements and the state reached a new high in the late 1970s. Following the 1975 *paro cívico* in

Barranca, the Colombian national government continued to implement aggressive policies of political repression, typified by the use of emergency legal measures. President Alfonso López Michelsen declared countrywide *estados de sitio* on three separate occasions between August 1975 and October 1976.[135] In June 1976 representatives of the Committee for Solidarity with Political Prisoners held a public meeting at the oil workers' union headquarters in Barranca to denounce arbitrary detentions and the militarization of the countryside.[136] The Conservative governor of Santander, Rafael Ortiz, again named an army officer as mayor of Barranca. During the following two years the city experienced another cycle of powerful social convulsions, including a *paro cívico* and an oil strike that has been immortalized by the phrase "That wasn't a strike, that was a war!"[137]

From November 1976 through November 1977 Lieutenant Colonel Álvaro Bonilla López, then commander of the Comando Operativo del Magdalena Medio, the counterinsurgency arm of the army's Fifth Brigade, served as mayor of Barranca.[138] Between 1922 and 1976 no fewer than ten army officers had served as mayors of the municipality.[139] Bonilla is nonetheless distinguished for having presided over one of the most polarizing years in the history of the *puerto petrolero*. It was the year of a major oil strike, organized by a resurgent USO. It was also the year of the first major national civil strike, or *paro cívico nacional*, in Colombian history. Both protests were violently suppressed by military force. As former mayor and national Liberal Party leader Horacio Serpa later recalled, Bonilla "divided our community between decent people [*gentes de bien*] and undesirables [*indeseables*], according to who supported him, opposed him, or were simply indifferent."[140]

During his twelve-month tenure, Lieutenant Colonel Bonilla undertook an intensive schedule of social reform. He visited poor *barrios*, organized sports tournaments, sponsored an agricultural fair, and created a "beauty committee" to lobby for Barranca's right to send a candidate to the Miss Santander pageant.[141] He also oversaw an unsuccessful attempt to institute price controls on basic food items such as beef and raw brown sugar, *panela*. Alongside Yolanda Sandino de Hoyos—the city's first woman *secretaria de gobierno*, the highest-ranking position after the mayor—Bonilla was determined to expose the "moral decay" that was corroding the foundations of Barrancabermeja society, beneath the din of the jukeboxes in the city's cafés and *whiskerías*.[142] In mid-January 1977, Bonilla ordered shut more than one hundred bars, many of which were located around the city's main marketplace, near the train station, and in a small congregation of businesses known as El Uno, located in the north end of the recently settled Barrio Primero de Mayo. Bonilla and Sandino informed bar owners that they would be closed or forced to relocate to a designated "tolerance sector" in Barrio el Campestre.[143] This *campaña de saneamiento moral* continued the following month, with more bar closures along the city's main avenue. Bonilla put unauthorized lottery ticket sellers and street vendors out of business, and closed cinemas for being "unhygienic" or for allegedly screening pornography.[144]

Inevitably, the government came into a head-on collision with the oil workers as well. On March 26, 1977, the USO signed a new collective agreement with Ecopetrol. Almost immediately, the union began to protest the company's noncompliance with the approved conditions. The union submitted a long list of demands to Ecopetrol concerning the fair treatment of contract workers, access to medical services, and the subsidized sale of meat and other basic foodstuffs. Union organizers demanded right of entry to the refinery in order to consult with members.[145] The USO also accused the company of offering workers wage increases on the condition that they renounce their union membership. Eventually, the USO called hour-long sit-down strikes on July 26 and again on August 5. One week later Minister of Labor Óscar Montoya issued a resolution suspending the legal status of the USO.[146] On August 25, 1971, a full-fledged strike began. The very next day, Presidential Decree 2004 was signed, asserting that all persons who organize or foment "in any way" labor strikes or *paros cívicos* that threaten to "dislocate" the government could be subject to detention for up to 180 days without trial. Enacted under the terms of Colombia's longstanding state of siege legislation, this decree could be enforced on orders from political officials including mayors or departmental governors.[147] Undeterred, the USO made clear that its grievances were of concern to all Colombians. Besides the long litany of complaints against the company for its apparent violations of the collective agreement, the USO complained that Ecopetrol was unlawfully lending drilling equipment to foreign companies operating in the Magdalena Medio.[148] The union also highlighted the arbitrary manner in which Ecopetrol interests, including natural gas reserves in the department of La Guajira, had recently been sold to U.S. companies. The union demanded the immediate restoration of its legal standing, as well as amnesty for jailed union members. The strike was comprehensive, shutting down not only the refinery at Barranca but also Ecopetrol installations in El Centro, as well as Cantagallo (Bolívar), Yondó (Antioquia), and Tibú and Cicuco (Norte de Santander).

The conflict in the refinery in Barranca came to a head in September 1977 during the lead-up to a *paro cívico nacional*. All of Barranca's political parties, including the Communists, ANAPO, Conservatives, and Liberals, sent a letter on September 5 to President López demanding the removal of Lieutenant Colonel Bonilla as mayor.[149] The oil strike was now into its second week, and nerves were beginning to fray. The supervisor of the Barranca refinery, Ismael Rincón Rodríguez, was assassinated. Bombs were set off in the city, including several at the homes of oil workers.[150] The mayor accused the union of intimidating workers who refused to participate in strike activities, distributing incendiary leaflets, throwing stones, and shooting at the homes and vehicles of Ecopetrol officials.[151] A group of young activist lawyers—including the future founder of the human rights organization CREDHOS, Jorge Gómez Lizarazo—published a letter accusing Bonilla of excesses in the name of public order, including the unnecessary extension of a curfew and other restrictions of basic freedoms.[152] The *paro cívico nacional* then took place on September 14, with massive participation in Barranca.

The final weeks of the 1977 oil strike proceeded amid escalating repression. Thousands of soldiers were sent to Barranca, public meetings were banned, and strike leaders were jailed. Civic groups, opposition political parties, and other unions joined forces with the USO in early October to stage a *paro cívico* in solidarity with the strikers. Police and armed forces personnel patrolled the streets of the city, enforcing a curfew. The union moved its center of operations every couple of days to avoid being shut down by authorities, and meetings of the union's executive committee were held in secret.[153] The oil strike finally came to an end on October 29, 1977, more than two months after it began. A total of 217 Ecopetrol workers were dismissed. A number of young people who had been detained during the *paro cívico* and strike were made to sweep the city's main avenues clear of *miguelitos*, the tacks thrown by protestors to discourage the circulation of cars and other vehicles.[154]

Another long hot season of protest in Barranca was coming to an end. But all of this social conflict was a mere prelude to the much more violent decade to come. The union was depleted, and the fledgling civic-popular movement was facing the cruel reality of ever more severe national security measures. More than a dozen presidential decrees intended to curtail union and civic organizing were signed during the first post–National Front government, led by the left-leaning Liberal Alfonso López Michelsen.[155] Presidential Decree 1923, better known as the National Security Statute, was then adopted by Liberal president Julio César Turbay Ayala in September 1978. The new law permitted the Colombian armed forces to exercise a variety of administrative functions, including the right to detain and prosecute Colombian citizens for organizing meetings deemed to be of a subversive nature. In the text of the National Security Statute, *paros cívicos* are equated with acts of armed insurrection. Notably, Article 7A bans the occupation of public or private buildings for the purposes of exerting pressure on "legitimate authorities" or "exhorting citizens to rebel."[156]

Conclusion

In the 1960s new social actors and new forms of social action emerged in Barrancabermeja as a result of major political and demographic change. Of the new forms of civic protest practiced in the period immediately after La Violencia that would come to characterize popular life in Barrancabermeja, the *paro civico* proved the most important.[157] The 1963 oil strike constituted a flexing of muscles by the once mighty union, after years in forced hibernation. The very first *paro cívico* in Barranca history was also organized in 1963. The end of civil warfare in 1958 and the nationalization of the oil refinery in 1961 had brought little relief to citizens of the Magdalena Medio. In response, local elected officials, *campesinos*, progressive Catholic priests, and urban squatters all began to assert themselves. At the same time, guerilla groups formed in the region became a focus of Cold War counterinsurgency concern on the part of the Colombian military.

The 1970s were a period of setbacks for Unión Sindical Obrera; the main leaders of Barranca's trade union movement were removed from their positions, arrested, imprisoned, or exiled during the major strikes organized in 1971 and 1977. A civic-popular movement emerged in the course of the decade that succeeded in mobilizing grassroots community groups in the poor *barrios* on the outskirts of the city. During the course of historic civic protests in 1975, a coalition emerged that was capable of crossing class and occupational lines in Barranca. In October 1983 representatives of a newly established civic-popular movement front, the Coordinadora Popular de Barrancabermeja, attended the First National Congress of Civic Movements, in Bogotá. The main thrust of the meeting was to identify the problems affecting poor urban Colombians, from water services to unemployment. For several years into the next decade, civic movements would continue to meet on a national level to exchange experiences and information.[158] As official repression increased, especially in the countryside, insurgent groups also expanded their influence. The distinction between urban and rural issues was blurred by the ensuing displacement of peasants to urban areas, and the dynamic of the civic-popular movement changed forever. Its focus would soon shift from social rights and poverty to the problem of violence.

3

War in the Countryside and the Transformation of a Company Town

> They started to kill us everywhere. I realized that I could not go on living in my home town, so I had to leave in secret. We went to a small town called Puerto Claver, where I spent six months. I never felt comfortable. So we went to Barranca. When we arrived, we met up with many *campesinos* who were our friends, neighbors who had fled looking for refuge. They were living in different *barrios*. In all of the *barrios* in Barrancabermeja you find displaced people, but in El Progreso there were 23 families from the same village where I used to live.
>
> *Campesino* leader displaced from Vuelta Acuña, Santander, in 1984[1]

Introduction

The massacre of eight *campesinos* on January 12, 1984, in Vuelta Acuña—a small farming and fishing settlement located just south of Barranca, located in the *municipio* of Cimitarra—was a wake-up call for social movement activists in the city. Perpetrated by a combined force of military and paramilitary troops, the Vuelta Acuña massacre was a pivotal moment, after which the history of the city of Barrancabermeja became incontrovertibly linked to armed conflict.[2] Following the massacre, hundreds of people from Vuelta Acuña were joined by hundreds more from the Cimitarra River Valley, southern Bolívar, and settlements along the Opón River in a mass exodus to Barranca to protest paramilitary terror in the region.[3] Other residents of Vuelta Acuña fled initially to neighboring towns, only to eventually converge on Barranca. The central government in Bogotá set up a special commission of enquiry into events unfolding in the area around Vuelta Acuña. For the individuals who participated in the commission, including several social activists from Barranca, it was a transformative experience. The massacre shed a cruel light on violence in the countryside, and human rights would emerge as the most important paradigm of protest in the city.

Barrancabermeja's human rights movement was the product of the encounter between violence-affected rural communities and urban social movements. Human rights discourses were circulating among small groups of activists in the Magdalena Medio, Bogotá, and beyond since the early 1970s. Indeed, the oil workers' strike and its aftermath had been the flashpoint for the creation of the county's first human rights organization. Yet Barranca's civic-popular movement remained focused on water quality and other public services through the end of the decade. The real turn to human rights began with the arrival of organized displaced *campesinos*. The counterinsurgency war based out of Puerto Berrío, Puerto Boyacá, Cimitarra, and other *municipios* to the south of Barranca was supported by drug traffickers and cattle ranchers with investments in the region.[4] In response, tens of thousands of *campesinos* abandoned the war-torn countryside.[5] Many of these newcomers participated in organized *éxodos* or were members of peasant associations. Once in Barranca, they were approached by officials from Barranca's left-leaning municipal council, as well as by established Church-sponsored community groups. The peasants who came to Barranca during the early 1980s did not seek merely to escape the violence. *Campesinos* squatted in public buildings in Barranca to call attention to their plight and demanded that the national government in Bogotá guarantee their safety. This led many local activists to take a longer look at events in the countryside, even traveling to war-affected areas to observe the crisis for themselves.

Barranca cast off its "company town" past as displaced peasants and other poor urban residents, seeking political recognition, called on the Colombian government to protect basic human rights.[6] The oil workers' union had been weakened during the repression of the 1971 and 1977 strikes, leaving space for other social actors to be heard. As the number of squatters grew, the importance of new social movements increased.[7] In 1980 there were forty-eight officially recognized *barrios* in the city of Barranca. By 1985 there were twice as many. At the height of violence in the region, between 1984 and 1985, the population of Barranca increased by 22 percent, from 128,685 to 156,917.[8] An estimated 80 percent of new neighborhoods were established through land invasions organized by migrants fleeing the countryside because of death threats, selective assassinations, or massacres.[9] Squatters were stigmatized by military authorities in the city because they had come from areas with a guerrilla presence. The actions taken by these migrants raised awareness around political violence. The fact that the new residents of the city identified with the radical stance of the civic-popular movement energized hopes for social and political change.

It was a time of powerful indignation toward the state in Colombia. The repression of the oil workers' union in the 1970s had been severe, and the national government was perceived by many in Barranca as obstructing the realization of social justice. Activists' resentment toward Bogotá was matched by their faith in the power of popular protest. Across the country Colombians expressed their antipathy to the restriction of civil and political rights under the National Security Statute. Local activists looked to the Sandinista revolutionary victory in Nicaragua in 1979 and the persistence of movements for national liberation in other parts of Latin America for inspiration. Yolanda Becerra, leader of the Organización Feminina Popular (OFP), recalls that when she became active in the city's student and women's movements in her early twenties, the prospects for change seemed immediate: "I got married in 1981, and I didn't have children until 1984 because I thought that social change was about to happen. I didn't want to be tied up with raising children. . . . First I am going to do this, and then I'll have children. Because we didn't see it happening tomorrow, it was going to happen today! This hope . . . to see this door opening up. That motivated us, made us strong. Dreaming of the world, dreaming of many things."[10] Becerra's almost unassailable belief that the opportunity for transforming Colombian society had arrived was shared by many of her fellow activists. It was a conviction that came from the experience of a growing broad-based social activism on the streets of Barranca over a period of more than a decade.

The individuals interviewed for this book came of age amid political turmoil. Many had activist parents and neighbors and were shaped by the confrontation between local social movements and the state. All partook of the *mística* of Barrancabermeja. This chapter brings together multiple personal, local, and national histories that constitute the geneses of human rights organizing in Barranca. Barranca's early human rights activists narrate journeys through fear, anger, frustration, and persistence. In the countryside, embattled *campesinos* mobilized their communities around the issue of violence. As paramilitary groups encroached on Barranca, urban social movement leaders in the city would address the issue with increasing seriousness. Resistance to state-sponsored violence resonated beyond the Magdalena Medio region, as national and international NGOs, the Organization of American States, and the United Nations responded to local groups' appeals and began to address human rights in the region.

The Human Rights Crucible in Colombia

There is a direct line between popular responses to the violent repression of social protest in Barrancabermeja and the development of a human rights activist agenda at the national level. The Colombian national human rights movement was born in the early 1970s, at a time of highly conflictive relations between the state and civil society. The first Colombian human rights organization, the Committee for Solidarity with Political Prisoners (CSPP), was established in 1973 to defend the rights of jailed social activists, including members of the Unión Sindical Obrera. A number of luminaries, including the future Nobel laureate Gabriel García Márquez, participated in its creation. The CSPP is credited with issuing the first "urgent action" out of Colombia addressed to the international community.[11] The first major documentary project undertaken by a human rights group in Colombia was the 1974 *Black Book of Repression*, published by the CSPP.[12] The Permanent Committee for the Defense of Human Rights, a Bogotá-based NGO associated with the Communist Party but with a broad mandate to defend human rights throughout Colombia, was established in 1979 in response to rising counter-insurgency violence, as well as the suppression of civilian and political rights. One of the first regions outside the capital to organize local chapters of the Permanent Committee was the Magdalena Medio.[13]

By the end of the 1970s, Colombians' denunciations of political repression had begun to attract the attention of international human rights groups. The United Nations Human Rights Committee expressed concerns about Turbay Ayala's National Security Statute in 1979.[14] Amnesty International carried out its first mission to Colombia in January 1980 to investigate allegations of torture, arbitrary detention, and extrajudicial killings by the Colombian state.[15] The resulting 258-page report to the Colombian government listed more than six hundred individual cases of abuse, backed by archival, testimonial, and forensic evidence.[16] A medical doctor traveled as part of the Amnesty team, undertaking examinations of twenty-seven victims of torture in eleven prisons, two military detention centers, and two hospitals in seven different cities. President Turbay Ayala described the Amnesty report as "libelous" and an affront to Colombian sovereignty, adding that the international human rights experts had undertaken their work with a "belligerent spirit."[17] The Inter-American Commission on Human Rights undertook its first visit to Colombia in April 1980.[18] Much to President Turbay Ayala's dismay, the commission's report vindicated the claims made by Amnesty International.[19]

This opening of Colombia to international scrutiny was part of a pattern of increasing concern for civil and political rights across Latin America. The

Figure 4. President Julio César Turbay Ayala's visit to Barrancabermeja, 1980. Courtesy of Foto Estudios Joya.

Argentinian Adolfo Pérez Esquivel won the Nobel Peace Prize in 1980. A fierce opponent of the military *junta* in Buenos Aires, Pérez Esquivel was one of the first Latin American human rights activists to receive international recognition. The Inter-American Commission published twelve country reports between 1978 and 1981, equal to the total number of reports over the previous sixteen-years. In Colombia, a handful of new human rights initiatives emerged in this period, mostly working out of Bogotá. The kind of reporting published abroad about human rights in Colombia dealt systematically with wrongful detentions, unfair trials, and torture. This tendency to emphasize civil and political liberties reflected international concern about authoritarianism in Latin America, as well as the main concerns of social movement activists subjected to the National Security Doctrine. At the time, a majority of Latin American countries were still under some kind of direct military rule.[20] The shadowy dynamics of paramilitarism, while also present in the Southern Cone of South America, were difficult to investigate and still little understood. Accessing conflict zones in the Magdalena Medio would have been practically impossible for international organizations

President Turbay Ayala governed Colombia under a permanent state of siege, allowing military authorities to overrule local civilian governments on issues of public order, restrict freedom of movement, and quietly cede power to paramilitary groups.[21] On July 20, 1980, just two months following Amnesty

International's first visit to Colombia, five army officers published a repentant open letter admitting their participation in the American Anticommunist Alliance (AAA). The AAA was a paramilitary group established in 1978 by Jorge Robledo Pulido, then commander of the Colombian armed forces. The Colombian officers who had worked with the AAA confessed to the torture and killing of members of left-wing opposition parties and the bombing of three Bogotá-based periodicals (including *Alternativa*, edited by Gabriel García Márquez and the sociologist Orlando Fals Borda, and *Voz Proletaria*, the official newspaper of the Communist Party of Colombia). The AAA, named after an Argentinean death squad that existed in the mid-1970s, was disbanded after one year.[22] But a new tendency had emerged. In late 1981 another new paramilitary group emerged, known as Death to Kidnappers, or Muerte a Secuestradores (MAS). Centered in the southern Magdalena Medio, MAS included among its members the future commanders of Colombia's national paramilitary, including Carlos Castaño.[23]

Paramilitarism posed a number of serious problems for human rights advocates. The fact that terrorist actions were being carried out by clandestine forces, in relatively isolated areas, made what was going on difficult to expose. Moreover, social activists themselves were targeted by paramilitaries. In the late 1970s and early 1980s nearly all of the violence in the Magdalena Medio region was rural-based, centered in the municipalities of Puerto Boyacá, Puerto Berrío, and Cimitarra, followed by El Carmen and San Vicente de Chucurí.[24] According to statistics gathered by the Bogotá-based researcher Amanda Romero on behalf of the Jesuit-run Center for Popular Education and Research (CINEP), between 1980 and 1985 the *municipios* of Cimitarra and Puerto Boyacá accounted for 450 assassinations.[25] Human rights complaints against the Colombian armed forces decreased dramatically in these same areas in direct proportion to the increase in paramilitary groups' strength.[26] As social movement organizations were silenced, and paramilitaries took over, there was simply nobody left to denounce human rights violations.[27] On January 27, 1983, unknown assailants presumed to be working with MAS murdered Fernando Vélez Méndez, a Liberal town councillor and president of the human rights committee in Puerto Berrío, affiliated with the national Permanent Committee for the Defense of Human Rights.[28] By the end of 1983, there was no human rights committee in Puerto Berrío, and the Communist Party had closed its office. There were no reported human rights violations in Puerto Boyacá, Cimitarra, and Puerto Berrío in the late 1980s. Local authorities yielded to the paramilitary, and the circle of impunity was complete. As union leader and CREDHOS cofounder Rafael Gómez recalls, it was a pattern repeated right across the region: "If you look at *municipios* like La Dorada,

Puerto Berrío, the rates of violence decrease at the moment that the *autodefensas* take control. People submit to the *autodefensas*."[29]

Early efforts to organize around human rights in Barranca itself were modest but productive. A small ad-hoc group of Barranca activists began working on human rights issues in 1980 in response to events in the region. That year they wrote a report documenting cases of torture, forced disappearances, and illegal detentions in the Magdalena Medio and submitted it to visiting delegates from Amnesty International.[30] In 1982 a group called the Comité de Derechos Humanos was formally established in Barranca. The committee functioned as a small collective of concerned individuals, and it did not carry out any public activities. It folded within one year. In 1983 the Pastoral Social organized a small human rights gathering in a lecture hall at the Universidad Cooperativa de Colombia, Barranca's main public university at the time. The speakers at the city's first Foro pro-Derechos Humanos included the future CREDHOS president Jorge Gómez Lizarazo, the future FEDEPETROL president Fernando Acuña, and the Jesuit priest Mario Calderón. Calderón was a prominent human rights activist and liberation theologian visiting Barrancabermeja from Bogotá, where he worked as a researcher for the Jesuit-run think tank and popular education center CINEP.[31]

Despite the growing interest in human rights, concerns around social services, infrastructure, and labor continued to drive the agenda of Barranca's civic-popular movement. Small groups of *barranqueños* were becoming aware of the seriousness of the counterinsurgency repression being carried out in the countryside. Yet the violence seemed somewhat distant, formless, or intangible. That is, until *campesinos* concerned with human rights began arriving in the city in far greater numbers and expressing themselves more forcefully. The relationships fostered between labor, the church, and other social activists during the early 1980s would prove important to the development of wider interest in human rights in the years to come.

Denouncing Paramilitarism in the Southern Magdalena Medio

Campesino organizations were the first to experience counterinsurgent violence in the Magdalena Medio, and the first to elucidate it. In 1979 at a meeting of the government-created National Agrarian Council, the National Association of Peasant Users (ANUC) described the situation in the Magdalena Medio region as "agrarian militarization." By this time, ANUC functioned as an autonomous organization, with factions or "sectors" representing different regions. ANUC decried the mechanisms of control being imposed on the local economy by the Colombian military, as well as an increase in arbitrary detention, torture, and disappearances.[32] ANUC's articulation of human rights concerns was closely bound to their disputes with the national government over access to land and markets. Military roadblocks were set up near major town centers, and the movement of people and goods was controlled by means of army-issued and enforced travel passes and quotas. A pamphlet distributed by the army in Puerto Boyacá read: "Peasant: collaborate with the Army, avoid restrictions, do not allow your land to lose its real value, and your children's future to be put at risk."[33] The pamphlet listed specific restrictions on the transport of food in the region, ostensibly as a means of preventing *campesinos* from supplying the guerrillas.

At public and internal meetings, peasant organizers in the Magdalena Medio linked paramilitary terror to the issues of land and economic justice. On the occasion of the First Agricultural Forum for the Magdalena Medio— held in Barranca on July 23, 1983, with the participation of the minister of agriculture, the director of the National Peace Commission, the governors of Santander and Antioquia, military officers, and local political officials— ANUC leader Ángel Tolosa stated that violence and repression threatened the survival of the peasant way of life. In his keynote address he stated: "The old magnificent Magdalena River . . . is now a peasant graveyard; not a day goes by in this port that we do not witness a parade of horribly mutilated and savagely tortured cadavers tossed aside by the death squads."[34] Tolosa, leader of ANUC's Barranca-based Sector Independiente, called on the government to guarantee the peasants of the region "respect for life and self-determination."[35] Tolosa said that peasants were being forced to abandon their parcels of land or sell them off "for the price of a scrawny chicken."[36] At their 1984 national gathering ANUC leaders in Barranca again emphasized the connection between basic rights and economic justice. This time "detentions, cases of torture, and all kinds of abuses that are committed against the peasants" were mentioned, together with concerns about the titling of land and access to credit, technical, and social services.[37]

Peasant activists laid bare the complexities of rural violence at a time when few Colombians knew what was transpiring in the Magdalena Medio. ANUC documented arbitrary detentions and extrajudicial killings. They made the case that fighting in the region was not in fact a war between belligerent groups but a conflict over control of land involving multiple actors. Access to land was a key concern for peasants in the Magdalena Medio due to encroachment by drug traffickers and highway construction. Farms abandoned by forcibly displaced peasants in the areas around Cimitarra, Puerto Berrío, and Yondó were claimed by absentee landowners, including members of the Medellín cartel. In the early 1980s small producers' parcels on both sides of the river were also being expropriated to accommodate road building. At a meeting of social movements in Bogotá in July 1984, ANUC shared their unique perspective on the conflict: "Contrary to what politicians say . . . that the violence in the Magdalena Medio and other regions of the country is due to confrontation between the guerrillas and the army, that is to say a battle between "bad guys" and "good guys," we maintain that the conflict is fundamentally socio-economic and political and essentially a dispute over the primary means of production: THE LAND."[38] As Nazih Richani describes, what was occurring in the Magdalena Medio was a process of forced concentration of landholding.[39] ANUC estimated that more than 51.7 percent of private land in the Magdalena Medio was held by just 4 percent of landholders.[40] The country's most prominent drug traffickers, including Pablo Escobar and José Gonzalo Rodríguez Gacha, hastened the rise of paramilitarism in the Magdalena Medio through their investments in cattle ranching over the next decade.[41] It was also the site of paramilitary training programs paid for directly by members of the Medellín Cartel.[42] Peasant farmers lived in fear. Those peasants who were not displaced were unable to meet increased leasing and purchase prices.[43]

The first sustained right-wing paramilitary organizing to be carried out in Colombia since the outbreak of guerrilla violence in the mid-1960s was based out of the southern Magdalena Medio. MAS was conceived by drug kingpin Pablo Escobar in response to the December 3, 1981, kidnapping by M-19 insurgents of the daughter of Medellín Cartel associate Fabio Ochoa. Although the kidnapping of Blanca Nieves Ochoa had been carried out on the campus of the University of Antioquia in Medellín, Escobar was far more concerned with securing control of territory in the Magdalena Medio. Dozens of people were killed by MAS paramilitaries in the first two months, leading up to Blanca Nieves Ochoa's release by the M-19 on February 16, 1982. The MAS leadership then turned their attention toward territory disputed by the more formidable FARC guerrillas. In 1978 Escobar had purchased a 7,400-acre estate in Puerto Triunfo, on the Magdalena River. A number of other high-level drug traffickers had also bought land in this area, for the purposes of investing their outsize profits. Drug traffickers' interests coincided with those of ranchers and other businessmen who had fallen victim to extortion by the FARC and local military officials. The paramilitary group MAS established a presence in the Magdalena Medio in 1982 with the cooperation of army captain Óscar Echandía, then acting mayor of the *municipio* of Puerto Boyacá.[44] Within a year there were a dozen or more paramilitary units operating in the region, targeting civilians living in bastions of leftist politics.

The FARC had expanded in the southern Magdalena Medio through the late 1970s and early 1980s, building on the electoral support garnered by the Communist Party, in keeping with a tradition of combining "all forms of struggle."[45] The Communist Party had secured influential minorities in the elected municipal councils of Puerto Berrío, Puerto Boyacá, and Cimitarra. In the countryside, the FARC sought and received the cooperation of peasants and cattle ranchers alike, at least initially. The FARC implemented a system of rent collection, the most lucrative of which were taxes charged to large holders. As the ambitions of the organization grew, so did its demands on local elites. Some ranchers feared being kidnapped or worse, and a number left their properties to live with their families in Medellín and other cities. The emergence of what the political scientist Carlos Medina Gallego has called the "economy of flight" put pressure on the overseers who represented absentee investors' interests in the region.[46] The FARC's influence became untenable when newer investors flush with the spoils of the drug trade began to buy land. These new elites were armed and in no mood to bargain.

The rise of paramilitarism coincided with a significant shift in the overall approach of the FARC toward its revolutionary war. At the guerrillas' watershed Sixth Conference in January 1978 a decision was taken to shed their identity as a "self-defense" force and to pursue a more expansive strategy of territorial and political control. Following its Seventh Conference in May 1982 the FARC announced its transformation into a mobile army to directly challenge the central state. It was at this point that the FARC added the initials EP—meaning Ejército Popular, or People's Army—to its name.[47] The FARC-EP would now focus on the military conquest of new territories and take the fight to the enemy. This meant directing energy where it would be most effectively spent. In the Magdalena Medio, the newly christened FARC-EP retreated from certain areas under paramilitary pressure, preferring to establish bases to the southeast and the west of Barranca, and eventually Barranca itself. It opened new fronts in Antioquia and Bolívar, where the remoteness of the terrain allowed the guerrillas to operate in relative calm.

While the FARC moved into new areas, activists in its traditional territories in the southern Magdalena Medio were under siege. The Communist Party and other left movements, including trade unions, were especially hard hit by MAS in the *municipios* of Puerto Boyacá and Puerto Berrío. It was reported at the time that MAS agents committed 250 political murders in its first two years of operations.[48] As the political scientists Michael Shifter and Jennifer Stillerman write: "The organization's initial objective—to free the region of subversives—soon expanded to include attacks on any person or organization that resisted it."[49] Military and paramilitary troops killed six town councillors and dozens of political activists in Puerto Berrío in 1982 and 1983. The Communist town councillor Jaime Nevado was murdered on July 22, 1982, by an army sergeant with the local Bomboná Infantry Battalion.[50] Many Communist militants chose to abandon their work or flee the region altogether. In the words of one former commander of the FARC's IX Front, the guerrillas had committed a series of "strategic" errors by increasing pressure on local elites, underestimating drug traffickers, and abandoning their Communist allies. The upshot was the selective disarticulation of the political and military sides of the revolutionary struggle in the region.[51] The guerrillas' departure from areas of paramilitary influence had left their rearguard exposed.[52]

According to figures collected by researchers at the Centre for Popular Education and Research (CINEP), about one third of Colombian peasant protests between 1980 and 1985 were motivated by concerns about human rights violations, paramilitarism, and the escalation of armed conflict.[53] These included the first popular protests organized specifically in favor of human rights in Colombian history. Two pioneering events—La Marcha del Silencio (October 1982) and La Marcha de la Solidaridad (November 1982)—were organized in Puerto Berrío by local social and political movements, with the approval of the mayor's office and the Catholic Church. Perhaps the single most ambitious action of the era was the Marcha por la Vida y la Paz, during which thousands of people from the region gathered in Barrancabermeja and proceeded overland more than six hundred kilometers to the city of Cartagena, on the Caribbean coast.[54] The onset of paramilitary violence coincided with the beginning of a general trend toward increased peasant militancy. The Magdalena Medio region was the epicenter of peasant protest in Colombia during these years. Eight of the top ten Colombian *municipios* with the greatest number of peasant protests organized between 1980 and 1995 were located in the Magdalena Medio.[55]

Campesino mobilizations helped to bring the problem of rural violence to bear on national politics. Beginning in 1982, President Belisario Betancur had initiated peace talks with the FARC and M-19.[56] In the midst of negotiations, the president ordered the creation of a special commission of the inspector general to look into the rise of paramilitarism in Colombia. Published on February 20, 1983, the inspector general's report was surprisingly forthright. Notably, the report exposed links between the military and paramilitary groups: "The MAS is a genuine paramilitary movement. . . . It is composed essentially of [state] officials who commit excesses when faced with the temptation to increase their capacity by making use of private forces."[57] The inspector general claimed that more than one-third of MAS paramilitary members under investigation were active Colombian military or national police personnel.[58]

War and Transformation

However, the results of the commission were muted by differences between the Betancur government and military authorities in the Magdalena Medio who sought a free hand in dealing with guerrillas. In December 1983 President Betancur personally sponsored a public rally described as a "March for Peace" in Puerto Berrío. He traveled to the region to demonstrate his commitment to human rights, accompanied by a large retinue of senior government officials, including the ministers of education, justice, and government, the head of the Institute for Natural Resources, and the National Peace commissioner.[59] It would be the last public demonstration in favor of human rights in the southern Magdalena Medio.

National government action on peace and human rights would prove ineffective and occasioned serious risks for social movement activists in war-affected rural areas. Beginning in the middle of the 1980s supporters of left-wing political parties energized by peace negotiations were persecuted with special ferocity. In April 1984 the Agreement of La Uribe was signed between the FARC's high command and the government of President Belisario Betancur, leading to the creation of a political party known as the Patriotic Union (UP). The Patriotic Union was a hybrid movement composed of members of the Communist Party, as well as unionized workers, teachers, peasants, and students. But rank-and-file activists' hopes for a democratic transition in Colombia would quickly be shattered. More than five hundred members of the Patriotic Union were killed during the 1980s. While this included presidential candidates, the victims were disproportionately grassroots members in places such as the Magdalena Medio.[60]

The killings of Communist, Patriotic Union, and other legal political activists in the Magdalena Medio obeyed the logic of counterinsurgency. Two specialized units of the Colombian army held sway over the Magdalena Medio region from bases in Puerto Boyacá (No. 3 Infantry Battalion) and Puerto Berrío (Fourteenth Brigade). In 1984 the Colombian army sent one of its brightest stars, General Farouk Yanine Díaz, to lead the intelligence unit of the Fourteenth Brigade.[61] General Yanine, a graduate and former instructor of the School of the Americas in Fort Benning, Georgia, claimed that his mission was social as well as military: "Whoever wins over the civilian population will win the war with the FARC; if we win, we will have no need to fire a single shot in the future."[62] Yanine set out to exercise control over the thirty-two municipalities in his purview, spread out along the Magdalena River and in highland Santander, through a combination of armed force and highly visible social projects, such as road building and mobile health clinics.[63] If the pacification and development of the region were supposed to go hand-in-hand, military prerogatives trumped humanitarian ones. In January 1984

Yanine was promoted to command the Second Division of the Colombian army in Bucaramanga, overseeing all operations along the Magdalena River.

As progressive popular movements declined in the southern Magdalena Medio, anti-Communist ranchers and politicians created their own socio-political organizations. Tearing a page from General Yanine's playbook, pro-paramilitary landholders joined forces to promote combined military and social tactics. The effect was to both spread and legitimize the nascent paramilitary movement. In 1984 the Asociación Campesina de Agricultores y Ganaderos del Magdalena Medio (ACDEGAM) established under the leadership of Puerto Boyacá's Liberal mayor Luis Rubio. ACDEGAM was a legally registered business association led by local powerbrokers such as Alejandro Echandía, the brother of Boyacá's former military mayor, Captain Óscar Echandía.[64] ACDEGAM published reports on current events, hosted conferences, sent delegations to Bogotá to speak with President Betancur on issues of economic development and security, and organized marches in support of local military officials or to protest the presence of the FARC in the region.[65] It also set up rural schools and organized "medical brigades" in poor and isolated areas that could provide them with intelligence on left-wing activities.[66] On balance, ACDEGAM was less interested in charity mongering than in propaganda. The organization was also key to the provision of logistical support to para-military organizations in the region.[67] The group's medical staff attended to sick and injured paramilitary fighters and spread the word about the dangers of Communism. ACDEGAM offices were used to stash weapons and orga-nize recruitment. Several indicted paramilitary leaders of that era have spoken openly of ACDEGAM members' participation in military planning sessions.[68] ACDEGAM even operated a small shop where paramilitaries could buy boots, clothing, and basic equipment.[69] In a very short period of time, it built a strong network of economic, political, social, and military forces around an anti-Communist ideology.

While paramilitary networks put down roots in the southern Magdalena Medio, social movement activists in Barranca began to sense that something was going horribly wrong. As the CREDHOS cofounder and oil workers' union leader Rafael Gómez recalls, Barranca activists were watching as the bodies floated downstream:

In Barranca we started to become aware of the deaths of many people, from the river . . . toward the south. In Puerto Boyacá and all of that region, Puerto Boyacá, Puerto Berrío, El Carmen, and San Vicente . . . the paramilitaries basically began their campaigns there. The dead floated down the river. Many displaced people who had suffered in those places . . . the paramilitaries took their land. That was, let's say, around 1983–1985, around that time, you could see that a lot of killings were being carried out in that region.[70]

In the first half of the 1980s, Barranca registered a total of ninety-nine political murders: high for a city of one hundred thousand, but very low compared with what was to come.[71] The violence taking place outside of the city loomed ominously but was not yet a direct threat to *barranqueño* activists. Peasant groups, on the other hand, were speaking out against the violence. By necessity, if not by vocation, peasants were the first human rights activists in the Magdalena Medio. In the meanwhile, urban activists still did not quite understand the seriousness of the threat they would soon face. And so for the time being, the civic-popular movement continued to mobilize around demands for improved public services.

The Coordinadora Popular de Barrancabermeja

Barrancabermeja's most important activist coalition, the Coordinadora Popular, was established in 1983. The Coordinadora Popular built upon the social bases of the *paros cívicos* of the 1970s, in a context of increasing confrontation with the national government. Recognizing that the state of emergency in which they lived was ongoing, these activists sought to create a permanent structure that could go beyond the temporary functions of a *comité de paro*. The Coordinadora Popular was born out of a protracted series of protests for public services. During two grueling months in 1983, the national government demonstrated its seemingly undiminished determination to repress popular protest in Barranca. The Coordinadora Popular was formed to engage with authorities during and in between crisis peaks, to counter state-sponsored repression, and to address the perennial issues of poverty and social exclusion.

Early experiments in coalition building had been short-lived in Barranca, despite the intensive work required to stage *paros cívicos*. A number of civic-popular movement groupings had been convened through the 1970s, notably the Alianza Obrero Campesino Popular y Estudiantil. The persistent drive for improved public services, including potable water, proper roads, schools, and sanitation, led civic leaders to work toward the unification of labor and new social movements. Led by the USO and FEDEPETROL, the Coordinadora de Solidaridad was established in 1980 as a way for unionized oil workers to build bridges between themselves and the broader community. According to the Coordinadora de Solidaridad's founding statement, equal emphasis would be placed on addressing poverty, political violence, and the curtailing of civil rights under the National Security Statute.[72] However, this new alignment did not succeed in engaging activists from the Pastoral Social or the Juntas de Acción Comunal (JACs, Community Action Councils), which were the pillars of neighborhood politics at the time.[73] It lasted about one year. The first effort to organize community-based groups in Barranca's poor squatter settlements was the Coordinadora del Sector Nor-oriental, established in 1981 in the city's northeastern *barrios* under the leadership of the Pastoral Social.[74] After some initial success lobbying the municipal government for bus service and road repairs, it participated in a national *paro cívico* in 1981 that failed to make an impact in Barranca. Discouraged by the lack of results and concerned about attracting unwanted repression, the Coordinadora del Sector Nor-oriental was dissolved in 1982. The successive collapse of these efforts suggested that a new strategy was needed to mobilize poor *barrio* residents, unionized workers, and local elected officials.

The Coordinadora Popular came together in early 1983, during prepara-tions for a *paro cívico* for improved public services. Over the course of a series of four *paros cívicos* that lasted several months, it became a major force in the daily life of the city. The new coalition was intended from the outset to have functions beyond the temporary mandate of a simple *comité de paro*, and its membership was far broader than the union-led Coordinadora de Solidaridad or the *barrio*-specific Coordinadora del Sector Nor-oriental. As Barranca civic leaders wrote in a report on Coordinadora Popular activities: "The organizers and participants were essentially the same during the civil strikes of 1975 and 1977 and with the *Coordinadora de Solidaridad*, but the nature and structure were different. It was conceived as a broad-based coordinating effort, in which neighborhood committees and representatives played important roles, political parties were represented and *campesinos* and popular organizations took active part."[75] While the Coordinadora Popular used protests to demand recognition, member groups met regularly to exchange views and information. They were thus able to present a united front when making demands of different levels of government. The Coordinadora Popular was composed of Barranca's most important popular organizations, which included the oil workers' union, as well as groups linked to the Catholic Church, such as the Organización Feme-nina Popular, and political parties, such as the Juntas de Acción Comunal. The direct participation of elected officials gave the Coordinadora Popular a voice on the city council, and links to regional and national networks. The regional wing of the national peasant association was also present, although their concerns around violence in the countryside were not central to the first actions carried out in the name of the Coordinadora Popular. The breadth of the effort was without precedent. But it was grassroots participation that distinguished the Coordinadora Popular from previous efforts.

More than just a way of bringing established groups together, the Coordinadora Popular was structured to carry out ongoing community work, emphasizing preparedness. This would allow for a more agile mobilization of citizens, when the time came. Individuals could become involved in the Coordinadora Popular through its various commissions responsible for finances, communications, health, and *guardias cívicas*, which ensured public safety and discipline during protests. The *guardias cívicas* had permanent functions at the neighborhood level as well, including crime prevention and conflict resolution. According to a study authored in 1991 by a group of Barranca activists with ties to the Coordinadora Popular: "With the job of maintaining control and neighborhood order . . . the *guardia* named a *Comandante de Guardia Cívica* who was a member of the Neighborhood Committee. One of the tasks of the *guardia* was to prevent attacks against property within the neighborhood. . . . It also provided protection to demonstrators when the security forces were present by designating someone to speak to the military."[76] The *guardias* demonstrated the importance of neighborhood-level activism. Unlike the coalitions organized in the past, the Coordinadora Popular attempted to sustain a direct link between urban squatters and the leadership of the civic-popular movement. The Coordinadora Popular was governed by a board of directors and a central committee, which included the representatives of community-based projects, namely those linked to the Pastoral Social and Juntas de Acción Comunal. But major decisions concerning the organization of *paros cívicos* were oftentimes taken at open-air public assemblies, usually held at the Parque Infantil, located in Barranca's main commercial district in front of the diocese.

From these local processes emerged an effective network of coordinated popular mobilization that impacted the entire Magdalena Medio. The April 13, 1983, *paro cívico* was planned by the Coordinadora Popular in coalition with the oil workers' union and the Catholic Church as a protest against the quality of the water supply in Barranca. The *paro* was approved at a general assembly of the Coordinadora Popular held in the Parque Infantil on April 7, 1983, attended by an estimated five thousand people.[77] The thirty-five organizations represented by the Coordinadora Popular gave the national government a long list of demands related to multiple deficiencies in public services. They demanded that water and electricity be subsidized for low-income households.

Further demands were made to improve bus service to the north and south-eastern *barrios*; to improve the quality of care provided by Barranca's sole public health facility, Hospital San Rafael; to ensure that an adequate number of teachers were employed in the local school system; to undertake road repairs; to resolve simmering labor conflicts at Ecopetrol, the hospital, and the sanitation works company; to dredge the Magdalena River in order to remove accumulated silt around the area of the city's main port area; and to resolve seven different land disputes involving organized peasant groups in the rural Magdalena Medio.[78] The concerns of poverty, labor rights, and economic underdevelopment resonated throughout the region. On the eve of the *paro cívico*, the departmental trade union federation, the Unión Sindical de Trabajadores de Santander, declared its solidarity with the strikers, calling on transport workers to respect the protest. The same day, Colombia's largest palm oil plantation and processing center, located in San Alberto, Cesar, in the northeastern corner of the Magdalena Medio, was shut down by workers striking for better wages and improved health and other social services.[79] The oil workers' union then announced that it would hold a national strike in solidarity with Barranca, involving all of its affiliates. Guerrilla groups in the region also issued communiqués expressing support for the *paro cívico*.

The prospect of the first major civic protest in nearly half a decade raised government fears around security. With the guerrillas expressing their support for the protests, municipal Liberal and Conservative Party representatives sought to distance themselves from the Coordinadora Popular. Some individual councillors spoke out against the *paro*, and the governor of Santander called for calm. Then-mayor Jaime Barba Rincón remembers working on behalf of the Liberal Party alongside the Coordinadora Popular to establish a more direct and permanent relationship between the municipal government and people living in *barrios de invasión*, or new squatter settlements. This entailed contact with activist groups with whom he had fundamental ideological differences. Barba Rincón recalls that "there was a movement called the Coordinadora Popular that was a civic movement . . . but behind this apparent civility we knew that there were leftist leaders."[80] The commander of the Fifth Brigade of the army in Bucaramanga said that his troops would provide security during the course of the *paro* in case subversives attempted to infiltrate or take advantage of the event.[81] In response to growing apprehension, the organizers of the *paro* announced that *guardias cívicas* would patrol the streets. Anxiety increased as the hour of the *paro* approached. On the evening of April 12, 1983, local markets and shops were overwhelmed as people stocked up for what they feared could be a prolonged breakdown of public order. Taxi drivers increased their fares overnight, and most people stayed indoors.

By taking responsibility for the organization of the protest, the Coordinadora Popular was able to mitigate the potential for violence. The first barricades were set up at 7:00 p.m. on April 13, some five hours earlier than had been planned. Small groups of mostly young men and women shut down all of the main entrances to the city and cut off rail and river transport. Passengers arriving on a flight from Medellín had to walk in 40-degree heat nine kilometers from the airport into town. Demonstrators burned tires at the barricades and threw tacks onto the city's main streets. The Coordinadora Popular mobilized dozens of small *barrio*-level committees to ensure the fullest participation possible. A crowd of thousands convened in front of the offices of the water services company the following morning. But no acts of violence were reported. Men, women, and children gathered at the barricades, chanting and raising their hands in victory. The day ended as planned, with a general assembly in the Parque Infantil. The army kept its distance. One week following the conclusion of the *paro cívico*, the municipal government of Barranca announced that it would make new investments to repair and expand the city's aqueduct and telephone networks.

The anniversary of the founding of the municipality of Barranca was marked on April 26, 1983, at which the governor of Santander announced that a "high-level" government commission would soon visit Barranca to seek solutions to the city's chronic problems.[82] Yet even as calm was restored, the crisis resumed. Another *paro cívico* was staged by the Coordinadora Popular, timed to coincide with the annual May Day celebrations.[83] While May Day celebrations were traditionally convened by the city's labor unions, this time the motivation for the protest came straight out of the southeastern *barrios* of the city. The residents of the neighborhoods of María Eugenia, El Cerro, Santa Barbara, and others had been without water for a grueling twelve days. Within twenty-four hours, trucks were dispatched to distribute water to the southeastern *barrios*, and the *paro* ended.[84] Although the second stage of the *paro cívico* also ended peacefully, some parts of the city remained without water. In short order, tensions between frustrated local residents and government authorities boiled over for a third time. On May 2, residents of the southeastern *barrios* blockaded the road connecting Barranca to Bucaramanga by dumping stones and logs onto the highway.[85] The acting mayor, José Domingo Villa, responded on behalf of the local administration, enforcing a curfew and suspension of liquor sales. The mayor's decree also allowed the police to detain persons suspected of subversive activity for up to five days without charges. Villa stated: "In light of behavior that has upset public order and the freedom of movement . . . it has been decided to impose severe security measures."[86] The police urged parents to keep their children at home as teachers went on strike for two days, and additional riot police were dispatched from Bucaramanga to patrol the streets. The teachers were joined by hundreds of defiant student supporters and parents demanding increased funding to meet the growing demand in the city. Students from Diego Hernández de Gallegos high school protested in front of the city's private schools until they too declared classes canceled.[87]

On May 12, 1983, the Coordinadora Popular announced a full and detailed platform of demands directed at local and national levels of government, centered on broken promises. Water, health, education, roads, good government, and land titles for new urban settlers were all highlighted. The Coordinadora Popular organized an outdoor assembly in the Parque Infantil on May 18, attended by thousands, at which yet another *paro cívico* was approved.[88] The next day a group of four people representing the Coordinadora Popular, including the well-known Communist Party organizer Leonardo Posada and Father Eduardo Díaz, went to Bucaramanga to meet with Governor Rafael Moreno Peñaranda and Congressman Horacio Serpa Uribe. On May 24, a committee of Barranca elected officials, trade unionists, and representatives of the Chamber of Commerce was flown to Bogotá to meet with President Betancur. They presented him with a petition calling for major government investments in water, sewage, garbage collection, health care, education, roads and bridges, and job training.[89] Led by mayor Jaime Barba Rincón, the committee warned the president that the crisis in Barranca was "promoting movements against the lawfully constituted civic authorities."[90] The governor of Santander requested urgent national government intervention to address the city's "delicate" security situation.[91] The commander of the Nueva Granada Battalion in Barranca, José Manuel Bonnet, said that the *paro cívico* was being promoted by "political interests," and that *barranqueños* were pawns in a game designed to destabilize the city's legitimate public institutions.[92]

Many different agendas converged around the Coordinadora Popular. The lists of demands presented to Bogotá by the Coordinadora Popular were long because there were many problems that needed to be addressed. The rapid growth of the city had continued to outstrip the municipality's capacities, causing major social instability. The former mayor Jaime Barba Rincón had recently returned from a stint in the planning office with the departmental government in Bucaramanga when he was appointed mayor of Barranca in 1982. He recalls: "It was a terrible dynamic, with problems related to public services, such as the lack of clean water, plus there were negotiations around collective agreements with Ecopetrol, which always caused social turmoil, and there were many demonstrations."[93] The historical grievances that had inspired *paros cívicos* in Barrancabermeja in the 1970s remained unresolved through the 1980s. It is into this context of social movement fervor that ever-larger waves of displaced peasants arrived. The Coordinadora Popular fulfilled the important task of engaging frustrated ordinary citizens, including many new arrivals. Its polyglot character would become the basis upon which the human rights movement would be built.

The Vuelta Acuña Massacre

The first episode of rural violence to rouse the urban activist community in Barranca, including several future members of the Regional Committee for the Defense of Human Rights (CREDHOS), was the massacre of eight people by paramilitary forces in the rural farming settlement of Vuelta Acuña on January 12, 1984. It is during this period that strategically located communities adjacent to Barranca began to feel the pressures of counterinsurgency actions carried out by the Colombian military and paramilitary groups. During this same period there was growing apprehension among provincial elites and military leaders concerning political negotiations between the FARC and the government of President Belisario Betancourt.[94] Civic leaders in Barranca helped investigate the events at Vuelta Acuña, and over the course of the next year would draw links between national politics, paramilitarism, and violent encroachment on the city. The FARC and the government would agree to a ceasefire in March 1984, yet counterinsurgency attacks continued against alleged guerrilla sympathizers. The main fight against the FARC was being played out in frontier zones of strategic importance, including the territories to the south of Barranca.

The massacre at Vuelta Acuña prompted an exodus of *campesinos* to Barranca that obliged urban activists to confront what was occurring in the countryside. News of the massacre first arrived in Barranca via newspaper and radio reports. A short article appeared in the January 14, 1984, edition of the *Vanguardia Liberal*, where the eight dead were described as guerrillas killed in combat.[95] Located approximately forty kilometers south of the city, Vuelta Acuña is a rural fishing and peasant farming community. The name "Vuelta Acuña" refers to a narrow meander in the Magdalena River. The *vereda* of Vuelta Acuña is traversed by the Barranca-Medellín railway line and a major highway. It is located in the *municipio* of Cimitarra, which had been under FARC influence since 1968. Given its strategic location and the historic presence of the FARC in the area, reports of an army-guerrilla firefight seemed credible.

But the official story would soon be refuted. During the two weeks following the Vuelta Acuña massacre, more than a thousand people fled the area and headed for the city, where they briefly occupied the courthouse before setting up camps on the grounds of a high school. In a press release, spokespeople for the displaced invoked the "right to life," stating "we are Colombians and human beings too."[96] The massacre at Vuelta Acuña might have gone unnoticed if it had not been for the pressure exerted by this *éxodo campesino*, or peasant exodus.

The national government in Bogotá acted swiftly to organize a commission of enquiry to Vuelta Acuña. Without precedent, the commission included national and local government and nongovernment members. Coming just weeks after President Betancur's participation in a "March for Peace" in Puerto Berrío, events in Vuelta Acuña could not easily be ignored. The commission was composed of local Catholic Church and municipal council representatives, as well as high-ranking central government functionaries, including the attorney general and the high commissioner for peace. For several individuals who participated in the commission, this was their first experience of human rights work. CREDHOS cofounder Jael Quiroga recalls her unease visiting the area to meet with survivors who had stayed behind:

> All of the people that left Vuelta Acuña . . . I remember I went with Nel Beltrán.[97] Nel Beltrán was a regular priest; he invited me to go there to Vuelta Acuña, and I met with such desperate people, who no longer believed in the Church. Nel Beltrán started to say Mass . . . and they were so untrusting. Vuelta Acuña was sadness, because at that time the people who stayed behind in Vuelta Acuña in the rural areas had to live with the paramilitaries. Many families came to Barranca and left children behind there, and other children they brought with them. . . . The trauma that mothers in Barranca have suffered, it is just terrible.[98]

The circumstances of the Vuelta Acuña massacre were far too complex for the commission to sort out on their short visit. Conversations with survivors revealed just how difficult it was to document and interpret crimes carried out in remote rural areas, and the kinds of pressures to which *campesinos* were subject. Some families had left members behind to take care of crops and animals. It was said that some people may have chosen to stay behind because they sympathized with the paramilitary project. Participation in the commission provided urban activists with direct exposure to the effects of political violence.

Critically, the commission would also give government and nongovernment officials the experience of working alongside one another on issues of basic human rights.

Unconvinced that it would be safe to return to Vuelta Acuña, the majority of the displaced ended up staying in Barrancabermeja, settling into the hard-scrabble northeastern *barrio* of El Progreso. In her novel *En el brazo del río*, Marbel Sandoval Ordóñez captures the fear, confusion, and incredulity experienced by two teenage girls from Vuelta Acuña.[99] Sierva María, a thirteen-year-old who settles in Barranca with her family following the massacre, questions whether government-led investigations can serve any purpose: "I thought about the news that I read about the Special Commission charged with finding out what happened in Vuelta Acuña . . . but that was justice after the fact, the kind that gets applied after things have happened. . . . Did people have to die to be taken care of? What would be the truth? My truth was that I was not yet fourteen years old and a day. All at once my eyes were opened, only I did not like the light that I saw."[100] Killings continued in Vuelta Acuña over the next few months, as the XIV Brigade and paramilitary groups consolidated their control over the entire *municipio* of Cimitarra. In total, an estimated forty people were killed or disappeared in paramilitary operations in Cimitarra in 1984. Over the following year charges were laid against thirty-five soldiers accused of massacring *campesinos* in the area of Vuelta Acuña. The charges related to several different incidents, including the events of January 1984. But all of the charges were eventually dropped.

The presence of displaced people from war-torn rural areas like Vuelta Acuña fundamentally transformed the political geography of Barrancabermeja. The new arrivals alerted the rest of Barranca to the war being waged in the surrounding countryside. Migrants from Vuelta Acuña and other rural zones were marked by the stigma of subversion. Displaced *campesinos* in Barranca's southeastern and northeastern *barrios* then became targets of a new urban variant of the paramilitary violence they had fled. *Campesino* leader Ángel Tolosa, himself a migrant to Barranca from rural Antioquia, was the target of an attempted assassination inside the ANUC office in Barranca on February 25, 1985. Had Tolosa been killed, it would have been the highest profile assassination of a Barranca-based activist to that point. In response, ANUC members organized a march through the streets of the city. They were joined by trade union members, and together they occupied the local headquarters of the Internal Affairs Agency of the national government, which at the time was the highest judicial authority responsible for human rights and public security.

Conclusion

In the late 1970s the first paramilitary death squads made their presence known in the Magdalena Medio. Simultaneous to this development, the FARC guerrillas moved to expand beyond their traditional self-defense strategies. The guerrillas' restructuring as an Ejército Popular in 1982 had serious consequences for local progressive political and social movements.[101] As the FARC gained political recognition, initiated peace talks with the government, and established a party to contest elections, people living in guerrilla-dominated areas became vulnerable to a powerful backlash on the part of an alliance of narcotraffickers, landholders, and military. On the eve of a ceasefire agreement between the FARC and the national government, paramilitaries in the region become more and more aggressive, leading to events such as Vuelta Acuña. Several Barranca civic leaders were drawn into the subsequent investigations. Peasants occupied public spaces and marched through the streets of the city to raise awareness and demand justice. But as described in the next chapter, the civic-popular movement would not undertake sustained collective action on human rights until killings were carried out on the streets of Barranca itself.

The massacre at Vuelta Acuña served as a warning that the counterinsurgency war being waged in the southern Magdalena Medio was drawing nearer to the city. The decision taken by peasants in the area to flee to Barranca ensured that the seriousness of the paramilitary threat would be acknowledged by urban activists who worked with poor squatters and peasant groups. Through the mid-1980s the human rights issues raised by displaced peasants would resonate with an increasingly broad circle of groups and individuals in Barranca, represented by the Coordinadora Popular coalition. A massive *paro cívico* for public services in 1983 would demonstrate the breadth and depth of the civic-popular movement, although human rights was not yet central to the demands formulated by member organizations. The former Barranca city councillor and CREDHOS president David Ravelo remembers how the influx of families from Vuelta Acuña and other rural conflict zones then changed Barranca: "These peasant marches began to generate links to workers' organizations in Barrancabermeja, to the people of Barrancabermeja, and oil workers; it was a relationship of solidarity with the peasants."[102] This period of transformation was a direct prelude to human rights organizing in Barranca. Chased from their homes, people from the rural areas and small towns of the Magdalena Medio articulated their concerns in terms of human rights. Rural migrants established new neighborhoods and breathed life into ongoing struggles for potable water, land titles, housing, and education. Imagining Barranca's civic struggles within a broader historical vision of where Colombia was headed, local social movements forged or renewed linkages to rural groups, including the Asociación Nacional de Usuarios Campesinos, the Coordinadora Campesina del Magdalena Medio, and rural Juntas de Acción Comunal, or elected community action councils. Displaced persons from violence-stricken areas thus changed the city's civic-popular movement.

4

Popular Protest and Human Rights Activism

We have had very tough times in Barranca and in the whole country, and the feeling of unity seems farther and farther away . . . but we have also been capable of coming together as a people during tough times, of being strong in the face of this, building movements that we can identify with and support.

Yolanda Becerra, president of the Organización Femenina Popular[1]

Introduction

Most Latin American human rights movements in the late twentieth century were born in response to the repression of social movements. As the Peruvian activist and sociologist Carlos Basombrío Iglesias writes: "Latin American human rights movements have emerged almost exclusively as responses to abuses by the state."[2] At the start of the 1980s, Guatemala, El Salvador, Honduras, Argentina, Uruguay, Chile, Brazil, Haiti, Paraguay, and Bolivia were ruled by right-wing military dictatorships. Guatemala was on the verge of a period of genocidal state terror. Peru had just emerged from a period of left-populist military rule, only to be plunged into a guerrilla conflict that would claim tens of thousands of lives. One of just a few formal democracies in the region, Colombia was governed by the repressive legal regime known as the National Security Statute that gave extraordinary powers to the security forces, while curtailing the rights to freedom of movement and assembly. One of Colombia's leading human rights organizations, the *Comisón Colombiana de Juristas*, estimated that no fewer than eight thousand people were legally prosecuted under the National Security Statute during President Turbay's term in office between 1978 and 1982, most of them by court martial.[3]

Human rights movements cannot be viewed as simple axiomatic responses to political repression. The advent of human rights in Barrancabermeja must be understood with respect to a long history of popular movement struggle around civil and political rights dating back to the early twentieth century. Human rights represented the outcome of the direct violence perpetrated by state agents on organized communities of activists, and a clash of worldviews. For twenty-three out of twenty-five years between 1958 and 1990, Colombia was governed under the terms of extraordinary legal measures that concentrated power in the hands of the executive, restricted the activities of trade unions and progressive political parties, and empowered the military to suppress popular protest when it was interpreted as allied with or supportive of Marxist subversion.[4]

The ascendancy of human rights activism in Barrancabermeja during the 1980s is closely linked to the onset of a state-sponsored dirty war against popular movements, in a region with strong presence of national government and military authorities.[5] The term "dirty war" gained currency among activists, journalists, and scholars across Latin America after it was adopted by the military junta that ruled Argentina from 1976 to 1983.[6] Junta spokespeople had argued that they had no choice but to carry out a "dirty war" of covert operations in order to defeat the shadowy guerrilla groups that posed a threat to Argentina's national security.[7] However, Argentinian rights groups pounced on this notion, stating that the "dirty war" against the guerrillas was in fact cover for an undeclared war on social movements. The use of the term has been defined by many scholars with reference to official forces' specious portrayal of a war on political opponents as a war between belligerent forces. But the phrase has long since entered the vernacular of human rights activism as a condemnation of covert operations, generally. In Colombia, the term has mainly, although not exclusively, been used by activists. The Comisión Andina de Juristas published a 1988 report alleging that national security forces were using "dirty war" tactics under the guise of counterinsurgency.[8] An Americas Watch researcher touring Colombia in 1988 documented threats against members of the UP political party by a death squad calling itself "Guerra Sucia."[9]

In Colombia, as elsewhere in Latin America, the turn to human rights took place during the late Cold War, as popular movements sought to change the behavior of abusive states. Guerrilla groups also expanded during this period, although the concurrence of violent and nonviolent movements such as existed in Barranca was distinctive. Unlike human rights defenders in Buenos

Aires, activists in Barrancabermeja were confronting the problem of a dirty war in a geographically isolated conflict zone, and they did so through mass mobilization. The decision by a diverse coalition of Barranca-based activists to establish a human rights committee in 1987 was a deep-seated refutation of state-sponsored violence, as well as an attempt to maintain the space for social movements to continue their work. It was a radical impulse, but one that drove the everyday business of social change. Régulo Madero—a former CREDHOS president and former elected representative of the Patriotic Union (UP)—says that in the 1980s many Barranca activists saw a link between human rights and the struggle to radically transform Colombian society: "Many people saw it up close, they touched it. They lived it. I think we got ahead of the facts. Many of the social movements and human rights movements in this country, not just in Barrancabermeja, sympathized with this, and so in large part one of the goals of the social movement was to overthrow the state, albeit with words instead of guns."[10] Human rights activism was a new means of mobilizing ordinary citizens and challenging political and economic power. Madero's suggestion that many activists sought to overthrow the state, "albeit with words," hints at a profound disillusionment with traditional politics. The fact that some people in Barranca looked toward a revolutionary horizon did not prevent the city's civic-popular movement from making claims on the state. Writing in 1989, community organizer Juan de Dios Castilla argued that "even the most radical" popular organizations in Barranca sought to influence government policies on social, economic, and security issues.[11]

CREDHOS is exceptional in the history of human rights organizing in Latin America because it was established by frontline activists in an area of armed conflict. This chapter aims to better understand the onset of the dirty war and the growth of human rights activism in Colombia through the late 1980s from the perspective of Barranca-based social activists. Due to the presence of armed groups in the city and surrounding region, Barranca's popular movement was subject to direct and indirect pressures that shaped the way in which human rights would be debated for years to come. While the worst abuses were being committed by military and paramilitary forces, during this period we also get a glimpse into how guerrilla groups' actions contributed to the volatility of relations between citizens and public authorities, and exposed rifts within Barranca's civic-popular movement.

Under extreme circumstances, CREDHOS brought a coalition of social and political movements together for the purposes of exposing human rights violators, advocating on behalf of victims and their families, and calling on the state to protect its citizens, while addressing deeper social and economic in-equalities. By utilizing the language of human rights, Barranca's civic-popular movement rendered the political violence being committed by state and para-state agents in Barranca apparent and legible to ordinary citizens within and beyond the Magdalena Medio.[12] This chapter begins with the interconnected stories of the 1985 murder of the former guerrilla commander Ricardo Lara Parada, the 1986 murder of the UP senator Leonardo Posada, and the 1987 murder of the teenager Sandra Rondón, leading directly to the establishment of CREDHOS.

Who Fired the First Shot in the Dirty War?

There have been many politically motivated homicides in Barranca's short history, but few as significant or as confounding as the murder of the Ejército de Liberación Nacional (ELN) cofounder Ricardo Lara Parada. The late 1980s was a period of rapidly escalating violence by military, paramilitary, and guerrilla forces. Competition between armed actors for influence in Barranca had serious consequences for social activists. Lara Parada's assassination on November 14, 1985, in Barranca by members of the ELN marked the start of the dirty war period within the city. Ricardo Lara's murder was a violation by the guerrillas of Barranca's autonomous civic-popular movement. It also revealed ideological contradictions and cleavages within and between the country's main guerrilla groups that would trouble local social movements for more than a generation. The ELN had purged its ranks of "traitors and *sapos*" before, most brazenly in the early 1970s under the leadership of Fabio Vásquez Castaño.[13] But Lara Parada's status as a local hero makes his case stand out.

The story of Ricardo Lara Parada's rise to prominence, capture, exile, return, and murder is a parable, symbolizing the tragic arc of many Barranca activists' aspirations to build a pluralist civic-popular movement. Lara Parada's story reflects the pressures under which social movement initiatives are subject in times of war. To his friends, such as the law professor Jairo Vargas León, Lara Parada was the personification of Barranca's exuberant activist culture. In this passage he likens Parada to Salsa singing great Ismael (El Sonero Mayor) Rivera: "[Lara Parada] was profoundly humanist, he expressed solidarity with the people, he was joyful like no one else I know, of a singular charisma, at times naive, unaware and without fear, an advocate for diversity, an interpreter of the heterogeneity in our society, convinced that it was important to put a person's humanity above political ideology, anonymous poet, frustrated accordionist and life of the party [*rumbero*]. The many melodies he created are still resonating in the hearts of *barranqueños*. Ricardo Lara: *el sonero mayor*."[14]

Many activists remember the larger-than-life Lara Parada as the first victim of the epidemic of violence that would consume the city in the late 1980s. One longtime community organizer and Barranca resident recalled: "After the assassination of Ricardo Lara Parada, it was as if they had opened the floodgates to kill and kill."[15]

Lara Parada was an idealist who gave up civilian life to pursue the cause of a new revolutionary movement that claimed direct links to a regional history of popular radicalism. Born in Barranca in 1940 the son of an oil worker and union activist father, Lara Parada left his hometown in 1960 to study at the Universidad Industrial de Santander (UIS) in Bucaramanga. While attending the region's most important public university, Lara Parada became a leader of the Juventudes Movimiento Revolucionario Liberal, a regional youth wing of the Liberal Party that drew inspiration from the experiences of the Comuna de Barranca uprising in 1948 and the guerrilla campaigns led by Rafael Rangel during La Violencia in the 1950s. While at the university Lara Parada met and worked alongside several cofounders of the ELN insurgency, including his future nemesis Fabio Vásquez. Lara Parada would play a key role in building the ELN. He was trained in guerrilla tactics with five other student activists in Cuba in 1962. Lara Parada also helped to establish the precursor to the ELN, the Brigada Pro Liberación José Antonio Galán, named after the popular nationalist leader of the eighteenth-century Comuneros revolt.[16] On January 7, 1965, he participated in the ELN's first military action, the armed seizure of the town of Simacota.

Lara Parada's military career was fraught and ended amid accusations that he had betrayed the guerrillas' cause. In 1967 Lara Parada was chosen to lead the Frente Camilo Torres Restrepo and became a member of the ELN's Central Command. In 1968 he was promoted to the rank of deputy national leader. However, Lara Parada lasted just one year in that position, replaced by Fabio Vásquez. Like other young and idealistic students who joined the guerrillas in the 1960s, Lara Parada had little military training. He was recognized for his political intelligence and communications skills, but this did not compensate for his deficiencies in terms of battlefield acumen. The ELN historian Milton Hernández writes:

> Ricardo Lara Parada demonstrated a total lack of aptitude as a member of the ELN Central Command; his irresponsibility led to the annihilation of the Frente Camilo Torres Restrepo; which was one of the worst blows to the ELN in 1969. That annihilation provoked a profound personal crisis in Lara Parada, forcing Fabio Vásquez Castaño to relieve him of his command. . . . In November 1973, at the time of the worst moment in our

history, caused by the events of "*Operación Anorí*," that we were only beginning to understand, he deserted our ranks in what constituted a profound act of cowardice.[17]

Implicit in Hernández's critical view of Lara Parada is that the young *barranqueño* lacked discipline and was too soft for serious guerrilla work. Lara Parada was captured along with eighteen other ELN guerrilla fighters on November 25, 1973, in Nechí, Antioquia, during the final days of the Anorí disaster. The commanders of the army's Medellín-based IV Brigade were thrilled by Lara Parada's detention, apparently convinced that he would provide intelligence regarding the ELN's network of urban supporters and the whereabouts of the group's leadership.[18] Reeling from their historic defeat at the hands of the Colombian army in 1973, leaders of the ELN speculated that Lara Parada had willingly surrendered to authorities and then traded information for favorable treatment.

Following his detention by the military, Lara Parada embarked on a circuitous journey back to Barrancabermeja, during which he would all but shed his past connection to the ELN. Lara Parada spent the next five years in La Picota prison in Bogotá before being released and exiled to Central America. He traveled to Panama in 1978, where he had made personal contact with the left-leaning Panamanian president Omar Torrijos through a mutual friend, the novelist Gabriel García Márquez. One year later, Lara Parada moved to Nicaragua to work on behalf of the newly formed Sandinista revolutionary regime. In 1980 he was employed as a bodyguard for the Sandinista minister of the interior when he received a visit from the Movimiento 19 de abril (M-19) guerrilla leader Jaime Bateman. Lara Parada secretly returned to Colombia in late 1981, this time to the southern department of Putumayo, to work with the M-19. In 1982 he journeyed to Bogotá as a participant in peace talks involving the FARC, M-19, and the government of President Belisario Bentancur.[19] Lara Parada had joined the process despite his belief that the Betancur government was untrustworthy. For their part, the ELN denounced the negotiations and had refused to participate. Negotiations ultimately soured, violence in the countryside escalated, and the M-19 remained at arms. Lara Parada, however, was granted amnesty for having played a role in the process, and returned to civilian life.

Despite everything, from allegations of incompetence and treachery, and the time he spent in exile, Lara Parada was enthusiastically received upon his return to Barranca. He very quickly became caught up in the romance of the civic-popular movement. Visiting his hometown in May 1983, Lara Parada was asked by friends to give an impromptu address to an assembly of the

Coordinadora Popular, convened in the final days of the *paro cívico* that would define the lives of many talented young popular leaders. It was Lara Parada's first public appearance in the city. Encouraged by the warm welcome from the activist community, and impressed with the achievements of the civic-popular movement, Lara Parada decided to stay. He planned to open a bookstore that he hoped would become a hub for radical intellectuals, activists, and students. His first political involvement was to join the small but growing campaign to establish a new public university in Barranca. Lara Parada planned to connect with members of Coordinadora Popular involved in developing spaces for the arts. Many of his new comrades worked with the Casa de la Cultura, a community center where socially engaged poetry readings, music events, and theater performances were organized. Dozens of people passed through the Lara Parada household to talk about the civic-popular movement, *paros cívicos*, and recent violence in the countryside. Within the first month he had abandoned his idea of settling into a life of debate, poetry, and *tertulias* and decided to get involved in local politics.

Lara Parada launched his new activist career in Barranca by establishing a regional political party with strong ties to local social movements called the Frente Amplio del Magdalena Medio (FAM). Jael Quiroga remembers the FAM as a reflection of its charismatic leader: "The FAM was *cheverísimo*, it was *macondiano*. . . . It was not dogmatic, or disciplined for that matter, totally undisciplined, I loved it!" Despite its apparent intemperance, the FAM achieved a great deal in a short period of time. Not only did it elect city councillors, but it also helped to organize public protests, participated in Coordinadora Popular de Barrancabermeja coalition work, and helped to articulate a regional vision of political, social, and cultural development. The FAM message touched on all of the major issues being raised by the Coordinadora Popular and *campesino* groups. Indeed, the FAM was perhaps the first attempt to reframe the civic-popular movement struggle in Barranca in regional terms. In their campaign literature, the FAM stated: "We simply take up the struggle developed by the people during *paros cívicos* and by *campesinos* from the region in defense of the land and the right to life."[20] The FAM stood for peace processes and demanded the "dissolution of paramilitary groups" by the state, which would become a major tenet of human rights activism in the years to come.[21] In March 1984 the FAM ran its first slate of candidates in Barranca's municipal elections, with plans to run candidates in other *municipios* around the region. Despite FAM supporters' fears that they would be stigmatized as "subversive" because of Lara Parada's involvement, and despite the presence of a well-funded Liberal Party, the FAM made a breakthrough. Two FAM candidates were elected in Barranca. For the first time since the 1940s, the Liberal Party was reduced to minority status on the municipal council.

The ELN has maintained that while the decision to assassinate Lara Parada was justified, the timing may have been ill-advised. In September 1983, at a national gathering commemorating the tenth anniversary of the defeat at Anorí, ELN guerrilla commanders named a squad of assassins to travel to Barranca and execute Lara Parada. But the plan was not carried out for two more years. Lara Parada was gunned down on the streets of Barranca in November 1985.[22] The alleged betrayal he had committed in 1973 had evidently not faded from memory. His rise to prominence as a spokesperson for the M-19 guerrillas and his ambitions as a political leader may have been too much to ignore. There may also have been concerns around his association with Barranca activists working for rival leftist factions, namely the Communist Party and Patriotic Union. The ELN has denied that the murder of Lara Parada was intended as an attack on the FAM in particular, or as a message to the city's social movements, or their rivals for that matter. The ELN has nonetheless admitted that it "acted without considering the political context at the time, appeared disconnected from the conjuncture and caused a strong polemic at the national level."[23]

The killing of Lara Parada drove a wedge between factions of the left in Barranca, and gestured toward armed groups' encroachment on civilian organizing spaces. Those sympathetic to the ELN may have been at pains to explain the rationale behind the killing. Those sympathetic to the FARC rallied behind Lara Parada's memory, and within two years the orphaned FAM entered into an official alliance with the political wing of the FARC, the Patriotic Union.[24] According to Irene Villamizar, a founding member of CREDHOS and long-time activist with the Pastoral Social, the murder of Lara Parada by his former comrades anticipated an increase in guerrilla actions that ran counter to Barranca's tradition of pluralist social protest:

When the guerrillas began to take control of the *paros cívicos*, many leaders were afraid. If [the guerrillas] had behaved differently, in a more civilized way, the history of Barrancabermeja would have been very different from what it is now. I am totally convinced that the death of Ricardo Lara Parada changed everything. The ELN killed Lara Parada, and that intolerance, that thinking that the armed struggle was going to lead to liberation . . . the guerrillas just were not capable of seeing the very important role that Ricardo Lara was playing. This changed the struggle in Barranca. Because until that time, everyone, ELN [*elenos*], FARC [*faruchos*], right wing, left wing, whatever . . . we could listen to one another and tolerate one another. But the death of Lara Parada brought out the differences between us. In spite of all of this, and I think again that the Church plays a big role, we were able to join together, organize ourselves and defend our lives. But we lost leadership.[25]

The battle for Barranca that unfolded in subsequent years might have been less complicated had the guerrillas not attempted to constrain social movement initiatives. While such conjecture may not be demonstrable, the Lara Parada murder has been remembered in this way. The activist Jesuit priest and long-serving Pastoral Social director Eduardo Díaz observed in a 1990 interview: "I think that the death of Lara Parada was one of the gravest political errors. In Barranca there has always been political confrontation, but the death of Lara Parada broke the barriers down, opened the floodgates."[26]

When the guerrillas established a military presence in Barranca in the mid-1980s, there began a violent contest over the urban territory that the civic-popular movement had fought to keep safe for public protests. The record shows that gunfire was rarely exchanged between the guerrillas and security forces. Rather, the struggle between the two sides over the city's diverse zones was played out mainly in the shadows. Before the close of the decade, there were hundreds of paramilitary attacks on alleged guerrilla sympathizers, including social activists, members of legal political organizations, and young people from the popular *barrios*. National Police continued to carry out spot checks, raids, and arrests of ordinary citizens. But the guerrillas also initiated what some activists in Barranca would come to view as a misguided military occupation of civilian spaces, most significantly the *paro cívico*.[27] Over the course of the next decade, the city would be carved up by both state and non-state armed actors claiming to control its main avenues, intersections, and plazas. As we shall see, the civic-popular movement was directly implicated in this contest, asserting its sovereignty, and the importance of maintaining space for nonviolent forms of social protest.

With deep roots in the Magdalena Medio, the ELN guerrillas enjoyed widespread but not unconditional support among poor urban and rural people. The way in which the guerrillas were perceived by progressive social movements was complicated by serious ethical concerns. One Bogotá-based activist, who worked as a "fixer" for journalists seeking interviews with ELN leaders in Barranca during the 1980s, maintains that the guerrillas were sincere in their desire to contribute to processes of change. However, she notes that while the guerrillas coveted popular support, they never recognized the tenuousness of the relationship between the civic and military struggles. Indeed, the question of whether or not it was a good idea to combine "all forms of struggle" was not debated as such.

> This was the 1970s and 1980s, the period of revolutionary fervor in Latin America. I mean, even the Catholic Church! There were all sorts of reasons for this fervor, in the sense that change was absolutely necessary in terms

of improving peoples' lives, and that revolutionary struggle involving arms was legitimate. In terms of my own experience, it was very much about the discourse that it was a peoples' revolution, it was not about ten thousand guys in arms taking power. It was about building a base of support for revolutionary change. That was the discourse. I think questions were raised internally . . . but there wasn't a questioning yet about the validity of the revolutionary struggle. . . . It didn't make sense to ask them at that point.[28]

In the mid-1970s the ELN had recast itself as a popular movement. The group abandoned the *foquista* approach, which maintains that the guerrillas should constitute a political vanguard for others to follow. The establishment by ELN supporters of the group ¡A Luchar! in 1985 as a national political organization was emblematic of this shift.[29] Some Barranca activists joined ¡A Luchar! for the same sorts of reasons that others joined the UP. The Lara Parada case demonstrated that there were fundamental contradictions between violent and nonviolent means of achieving social justice.

The murder of Ricardo Lara Parada laid bare some of the unique challenges inherent to social movement organizing in the midst of armed conflict. From the ELN's point of view, Lara Parada had committed an unpardonable offense. Members of the UP took the opportunity to take over Lara Parada's movement, the FAM. The assassination was therefore a divisive event, after which all armed actors extended their reach. To many *barranqueño* activists working for social change today, Lara Parada's murder would come to represent the opening of a dark chapter in the city's history and the realization of their own vulnerabilities. The Coordinadora Popular would ask the guerrillas to restrain themselves during social protests. As violence increased, human rights became the main discourse the civic-popular movement.

The Advent of Human Rights Activism

The specific genesis of the Regional Committee for the Defense of Human Rights (CREDHOS) in 1987 can be linked to a sequence of murders that brought clarity to Barranca's social movements on the issue of political violence. The first of these events was the slaying of the respected community organizer and UP congressman Leonardo Posada on August 30, 1986. Riding a long wave of support for radical politics coming out of Barranca, Leonardo Posada was a popular figure who embodied the *mística* of the Colombian oil capital. Posada was also one of the first prominent urban activists to publicly denounce violence against *campesinos* in the Magdalena Medio. Massacres in the countryside had shocked many urban activists but did not immediately compel them to action. The killing of Ricardo Lara Parada had been deeply distressing, but it was viewed at the time as somewhat of an anomaly. Indeed, the guerrillas would kill no other prominent activist figures during this period of time. One CREDHOS cofounder describes the awakening that many individuals experienced following Leonardo Posada's murder, as a city once considered to be a haven for social activists became a dangerous place: "Previously, deaths occurred all over the Magdalena Medio, but not in town. Barranca was a city that took in *campesinos* displaced by the violence, but then death appeared on the street corners of the city, everywhere. . . . The violence convinced us to look for a way of fighting for human rights."[30] Each subsequent death referenced the violence that had come before it, added to the overall impact, and proved unifying. The campaign of paramilitary attacks that began with the murder of Leonardo Posada, and culminated with the murder of Sandra Ronón, set new forces in motion.

Leonardo Posada was already one of the brightest stars of the Colombian left before he moved to Barranca. He was raised in Barrio Quiroga, a working-class neighborhood in central Bogotá that had been the site of one the first major state-led urban renewal projects in Colombian history. Posada was exposed at an early age to the type of city politics that was being debated in Barranca, including the unequal development of housing and infrastructure. Posada's parents were both active members of the Communist Party of Colombia (PCC). While studying at the National University in Bogotá during the 1970s, Posada immersed himself in a bohemian world of student politics, poetry, and late nights listening to tango music. He became a prominent organizer with the national directorate of the Communist Youth (JUCO). He was promoted to the Central Committee of the PCC in 1980. That same year, party officials asked Posada to relocate to Barranca in order to work with the city's popular movements.

The transition to community-based activism in the small city suited Posada, and like many other *barranqueños* he became concerned with the widening circle of violence consuming the region. Posada was a founding member and spokesperson of the Coordinadora Popular coalition. He participated alongside Ricardo Lara Parada in the regional movement FAM and served three terms as a municipal councillor before running for national office. Posada was strident in his views and a captivating public speaker. While the notion of a human rights movement had not yet taken shape, Posada spoke openly at protest rallies about state-sponsored attacks on *campesinos* and called for the dissolution of MAS death squads. In a 1995 interview with longtime social activist Ubencel Duque, one Barranca resident recalled Posada's early attempts to draw attention to the human rights crisis: "I remember that one day Leonardo Posada took it on himself to retrieve dead bodies from the river, because he could not accept that in Barranccabermeja we were so indifferent to what was happening all around us."[31] In 1986 he was elected to the House of Representatives as a candidate from the Department of Santander on behalf of the UP.[32]

Leonardo Posada's standing as an elected official was not enough to protect him. He was gunned down in Barranca on August 30, 1986. The murder was carried out just a few days before he was scheduled to move to Bogotá to begin his work in Congress. In the previous week, threatening graffiti had appeared in Barranca calling for Posada to leave town, signed by MAS paramilitaries, "*Fuera communistsas, fuera Leonardo Posada.*" He had started taking precautions, avoided sleeping in the same bed two nights in a row, but otherwise worked tirelessly to prepare himself to represent the Magdalena Medio on the national political stage. It was 6:00 p.m. Leonardo Posada came out of a meeting and walked into the warmth of his last Saturday night in Barranca. Before he could take even a few steps, he was shot multiple times at close range by a gunman riding on the back of a motorcycle. According to reports, the assassin paused briefly, was exhorted by the driver to finish him off, and then unloaded several more shots. Nobody was ever charged with his murder.

Like many of Barranca's martyred popular leaders, Posada is remembered not only for his leadership qualities but also for his love of life. In 1987 the main commercial street in central Barranca was named after Leonardo Posada. A sign was put up, inscribed with lines from the poem "Winds of the People Carry Me" by Spanish anti-fascist writer Miguel Hernández: "Singing I await death / for there are nightingales that sing / above the guns / and in the midst of battles."[33] One close friend in Barranca remembered him with a few lines of verse: "Leonardo, *el viejo man, salsero, bolerista,* man of a thousand and one *tertulias,* he was a man who came into your life unexpectedly, those of us who loved him, and those who hardly knew him."[34] Posada was regarded in activist circles as a gifted organizer, charismatic speaker, and *rumbero*. In his last interview with a local journalist, Posada said: "I want them to sing *boleros* at my grave."[35] A *paro cívico* was organized by members of the PCC and UP in Barranca, and an estimated ten thousand people attended Posada's funeral in his hometown of Bogotá.[36]

The murder of Leonardo Posada augured poorly for the UP in the Magdalena Medio, as it did for popular movements in general and the wider population. Hundreds of UP militants were killed or disappeared across Colombia in the first few years of the party's existence.[37] The departments of

Figure 5. Meeting of the Unión Patriótica political party in Barrancabermeja, late 1980s. Courtesy of Foto Estudios Joya.

Santander and Antioquia, ground zero for paramilitary repression, accounted for approximately one-third of all attacks on the UP. On the evening of April 23, 1987, three prominent Barranca-based social activists and five other people were injured by the explosion of a hand grenade thrown into the busy Monte Blanco ice cream shop located in the central Barranca neighborhood of La Campana.[38] At the time, most people in the city were either gathered in their homes or in public places watching Colombia win the South American youth soccer championship. César Martínez, Alirio Traslaviña, and Miguel Castañeda were the intended targets. Martínez, a city councillor and member of the Patriotic Union, lost his legs as a result. Traslaviña, the president of the Magdalena Medio Peasant Coordination who had helped to lead the 1985 *marcha campesina* to Cartagena, was rushed to the hospital unconscious. Castañeda, a UP organizer, suffered serious wounds to one of his legs. Five other people, including two children, were injured by shrapnel. It was the first time that such a reckless attack had occurred in a public place in the city, spreading fear among the general population.

The Monte Blanco incident was met with a spontaneous and angry *paro cívico*, led by local UP and PCC members, but with broad participation.

Within six hours of the attack, barricades of burning tires and scrap wood were set up in front of the As de Copas, the convenience store at the edge to the city center that had served as a gathering place for demonstrators since the 1970s. Longtime PCC activist David Ravelo remembers how quickly the protests unfolded.

> I was at home, not far from the San Rafael Hospital. . . . It was about 7:30 or 8:00 p.m. We met just outside the hospital and said that we had to do something, because this just cannot go on any longer. . . . At about 10:00 p.m. we all got together at a strategic spot known as the As de Copas, on the way out of Barrancabermeja. We blocked the road, more people came, the police came. . . . A couple of guys with guns showed up, we figured it was the security forces, threatening, and the people just jumped on them, burned their motorcycle. Because the people were furious. At 10:00 a.m. the mayor of Barranca, a Liberal mayor, called [UP municipal councillor] Ismael Jaimes and myself, and we went down to City Hall. And while we were talking to the mayor, the police descended on the barricades, and the people were dispersed. They used tear gas, fired shots into the air. And by the time we got back we found that the police had overturned the pots [of *sancocho*], and the protestors were radicalized. We had only occupied the one spot, the As de Copas. After that, though, the thing spread to the entire city. The entire city was paralyzed, all because of the aggression against the protestors who had been at the barricades.[39]

Hundreds of ordinary citizens joined the barricades, demanding an end to political repression and other human rights abuses. They seized the moment to denounce Barranca's persistent contaminated water and other social problems. In the aftermath, UP and other municipal councillors sat down with the mayor and regional military authorities to negotiate the release of thirty protestors who had been detained by police.[40] The *paro* ended within twenty-four hours, and a tense calm came over the city. There would be no mass meetings in the Parque Infantil, no delegations to the capital, and no immediate plans to organize another *paro cívico*.

The indignation felt by many activists in the wake of the Monte Blanco attack animated a series of increasingly spontaneous protests in the days that followed. The very next week, traditional May Day celebrations turned into another citywide *paro cívico*, with union-led marchers setting up barricades and blocking the flow of goods and transportation. In an effort to quiet May Day protests, Mayor Rafael Antonio Fernández declared a curfew, as well as a temporary prohibition on alcohol sales and on the bearing of arms.[41] The army and police mobilized to keep people off the streets from 10:00 a.m. to 5:00 p.m. May Day protestors in Barranca were labeled "extremists" by the national press.[42] May Day in Barranca had always been a platform for the expression of a variety of grievances. A major cultural event in the calendar of the local labor movement, May Day typically involved a march through the streets of the city and a rally in front of the national headquarters of the USO. Celebrations—including stirring speeches, live music, refreshments, and *sancocho*—were well attended by union members, other activists, and their families. The mayor of the city and the bishop would often attend, and dignitaries might be invited to join in singing the Internationale. National union leaders would travel to the city from Bogotá, and the full gamut of local social and political groups would be present. However, the mood of the 1987 May Day demonstrations reflected the deepening anxiety felt by many participants. The traditional party atmosphere was dampened by strict security measures, replaced by fear and anger.

A major transformation was taking place in the politics of protest in Barranca. The focus was now squarely on the issue of political violence, and the ordered rituals of the *paro cívico* had given way to spontaneous outbursts of popular anger and mourning. Whereas previous *paros cívicos* were carefully choreographed events, preceded sometimes by weeks of negotiations between social movements and the national government and requiring extensive planning on the part of activist groups, in the late 1980s there was a tendency for human rights protests to be convened without preparation, in response to specific events. Along with shifts in the discourse and form of *paros cívicos* was a change of purpose. The historian Alejo Vargas observes: "There was a transformation in terms of the demands, the mechanisms of organization, which started to become quite spontaneous, and also in terms of objectives. . . . It was no longer about winning tangible demands but rather to express protest and disagreement in the midst of a social environment that was starting to become chaotic."[43] The concomitant radicalization of the *paro* reflected the rising tide of frustration and an increasingly unstable mix of revolutionary politics. As Vargas suggests, protestors' actions demonstrated a rejection of the state itself, in light of paramilitary activity and consistently high levels of impunity for crimes being committed in the region.[44] It was through this volatile process that human rights was introduced as a new paradigm of social activism.

Anguish and Popular Protest
in the Aftermath of Violence

As street protests become less constrained, and citizens came together to denounce the dirty war being waged on the streets of Barranca, the term "human rights" was used as a rallying cry. The protest denouncing the killing of Leonardo Posada was well attended by Barranca residents. However, Posada's murder did not seem to indicate that ordinary people in the city would become targets. The attack on UP members at the Monte Blanco ice cream shop was more alarming in this regard. It was carried out in a public place frequented by children and families, and several bystanders had been injured. While peasants had been killed simply because they lived in areas of guerrilla influence, similar dynamics had not yet been present in the city. The killing of Sandra Rondón revealed that this was about to change.

The massive *paro cívico por la vida* organized to denounce the murder of the teenager Sandra Rondón differed significantly from the protests triggered by the murder of Leonardo Posada and the attack at the Monte Blanco ice cream shop because it explicitly and exclusively focused on human rights. Sandra Rondón was a fourteen-year-old high school student whose only involvement in currents events in Barranca was having been witness to the April 23 attack on UP members at the Monte Blanco ice cream shop. Rondón was killed on May 2, 1987, while walking with her sister on their way to church. She was neither a political activist nor a displaced peasant, and she had no links to the Patriotic Union or other leftist movements. Her murder was committed in a central Barranca neighborhood, just a few minutes' drive from army barracks, the oil refinery, and city hall. The *paro cívico* engaged a wide swath of *barranqueño* society, gained the support of national political leaders and editorialists, and brought the fears and tensions present in Barranca to the attention of the rest of Colombia. On Tuesday, May 5, Sandra Rondón was buried. Thousands of mourners gathered in the Parque Infantil, the square located next to Barranca's Roman Catholic diocese that was often the site of popular assemblies. The huge crowd accompanied Rondón's funeral cortège on foot as it made its way to the old municipal cemetery a few blocks to the east.

The second day of the *paro cívico por la vida* reflected rising tension. In the Primero de Mayo neighborhood, a major center of activism since it was established by organized land invasion in 1975, protestors attacked symbols of power. A group of individuals vandalized a police station and attempted to do the same to a Mormon church.[45] That same afternoon, thousands participated in a silent vigil and march that wound through the streets of the city, led by Father Gabriel Ojeda, the parish priest for the neighborhood of Torcoroma where Sandra Rondón's family attended church. At the end of a prayer for the murdered teenager, Father Ojeda passed the microphone to representatives of the *comité del paro*, who urged those assembled to abstain from acts of anger or violence. Defying the *comité del paro*, ELN members made an appearance on 28th Street, near the barricades at the As de Copas. They were armed and carried a banner bearing the name of the group. One eyewitness recalls people dispersing at first, perhaps because they could not be sure who the armed men were, or perhaps because they feared confrontation with security forces.[46] Soon afterward, some of the people who had dispersed returned to the barricades, and a few even applauded the *muchachos* from the ELN. The first ever *paro cívico por la vida* ended forty-eight hours after it began, on the evening of May 7, with a large and emotional assembly in Parque Camilo Torres.[47]

Barranca residents rose up in protest on numerous occasions during the late 1980s in response to politically motivated killings carried out by military and paramilitary forces. Between the murder of Sandra Rondón in April 1987 and December 1988, nine *paros cívicos* were staged to denounce political violence in the city.[48] The broad appeal of these demonstrations for human rights was without precedent. The uprising known as La Comuna de Barranca that took place following the murder of Jorge Eliécer Gaitán on April 9, 1948 was improvised in response to a specific event. The oil workers' strikes in the 1970s had been triggered by particular grievances. There had been pockets of turmoil within the *paros cívicos* for public services and infrastructure of 1975, 1977, and 1983. Rioting and other expressions of frustration were part of the dynamic in each case, as were mass arrests and other repressive actions on the part of security forces. Nevertheless, social protest in Barranca had been built on consensus between the diverse social, labor, and political groups that made up the city's civic-popular movement. Sustained state-sponsored violence in the 1980s would give impetus to social movement activists to organize collectively around human rights principles. The severity of the violence would eventually erode the foundations of the civic-popular movement itself and make way for the military and paramilitary to increase their power. But in the meantime, the same organizations and communities that had converged around the Coordinadora Popular gained a sense of focus to confront the state directly about political violence.

Human rights activists forced the Colombian government to recognize that political killings were on the rise in the country's most important industrial center. Moving beyond the acknowledgment of the problem would be an entirely different issue. In May 1987 the Colombian Supreme Court announced the creation of a Tribunal Especial de Instrucción, a judicial commission charged with investigating human rights crimes. The murder of Sandra Rondón was the main catalyst behind the initiative. However, expectations and pressures on the Tribunal Especial were heavy, and no one was willing to serve on it. Three of the country's top jurists turned down the offer. One recused himself for personal reasons, and another said he believed that the Tribunal Especial would interfere with ongoing peace negotiations. Eduardo

Umaña Luna—the esteemed defender of political prisoners and one of the most prominent figures in Colombia's nongovernmental human rights movement—also declined the position.[49] Some observers suggested that the whole enterprise was dangerous and naive. Others pointed out that because the Tribunal Especial was not mandated to prosecute crimes committed by the Colombian security forces, its ability to combat impunity was very weak. The impact of this disappointment was to reinforce the belief held by many social activists that the Colombian state remained unwilling to directly address the armed forces' role in human rights atrocities.

Human Rights and Revolution

Popular movements in Barrancabermeja and across the Magdalena Medio region had to reconcile human rights with longstanding political and social struggles. In Colombia in the 1980s, progressive academics, trade unions, *campesino* movements, and the Catholic Church arrived at human rights activism on distinct paths. Different registers of human rights discourse were being used by local activists, elected officials, rebel groups, and even the Colombian military.[50] Just as political violence was the impetus for people to organize collectively around human rights, the sustained pressure suffered by social movements in the Magdalena Medio fuelled ideological and tactical debates that were not easily resolved.

The first major test of the consensus for human rights in Barranca occurred when the agenda of the *campesino* movement collided directly with the agenda of the civic-popular movement. In early June 1987, just three weeks following the *paro cívico por la vida*, Barranca became the focal point of a massive regional *campesino* strike. Tens of thousands of peasants from the departments of Cesar, Bolívar, Santander, Norte de Santander, and Arauca marched on major cities on June 8. It was an ambitious protest that had been months in the planning. In the lead-up to the *paro del nororiente*, some peasant groups expressed fears that the *paro cívico por la vida* unnecessarily raised political tensions and insecurity in the region. Some argued that the *paro cívico por la vida* was a distraction from the historic class struggle being waged by *campesinos*. Others suggested there would simply not be enough momentum to carry out both protests.[51] On the other side of the argument, there were concerns around the more militant agenda embodied by the *paro del nororiente*, which shut down the rural economy across five departments and was denounced as "subversive" by national politicians.[52] Barranca-based social and trade union activist Jairo Chaparro recalls: "Here in Barranca the *paro del nororiente* was different than other *paros*. It did not have the same support and the Bishop said that the movement had a hidden agenda. Business owners were pissed off [*andaban cabreros*]. Ecopetrol and other companies in the city paid for small planes to drop pamphlets denouncing the protest. . . . In the lead-up to the protest there was a brutal psychological war, brother [*viejo man*]. Raids, people taken out of their homes and the like. It was heavy, extremely heavy. . . . It was a confusing and frightening protest."[53]

Notwithstanding unresolved differences of opinion, and the fact that the *paro del nororiente* was being stigmatized, both protests were carried out. The *paro del nororiente* required a high level of coordination among *campesino* participants and between the *campesinos* and their urban counterparts. During the *paro del nororiente*, more than a thousand *campesinos* arrived in Barranca on June 9, 1987, and occupied a church in the Barrio Palmira, where they would stay for five days. On the second day, the city's commerce and transport was shut down because of protests organized by civic groups in solidarity with the peasants. Local urban movements took advantage of the opportunity to underscore their perennial demands for investments in the city's physical and social infrastructure. Protestors set up barricades at the traditional entry points to the city, and a solidarity march was carried out by the Coordinadora Popular de Barrancabermeja. As army helicopters flew overhead, violence broke out between some of the demonstrators and police.[54] In a press release the Coordinadora Popular condemned the behavior of the police, whom they accused of acts of intimidation against a peaceful march for which the mayor's office had given a permit.

Despite their capacity for joint action, local movements were unable to stop the advance of paramilitarism. In the late 1980s it seemed nobody was untouchable, not even priests. A major setback for the civic-popular movement was the departure from Barranca of Father Eduardo Díaz after seventeen years at the head of the Pastoral Social. Díaz left in April 1987, just prior to the murder of Sandra Rondón, due to death threats and an attempt on his life.[55] Barranca's Bishop Juan Francisco Sarasti publicly supported Díaz and his work with Pastoral Social, but it was not enough to convince Díaz to stay. Díaz would describe his departure from Barranca as "very painful."[56] Other activist priests linked to the diocese of Barrancabermeja would be attacked in the coming months. In April 1987 Javier Álvarez, a member of the De La Salle Order of teachers, was assassinated in northeastern Antioquia, a few kilometers from Barranca. Álvarez, a lay missionary, had spent more than a decade working in *campesino* communities in the Magdalena Medio.[57] In May 1987 Father Bernardo López was murdered in the department of Sucre.[58] Four years earlier, Father López had been a key witness in helping judicial authorities identify and investigate the activities of the paramilitary group MAS. In September 1987, Father Bernardo Marín was forced to flee his parish in the Magdalena Medio because of his condemnation of paramilitaries.[59] Also in September it was announced that Eduardo Díaz was one of thirty-three social activists on a list of people slated to be killed by MAS paramilitaries. This would precipitate his departure from Colombia.[60]

The silencing of progressive voices augmented the power of armed movements. On October 11, 1987, Patriotic Union chief Jaime Pardo Leal was murdered in the countryside just west of Bogotá.[61] The previous year, Pardo had won 328,753 votes as UP presidential candidate in the largest show of voter support for any left-wing candidate in Colombian history to that point. His death sparked a four-day *paro cívico* in Barranca. It was unlike any *paro cívico* that the city had experienced in the past. From the very first day, armed men joined the protest in the name of both the FARC and the ELN. For the first time in the city's history, there was combat between the guerrillas and the army in the streets of the city during a popular protest. The guerrillas set up checkpoints on the outskirts of the city and patrolled the streets of the north-eastern and southeastern *barrios*.[62] Army reinforcements were sent from Bucaramanga. It was a remarkable moment of shared fury that united *milicianos* from the ELN and the FARC.[63] It was also a key turning point that saw the rise of the guerrillas at the expense of civil society.

Independently of the strategies adopted by local social movements, the guerrillas had seized the initiative. Through the middle of the 1980s, the guerrillas, most notably the ELN, had established themselves among the residents of the popular *barrios*. As one Barranca activist said in an interview: "the guerrilla came in saying 'we have come to fight for the same thing, you can count on our support,' so there was a feeling among the people, that we are protected, but nobody ever said that we are allied with the guerrillas, that we are *elenos*."[64] Toward the end of the 1980s, as the circle of military and paramilitary repression closed in on Barranca, the guerrillas would make increasing use of the *paro cívico* as a tactic of the armed struggle. As we shall see in the next chapter, it was during this time that the *paro armado* or "armed strike" was invented. It would be misleading to separate the history of the guerrillas in Barranca from the history of all other political and social forces. The origins of the guerrillas can be traced through the history of the city. It is nonetheless crucial to differentiate between *convivencia*, *simpatía*, and *militancia*. These terms reflect different levels of interaction with the guerrillas, ranging from forbearance to sympathy and direct involvement. As human rights activists have long argued, it is one thing to live in a city or rural area where the guerrillas are present, another thing to identify with the goals of a revolutionary movement, and quite another to carry a weapon. The line between violent and nonviolent struggles was intentionally blurred by paramilitary attacks on legal groups such as the UP, but also on the civilian population. As the violence escalated, the guerrillas made use of the *paro cívico* in order to demonstrate their solidarity with the popular movement, and to increase their own influence. Human rights activism thus emerged at a time when the civic-popular movement's social bases were in play.

Conclusion

The decision by Barranca activists to take up the cause of human rights arose out of a rapidly evolving crisis. During the late 1980s, counterinsurgency forces opened an urban front in Barranca. At the same time, the guerrillas began to consolidate their presence in the city. While the ELN and FARC expressed some of the same frustrations with traditional politics held by the general population and the civic-popular movement, the rebels' actions contributed to the militarization of the city. There had never before been a moment of such fervor mixed with such fear for Barranca's civic-popular movement. Record numbers of people took to the streets in response to political killings, and protests became increasingly spontaneous. In conversation with historian Alejo Vargas in the late 1980s, Ezequiel Romero, long-serving municipal councillor in Barranca on behalf of the Communist Party and former trade union leader, said: "It is part of the culture of the people of Barrancabermeja. So much so that when something violent occurs, if they kill a leader, the city automatically stops. Before, you had to go into the neighborhoods and organize people into committees."[65] Sudden outbursts of grief, anger, and frustration reflected a fundamental change in the relationship between social movement organizing and popular protest.

The decision on the part of Barranca activists to organize a human rights committee in late 1987 was an attempt to channel popular indignation into collective civic action. Notwithstanding the strong historical ties to both of Colombia's main guerrilla groups among many citizens of Barranca, the civic-popular movement had hitherto maintained its autonomy and maintained space for broad-based popular protest to take place. Anchored by the Coordinadora Popular civil society coalition, the nascent human rights movement inherited a commitment to challenging structures of power, not simply protecting lives. Jairo Chaparro reflects on the legacy of the protests of the late 1980s: "Our culture of fraternity and solidarity, our culture of the *paro* could be felt on every street corner, in every house, in all of its strength. That will never end."[66] The challenge would be to carry out an agenda of human rights protection in a context of increasing complexity, tension, and violence.

As we explore in greater detail the impact of the human rights turn in Barrancabermeja, we should not underestimate the contribution that front-line activists have made to our understanding of political violence. Human rights activists in Barrancabermeja and elsewhere successfully challenged the deniability of war crimes, even as armed groups engaged in acts of subterfuge. This may prove to be the most important contribution that human rights activists have made to the understanding of armed conflict. This insight has allowed scholars to undertake a deep revision of the historical record. Human rights activists have successfully challenged the fiction that Colombia's decades-old armed conflict is fundamentally a clash between belligerent armies. Because of the efforts of groups like CREDHOS, no discussion of the Colombian conflict can overlook the ways in which armed groups target civilians.

5

Biography of a Movement

We have become specialists in the defense of human rights because of the armed conflict in Barranca, and in the definition of human rights, both conceptually, and in practice. In the process of daily struggle we have created many ways of defending human rights.

Yolanda Becerra, Popular Women's Organization[1]

Introduction

In the late 1980s, paramilitary forces attacked social activists and ordinary citizens in Barrancabermeja with shocking brutality, inspiring popular protests that opened pathways to collective grief and anger. The Regional Committee for the Defense of Human Rights (CREDHOS) was conceived in 1987 by like-minded activists during a series of informal encounters at *paros cívicos* and rallies.[2] Through the leadership of a highly regarded young lawyer, a charismatic city councillor, an oil workers' union leader, a teacher, and several prominent community organizers, CREDHOS soon became the central node in a regional human rights network that involved most of the major social and political groups in the Magdalena Medio. CREDHOS's early success was evidenced at the meetings it organized in 1988 and 1989, which brought together hundreds of individuals representing the most important civil society organizations and government human rights bodies in the Magdalena Medio and Bogotá. Though initially put forward by a small core group, the idea of a human rights committee captured the spirit of the time. CREDHOS functioned both as an advocacy organization and a rallying point around which the community-at-large and local activists could convene and develop strategies for human rights protection.[3] CREDHOS provided legal advice, undertook research, carried out educational activities, and acted as interlocutor with authorities, including the military, on behalf of the victims of political violence.

By 1988 the defense of human rights had become the main reason for popular protest in Colombia.[4] The country was on the brink of a profound crisis. Paramilitary and guerrilla organizations were expanding their interests and influence, fueled by the illegal trade in cocaine and protection rackets. Conflict-related deaths rose sharply. The national homicide rate in 1988 was 62 per 100,000 people, triple what it had been a decade earlier when President Julio César Turbay Ayala introduced the National Security Doctrine.[5] The creation of CREDHOS in December 1987 was a direct response on the part of activists in Barrancabermeja to the fact that violence was remaking their city. It was an attempt to renew and defend Barranca's tradition of popular protest, bolstering the drive for social change. By demonstrating the link between violence and structural inequalities, CREDHOS set out to define human rights in the context of the struggle for social justice. Its founders aspired to create a consensus among social movement activists in Barranca. The work of documenting and denouncing state repression begun by activists in small towns and villages in the Magdalena Medio in the early 1980s was now being undertaken by their urban counterparts. Through CREDHOS, Barranca-based groups added their voices to a national conversation on human rights.

CREDHOS emerged at a time when the Colombian national government was also creating discourses and structures that promoted human rights. On December 1, 1987, in Bogotá a group of leading academics was joined by national NGOs and government officials for a day-long colloquium to reflect on human rights in Colombia. The opening address was delivered by the country's first presidential adviser on human rights. The Consejería Presidencial para los Derechos Humanos was established in 1987 by the Liberal president Virgilio Barco in response to the grave crisis facing the country. The first person to fill the position was Álvaro Tirado, a progressive Liberal lawyer and historian. Tirado had been a member of the nongovernmental Comité Permanente para los Derechos Humanos since it was established in 1979.[6] In his speech at the colloquium, Tirado rejected the small-minded policies of previous governments: "The government of Colombia through the practice of tolerance and conciliation has rejected the National Security Doctrine and broken with it."[7] Tirado pointed to a shift in Colombian politics toward the acceptance of human rights. However, the demobilization of paramilitary groups and the disentangling of state from the logic of counterinsurgency were not forthcoming, as events in the Magdalena Medio would continue to prove.

The state worked to promote human rights, while it also undermined them through its repressive apparatus. The Colombian government had recognized the compulsory jurisdiction of the Inter-American Court of Human Rights in 1985, effectively allowing international legal intervention in Colombia's domestic affairs.[8] One year later, President Belisario Betancur created the Permanent Commission for the Defense of Human Rights, a mixed government-NGO initiative led by the attorney general and representatives from Colombia's best-known human rights groups.[9] The Consejería Presidencial para los Derechos Humanos was established in 1987 as an interface between the government and civil society. President Barco officially declared paramilitary groups illegal in 1989, signed a peace agreement with the M-19 guerrillas that same year, and convened the constituent assembly that would produce a new constitution.[10] Colombians were experiencing a human rights "norm cascade," characterized by the diffusion of human rights discourse by civil society organizations and government agencies and the creation of new laws and institutions.[11] It might have been an ideal scenario for real improvements, except for the simultaneous emergence of new and virulent forms of paramilitary violence. Journalist Alfredo Molano writes: "The clear collaboration among the official military, the police and paramilitaries is well-documented. In fact, some observers have likened the increase in paramilitary activity to "privatization" of the state's repressive apparatus, providing the government with "plausible deniability" while it seeks to wipe out guerrilla and other challenges to its rule."[12] Whereas human rights language rendered political violence committed by state agents legible, and the number of lawyers working on behalf of the state in the area of human rights proliferated, paramilitarism rendered violators injusticiable.[13]

In Colombia in the late 1980s human rights activists aspired first and foremost to expose the "killer networks" composed of regular military and private paramilitary forces that were responsible for the vast majority of threats and attacks on civilians.[14] Notwithstanding the murder of Ricardo Lara Parada one year earlier, the guerrillas claimed an ethical position, courted popular support, and appeared comparatively restrained in their use of violence within the city. Generally speaking, governments do not seek negative attention for the abuse of human rights. Human rights activists aim to maximize the "unacceptable costs" of carrying out attacks.[15] In political and legal terms, this means human rights activists work to expose human rights violators and challenge impunity. This would prove extraordinarily challenging, as the Colombian military withdrew into the shadows, and paramilitary forces gained notoriety.

This chapter takes an in-depth look at the possibilities and constraints of human rights organizing in a conflict area. The focus here is on the earliest stages of such an endeavor, during which social movements make choices about the very nature of their work. The contentious politics that give rise to human rights movements, their social origins, are often eclipsed by the violence, both discursively and literally. While the history of human rights activism cannot be decoupled from the prevailing narratives of atrocity that human rights movements themselves reproduce, we can take a critical look at how and why people organize collectively around human rights. In the first half of the chapter I trace the formation and early activities of CREDHOS, with a focus on the organization's attempts to rally social and political forces in the city around the cause of human rights. CREDHOS attempted to bring pressure to bear on the state to curb abuses by military and paramilitary forces through a combination of documentation, denunciation, and dialogue. Simultaneously, the Coordinadora Popular coalition would continue to play the role of mobilizing ordinary citizens. In the second half of the chapter I look in detail at the forms that the dirty war took in the region, with a focus on repressive actions targeting popular protest in both urban and rural contexts.

While CREDHOS's energies were absorbed by events in Barranca itself, the organization aspired to shed new light on the problem of rural violence. The massacre of peasant protestors at Llana Caliente, a small hamlet in the foothills of the *cordillera oriental*, revealed ongoing processes of violent transformation in the Magdalena Medio. The protestors were in the process of marching to mark the first anniversary of the *paro del nororiente*. They had chosen a path that led right through the heart of the region's newest paramilitary territory when they were blocked by army troops. Llana Caliente is situated on the road between Barranca and Bucaramanga in what had once been an ELN stronghold. The massacre at Llana Caliente was evidence that the counterinsurgency war was advancing on Barranca. During this period CREDHOS created new rural *promotorías*, or advocacy teams, to address the crisis in the countryside directly. As the peasant leader Ángel Tolosa recalls, while ANUC did not participate formally in CREDHOS, it worked closely with the new organization and was represented by its president Jorge Gómez Lizarazo. Peasant challenges to the expansion of the counterinsurgency war, including *marchas*, *éxodos*, and *invasiones*, would continue to shape urban activism.

A New Paradigm of Social Protest

In a special issue of the Bogotá-based activist newsmagazine *Opción* published in 1988, the editors wrote: "In order to understand the civic movement in Barranca we must analyze four indissolubly linked phenomena:

land invasions, trade unions, *paros cívicos*, and the defense of human rights."[16] CREDHOS was born out of spontaneous *paros cívicos* and mass commemoration of the victims of violence and thus reflected the popular zeitgeist. Capturing that energy and translating it into a workable formula for social and political action would prove tremendously complicated. Through detailed accounts of the impact of political violence in the Magdalena Medio, I explore the extraordinary challenges that face human rights groups in areas of armed conflict. As we shall see, Barranca activists took up the struggle with characteristic flair.

Understanding the sources of social movement formation in Barranca is critical to explaining how human rights discourse took hold there. It is therefore important to get to know the people who established CREDHOS, the processes in which they were engaged, and how they articulated their objectives. In his authoritative treatment of popular protest in Colombia during the Cold War era, the historian Mauricio Archila defines social movements as collective processes that confront various forms of injustice and inequality, whose identities cannot be reduced to economic or class factors alone.[17] Charles Tilly defines a social movement as "a sustained campaign of claim making, using repeated performances that advertise the claim, based on organizations, networks, traditions, and solidarities that sustain these activities."[18] Tilly posits that social movements are composed of diverse individual actors, including professional campaigners, organizers, and lobbyists, as well as rank-and-file members of large groupings such as trade unions. Joe Foweraker observes: "Despite the range of social movement theory, a satisfactory definition of social movements remains elusive. Nonetheless, there is some agreement that the social movement must be defined not as a group of any kind but as a process."[19] In this perspective, CREDHOS does not constitute a social movement in and of itself. Rather, CREDHOS must be seen as a specific expression of the wider social movement that coalesced in war-torn Barrancabermeja in the 1980s.

Activists from Barranca have long taken special pride in their capacity to combine politics and pleasure, and this influenced the way in which they spoke about human rights. From 1985 to 1992 the Communist Party activist Ismael Jaimes published *La Opinión*, a monthly newspaper dedicated to reporting human rights and social movement news in Barrancabermeja. *La Opinión* was initially conceived as the official newspaper of the Patriotic Union (UP) political party in the Magdalena Medio region, although it reflected a broad diversity of views. Right up until his murder in 1992 Ismael Jaimes lived, breathed, ate, and drank local politics, and he counted people from across the political spectrum among his close collaborators and friends. In *La Opinión* he wrote a special column dedicated to gossip and humor called "El Rincón de la social-bacanería." The term *bacanería* is derived from the word *bacano*, which is an adjective that translates as "cool," "amazing," or "brilliant." In Barranca it is the kind of thing you might say to describe a hot new salsa record, a great night out on the town, or an inspiring speech at a May Day rally. In July 1987 in "El Rincón de la social-bacanería," Jaimes published a manifesto for an imaginary social movement, the Frente Único de Macondo.[20] Among the tenets included in Jaimes's manifesto were the following: "1. Up with life, 2. No prohibition on love at the barricades, 3. No prohibition on partying." And it ends with "For the right to invent things, to be creative and to give flight to dreams, onwards."[21] Across the country, many Colombian activists were caught up in the romance of Barranca radicalism, as evidenced in the title of a 1988 editorial from the Bogotá magazine *Opción*: "Barrancabermeja, colorful Barranca, I love you for being free, strong and honest."[22]

Toward the end of the 1980s, daily life for activists in Barranca was a surreal mix of freedom and fear. Friends, coworkers, and family were being killed, yet social movements surged. People fell in love at the barricades and at the parties that sometimes lasted through the night in defiance of curfews. Francisco Campos, a student leader at the time, observed that his early involvement with CREDHOS taught him to "love life . . . to have the social sensibility that you need to be a human rights defender. . . . I took a chance on life, on the trans-formation of this society."[23] The exiled *barranqueña* Luisa Castro, former CREDHOS member and trade union activist, describes Barranca as a place of opportunity, of solidarity, and of hedonism:

> My view of Barranca is that it is a school for citizen convergence. There are exceptions to prove the rule, but I think that this is something that has been maintained. This joyful spirit, festive [*parandero*] in a way. Nobody would kill you over a difference of opinion. That is something that came from outside. I did not have to live through what came afterward, the *narcos*, the *paracos*. You could dress however you wanted, you could put an earring in your ear whether you were a man or a woman, wear your hair long or short. Barranca is a libertarian place; that is part of its charm. This land of joy, of solidarity, diversity is part of that. It seduces. I know it sounds sexist . . . but Barranca takes hold of you, you are seduced.[24]

Barranca was for many decades a place where people had come to escape violence, where authority could be snubbed and life celebrated. It is per-haps one of the greatest achievements of the many individuals who took up the struggle for human rights that they were able to sustain this sense of defiance.

CREDHOS functioned autonomously, yet expressed a large number of groups' determination to confront the problem of political violence. Twenty-three local organizations participated in CREDHOS's first assembly in January 1988. From the outset, CREDHOS's founding members hoped to build a consensus in the Magdalena Medio region around the importance of rights and the responsibility of the national state to protect people from violent and arbitrary treatment. In order to do so, they had to work with a variety of social and political actors at the local, regional, and national levels. Many of these were established forces in the Magdelana Medio, with long histories of claims making on the state. The participation of the Pastoral Social was fundamental, as was that of the oil workers' and teachers' unions. All of the groups that participated in the Coordinadora Popular de Barrancabermeja participated in CREDHOS. The collective therefore included representatives of all the major political parties present in Barranca, from Conservatives to Communists. In its first year of work, CREDHOS was financed by the Bucaramanga-based Foundation for the Promotion of Popular Education and Culture (FUNPROCEP), an NGO established in 1982 by progressive lawyers, educators, and activists that provided support to community-based initiatives.[25] The Bogotá-based CINEP, which had been visiting Barranca since the late 1970s, also collaborated with CREDHOS in this early period, sharing ideas around the recording of data, writing *denuncias*, and organizing public meetings.

The founding members of CREDHOS comprised a group of young professionals, politicians, and social movement leaders whose standing in the community would help propel the group to prominence. The lawyer Jorge Gómez Lizarazo and the municipal councillor Jael Quiroga were among the first to discuss the idea of a human rights committee in Barranca. Quiroga arrived in Barranca in 1981, having recently graduated from the National University in Bogotá. She was married to a petroleum engineer and lived in the Ecopetrol camp at El Centro, an enclave set up decades earlier by Tropical Oil where oil company managers and their spouses enjoyed a country club lifestyle. Quiroga was initially isolated from the real Barranca and seemed an unlikely candidate to lead a human rights organization. She remembers well having to earn the trust of the wider Barranca community. How could this pampered "engineer's wife" from Bogotá possibly appreciate the struggles of local people, she wondered? But previous activist experience at the National University in Bogotá served her well, as did her self-confidence. She soon ventured outside of the protected walls of El Centro and into the city, where she became involved in local politics. In 1986 she was elected to city council as a Conservative and was named head of Empresas Varias, the influential municipal public works department.

City Hall was itself a meeting place for many activists. The public works department managed Barranca's marketplaces, slaughterhouse, street cleaning and maintenance, water, and many other services that had for years been central concerns of local politics. Quiroga was therefore in a unique position to experience the tensions that arose around basic issues of services and infrastructure. She worked directly with all of the main community, business, labor, and professional organizations in the city. Quiroga saw the disputes that pitted Ecopetrol against the city from both sides, but soon came to identify with the prevailing culture of protest.

From the beginning CREDHOS functioned out of Jorge Gómez Lizarazo's storefront office, located on the second floor of a small commercial block overlooking Barranca's historic food market. Jorge Gómez Lizarazo was CREDHOS's president and its most visible spokesperson from 1987 through 1992. Born in Bucaramanga and trained at the National University in Bogotá, Gómez graduated from law school in 1974 and moved to Barranca to assume a post as a judge at the Barrancabermeja Municipal Court. After 1977 he served as legal counsel to *campesino* and trade union movements, as well as to political prisoners and squatters.[26] For the decade prior to the founding of CREDHOS, Gómez's office had been a hub of social justice work in the city. Significantly, Gómez had no political affiliation and was perceived by his peers to be an independent thinker. As the original CREDHOS member and Pastoral Social activist Irene Villamizar asserts, many organizations, including CREDHOS, were accused of being subversive, but not Jorge Gómez: "Nobody could pin him down, as belonging to one political movement or another."[27] Quiroga remembers developing a friendship with Gómez at demonstrations: "We met there, in the middle of the excitement of the *paro cívico*, of the *éxodos campesinos*. We saw each other at events, when the peasants came over from Yondó, from the Cimitarra River Valley, from the south of the department of Bolívar. They came to Barranca and took over the Parque Infantil, and they lived there. Right there they slaughtered their animals for food and prepared their meals . . . annoying local business owners and all of that. . . . That is where we started to work with Jorge Gómez Lizarazo."[28] Through informal conversations held over a period of months, Quiroga and Gómez were joined by Villamizar and others. Together they agreed to launch a committee in which all expressions of social and political activism would be welcome. Thus, while the inner circle of CREDHOS was small, they hoped to have a broad reach.

From the beginning CREDHOS's greatest asset was that it was immersed in a deep current of activism. Jorge Gómez Lizarazo recalls: "I was joined by some of the people from social movement organizations that I had worked for, and individuals on the municipal council . . . and together we started to look at creating a human rights committee."[29] The pillars of Barranca's popular movement in the 1970–1990 period were organized labor, peasants, the Catholic Church, and urban squatters. All were present at the formation of CREDHOS. Even the Liberal mayor of Barranca was present. As CREDHOS cofounder Irene Villamizar suggests, CREDHOS aspired to rise above partisan squabbling: "At that time Jorge Gómez Villamizar was mayor of Barranca, who later became governor of Santander. He participated in CREDHOS. He supported us and said that he was in agreement with what CREDHOS was defending . . . so he played a positive role, with the support of a recognized authority. CREDHOS played such an important role, CREDHOS had more authority than the Coordinadora Popular de Barrancabermeja. It could rise above the political parties. It was a pluralist project; it was not defined by politics, but by the defense of human rights."[30] Four institutions—the Unión Sindical Obrera oil workers' union, the Pastoral Social program of the diocese of Barrancabermeja, the National Association of Peasant Users, and the Juntas de Acción Comunal neighborhood councils—were the greatest contributors to the development of an autonomous and progressive civil society in Barranca. Each was a key link to a broader network, and each participated in CREDHOS's earliest activities.

On September 28, 1988, CREDHOS convened a public event in favor of "peace and human rights" in the Magdalena Medio region. The forum was held at the offices of the municipal council, with a number of city officials participating. Dozens of local activists from the trade union movement, progressive Catholic organizations, left-wing and mainstream political parties, and other community groups were present. A sizeable number of delegates representing prominent national human rights organizations were also in attendance. The Bogotá-based Permanent Committee for the Defense of Human Rights, the Association of Families of the Detained-Disappeared, the Jesuit-run Centre for Popular Education and Research (CINEP), the "José Alvear Restrepo" Lawyers Collective, and Colombia's oldest human rights NGO, the Committee for Solidarity with Political Prisoners, were joined that day by Bernardo Echeverry Ossa, delegate for the Internal Affairs Agency of the Colombian government. Local police and army commanders, media, and the general public were also invited to participate.

At its first public forum, CREDHOS called on participants to fight for human rights in terms that took the debate beyond civil and political liberties, or a mere denunciation of violence. They asserted that human rights were central to processes of social and political change. In the conference's final declaration, participants agreed that the current state of affairs in Barranca qualified as a "dirty war" because of the fact that it amounted to an undeclared and clandestine campaign of violence against civilians. Their list of demands included the following points:

1. Respect for the right to life.
2. Compliance with and monitoring of all international human rights instruments signed and ratified by the Colombian State.
3. The lifting of the State of Siege.
4. The dismantling of paramilitary groups.
5. Full respect for International Humanitarian Law by all sides in the conflict, including insurgent groups.
6. The implementation of political and economic reforms that assure greater democracy and social justice.

The inclusion of the two points concerning illegal armed groups was a reflection on the particularities of the Colombian conflict, which was being fought on multiple fronts by a multiplicity of right- and left-wing groups, in addition to the armed forces, National Police, and secret services. The final declaration of the conference clearly stated that the defense of human rights was "a struggle . . . understood in sociopolitical context."[31] It was a good point, considering the enormous complexity of the problems facing Barranca, and the civic-popular movement's history of struggle for public services. Echoing longstanding concerns about Colombia's relationship to foreign oil companies, CREDHOS even called for a debate on the exploitation of petroleum and other natural resources "*in defense of national sovereignty.*"[32] To advance these goals, CREDHOS would have to create structures for the socialization of human rights issues.

CREDHOS defined education and outreach as the group's main activities.[33] When CREDHOS registered as an independent not-for-profit corporation in April 1989, included in its incorporation papers was a commitment to "the preparation and training of promoters of social rights and human rights through popular organizations working in the community, in order that their knowledge be used to engage in the defense of their rights" and "to carry out appropriate legal actions and denunciations, in order to make visible the effective defense of human rights."[34] The decision to register CREDHOS and establish democratic internal governance rules served to legitimize the organization as an independent voice for human rights. Giving CREDHOS a formal structure that included a board of directors and a general assembly guaranteed that citizens from diverse backgrounds could participate in decision making. The challenge moving forward would be to maintain this sense of purpose, the sense of openness established by Jorge Gómez Lizarazo, as attacks against the social movements intensified.

The Murder of Manuel Gustavo Chacón

The nine *paros cívicos por la vida* organized in 1987 and 1988 demonstrated that there was an appetite for change among a substantial proportion of Barranca's citizens. There was a great deal of interest in what CREDHOS had to say, reflected in the level of participation in CREDHOS-organized events. But the violence from military and paramilitary forces also threatened to undo the consensus that brought people together in the first place. A number of key leaders who embodied the spirit of the city's civic-popular movement were killed. The resulting protests were dynamic, but practically impossible to influence or control. The city's civic-popular movement would be elbowed aside in the ensuing street fight between security forces, paramilitaries, and the guerrillas.

One of the most significant assassinations in Barranca's history took place just one month after CREDHOS's launch. The murder of the Unión Sindical Obrera leader Manuel Gustavo Chacón on January 15, 1988, remains symbolic of the price that social activists pay for their work in Barranca.[35] The story of Chacón's murder, and the way he is remembered, tells a great deal about the importance that activists in Barranca give to their shared history. Portraits of the fallen leaders of the USO are displayed prominently in the front foyer of the national headquarters of the oil workers' union in Barranca. Chacón's likeness stands out. His hair is long, and he is depicted clutching a microphone, looking more like a singer than a union organizer. Chacón was a legendary orator and a folk hero in Barranca, along the lines of other romantic figures such as Ricardo Lara Parada and Leonardo Posada. Born and raised in the historic sugar-growing center of Charalá, Santander, Manuel Gustavo Chacón had married María Elsa Uribe in 1976. Twenty-four years old when he arrived in Barranca from Bogotá in 1977, Chacón was a rugged and dashing rebel with a Che Guevara beard. He attended technical college in Barranca and soon took up a position as a machinist with Ecopetrol. Chacón rose to a leadership position within the oil workers' union, and eventually to the position of shop steward, and then to the National Executive. Chacón is fondly remembered as "El Loco," a larger-than-life character who composed poetry, sang, and inspired confidence in his comrades at Ecopetrol. As his portrait in the USO suggests, Chacón was indeed an accomplished musician who epitomized the exuberance of Barranca. He was not just a symbol for oil workers, but for the city itself.

The day Manuel Chacón was murdered was like any other. And like any other day, Chacón strode energetically through the streets of Barranca, seemingly oblivious to the dangers he faced. At about 9:30 a.m. a phone call came through to the main reception at the union office from a man calling himself

Juan, who said he was an Ecopetrol employee in need of assistance clarifying a problem with his paycheck. Chacón and fellow USO official Luis Eduardo Galindo Saavedra drove to the Banco de los Trabajadores in the city's commercial district to help out. But they could not find Juan anywhere, and the bank staff did not know anything. He and Galindo shrugged off what seemed a misunderstanding and decided that they might as well do their own banking. Galindo waited for Chacón outside the Banco de Bogotá. When Chacón was finished, Galindo went into the Banco Popular next door. Chacón then waited outside talking to a friend. Galindo remembers thinking how typical it was for Chacón to stop on the street to chat with people he knew or who recognized him. About ten minutes later, as Galindo was finishing his transaction at the teller's window, a woman burst into the bank shouting, "They've killed Chacón."[36]

The nonchalance and confidence with which Manuel Chacón walked the streets of Barranca seemed to show that he did not expect to be targeted. Yet Chacón had received multiple death threats and survived two previous assassination attempts. The assailants had fled the area in an unmarked blue pickup truck. Nobody pursued them, despite the fact that the murder took place at the busiest intersection in the city center, and there were a number of police officers in the area. Chacón was quickly rushed to the hospital, where he soon succumbed to his injuries. No suspects were detained, and no eyewitnesses identified at the scene, in spite of the fact that a crowd had gathered on the sidewalk. Investigators later confirmed that two police were inside the Banco Popular at the time, just a few meters away.[37] The two officers would testify that they heard shots but saw nothing.[38] At about 10:00 a.m. Chacón's wife, María Elsa Uribe, was told her husband had been shot when a neighbor burst into the house with the news. She made her way to the hospital, where her husband was still being treated. Ten minutes later, she was informed he was dead.[39] Among the personal effects found on the body of Manuel Chacón was an unsigned letter dated October 27, 1987, from a man claiming to be a police officer from Santa Rosa de Simití, located a few hours downriver from Barranca. The letter stated that the Colombian navy was plotting to kill Chacón.

Chacón's murder was perceived as an act of war on the city's social movements. In the hours following Chacón's death, conflict between the city's nascent human rights movement and the military came to a climax. The oil workers' union collaborated with the Coordinadora Popular to organize a *paro cívico*. The protest lasted four days, from January 15 to January 18, 1988. The Coordinadora Popular's accusation that state security forces had been complicit in Chacón's murder was met with stiff opposition. On January 23, 1988, the president of FEDEPETROL, Fernando Acuña, received a threatening letter signed in the name of the MAS paramilitary organization. The letter threatened Acuña, as well as David Ravelo, Álvaro Solano, and Wilson Ferrer, all named as spokespeople for the Coordinadora Popular. The letter stated that the MAS would not tolerate accusations of responsibility for murder or reprisals against the military, Ecopetrol, the government, or Barranca's business community: "your life or the life of your family, will be the retribution, if anything unfortunate should happened to the aforementioned entities."[40]

Manuel Gustavo Chacón's murder was the first in a terrible series of paramilitary actions carried out in central Barranca against popular leaders between 1988 and 1992. The navy serviceman Pablo Francisco Pérez Cabrera was arrested in February 1988 and sentenced to sixteen years in the La Picota prison in Bogotá for his involvement in Chacón's murder. But that is where the investigation stopped. Despite the arrest of one of Chacón's alleged killers, the level of violence increased. More than three thousand politically motivated killings were reported in Colombia as a whole in 1988, including four hundred in Barranca.[41] These included some of the highest profile activists in the city. On May 24 an attempt was made on the life of Doris Molina, secretary of the oil workers' union.[42] The vice president of the oil workers' union local at El Centro, Hamet Consuegra Llorente, was shot and killed on May 25, 1988, at approximately 11:00 p.m. while participating in a protest on one of Barranca's main roads.[43] Two months later, two eyewitnesses to the Consuegra murder who had been asked to make declarations to police investigators were shot and killed in front of a café on the city's main thoroughfare, the Avendia del Ferrocarril. The murders of Manuel Gustavo Chacón, Hamet Consuegra, and others demonstrated that the military and paramilitary could act with impunity in the city's highly controlled commercial center, a short distance away from national police and army bases.

City and Region under Siege

CREDHOS joined *campesino* groups and progressive Catholic priests in documenting and denouncing the spread of paramilitarism in the city and across the Magdalena Medio. Attacks on peasants were now being carried out in the rural periphery of Barrancabermeja, and in neighboring *municipios*. The distinction between rural and urban violence was blurred. A number of the paramilitary actions carried out in 1988 specifically targeted *campesino* activists living in Barranca, including several individuals who had been involved in the *paro del nororiente*. On May 23, several people preparing to join a *marcha campesina* were shot and killed by the Colombian army on the outskirts of the city. Following these killings, hundreds of peasants took refuge inside the national headquarters of the USO. This led immediately to a *paro cívico* in solidarity with the peasants, led by members of the USO and CREDHOS. Just a few days later another massacre of peasant protestors was carried out by the Colombian army at Llana Caliente, on the road to San Vicente de Chucurí. It was during this time that the pattern of paramilitary expansion into new territories became evident, notably into the foothills of the Cordillera Oriental in Santander. The tensions and the popular outcry against paramilitarism were such that *campesinos* and the military soon found themselves in direct and deadly conflict.

CREDHOS was conceived to carry out work at the regional level. In its first year CREDHOS organized activities in Barrancabermeja, as well as in the *municipios* of San Vicente de Chucurí, El Carmen, Bajo Simacota, Sabana de Torres, and Puerto Wilches (Santander), Yondó (Antioquia), and San Pablo and Simití (Bolívar).[44] CREDHOS's work in rural zones and small towns outside of Barranca mainly consisted of fact finding. In order to establish themselves in small towns that were even more exposed to violence than was Barrancabermeja, CREDHOS also organized small workshops where human rights were discussed. These activities were facilitated by local *promotores*, or human rights advocates affiliated with CREDHOS. The work of preparing and delivering legal *denuncias* of human rights abuses committed outside of Barranca was carried out by Jorge Gómez Lizarazo and others at CREDHOS's main office. Recently displaced peasants living in Barranca would sometimes go to the CREDHOS office in person to register their complaints. In at least one locality, the oil-producing *municipio* of Sabana de Torres, a small human rights committee was established to carry out a fuller range of actions in situ. This gave the organization valuable insight into the extent of violence in the rural Magdalena Medio.

The massacre at Llana Caliente was one of the most notorious attacks carried out by security forces against activists in the Magdalena Medio during the late 1980s. On Saturday, May 29, 1988, soldiers from the Luciano D'Elhuyar Battalion based in San Vicente de Chucurí opened fire on unarmed peasant protestors who had occupied a rural crossroads connecting San Vicente to El Carmen de Chucurí and Barrancabermeja. The *campesinos* had gathered to protest government inaction on promises signed one year earlier at the resolution of the historic *paro del nororiente* national peasant protests. Seventeen people, mostly *campesinos*, were killed that afternoon. The massacre took place in broad daylight during a standoff between soldiers and *campesino* protestors, not under the cover of paramilitarism. The way in which the massacre occurred demonstrated the volatility of the situation in the region.

The Colombian military continued to carry out functions of social control and counterinsurgency in the Magdalena Medio, extending to the intimidation of civilian protestors. The Llana Caliente massacre showed the degree to which military personnel were on edge.

The Llana Caliente massacre was the tragic culmination of a drama that began one week earlier when thousands of peasants from the surrounding region began a march toward the capital of the department of Santander, Bucaramanga, to mark the first anniversary of the *paro del nororiente*.[45] *Campesinos* in San Vicente de Chucurí and El Carmen de Chucurí had spent the year enduring paramilitary incursions, resulting in the displacement of many people to Barranca. A paramilitary base had been established in the rural area of San Juan Bosco de la Verde, located just south of El Carmen de Chucurí, in 1981.[46] According to confessed paramilitary organizer and Colombian army major Óscar de Jesus Echandía Sánchez, San Juan Bosco de la Verde served as a training base for paramilitaries operating in the *municipio* of Simacota, where the Ejército de Liberación Nacional (ELN) had carried out its first military actions in 1964. The San Juan Bosco de la Verde paramilitaries' main area of influence was the Carare-Opón corridor and south toward Puerto Boyacá.[47] But by 1986 the paramilitaries were also pushing northward. In the five months preceding the massacre at Llana Caliente, twenty-two people from the *municipios* of San Vicente and El Carmen were either killed or disappeared in incidents involving military and paramilitary personnel.[48]

The standoff between the army and peasants at Llana Caliente was long and tense. On May 22, 1988, hundreds of *campesinos* from the surrounding area set off toward San Vicente from El Carmen in a convoy comprising 140 trucks and buses. They were stopped along the route by soldiers at a spot known as Llana Caliente, a tiny hamlet located at the intersection of roads linking the municipalities of El Carmen, San Vicente, and Barranca, fewer than ten kilometers from the San Vicente town center. A short bridge spans the Opón River as it winds down through the rocky hills of Santander, meeting up with the Magdalena River just south of Barranca. It is a narrow unpaved road, with lots of tree cover and steep sloping sides. Completed in 1932, it was until the end of the 1980s the most important land route connecting Barranca to the interior of the department of Santander. By Monday, May 31, there were nearly ten thousand *campesinos* from dozens of small communities backed up along the road. They stretched out in a line hundreds of meters long, with tents and makeshift shelters. By now, food and water were in very short supply. A few days later tensions started to boil over, with soldiers and protestors shouting at one another. Soldiers fired warning shots into the air.

After a long war of nerves, the stalemate was eventually broken. A commission of representatives from the departmental government arrived at the site and requested of the army that the *campesinos* be allowed to send a delegation to discuss their demands. On the morning of May 29, a small group of *campesino* leaders left for Bucaramanga. The brigade commander Lieutenant Colonel Rogelio Corea was celebrating his forty-fifth birthday over lunch that day, accompanied by the mayor of San Vicente and other municipal officials. Some have suggested that Corea was drunk by midday. Whatever the case, witnesses reported that the Lieutenant Colonel was angry as he made his way to the barricades separating the soldiers from the *campesino* marchers. He had been informed that the marchers demanded to see him, that they were accusing the army of having detained four *campesinos*. As he approached the barricades, he warned the protestors on the other side not to try and cross over. One man attempted to remove some tree branches that had been leaned up against the barricades. Corea gave the order to open fire. But at first nothing happened. Corea shot and killed soldier Luis Suárez Acevedo, who refused to carry out the order. A former FARC guerrilla-turned-army-informant known as "Comandante Camilo" then turned and fired on Corea himself. Comandante Camilo was struck by a flurry of gunfire. Soldiers then began firing at will on the *campesinos*, many of whom ducked behind trees along the roadside.[49] Four soldiers died, including Lieutenant Colonel Corea. Eight *campesinos* were declared dead at the scene, and twenty-seven were taken to the hospital, where at least five more would die. *Campesino* groups would later claim the number of dead and disappeared to be thirty-eight.

The Llana Caliente massacre reinforced the concerns of Barranca-based popular movements, all the more so as *campesino* families fleeing the San Vicente area began to arrive in increasingly large numbers in Barranca.[50] Lieutenant Colonel Rogelio Corea's actions at the barricades, the presence of a guerrilla informant, and the disconnect between civilian and military actions all contributed to an atmosphere of fear. It became known to human rights activists with connections in the area that as the paramilitaries advanced, a number of guerrilla militants, including commanders, were switching sides. During the first two weeks following the Llana Caliente massacre, the bodies of nine murder victims were recovered from the streets of the city. In response, the police stepped up armored patrols in Barranca's poor neighborhoods. In October 1988 a police station was opened along the main road in the Primero de Mayo neighborhood, and construction began on a new central police base, built inside a fortified compound adjacent to the city's largest power station. This process of militarization of the city was accompanied by even more violence. In November, the National Police reported to the municipal council that fourteen murders had taken place in a span of just three weeks.[51]

Conclusion

CREDHOS called on the national police and military to protect the local population, instead of treating civilians like enemy combatants. Jorge Gómez Lizarazo attended municipal council meetings, where he made statements denouncing arbitrary detentions by the army in Barranca, the physical abuse of suspects, and the denial of legal counsel to detainees.[52] The municipal council discussed human rights concerns regularly through 1987 and 1988. It became an important arena for debating potential solutions to the violence, and council meetings were sometimes filled to capacity (see fig. 6). For the first time in the city's history, human rights had displaced social services and infrastructure from local lawmakers' agendas.

The shift in Barranca to a focus on human rights coincided with the first-ever popular elections for mayors in Colombia in 1988. But the democratic opening that began with mayoral elections did not come without risks. In many regions, direct elections for mayor exacerbated political tensions. Some observers feared that the paramilitaries and guerrillas would seek to install clients in positions of power in local government. More than three hundred political activists were killed across Colombia during the 1988 mayoral campaigns. These included thirty-five candidates for mayor and ninety-four candidates for municipal councils.[53] Barranca was no exception. Political scientist María Emma Wills writes that in Barranca, the popular election of mayors "did not strengthen new political formations, nor did it widen citizen participation in local decision-making. On the contrary, parallel to the electoral process, the dirty war phenomenon became stronger in the *municipio*."[54] The killings of social and political activists in the late 1980s all but vanquished hopes that a viable nonviolent political alternative would emerge. In August 1988 the municipal councillor and CREDHOS supporter Orlando Higuita asked whether the mayor's office was prepared to take any special measures to help provide security to members of the council.[55] Higuita pointed out that the mayor was, from a constitutional point of view, the commander of the National Police assigned to Barranca. Over the course of the debate that day, the mayor admitted that there were no special security measures in place, and many city councillors admitted that they feared for their lives. In the end, Higuita's words were prophetic. Orlando Higuita—a member of the Patriotic

Figure 6. Standing room only at municipal council meeting in Barrancabermeja, circa 1987. Courtesy of Foto Estudios Joya.

Union, the Central Committee of the PCC, the Coordinadora Popular, and CREDHOS—was assassinated on June 12, 1989.

CREDHOS established a nonpartisan basis upon which to advocate for human rights. Buoyed by the mass protests against political violence that took place in Barranca in 1987 and 1988, CREDHOS rallied the city's civic-popular movement. CREDHOS was open to the general public and made use of its allies at the mayor's office. However, CREDHOS's early successes were realized through the collective efforts of established social movement organizations, including the members of the Coordinadora Popular. Irene Villamizar describes the dynamic: "We twenty-one leaders created CREDHOS together. We were leaders because we represented different organizations. We were twenty-one people worried about human rights. . . . We joined forces and created the human rights committee. I came from the Church, Juancho Castilla, Rosalba

Marín, and me, from the Church and the Organización Femenina Popular. Juancho and I worked for the Pastoral Social, and Rosalba the women's organization. That was when we met with Jael Quiroga. It was interesting work, but not easy; those were difficult times."[56] Working together as CREDHOS, these groups set out an agenda for human rights protection that included a strong social justice component. The pluralism embodied by CREDHOS at the time was a legacy of the civic-popular movement. Despite the fear experienced by many activists, there persisted in Barranca an established basis for communication between different groups.

The wider context that gave rise to human rights activism in Barranca can be linked to national and international political changes. On the one hand a democratic opening was announced, including important democratic reforms and the establishment of human rights institutions. On the other hand, activists in conflict areas such as Barranca experienced the breakdown of peace negotiations between the government and leftist insurgents, the rise of the drug trade, and a deepening of wartime paranoia. Barranca was stigmatized as a red zone, home to guerrillas and those sympathetic to them. Human rights workers were accused of being auxiliaries of the guerrillas. In the midst of the United States–sponsored War on Drugs, gangsters, guerrillas, and social movements were readily conflated. In a June 5, 1988, article published in the Bogotá newspaper *El Tiempo*, Barranca is described as an "enclave under siege" and "controlled by the guerrillas."[57] In response, the new director of the Pastoral Social, Father Nel Beltrán, declared: "Barranca . . . is not a guerrilla center. . . . It is not the same to endure the presence of a particular group and to be identified with it."[58] Jorge Gómez Lizarazo reflects on the challenge of human rights organizing in Barranca, and in Colombia, during the armed conflict: "Accusing human rights workers of working on behalf of the guerrillas is a national phenomenon. It is a way of discrediting them. But I think it is a mistake because what human rights workers do is to affirm democracy, to affirm the social rule of law. These types of things are not understood by the Colombian state."[59]

6

The War on Human Rights Defenders

We thought we were immune. We were racing with death. We were constantly clashing with the security forces. Because we had so much support. But we underestimated them. We didn't think they would kill us.

Jael Quiroga, human rights activist[1]

A Terrifying Message

On January 18, 1989, a combined military-paramilitary force posing as leftist guerrillas murdered twelve government human rights investigators in the small town of La Rochela, Santander. Judges and lawyers had been subject to attacks in the past.[2] But never had human rights officials been so audaciously targeted, and with such a deep impact on Colombian society. Most of the La Rochela commission members were based in the department of Santander, although none possessed direct firsthand knowledge of the small corner of the Magdalena Medio into which paramilitary groups from Antioquia and Boyacá were expanding. Had the commission been allowed to carry out its work, it would have been an important positive step for Colombia's justice system. Instead, La Rochela was the first major incident in the war on human rights defenders in the Magdalena Medio.[3] The fact that military personnel would conspire to murder government officials hints at the ways in which particular histories have shaped different branches of the Colombian state.[4] On the one hand, the Office of the Inspector General of Colombia was under pressure to fulfill its mandate as overseer of human rights. On the other hand, the Colombian military was deeply engaged in a Cold War counterinsurgency campaign in the Magdalena Medio. The La Rochela massacre confirmed the lengths to which the military was prepared to go to avoid scrutiny.

In the aftermath of La Rochela, activists in Barrancabermeja would have to carry out their work under a cloud of fear. It was a terrible omen for the recently established Regional Committee for the Defense of Human Rights (CREDHOS). But this did not dissuade CREDHOS from openly denouncing injustices. In July 1989 CREDHOS hosted the region's first major summit on human rights. It was attended by more than a thousand people representing local peasant, church, and labor groups, as well as the national government, armed forces, and nongovernmental organizations from Bogotá. All four of Colombia's main guerrilla organizations sent delegates.[5] The CREDHOS president Jorge Gómez Lizarazo spared no one in his address to the conference plenary. CREDHOS's president railed against the military, paramilitary, and drug traffickers, as well as the foreign investors that he described as waiting in the wings to plunder the region's natural resources:

> They are conspiring against the tranquility of this region: multinational interests want to plunder the riches of the subsoil without obstacles; agribusiness, ranchers and farmers need to guarantee the stability of land tenure; drug traffickers search for ways of legalizing their profits and the projects promoted by the most militaristic sectors of the armed forces to impose "National Security" doctrines. These are all factors that have led the State to lose its monopoly on the use of force . . . and its [ability] to impose the rule of law, as private interests take the "administration of justice" into their own hands.[6]

Gómez argued that leftist guerrillas' pursuit of power also compromised the security of the civilian population in the region.[7] It was a revealing moment. Public encounters between social movements, state officials, and insurgents were rare in Colombia.[8] Such forthright talk about the complexity of the human rights crisis was also rare. It would be the last time such a meeting would be held in Barranca.

CREDHOS had opened a window on political violence in the Magdalena Medio. The final declaration approved by participants in the 1989 Regional Encounter on the Human Rights Situation in Colombia stated unequivocally that "social injustice is the main cause of violence."[9] CREDHOS's regularly published newsletters, press releases, and annual reports constituted a comprehensive examination of violence. Their first major study, published in November 1989, began with a five-page analysis of the political economy of the region and ended with a twenty-five-page appendix listing the names of all the documented murders in the region since 1987, dozens registered simply as NN (no name). CREDHOS's correspondence with local and national government authorities presented painfully detailed accounts of specific cases of death threats, intimidation, and attacks on the civilian population, oftentimes accompanied by photographs of the dead. CREDHOS also provided legal support to victims and their families. Despite the threat of violence, CREDHOS received a steady stream of visitors at its office. People came from all over the city and from rural areas around the Magdalena Medio to file reports about missing people, deaths, detentions, and maltreatment at the hands of security forces personnel.

Guerrilla violence was on the rise as well, although attacks on civilians were still relatively rare. Insurgent actions posed a dilemma for human rights defenders, whose focus was squarely on the Colombian state. Jael Quiroga recalls being asked why she spent most of her time denouncing military and paramilitary crimes: "I didn't have any guerrilla cases to talk about. I don't know, maybe in other regions, but not in Barranca. In Barranca we did not know, and the guerrillas were not that depraved."[10] Quiroga's recollections are broadly substantiated by the available evidence. The guerrillas regularly engaged the Colombian armed forces in the city and carried out strikes on oil infrastructure. A handful of high-profile kidnappings were carried out by the ELN and FARC during this period, targeting Ecopetrol managers, police officials, businessmen, a former governor of the department of Santander, and, on at least one occasion, Italian engineers working at the Barranca refinery. Most of the kidnapped were reported released within days of being abducted, and many reported having been "tried" by the guerrillas for their alleged complicity with paramilitary or state crimes. In 1993 the ELN kidnapped and then killed the refinery production chief Óscar Tamayo.[11] Between 1990 and 1995 the national press reported fifteen oil pipeline bombings. The ELN's two Barranca-based urban militia, the Frente Capitán Parmenio and Frente Manuel Gustavo Chacón, occasionally took shots at police and army patrols on the city streets. The security forces counterpunched with armored incursions into poor neighborhoods and carried out mass arrests of young men.[12] Sometimes the back-and-forth between the two sides would play out over several days. The military would often identify the victims of armed actions in the *barrios orientales* as guerrillas.[13] However, in the aftermath of these dangerous altercations, Barranca's human rights activists received very few specific complaints against the guerrillas.

CREDHOS and other activist groups in Colombia gave lie to commonly held views that the Colombian conflict was mainly about drugs or was too complex to understand. As Winifred Tate recounts, human rights defenders

Figure 7. Oil pipeline sabotage to the south of Barrancabermeja, 1998. Photo by the author.

from Colombia who traveled to the United Nations Human Rights Commission in Geneva dedicated themselves to "shifting the framework used to describe Colombia, from drug trafficking violence in which the government is a victim needing support to a human rights crisis for which the government is at fault."[14] On the diplomatic front, activists had to counter the confusion encouraged by the Colombian government and its allies in Washington. There was a strong trend evident at the time toward the official conflation of political and drug violence. During a twenty-four-hour visit to Bogotá on May 24, 1988, the U.S. congressman John P. Murtha and the U.S. Army secretary John O. Marsh met privately with the Colombian president Virgilio Barco.[15] President Barco agreed with his guests that during his upcoming visit to Washington, DC, he should refrain from offering U.S. lawmakers a nuanced analysis of Colombia's armed conflict, "half jokingly noting that even he is not sure he fully understands the long history of guerrilla related violence in Colombia."[16] In preparing for the trip to Washington, the U.S. ambassador in Bogotá assured State Department officials that he would "send [President Barco] the Embassy's analysis of the connections between the insurgency and the [drug] traffickers."[17]

Recognized by Washington-based organizations for their knowledge of the links between the Colombian military and the paramilitary, CREDHOS spokespeople would find themselves contributing to debates around U.S. policies. But the momentum behind military cooperation between Colombia and the United States was strong. The U.S. government was convinced that the guerrillas were getting the upper hand and needed to be stopped. In a cable sent to the U.S. secretary of state on February 22, 1988, officials at the U.S. embassy in Bogotá describe the Colombian counterinsurgency war as a shambles: "Meanwhile the armed forces [are] stuck in a reactive mode . . . playing catch-up with the guerrillas. Their response has been piecemeal, reflecting the absence of a national strategy or framework."[18] In 1988 Colombia received $14.1 million in U.S. military aid. In 1989 the figure increased to $86 million.[19] U.S.-based rights groups were attempting to demonstrate that the Colombian military was not entitled to receive aid from the U.S. government because of their links to paramilitaries and human rights atrocities. CREDHOS's focus on the violence committed against social activists by the military and paramilitary provided an essential corrective to the official War on Drugs discourse of the state.

It was a decisive time in Colombian history, characterized by great promise and even greater peril. By 1991 the Cold War was officially over. The first comprehensive political reforms in Colombia in more than one hundred years were being carried out. The Colombian Constitution of 1991 recognized human rights and strengthened judicial independence.[20] It also created new mechanisms such as the *defensoría del pueblo* (human rights ombudsman) and the *fiscalía general* (attorney general) to monitor, promote, and enforce human rights.[21] At the same time, a war was being waged on numerous fronts and in different regional configurations, between the state, paramilitary forces, drug lords, and Leftist guerrillas. In 1991 CREDHOS counted hundreds of murders in the city for which no armed group had claimed responsibility and noted the increasingly frequent appearance of mutilated and unidentified victims.[22] As violence increased across the country, a generation of Colombian social activists were expressing themselves using the language of human rights. In response to pressure from below and unwelcome international attention, the Colombian government continued to express concern for human rights. The major players in Colombia's armed conflict were expanding their influence.[23] Indeed, even as human rights became the subject of national debate, the military deepened its involvement in paramilitarism. In short, the basic modalities of Colombia's current social and political conflict were taking shape. As CREDHOS's first president Jorge Gómez Lizarazo observed: "the situation was quite difficult, and in a way it went way beyond our capacity to respond."[24] Yet despite the escalating repression and violence surrounding them, CREDHOS members did not initially suspect that they themselves were in grave danger.

Paramilitary Violence in Barrancabermeja

The fact that Barranca had a strong state presence, including civilian and military authorities, made human rights work viable. In the first few years, CREDHOS and other groups delivered their reports personally to the local representatives of the national government agencies responsible for human rights, including the Barranca office of the Inspector General. They also met directly with army commanders when necessary. Following the approval of the 1991 Constitution, Barranca became the regional headquarters for the office of the *defensoría del pueblo* and the *fiscalía general*. Barranca also bene-fited from a large presence of news media, including two local weekly news-papers, *La Opinión del Magdalena Medio* and *El Sideral*, as well as a handful of radio stations. By 1994 there was also an independent television station in Barranca, Enlace 10. The *Vanguardia Liberal* newspaper, published out of Bucaramanga, began publishing a daily supplement on the Magdalena Medio in the mid-1990s. Barranca had become one of the most militarized urban areas anywhere on earth, measured in terms of the sheer number of military and police in the city, not to mention illegal armed groups.[25] The city served as a regional base of operations for two army battalions, naval and national police forces.[26] The Colombian government's efforts to control the city only increased when the guerrillas established urban militia within the city. Being able to monitor and denounce human rights violations under such tightly controlled conditions meant that CREDHOS was able to put state security forces under a relatively high degree of scrutiny.

The history of Barranca provides clear insight into the parallel rise of paramilitarism and human rights activism, and how these forces influenced one another. A small group of prominent Colombian scholars began writing about paramilitarism in the Magdalena Medio in the late 1980s, focused on rural areas.[27] These studies—which explore the relationships between armed forces, paramilitaries, guerrillas, social movements, drug traffickers, landowners, and left-wing political parties—were made possible by the work of human rights activists in places such as Barranca. In no other region of Colombia was frontline human rights reporting being done on a permanent basis. The work carried out by CREDHOS's rural *promotores*, as well as by Justicia y Paz, ANUC, and the Unión Sindical Obrera, to cite just a few examples, was hugely influential in defining human rights critiques of the Colombian state.[28] These groups' Barranca-based members provided firsthand evidence from contested peripheral zones that would inspire a fierce debate among activists, policymakers, and academics concerning state-paramilitary collusion. Beginning in the early 1980s in the southern Magdalena Medio, paramilitary groups enjoyed the cooperation of the Colombian military. The same basic patterns were documented during the expansion of paramilitary groups north into the mountainous areas of Santander from San Juan del Bosco in the mid-1980s. The rise of paramilitarism within the city itself likewise required the support of state security forces.[29]

There exists in Colombia a fierce polemic between those who argue that the paramilitaries are a clandestine arm of the state counterinsurgency apparatus and those who claim they are independent actors. Thanks to the work of CREDHOS and other groups in the Magdalena Medio, the extent of state complicity with paramilitarism became a matter of public debate. Paramilitary groups have taken on different forms in different regions of Colombia. As has been documented by the sociologist Mauricio Romero, in regions of Colombia where the state is less present, paramilitary groups developed some of the characteristics of autonomous armed actors.[30] Conversely, the interlacing of military and paramilitary power in the Magdalena Medio was highly visible to local area residents. As one activist priest recalls, paramilitary actions were often carried out directly by members of the armed forces:

In the 1980s I think that . . . the state and its security forces were in charge of what we would call a "dirty war." We all know about the death of Manuel Gustavo Chacón. . . . It was carried out by the famous navy "clan," and we know that naval officials went around pretending to be paramilitaries, what they used to call the "*masetos*," members of MAS, to annihilate union and social leaders. The UP [Patriotic Union] was hit hard in Barrancabermeja, in the Magdalena Medio, directly by the official security forces, whatever you want to call them . . . Departamento Administrativo de Seguridad [DAS], Policía Judicial [SIJIN], navy, army, police, etc. To the degree that they went ahead with this fight, the para-state forces grew closer and closer to the state and behaved more cynically and brazenly. In the Magdalena Medio the people can provide testimony of mixed patrols where the paramilitaries go around with state agents; the people have seen soldiers get down from their vehicles and forget to take off their [paramilitary] armbands.[31]

Human rights activists in the Magdalena Medio gathered a tremendous amount of anecdotal evidence linking the military to human rights abuses. This almost never led to prosecutions, however. In most cases, no crime scene investigations were undertaken, and no charges laid. This did not deter CREDHOS and other activists in the Magdalena Medio from gathering and registering information. Human rights work exposed the fine-grained details of daily life in a conflict zone, and how armed forces personnel were implicated in attacks on legitimate social activists.

The Massacre at La Rochela

During the 1989–1993 period, a number of important incidents in Barranca and the Magdalena Medio announced the intention of paramilitaries and the Colombian armed forces to suppress human rights activism. Some of these cases had an enormous impact in terms of clarifying relations between the military and paramilitary. The January 1989 massacre of the members of a government judicial commission at La Rochela was the subject of an international legal process led by Colombian human rights lawyers that lasted seventeen years, during which time thousands of pages of documents and testimony were collected.[32] In the end, a Colombian army general was accused of complicity in paramilitary crimes. La Rochela is of critical importance in terms of historical interpretations of the Colombian conflict, and the evolution of human rights work.

The judicial commission whose members were massacred at La Rochela was set up in response to pressure from grassroots human rights groups in the Magdalena Medio region and an Inter-American Court of Human Rights judgment ordering the Colombian state to look into illegal paramilitary activity in a rural area to the south of Barrancabermeja.[33] Following the disappearance of nineteen traveling merchants on October 3, 1987, along the Pan-American highway just south of Barranca, the Inter-American Court of Human Rights of the Organization of American States (OAS) ordered the Colombian government to undertake an investigation into paramilitary organizing in the region.[34] In December 1988 a commission was created by the Dirección de Instrucción Criminal (DIJIN), the investigative branch of the National Police, to look into crimes in the rural *municipios* of Bajo Simacota, Puerto Parra, and Cimitarra in the department of Santander and Puerto Boyacá in the department of Boyacá. The state's quick and positive response to the Inter-American Court judgment represented a potential breakthrough in terms of the effectiveness of the national justice system. The commission's job would be to interview public officials and local residents about the activities of paramilitary groups and report back to the inspector general's office.

The commissioners' work was troubled from the outset. The first judge assigned to coordinate the investigation, Camilo Navarro Velásquez from Bucaramanga, received death threats and quit.[35] By the end of December 1988, the replacement judges Mariela Morales and Pablo Beltrán Palomino were fed up with what they felt to be the noncooperation of Colombian army commanders in the region.[36] So they quickly made plans to undertake a visit to the Magdalena Medio to gather evidence. Apprehensive that the army might try to intimidate potential witnesses or otherwise hinder their work, the commissioners decided to proceed without notifying the Fourteenth Brigade in Puerto Berrío or the Second Division in Bucaramanga. They drove from Bucaramanga to Barrancabermeja on January 14. Over the next three days they collected testimonies in Barranca, in the nearby *municipio* of Puerto Parra, and made two brief reconnaissance trips to La Rochela. Seeking to delve deeper into the case, the commissioners planned to return to La Rochela the very next day. The evening of January 17, the night before she was killed, judge Mariela Morales called her husband to tell him that she felt nervous.[37]

The fifteen-person commission consisting of judges, lawyers, and other investigative staff set out for La Rochela from Barranca at 7:00 a.m. on January 18, 1989.[38] Arriving in the town of La Rochela just before 8:00 a.m., commission members proceeded to set up a temporary office inside the town police post and began taking testimony. But few local residents came forward to speak.

Three members of the commission, accompanied by the local police inspector, then decided to go to the neighboring village of Pueblo Nuevo to locate several other individuals they hoped would be willing to talk.[39] They were stopped en route by a group of armed, uniformed men claiming to be members of the 23rd Front of the FARC. The group's commander identified himself as "Comandante Ernesto." He was affable, pledged to cooperate in any way possible, and let them pass. Unnerved but undeterred, the commissioners continued on to Pueblo Nuevo, made some inquiries, and then returned La Rochela.

Soon afterward, a group of about forty armed men entered La Rochela and presented themselves to the commission as members of the FARC. Unbeknownst to the commissioners, this was turning into a gathering of some of the most important paramilitary commanders in Colombia. Within an hour a large SUV arrived, and several heavily armed men got out. One of them was Alfonso de Jesús Baquero, alias "El Negro Vladimir," one of the most notorious paramilitary commanders in Colombian history. He was not recognized by members of the commission, but something about his appearance was unsettling to them. He seemed too well dressed and was wearing too much jewelry to be a guerrilla fighter. It was now nearly noon, and the heat of midday was beginning to wear on everybody. One of the alleged FARC commanders announced that an army truck had been spotted on the road and insisted that the commission would have to leave the area. They took the members of the commission inside the police station and tied their hands behind their backs, explaining that they needed to pretend that the commission had been taken hostage in case they ran into authorities. The puzzled commission members were then loaded back into their vehicles and driven out of town, heading north on the Pan-American Highway. A few kilometers into the journey the convoy came to a stop by the side of the road.

The first shot was fired, followed by an all-out hail of bullets. The barrage lasted for nearly ten minutes. Twelve men and women were killed. Three men—Arturo Salgado Garzón, Manuel Libardo Díaz Navas, and Wilson Humberto Mantilla—survived by pretending to be dead. Díaz was shot several times, dragged from the truck, and left face down on the road. The assailants did not notice he was holding his breath. Several of the paramilitaries spray-painted "*Fuera el MAS—Fuera Paramilitares*" (MAS out—Paramilitaries out) on the trucks. Salgado, Díaz, and Mantilla waited in silence until they were certain that the armed group had left the area. They then found the keys in the ignition of one of the trucks and headed toward Barranca. But the truck quickly broke down, and they had to wait for help to come by. Salgado, the most seriously injured of the three, could not be moved. Díaz and Mantilla walked ahead and flagged down a passing tractor-trailer. They were taken to an army post, where they asked for assistance. Salgado was picked up several hours later, still alive.

In February 1989 government investigators from Barranca, Bucaramanga, and Bogotá confirmed that the perpetrators of the massacre had indeed been paramilitaries and not FARC guerrillas. It is now known that the massacre was carried out by paramilitaries under the command of Julio Rivera, also known as Julián Jaimes or "Comandante Ernesto," assisted by Alfonso de Jesús Baquero, alias "El Negro Vladimir." Julián Jaimes was a retired military police-man, originally from Barranca. Baquero was a former member of the FARC. Both men were well known to local army commanders and had been in touch with military informants in Barranca that same morning. Ramón Isaza Arango, sometimes described as the "oldest paramilitary in Colombia," also helped plan the massacre. Isaza Arango, born and raised in Antioquia, organized one of the very first private "self-defense" groups against the FARC in 1978. He led the self-proclaimed Autodefensas Campesinas del Magdalena Medio, which operated mainly in the area to the south of Barranca, until his arrest in 2005.

The story of the miscarriage of justice that ensued has been amply docu-mented by the 2010 publication of a book by the Historical Memory Group of Colombia's National Reparations and Reconciliation Commission.[40] The survivors, victims' families, lawyers, and low-ranking paramilitary and military members were scared silent, while the case was transferred to different juris-dictions multiple times within the country. Initially, however, there had been a few positive signs. Arrest warrants were issued for Julián Jaimes, Alfonso de Jesús Baquero, and fifteen other presumed paramilitaries. Nine were captured, including the two alleged masterminds. However, the trial was moved to a court in the faraway city of Pasto, in the department of Nariño.[41] On June 29, 1990, Jaimes and Baquero were found guilty of aggravated homicide and sentenced to thirty years in prison. Another eleven individuals were sentenced to between five and thirty years. Even as the first sentences were handed out, a reversal was being engineered. On November 14, 1990, the Tribunal Superior de Orden Público in Bogotá reduced or dropped most of the charges and sentences.

By their very existence, paramilitary groups obfuscated state responsibility for human rights abuses. It took two decades to officially clarify the events sur-rounding La Rochela. On May 11, 2007, the Inter-American Court of Human Rights held the Colombian state responsible for the La Rochela massacre. Years later it would be revealed that the massacre was planned in coordination with high-ranking Colombian army officers, including General Farouk Yanine Díaz, then commander of the Second Division in Bucaramanga. It was, in the words of one of the lawyers who represented the victims' families, "the first time that the state has been found guilty of collaborating in the murder of other agents of the state."[42] In the view of a disgruntled official who defended the government's case, "The entire Colombian judicial system is at risk of being replaced by the Inter-American Court."[43] The failure of the Colombian courts to effectively investigate and prosecute the massacre demonstrated that there was little political will in Bogotá to constrain paramilitarism, and little evidence to work with. Notwithstanding the hyperbole of the state being "replaced," this episode and its aftermath encouraged citizen-led efforts such as CREDHOS to take up the important work of human rights investigations at a time when judicial authorities were unable to do so.

Human Rights Spring

As the dirty war escalated in the late 1980s, Barranca's status as a center of labor, social, and civic movement organization grew. It was a period of forward-thinking creativity during which *barranqueños* integrated themselves more fully into national and international communities of human rights activism. There are three significant outcomes of this period in terms of the expansion of the horizons of human rights activism. First, longstanding local movements established their own intramural human rights committees, or embraced human rights as central to their ongoing work. Second, national organizations established human rights projects in Barranca, or initiated collaborations with local groups. Third, foreign groups began to develop ties of solidarity with Barranca-based human rights defenders.

Unions and social movements in the region contributed to the process of documentation and denunciation through their own channels. The oil workers' union set up its own human rights commission under the leadership of the Barranca community activist Ramón Rangel in 1989. The first National Association of Peasant Users (ANUC) publications to focus on violence from a human rights perspective, employing terms such as "impunity" and "dirty war," appeared in this period.[44] The Bogotá-based NGO Justice and Peace undertook pioneering monitoring work in the Magdalena Medio in the late 1980s, as did the Committee for Solidarity with Political Prisoners (CSPP) and the Latin American Institute for Alternative Legal Services (ILSA), maintaining contact with informants living in paramilitary-controlled areas.[45] In 1989 the United Nations Special Rapporteur on Extrajudicial, Summary or Arbitrary Executions visited Colombia for the first time, stopping in Bucaramanga, where UN officials met with peasants from San Vicente and oil workers from Barranca. Later on, the Colombian Office of the Andean Commission of Jurists also published reports on violence in the region.[46]

National activists drawn to Barranca learned valuable lessons in the politics and strategies of human rights protection. It was during this period that the Comité Ecuménico de Colombia—a national human rights organization known today as the Inter-ecclesial Commission for Justice and Peace, or simply Justicia y Paz—began working with displaced peasants in Barranca. The Refuge for Displaced Peasants, or Albergue para Campesinos Desplazados, was formally inaugurated by Barranca's Bishop Juan Francisco Sarasti on May 6, 1989.[47] The Albergue Campesino was the initiative of local representatives of the national peasant association Asociación Nacional de Usuarios Campesinos under the leadership of Ángel Tolosa and the Bogotá-based Comité Ecuménico under the leadership of Father Javier Giraldo, SJ.[48] With the support of the Catholic diocese of Barrancabermeja and the International Committee of the Red Cross, the Albergue Campesino was able to house dozens of families on short-term bases and occasionally provide aid to *campesinos* returning to areas from which they had been displaced.[49] The Albergue Campesino also received support from local union and social movements, including CREDHOS, the USO, the Barranca municipal council, and the department of Santander teachers' union.

Many of the first peasants to make use of the shelter were community leaders from areas affected by the spread of paramilitarism into upland Santander and rural municipalities north along the Magdalena River.[50] Flor Castro—a former CREDHOS member who worked closely with the Albergue Campesino—recalls that many of the people who came to stay at the shelter were extremely vulnerable: "It was mainly children and mothers, pregnant women, or widows, sadly. I remember that one week something like ten babies were born. It was impressive. The people who went to Barranca were the neediest. But in the midst of this, the idea of Father Javier Giraldo was to strengthen resistance movements."[51] Those *campesinos* who sought shelter in the Albergue Campesino were often accused by the army and the paramilitaries of being subversives, and shelter staff members were subject to threats and acts of intimidation.[52] To counteract these pressures, the Albergue Campesino relied on the support of the local civic-popular movement, and was one the first groups to help bridge the local, national, and international spheres of human rights action.

The basic principles of frontline protection for displaced people, of religious and international accompaniment, and of providing support for activist voices in the midst of armed conflict were progressive strategies that inspired more initiatives along these same lines. The long-term vision of the Comité

Ecuménico was to create a network of *albergues* or shelters for displaced people in different regions of Colombia. They did not consider the *albergue* to be a humanitarian project but rather a way of building political support for *campesino* organizations while denouncing the role of the armed forces in causing displacement in the Magdalena Medio. The idea of setting up a transnational human rights organization in a poor *barrio* of the city was an important innovation. The Albergue Campesino was set up along the main road in the furthest southeastern corner of Barranca, in one of the areas of most recent settlement by displaced peasants and other squatters. The facility consisted of one main building with several large rooms for communal sleeping and a fenced-in backyard. The Albergue Campesino's daily work was managed by a small group of Catholic nuns and a team of mostly young volunteers from Bogotá. Priests and lay workers from overseas connected to the Comité Ecuménico also spent periods of time living in the refuge. The importance of working in coalition with *campesino* groups, the Catholic Church, and undertaking human rights work as a form of social activism were all reinforced during this period. Together the *albergue* and CREDHOS attracted international attention.

National and international human rights organizations began organizing fact-finding trips to Barranca. North American and European trade union and church-based groups engaged in solidarity and human rights advocacy work on Central America began to look seriously at Colombia. The Toronto-based Inter-Church Committee for Human Rights in Latin America traveled to Barranca for the first time in 1989, initiating a relationship with the city's popular movements that would last two decades. One Bogotá-based social activist recalls working as a guide and translator for international visitors to Barranca. She recounts how Barranca was represented, and viewed, as a beacon of resistance:

> The myth was built in my mind about Red Barranca, but in a good way. I saw it as a place where popular organizations on the ground had really taken on political organizing in an important way. . . . There was an importance given to the civic organizing that took place in the *comunas* of Barranca as something to be followed, as something to be looked up to, as something that was significant. . . . It wasn't all myth, there were some very real things happening that were examples for the rest of the country, important examples. . . . Certainly Barranca was held up as a possibility. Look at what they are doing![53]

Through these experiences, outside visitors formed their first concrete opinions about the problem of paramilitarism in the country, and how it could be addressed through community-based actions.

Barranca would garner more and more international attention as violence increased in the early 1990s. At the invitation of the Barranca mayor and CREDHOS associate Jorge Gómez Villamizar, the Inter-American Commission on Human Rights visited the city in July 1992. It was the commission's first visit to Colombia since 1984 and came at a time when violence in the country was beginning to spiral. CREDHOS's president Jorge Gómez Lizarazo declared: "It is clear that the situation of human rights violations in our region has already transcended geographic borders."[54] In October 1994 Peace Brigades International, a human rights organization that provides unarmed protective accompaniment to social activists in conflict areas, arrived in Barranca at the joint request of CREDHOS and the Albergue Campesino. When a half-dozen volunteers from Spain, Belgium, and the United States began their work of accompaniment in Barranca, CREDHOS members were being protected by armed bodyguards paid for and licensed by the Colombian National Police. As a precondition stipulated by Peace Brigades, CREDHOS made the "remarkable" decision to renounce the use of armed bodyguards. In an interview conducted in 1995, CREDHOS's second president, Osiris Bayter, commented: "We have always told the government . . . that human rights work is incompatible with weapons; much less so with having them right in your office, where people would come, full of fear, to lodge their complaints and testimonies about abuses. After awhile the people stopped coming—seeing the police there and we had to start going to their houses to take testimony."[55] CREDHOS did not close its offices; neither did the Organización Femenina Popular, the Coordinadora Popular, or the Unión Sindical Obrera. As described in the next chapter, these organizations would nonetheless be fundamentally transformed by the violence. The adaptation of the civic-popular movement to the realities of living and working under constant threat included a greater reliance on international solidarity.

The Albergue Campesino closed its doors in 1996 following a process of internal reflection, and consultations with its Support Committee composed of CREDHOS, the USO, and various other groups. Flor Castro comments: "It was a pilot experience. That has been recognized. I left the country when the *albergue* was still open. I met up with Javier Giraldo in Toronto and I remember him telling me with tears in his eyes that they had been forced to close the *albergue*."[56] The Albergue Campesino had been struggling for several years. Staff and volunteers attributed a decline in usage of the facility by *campesinos* to several related factors: the diminished influence of *campesino* groups in the countryside due to paramilitary repression, harassment of the Albergue Campesino by the military and police, differences of opinion among its coordinators, and changing patterns of displacement in the region.

Increasingly, *campesinos* were seeking permanent refuge in the *barrios* of the city rather than temporary asylum. Threatened individuals visiting Barranca often elected to stay with extended family and neighbors from back home.[57]

The history of the transnational human rights projects that flourished in Barranca in the late 1980s and early 1990s has major implications for understanding the growth of human rights work elsewhere in Colombia. Peace Brigades International would begin work in the banana-producing frontier region of Urabá alongside Justicia y Paz in 1998, based in large part on lessons learned during the Albergue Campesino experience. The relationship between Peace Brigades and Barrancabermeja has endured for more than twenty years, inspiring other international organizations to take up similar work. The Colectivo de Abogados would continue to collaborate with CREDHOS for years to come. But the intensity of the conflict in Barranca and the Magdalena Medio would also force many organizations to make accommodations over time, retreating when necessary.

Attacking CREDHOS

The murder of the CREDHOS secretary Blanca Cecilia Valero in 1992 was a disturbing reminder that nobody was safe from the backlash of paramilitary terror. Valero was shot at 6:00 p.m. on the street in front of the CREDHOS office on January 29, 1992. CREDHOS's office was located at the busiest intersection in the city, and the streets were crowded with rush-hour traffic. Blanca Valero had served as the organization's secretary since the beginning and had previously worked as a secretary in the law office of Jorge Gómez Lizarazo, now CREDHOS's headquarters. Of the six CREDHOS staff members assassinated between 1991 and 1992, Valero's death remains the most discussed and debated. One account of the killing suggests that Valero was the victim of mistaken identity, that the bullets were intended for Jael Quiroga. Another version suggests that she was killed to send a message to her boss. A number of other CREDHOS associates have been killed over the years, as recently as 2005. In each case the victim's association with CREDHOS was a major factor in his or her death. But as with the killing of Sandra Rondón in 1987, Valero was perceived by the general public as an innocent bystander. It even garnered international attention.

On March 1, 1992, the *New York Times* declared: "Violence Takes Over a Colombian City." Written in response to the Blanca Valero murder, the article accurately described the unique combination of social and political conflict in Barrancabermeja in the early 1990s. Through the first two months of 1992 there had been an average of ten conflict-related murders per week in the city.[58] That represented a 33 percent increase from the previous year, and a rate several times the national average. Barranca was described by the *New York Times* as a gritty industrial town with a long history of left-wing political organizing. The article pointed out that all of Colombia's major armed actors were present in the city of Barranca, with one notable exception. Drug traffickers, the articles stated, were simply not a major presence in Barranca. This was no small detail in the heyday of the drug kingpin Pablo Escobar, then the world's most famous fugitive. The *New York Times* observed that Barranca's large poor population, mainly peasants displaced from the countryside by political violence, had been "denied the economic benefits" of oil.[59] Bitterness toward the state, the article concluded, strengthened the hand of the guerrillas in Barranca and across Colombia.

The war against human rights activists in Barrancabermeja in the late 1980s and early 1990s is central to interpretations of the Colombian conflict, the role of the state, the role of paramilitary forces, and relations among them. In the late 1980s in Barranca there emerged a model of paramilitarism that can best be described as a state-backed form of clandestine counterinsurgency. The Barranca model of paramilitarism depended upon the direct participation of members of the Colombian armed forces and national police. The Colombian security forces typically hired assassins, or *sicarios*, who dressed in civilian clothes, traveled by motorcycle, and carried out surgical strikes in broad daylight. These were not exactly the same as the paramilitaries of the rural Magdalena Medio, who worked in larger groups, carried high-powered automatic weapons, wore uniforms, and traveled by truck, car, or boat. The *sicariato* phenomenon is best known, and most mythologized, in the case of Medellín, where young gunmen for hire with no political allegiances and little training are contracted by drug lords or private paramilitary groups for shockingly small sums of money.[60] The *sicarios* who operated in Barranca came out of these same networks and had a similar modus operandi, but they were contracted by local security forces.

Human rights work in Barrancabermeja entailed great risks, and members of CREDHOS came under direct fire from the Colombian military. Between 1989 and 1992 six CREDHOS staff members were killed. In 1993 five key CREDHOS representatives fled the country to escape the pressure cooker that Barranca had become. Among those exiled were CREDHOS cofounders Jorge Gómez Lizarazo, Jael Quiroga, and Rafael Gómez, as well as newcomer Osiris Bayter. Jorge Gómez Lizarazo moved to Central America, during which time he worked on behalf of the United Nations. Jael Quiroga and Rafael Gómez moved to Bogotá, where they established a new human rights organization named Reiniciar, literally "begin again." Osiris Bayter fled to Chile for a few months but returned to Barranca to lead CREDHOS.

The very first of the attacks on CREDHOS members was understood in the context of a long war on leftist and progressive forces in Barranca. The year 1991 began with the murders of Patriotic Union city councillors in Barranca and nearby Yondó.[61] The first two killings of CREHDOS members took place just a few weeks later. Álvaro Bustos Castro was killed on February 27, 1991, in Barrio Las Granjas in the city's poor northeast district by a single gunshot to the head. Bustos Castro was a member of the Patriotic Union who had been hired by CREDHOS as a bodyguard just one month prior to his death. Bustos Castro's family initially told the press that they were unaware of any threats against him, but it would later surface that he had indeed been the target of an anonymous death threat.[62] The next CREDHOS victim was José Humberto Hernández Gavanzo, a retired oil worker who had been active with USO, ANUC, and CREDHOS. Hernández was shot in the back four times at close range on March 19, 1991, in Barrio el Paraíso, where he lived with his wife and three children.[63] In a tribute to the fifty-six-year-old veteran of the strikes of the 1970s, CREDHOS wrote: "Pain . . . yes, we give thanks that it exists. Pain does not allow us to forget, forgetting in these circumstances of violence, with so many deaths, is unforgiveable. . . . With your poet's laugh, with your philosophy born out of living for the moment, we hope that wherever you are, you will toast with us the drink of the Gods."[64] CREDHOS explicitly drew upon the themes of defiance, of the lust for life that had been embodied by the slain union and political leaders of the previous decade. It was the way in which certain figures had been celebrated in the past, and remained part of a culture of audacity among Barranca's popular leaders.

In 1992 clandestine agents working for the Colombian Navy carried out sixty-eight political murders in Barrancabermeja.[65] The case of the "07" naval intelligence network lays bare the close relationship that has always existed between paramilitaries and Colombian security forces in Barranca. It also demonstrates the double challenge that human rights defenders have faced in Colombia: that of investigating the links between clandestine and regular armed forces, while simultaneously trying to evade personal attacks. In 1991 the Colombian Defense Ministry signed Order 200-05/91, authorizing the creation of civilian intelligence networks to monitor the activities of suspected guerrillas and guerrilla sympathizers. Ostensibly, the legislation was meant to facilitate intelligence gathering. In practice, it allowed junior and midlevel security forces personnel to take advantage of their existing relationships with paramilitaries.[66] One former Colombian marine explained that 700,000 pesos would be withdrawn from a special fund, ostensibly to be paid out to an informant, but that 600,000 pesos of the total would be transferred to assassins.[67] The injection of resources into Barranca increased the *sicario* phenomenon beyond previous levels. The results were devastating, but incredibly difficult to investigate, let alone stop.

On the day Blanca Valero was killed, January 29, 1992, all of the highest-ranking military officials in the region were in Barranca attending a special meeting convened by the departmental government of Santander. CREDHOS's president Jorge Gómez Lizarazo had just returned from a three-month stay in Washington, DC, a few days before. He was living in the United States capital on a scholarship with the Inter-American Commission on Human Rights of the Organization of American States. While in Washington, he had been recognized by the Institute for Policy Studies with the Letelier-Moffitt Human Rights Award.[68] Gómez Lizarazo took advantage of his stay to undertake lobbying work on Capitol Hill with the Washington Office on Latin America (WOLA), a coalition of civil society organizations that carries out research and advocacy on U.S. foreign policy toward Latin America.[69] It was intended as a break from the near constant pressure to which he was subject back home. He returned to Barranca to find that the situation had deteriorated.

According to the most well-known version of events, Blanca Valero was the victim of mistaken identity. It was a Wednesday evening, about 6:30 p.m., and the CREDHOS office was still busy. Just past 6:00 p.m. Jael Quiroga had called for a taxi and spent a few moments finishing up some paperwork. Nothing unusual whatsoever. Except that Quiroga did not finish her work on time and asked Blanca Valero to cancel the taxi. Valero asked if she could take the taxi herself, so she could get home in time to prepare dinner for her family. Valero and another colleague left the office and descended the short, unlit staircase to the street below. Halfway down, Valero realized she had to go back upstairs to leave behind a package that she had been carrying around in her bag. Worried about missing the taxi, she asked her colleague to run back up to the office for her. Valero reached the street, where she was shot by a gunman riding on the back of a motorcycle. Eyewitnesses heard Valero shout, "It's not me!" before falling to the pavement.[70] The high-pitched drone of the motorcycle's two-stroke engine quickly faded as the assailants weaved their way through the late rush-hour traffic.

Not unlike the killing of Sandra Rondón, the murder of CREDHOS's secretary inspired a strong public outcry in Barranca. Blanca Cecilia Valero's husband did not recall his wife ever receiving a death threat. Even though she worked for CREDHOS, Valero did not consider herself to be an activist. Still, her association with the human rights group was an important factor in how forcefully her death would be denounced. The day after Valero was killed, a *paro cívico* was organized in her memory that lasted thirty-six hours. The oil workers' union shut down the refinery, and thousands of people took to the streets. Guerrillas set fire to two city buses and sabotaged an oil pipeline on the outskirts of town.[71] The day following the start of the protests, a letter in support of CREDHOS signed by ten members of the U.S. Senate was sent to the Colombian president César Gaviria Trujillo.[72] On February 5, just one week after the murder, the Inter-American Commission on Human Rights wrote to the Colombian foreign minister Nohemí Sanín to ask that emergency "precautionary measures" be taken to protect the life of the CREDHOS president Jorge Gómez Lizarazo. Gómez Lizarazo was described by the Inter-American Commission as having "received constant and serious death threats."[73]

The fact of international involvement, particularly from the United States and the OAS, was a significant development. Blanca Valero's murder was carried out the day after the publication of an opinion piece by Jorge Gómez Lizarazo in the *New York Times* in which the CREDHOS president linked U.S. military assistance to Colombia with an upsurge in political violence in the Magdalena Medio. In the article, Gómez Lizarazo asked the U.S. Congress to hold hearings on Colombia.[74] He argued that the escalation of paramilitarism should give U.S. lawmakers cause to halt the Andean Regional Initiative: "The U.S. must bear some responsibility for this situation. From 1988 to 1991, its military aid to Colombia increased sevenfold. . . . The main victims of Government and Government-supported military actions are not traffickers but political opposition figures, community activists, trade union leaders and human rights workers."[75] Gómez Lizarazo argued that the Colombian military was working with illegal paramilitaries and drug traffickers, "forcing human rights activists to abandon their regions and try to do their work from Bogotá or abroad."[76] His words would turn out to be prescient.

Paramilitary assassins paid by the Colombian Navy murdered another three members of CREDHOS in 1992. Ismael Jaimes was shot and killed on May 6, 1992, in the central Barrio Torcoroma, moments after dropping off his two small children at a daycare center. Thirty-eight years old at the time of his death, Jaimes was a city councillor, a member of the Patriotic Union, and the publisher of the influential local weekly newspaper *La Opinión del Magdalena Medio*. His funeral attracted hundreds of mourners, including dozens of the city's most prominent journalists, social movement activists, representatives of the Chamber of Commerce, and municipal government. Presidential Peace Commissioner Horacio Serpa Uribe even made the trip from Bogotá.[77] To commemorate the legacy of Ismael Jaimes, Barranca's four main radio stations produced a day-long coordinated simulcast of tributes to Jaimes and commentary on the situation in Barranca.[78] A former naval intelligence official linked to a series of political killings in Barrancabermeja later claimed that Jaimes was killed because of his work as a journalist uncovering abuses committed by state forces.[79]

Two more CREDHOS members were killed in May and June. Julio César Berrío was shot five times at close range on the street in central Barranca on June 25, 1992. Hired as a bodyguard by Jorge Gómez Lizarazo, Berrío had begun to take on investigative work as well and was very much identified as a member of CREDHOS.[80] Following Berrío's death, Jorge Gómez accused the Colombian government of deliberately trying to silence CREDHOS: "It looks like the goal is to throw us out of the Magdalena Medio."[81] Ligia Patricia Córtez Colmenares, the coordinator of CREDHOS's education program, was one of three people killed in a massacre at a popular restaurant on July 30, 1992. ANUC activist and coordinator of Barranca's recently opened Albergue Campesino, René Tavera Sosa, and the president of the San Silvestre Transportation Workers Union, Parmenio Ruíz Suárez, were the other two victims. At 11:30 a.m. the three colleagues were sitting together in Restaurante La Shannon when two men drove up on a motorcycle.[82] The assailants were recognized by eyewitnesses.[83] Ancizar Castaño Buitrago, alias "Cachetes," one of the most prolific assassins utilized by naval intelligence in Barranca, is said to have been the gunman in the killings of both Ligia Patricia Córtez and Ismael Jaimes.[84]

The shift to human rights activism was a response to extreme and confusing circumstances. It was a "state of emergency" declared by the city's social movements. Barranca social movements responded to the La Shannon massacre with a renewed cycle of street protests, work stoppages, and public denunciations made by CREDHOS through declarations to the press and communiqués sent to the national government. While not a full *paro cívico*, the protests organized by the unions, transport workers, and the Coordinadora Popular, including CREDHOS, prompted the cancellation of public school classes, bus services, and most commercial activities for a twenty-four-hour period. In addition to the city's social movements, the Barranca Chamber of Commerce, the Committee for Business Associations, and mainstream political parties publicly denounced the massacre through the press. The Coordinadora Popular blamed the massacre on the army. In response, the commander of the Nueva Granada Battalion, Colonel Fabio Luis García Chávez, suggested that the massacre was a guerrilla operation intended to look like a covert army or paramilitary operation. García claimed that the FARC and ELN were carrying out clandestine operations "to disturb public order and then blame the Armed Forces."[85] At the time, there were numerous cases denounced by CREDHOS of civilians killed by the armed forces and then either dressed in guerrilla uniforms or simply claimed by the army as enemy soldiers killed in combat. The investigations into the La Shannon case carried out by local investigators with the attorney general's office produced several eyewitness statements implicating army soldiers directly in the massacre, but no prosecutions.[86]

The initial response of Barranca's social movements to the war on human rights activists was to rally together. CREDHOS held its Third General Assembly in a conference hall on the top floor of the Hotel Bachué in downtown Barranca on the evening of June 17, 1993. The meeting began with a moment of silence for the members of CREDHOS who had been killed in recent years. The CREDHOS treasurer Evangelina Marín, a teacher and trade union activist, took a few moments to update the membership roll. She recounted how 7 members of CREDHOS had been killed, and 10 had left the city. A total of 115 of the 160 remaining individual associates retained their voting rights. At a meeting of the board of directors held the day before, an additional 141 people had submitted their membership applications. Another 78 people applied to join CREDHOS simply by showing up for the general assembly. In total, in June 1993, CREDHOS was composed of 379 members. In spite of, or perhaps because of, all of the fear surrounding CREDHOS, the organization had more than doubled in size in the space of two years. As the *Vanguardia Liberal* reported, CREDHOS members declared their intentions to "open the doors" and "achieve the direct participation of many civic organizations."[87] In order to respond to this greater interest, the general assembly voted to increase the number of people on the board of directors from 10 to 17. The board of directors included representatives of all of the major civil society organizations in the city. The general assembly also named representatives of CREDHOS based in the *municipios* of Sabana de Torres, Yondó, Puerto Wilches, and San Pablo. And they elected Osiris Bayter, a young activist born and raised in the northeastern neighborhoods of Barranca, as their new president. The group that would endeavor to bring CREDHOS forward included a strong contingent of teachers, oil workers, community organizers, municipal officials, lawyers, and Catholic priests.[88]

The crisis in Barrancabermeja was the subject of dozens of front-page news stories in Bogotá. This did not escape the attention of Colombia's Liberal president César Gaviria Trujillo (1990–1994). Gaviria visited the city three times while in office, on the last occasion declaring his intention to attend to the city's continuing social and political crises through major public investments. One week after the CREDHOS General Assembly, Gaviria announced a special development plan for the department of Santander aimed at addressing fundamental inequalities and quelling political violence.[89] Gaviria visited Barranca on July 9, 1993, to formally declare that 65 billion pesos would be invested in schools, health care, roads, water, sanitation, and a number of economic development projects, including a fish farm. While the plan was slated to cover all of Santander, the vast majority of the funds were going to be invested in the Magdalena Medio over an eighteen-month period. But even as Gaviria made the announcement, his government was in crisis due to escalating *narco* violence. The killing of Pablo Escobar in December 1993 would improve Gaviria's standing and assure his post-politics career as an international statesman. The Liberal Party presidential candidate Ernesto Samper Pizano then eked out a victory in the May 1994 elections. One year later, Gaviria's term as president was over, he was in Washington, DC, working as Secretary General of the Organization of American States, and none of the money promised to the Magdalena Medio had been spent.[90]

The violent repression to which rural residents of the Magdalena Medio had been subjected was now a mainly urban phenomenon. Of the 512 homicides reported by CREDHOS in 1991 for the Magdalena Medio region as a whole, 365 were committed in Barranca.[91] This was the same year that a new constitution was approved through an innovative process of national consultation.[92] But the enhanced status that human rights enjoyed in Colombia did not translate into improved protection of civilian populations. In a report published at the time, CREDHOS wrote: "Community leaders, lawyers, journalists, politicians from all parties and people who are critical of the state and the government in power, have all now become targets."[93] The daily newspaper *El Tiempo* reported frequently on events in Barranca, including a dozen or more articles every year about guerrilla actions. During this period, military and paramilitary actions dwarfed those of the guerrillas. However, there were now three guerrilla groups present in the city: the ELN, FARC, and the Maoist Ejército Popular de Liberación (EPL). Citing reports from confidential informants, army and National Police spokespeople claimed that a bloody battle between insurgent forces for control of the city's *barrios orientales* was underway.[94] It was popularly believed that urban *milicianos* lacked the training and discipline of the more prestigious fighters working in the *sierra*, or hills.[95] Separating fact from rumor and propaganda was practically impossible. Whatever the case, the city was now a theater of armed conflict.

The Changing Nature of Popular Protest

In her 1989 study of Barranca's municipal politics, María Emma Wills observes that the *paros cívicos por la vida* lacked the cohesiveness of past struggles. *Paros cívicos* were no longer locomotives of social movement organization, but "irregular and sudden explosions of grief that do not transcend the immediate moment."[96] The volatile nature of social protest in Barranca during the late 1980s was a reflection of the increase in political violence in the city. While the basic forms of protest did not change, the motives for *paro cívicos* were substantially different. Traditional struggles for social services and infrastructure were eclipsed by the struggle for basic human rights. And while there were examples of *paro civicos* that conformed to the disciplined standard that the Coordinadora Popular had established by 1983, the sheer number of protests through the mid-1990s was overwhelming.

There also occurred in this period a changing of the guard in Barranca's civic-popular movement and a trend away from the grassroots civil protest organizing of the 1970s and 1980s. The closure or retreat of important activist projects in the late 1980s and early 1990s, such as the Frente Amplio del Magdalena Medio, the Albergue Campesino, the Barranca office of the Asociación Nacional de Usuarios Campesinos, and the Coordinadora Campesina del Magdalena Medio represented a serious challenge to the future of popular movement organizing. The role of the Unión Sindical Obrera as an agent of social change had also declined. The oil workers' union had not gone out on strike since 1981. Between January 1988 and December 1993, at least eighty-seven USO members were murdered. A number of individual activists decided to leave the city around the same time. The departure from Barranca of Father Eduardo Díaz due to death threats was particularly hard to accept. As leader of the Pastoral Social, his exile to Vancouver left a serious vacuum. Barranca's Pastoral Social would continue to play an important role in local social movement organizing, thanks in large part to the leadership of Father Nel Beltrán. In 1987 CREDHOS was established, but it too lost its original leadership group to political repression. In June 1993 gunmen fired on a car carrying Jorge Gómez Lizarazo and two other members of CREDHOS as they made their way back from investigating a massacre.[97] Gómez Lizarazo left Colombia soon afterward. One of the positive developments of the time was the decision by Organización Femenina Popular organizers to break away from the Pastoral Social, establishing in 1987 the basis for what would become Colombia's most celebrated and largest grassroots women's movement. But on the whole, the armed conflict was escalating, and the civic-popular movement appeared to be in decline.

The "civic" character of the *paro cívico* was undermined by the process of militarization of the city. Invariably, *paros cívicos* prompted the mobilization of riot police, the army, and the guerrillas. Photos of armor-clad policemen, tanks, masked youth, and billowing black smoke appeared in the national press. Toward the middle of the 1990s guerrilla-imposed *paros armados* became common and *paros cívicos* increasingly rare. Rafael Gómez, a former leader of the oil workers' union and CREDHOS founder, observed:

> The people participating in the *paros cívicos* got scared, I think. They got scared. People went out into the streets to fight for water, electricity, whatever, but it was not their intention to become guerrillas, that was a negative. The *paro cívico* was supposed to be a popular struggle. In the heat of the moment, in the heat of the struggle, people took out guns . . . so people stopped coming out. Imagine a *paro cívico* near the As de Copas! Sometimes the street would fill up with people all the way to the USO. It was massive. People would go to the railroad crossing, guarding the barricades. Even at 2:00 or 3:00 in the morning there were people, but later on there would be shots fired, gunfights, military confrontations, and the people went home. People wanted to show that the problems were serious, but not everyone wanted to trade shots with the army.[98]

The tactics employed by the civic-popular movement in the carrying out of *paros cívicos* would be borrowed by the guerrillas. Guerrilla members would begin by contacting local radio stations, distributing pamphlets, or simply spreading the word among friends. The official start to the *paro armado* would often be announced with the torching of a city bus. Flames rising into the air would let everyone know that the *paro armado* was underway. As Francisco Campos stated: "The guerrillas started to take advantage of the spaces created by the Coordinadora Popular de Barrancabermeja and they started to organize what they called *paros armados*. That absolutely killed civic protest."[99]

Conclusion

The 1989 La Rochela massacre was a brazenly orchestrated attempt to frustrate investigations into joint military-paramilitary crimes. Understanding the circumstances surrounding the massacre can provide us with important insights into the impact of paramilitarism, both on the victims and on the Colombian justice system. In the wake of La Rochela, human rights activists in the Magdalena Medio region knew that they would have to carry out their work without a safety net. Over the next two decades, hundreds of Colombian activists and justice officials would be threatened, forced into exile, or killed. Attacks on social activism gave further impetus to human rights.

Events in Barranca reflected continued paradoxical national trends toward the spread of paramilitarism, on the one hand, and formal recognition of human rights, on the other. The U.S. government was already making policy decisions that responded to the complexities of Colombia's human rights problem, although they did not acknowledge as much. The rising tide of paramilitarism had not stopped U.S. congressional approval of President George H. W. Bush's "Andean Regional Initiative" in 1989, which included hundreds of millions of dollars in assistance to the Colombian National Police.[100] However, the money was directed to the National Police because the United States did not want to be perceived as supporting a progressively more shadowy counterinsurgency effort led by the Colombian armed forces. In order to sell the deal, the U.S. government needed a hero to step forward, who came in the form of the National Police chief General Rosso José Serrano.[101] That same year, the Colombian president Virgilio Barco signed Decree 815 formally banning the formation of "self-defense" or paramilitary groups. Barco also created a task force to combat paramilitaries, formally designated the "Advisory and coordinating commission of actions against death squads, gangs of assassins or self-defense or private justice groups, inaccurately referred to as paramilitaries."[102] It was during this period that the Colombian Supreme Court struck down the law that allowed for civilians to be prosecuted by military courts. In its ruling the Supreme Court also stipulated that soldiers who committed crimes "outside of military service" be tried by civilian courts.[103] Despite these legal advances, the bloodletting continued. In 1990 the Colombian army created its first mobile brigades for counterinsurgency purposes, two of which were deployed to the Magdalena Medio.[104]

Barrancabermeja's human rights movement emerged out of the tension between urban, rural, and transnational activism. CREDHOS was attacked both because it sought to expose human rights violators and because it represented an attempt by Barranca-based popular movements to advance an agenda of social change in defiance of military and paramilitary pressure. This deadly conflict between CREDHOS and the Colombian military is emblematic of a larger struggle over the meaning and applications of human rights in Colombia. The work of these early human rights defenders informed the way in which human rights struggles around Colombia were waged, and the way in which transnational activism for human rights in Colombia developed. Colombia became the focus of attention of international human rights advocacy in Latin America during the next decade, particularly in response to the growth of United States military aid. The challenge for Barranca activists would be to maintain the spirit of the civic-popular movement, despite the constant barrage of attacks against popular leaders.

In the late 1980s human rights became the language of a new generation of social activists who sought to transform Colombian society through nonviolent means. In Colombia there exists an interrelated set of conflicts involving various armed actors. By taking up the cause of human rights, social movements highlighted the fact that the majority of the victims of political violence in Colombia were in fact noncombatants. While this revelation was an extraordinary achievement, key human rights "truths" in Colombia, such as the complicity of the Colombian military with paramilitarism, would remain the subject of incendiary debates. The same could be said of the role of the guerrilla. As explored in greater depth in the next chapter, paramilitary violence provoked guerrilla violence. As the guerrillas fought to maintain their influence within the city, atrocities were committed on all sides. This would become the next major challenge of the city's human rights movement. As Winifred Tate writes: "human rights activism is an effort to bring certain public secrets into the public transcript, to make what is known but denied part of the general discussions about the nature and cause of violence and possible solutions."[105]

7

Social Movements Respond to Catastrophic Change

> People in this city think they live in the center of the universe. Many people say that peace in Colombia begins with the Magdalena Medio, begins with Barranca. That allows us to feel messianic, to build social processes, to crystallize our ideas. This messianic attitude has allowed us to dream in Barrancabermeja. Our life experiences, of solidarity, of liberation, of irreverence . . . these experiences of building a social network . . . these allow us to imagine the utopias and the proposals that we are advancing today.
>
> Régulo Madero, human rights activist, 2006[1]

La Toma de Barrancabermeja

Right wing paramilitary groups displaced the guerrillas from Barrancabermeja in late 2000 and soon came to dominate economic and political life in the city. In the first decade of the twenty-first century, paramilitaries across Colombia achieved official recognition of their hegemony: they received clemency from the government of Álvaro Uribe Vélez through a process of demobilization.[2] President Uribe's Justice and Peace Law of 2005 offered reduced sentences for paramilitary commanders and immunity from prosecution for rank-and-file fighters. Some officially demobilized paramilitaries in Barranca restructured to carry on the work of political repression and now use names such as the "Black Eagles" that evoke the specter of the death squads that operated in Colombia during La Violencia.[3] One group of demobilized *paras* banded together with ex-guerrilla *milicianos* in new criminal organizations that deal in drugs and contraband gasoline.[4] Another group even established an NGO called Seeds for Peace, which seeks to speak on behalf of victims of the conflict.[5] The adjustment for Barranca's human rights activists has been quite literally overwhelming.

Human rights defenders would continue to face an existential threat. There are a few incontrovertible facts worth reviewing, in order to properly understand the impact of the violence experienced during the final siege of Barrancabermeja by paramilitary forces. The research institute CINEP tallied more than three hundred death threats made against individuals or groups in Barrancabermeja between 2001 and 2012. According to the national government's central planning office, nearly 23,000 people were forcibly displaced from Barranca between 1998 and 2010 (including 5,967 in 2001 alone).[6] Formerly a haven for activists, Barranca was now a source of internally displaced persons. Approximately 97 percent of all of the acts of political violence committed in the *municipio* since 2000 can be attributed either to paramilitary groups or to state security forces. Of the more than one thousand homicides, death threats, disappearances, and other human rights violations counted by CINEP, a mere twenty-seven were committed by insurgent groups.[7] The decline in insurgent violence since 2000 corroborates the fact that the ELN and the FARC have withdrawn militarily from Barranca. Human rights activists would persevere through a reassessment of the political conjuncture.

In many respects, Barrancabermeja today barely recalls the city described in the preceding chapters. There is no monument to the victims. One of the only reminders of the period of violence is a cairn just outside the central market that bears the name of murdered CREDHOS secretary Blanca Valero. It is easily overlooked, and mostly is. The municipal council of Barranca officially renamed the city's main commercial street Avenida Leonardo Posada on the first anniversary of Posada's murder in 1987, although no signs were actually posted, and the gesture is forgotten. The plaza named after the rebel priest Camilo Torres Restrepo is known to cab drivers and people of a certain age as *el descabezado*, or "the headless man," after the fact that vandals twice removed the bust with blasts of dynamite. Yet even the facetious memory of Barranca's former status as a hotbed of radicalism is at risk. In 2006 the metal plaque on the base of the bust of Camilo Torres was removed, temporarily leaving no evidence of the park's origins. Even the old municipal graveyard, a constant, if neglected, reminder of the pain of the past, was relocated in 2004 to the outskirts of town, displacing from public view the graves of martyrs to the city's activist history. Public art has been erected elsewhere, including ironwork iguanas, caimans, and armadillos, and a statue of the Yareguíes cacique Pipatón. But there are no memorials to recent history.

This chapter explores the social memories of human rights activism in Barrancabermeja in the context of great upheaval. Between 1998 and 2002 Barrancabermeja endured a *limpieza política*, a political cleansing. By some estimates, more than one thousand people were killed in the city and surrounding area during that period.[8] In Michael Taussig's book *Law in a Lawless Land: Diary of a Limpieza*, we see through the eyes of a concerned outside observer the process by which paramilitaries lay siege to a town in the Valle de Cauca.[9] Confusion, dread, resentment, and accommodation are all dynamic forces in Taussig's narrative, as they are in activists' accounts of the *toma de Barranca*. The recent history of Barrancabermeja allows us to observe how human rights defenders working in conflict zones adapt to catastrophic shifts in the balance of power. Armed groups demonstrate that they are capable of adopting new strategies of repression and subterfuge in response to social and political change, even reinventing themselves. Are human rights defenders as flexible? How are the memories of past social movement struggles impacted by the paramilitary occupation and its attendant pressures? What is the relationship between historical memory and social movement responses to current events? In this chapter I provide an overview of the main events and developments in the ongoing struggle for Barrancabermeja since 1998.

Not simply was Barrancabermeja the most violent city in Colombia from 1998 to 2002, but it also experienced a profound political transformation during that time. The new reality of paramilitary dominance that began in 2001 has caused many activists to reflect on the losses suffered during one of Latin America's longest and bloodiest dirty wars. In my interviews with social movement leaders conducted in 2005–2007, many people relived the circumstances that gave rise to the crisis and asked tough questions about the way in which events unfolded. Our conversations were pulled time and again into the present, as we sought to make sense of the takeover of the city by paramilitary forces. How could we avoid it? Determined to renew the city's social movements, local activists asserted that they will have to learn from the past and rethink their expectations. First-person accounts give us valuable insight into the possibilities and limitations of human rights organizing in this conflict zone. It is a way of accessing the hidden transcript, not just of resistance, but also of disillusionment.[10] Through these interviews, we are witness to a process of coming to terms with loss of friends and colleagues, and of long-held certainties.

Barranqueños display a strong sense of democratic entitlement that is exceptional in a country where many communities and social movements have been devastated by decades of dirty war. In the current context, many individuals and groups are asking whether or not Barranca has exhausted its reserves. Many of the city's best and brightest have been killed or have left. Many others remain, of course, but under totally changed circumstances. The balance of power between insurgent and counterinsurgent forces has been upset in favor of the latter, and the paramilitaries have imposed serious restrictions on activists who are associated directly or indirectly with left-wing causes and on the population in general. As the sociologist Martha Cecilia García writes: "In order to maintain control over the territory, the paramilitaries use networks of informants . . . and enforce a system of 'law.'"[11] Since 2003 "codes of conduct" for youth have appeared on pamphlets signed by the paramilitaries.[12] The culture of street protests has been dampened, yet popular movements remain committed to the same basic principles of social justice and human rights. Barranca is still an area of social struggle and political violence, and the outcomes of these processes remain unclear.

Human rights activists in Barranca continue to see themselves as agents of social change and carriers of a longstanding tradition of popular social and political activism. The tension between loss and defiance informs the way in which activists evaluate their own role in the crisis. What lessons can be learned from the *toma de Barranca*? In order to situate activists' experiences and reflections in a broader context, I make use of selected primary sources (e.g., judicial records, U.S. consular correspondence, and international human rights reports, as well as reporting on the situation in Barranca by local civil society organizations). I also draw on contemporary scholarly contributions, such as Colombian social scientists' and historians' analyses of the significance of Barranca. I also make use of the accounts of foreign journalists and researchers who have reflected on what is often referred to as the "degradation" of the Colombian conflict.[13]

The May 16, 1998, Massacre

The killing and disappearance of thirty-two mostly young men from the poor *barrios* of Barranca in May 1998 provoked a major crisis in the city and a realization among activists that they would have to change their approach to human rights work. The shock was comparable to that experienced during the first wave of political assassinations that took place in the city a decade earlier. Although surrounded by violence, and working under conditions of tremendous stress, human rights activists in Barranca in 1998 did not imagine that an attack could be carried out with such brazen force in the heart of the city. In the days prior to the most devastating massacre in Barranca's history, a *calma chicha*, or false calm, reigned over the city. Some rumors had circulated that paramilitary groups were preparing an attack. As per usual, letters and phone calls had been made from CREDHOS and other groups to local military authorities, informing them of possible danger. The massacre came as a swift kick in the teeth to members of CREDHOS and others who saw themselves as the last line of protection for local citizens, and it would occasion immediate and long-term changes in the practice of human rights protection.

The massacre was audacious. At 9:00 p.m. three trucks carrying approximately forty heavily armed men dressed in black and green military fatigues, their heads covered to conceal their identities, drove past an army post at the southern entrance to Barranca. The trucks continued along the main thoroughfare leading into the city and stopped at a popular roadside bar. Upon entering the Estadero La Tora, they turned up the lights and turned off the music. Two people were seized and taken away. The trucks headed back toward El Retén, stopping briefly at another bar located across the street from the army post. The trucks then turned around and took a hard right turn into the *suroriente*, the sprawling low-income district known as a stronghold of the Ejército de Liberación Nacional (ELN). The paramilitaries arrived at the soccer field that serves as the main plaza or meeting place in the area, where a large party was underway. Most of the people in attendance were teenagers. The men jumped down from the trucks, brandishing guns and shouting, and started rounding people up, separating the men and boys from the women and girls. Eyewitnesses reported that among the attackers was at least one person in civilian clothes, her face covered by a hood, who helped identify individuals from a list of names.[14] Seven people were killed and twenty-five people abducted in less than one hour. Around 10:00 p.m. the men got back onto the trucks and left by the same route by which they had come. They passed El Retén and drove out on the main highway in the direction of Bucaramanga.

It was the single boldest act of paramilitary violence ever committed in the city, and a message to local residents that the tide of history was turning. The people abducted that day would never be seen again, although rumors of their return to the city circulated freely for some time afterward. Over the next five days Barranca was gripped by the largest civic protests in a generation. More than ten thousand people attended the funeral for the victims whose bodies were recovered at the massacre site. Immediately after the funeral, large public assemblies reminiscent of the *paros cívicos* of the past were held in the Parque

Infantil in the center of town and at the oil workers' union headquarters, while groups of young men and women set up barricades of burning tires at the As de Copas and Puente Elevado. By the end of 2001, the guerrillas who had held sway in Barrancabermeja's poor neighborhoods for two decades were in full retreat. People were now being displaced from the city or, within the city, from one *barrio* to another.[15] And the oldest and most vibrant social movements in all of Colombia were at risk. Human rights activists were targeted with a ferocity reminiscent of the first wave of attacks against CREDHOS in the early 1990s.

According to Sergeant Mario Alberto Fajardo Garzón, who was in charge of the army unit stationed at El Retén that night, his troops were in place until 9:30 p.m., at which time they were called to return to the main army base located several kilometers away.[16] They had noticed nothing untoward the entire evening, only a few trucks, a car, a few motorcycles, and an armored truck belonging to the National Police. No vehicles had been stopped or searched. A small permanent military post known as Pozo 7, or "oil well number 7," is located a few hundred meters from where the massacre took place, on the beltway road that connects the *suroriente* to the *nororiente*. El Retén and Pozo 7 are located at key points of entry into the district, making it difficult to believe that a large truck full of paramilitaries could go by unobserved.

The head of the National Police in Barranca, Lieutenant Colonel Joaquín Correa López, said that he first received reports of a disturbance in one of the city's outlying *barrios* at about 11:00 p.m. Correa was the commander, not just of Barranca but of all National Police present in the area covered by the Comando Operativo Especial del Magdalena Medio, including twenty-seven *municipios* well known as areas of both paramilitary and guerrilla presence. Later, in an interview with investigators from the attorney general's office sent from Bogotá, Lieutenant Colonel Correa said that he did not respond to these reports because he feared they might be false alarms made by the guerrillas in order to lure police into an ambush.[17] The police only entered Barranca's poor *barrios* in armored vehicles, mainly out of fear of being shot at by the guerrillas. As Correa put it, after all that the police had done to help the people of Barranca, he was not going to lead his men into a trap.[18]

The investigation conducted by the Office of the Inspector General in June 1998 concluded that Barranca's security forces had in fact received timely and detailed information about the events leading to the massacre. Earlier in the day, the commander of the Batallón Nueva Granada in Barranca had issued "Operations Order 100" to army field commanders responsible for urban areas, warning of possible paramilitary maneuvers. It ordered armed forces personnel to "carry out military operations to neutralize or destroy the actions of narcobandits and private justice groups" and "undertake searches of people and vehicles."[19] Just past 10:00 p.m. relatives of the victims traveled six kilometers across town to National Police headquarters. They gave detailed reports of what had just transpired and requested immediate assistance. But Lieutenant Colonel Correa did not respond. No police were mobilized to investigate, secure the area, or pursue the fleeing perpetrators. The commander made no phone calls to other security forces in the area. No coroner was summoned to the scene. In the end, the bodies of seven people were picked up by family and neighbors and transported to funeral homes in central Barranca. One funeral home owner told investigators that he called the police in the small hours of the morning to see if they were aware of what had just happened.

Before sunrise on May 17, CREDHOS's president Osiris Bayter Ferias was called at her home by the owners of Funeraria la Foronda. When Bayter arrived, wearing the T-shirt she had slept in, she was sought after by the victims' families, embraced, and entreated to deliver justice. Bayter was at the time the most recognizable figure in the city's civic-popular movement and the soul of CREDHOS. A longtime friend and colleague, Jael Quiroga, observed: "Osiris is an extraordinary woman. She is magic. *Tiene mística*. She has a commitment inside of her. Because she loves her people, she loves her struggle, she is sincere and brave."[20] Bayter was raised in the *barrios nororientales* of Barranca. Her father was a former oil worker who had been sacked by Ecopetrol along with dozens of his comrades following the great strike of 1963. Her parents, both of *costeño* origin, spoke passionately about the struggles of Colombian working peoples and followed politics closely. Bayter was known to attend victims' funerals, where she attracted much positive attention. In the hours and days that followed, she would act as spokesperson for the people of Barranca to the national journalists and government officials who descended on the city to investigate the massacre.

Osiris Bayter accused the Colombian military of responsibility for the massacre. Her boldness would provoke a terrible backlash. Less than one month following the massacre, Bayter fled the country. The paramilitaries that claimed responsibility for the massacre sent a threatening letter addressed to Bayter and the president of the oil workers' union, Hernando Hernández: "Conscious of the grave harm that you, Osiris Bayter, are causing with your work which benefits the guerrilla and in detriment to Human Rights we are telling you that we have decided to declare you a military target as well as Mr. Hernando Hernández Pardo, President of the USO."[21] The remaining team of CREDHOS staff and *promotores* had to take over where Bayter left off, sorting out the case against the Colombian state and lobbying on behalf of the victims' families. Though not as well known as Bayter, they were experienced activists in their own right. They also relied on a strong network of support to carry out their work. But the pressure continued to mount, as rumors swirled around the city's popular movement, and more death threats were issued against CREDHOS in the name of the paramilitary group that claimed responsibility for the massacre, the United Self-Defense Forces of Santander and Southern Cesar, or Autodefensas Unidas de Santander y Sur de Cesar (AUSAC).[22] CREDHOS's activities in the rural *municipios* of San Pablo and Cantagallo, both in southern Bolívar, had to be closed by the end of the year. Over the next three years, seven CREDHOS staff abandoned the region. Several would return to Barranca, only to be forced to leave again. While some did manage to stay in Barranca, they eventually quit CREDHOS.

Government investigations into the events of May 16, 1998, in Barranca began within a week. National Peace Commissioner José Noé Ríos flew to Barranca a few days following the massacre. But when Ríos appeared on the balcony of Barranca's City Hall to address the thousands of protestors who had come to greet him, there was a sense of anger among many local activists. The feeling of impotence was excruciating. The protestors chanted: "*¡Vivos se los llevaron, vivos los queremos!*" They took them alive! We want them back alive! "*¡El pueblo lo dice y tiene la razón—militares y paramilitares, la misma mierda son!*" The people say it, the people are right—the army and the paramilitary are the same shit! The oil workers' union president Hernando Hernández appeared in front of the crowd on the steps of City Hall to denounce the national government's complicity with paramilitarism (see fig. 8). Under constant threat, Hernández was flanked by bodyguards. It was rumored that the twenty-five people abducted on May 16 were being held at a nearby farm. The military only had to drive a few kilometers up the road toward Bucaramanga to investigate. A few weeks later José Noé Ríos announced that the twenty-five missing people had been killed, although no evidence was produced.[23]

The final assault on the city had been foretold. One of the most famous phrases ever attributed to Carlos Castaño, former leader of the United Self-Defense Forces of Colombia, or Autodefensas Unidas de Colombia (AUC), was his intention to sit in a hammock and drink a cup of coffee in Barranca's northeastern *barrios* by Christmas 2001.[24] The AUC was a national umbrella organization for right-wing paramilitary forces across Colombia, established in 1997. It is unlikely that Castaño ever visited Barranca, let alone put his feet up to drink a triumphant cup of *tinto* in the former guerrilla stronghold, but Castaño clearly identified Barranca as one of the most important battlegrounds for the AUC. The AUC saw Barranca as important because it was the

Figure 8. Oil Workers' Union leader Hernando Hernández speaking at a rally in protest of the May 16, 1998, massacre. Photo by the author.

capital of Colombia's oil industry and because it was so closely identified with the ELN. In the book-length interview with Castaño published in 2001 titled *Mi confesión: Carlos Castaño revela sus secretos*, the paramilitary commander recounts winning the war against the guerrillas "block by block," beginning with Barranca's commercial district.[25]

Carlos Castaño describes the siege of Barrancabermeja as having been carried out in two stages: the enforced co-optation of the city's commercial center, followed by a dirty war in the city's poor *barrios*. Castaño first sought to seize control of protection rackets run by the guerrillas in Barranca's downtown core and then set about to demoralize the residents of guerrilla-dominated poorer districts through massacres, targeted killings, and threats. Neither task would prove simple. According to Castaño, the guerrillas had achieved a high level of penetration into the daily commercial life of the city. But as more and more shopkeepers and businesspeople accepted the paramilitaries' protection, a tipping point was reached, and the guerrillas lost control over an essential support network.[26] Overturning guerrilla influence in the eastern *barrios* of the city would be an entirely different matter. Defeating the guerrillas on their turf was less a question of winning hearts and minds, and more a question of bloodshed: "That is how we gained trust and credibility with decent people [*la gente buena*]. Afterwards we recuperated the *barrios nororientales* block by block. There the urban war between the Self-Defense Forces [AUC] and the guerrillas was fought with pistols, rifles and 45 millimeter grenades. Tremendous battles were fought in the *barrios*, we even went into the homes of *milicianos* to seize them."[27] Castaño is quoted as saying that about one hundred members of guerrilla militia were killed in the first two years of the battle for control of Barranca. He then adds: "Between two and three executions every week. For sure. Counting those who really were subversives."[28]

The AUC could not gain control of Barranca in a vacuum. On the contrary, the paramilitary coopted key economic and social sectors, creating new webs of power as they advanced through the countryside and eventually from central Barranca out to the poor suburbs of the city. Jorge Gómez Lizarazo returned to Barranca in 2002 after ten years in exile to take the job of regional human rights ombudsman, or *defensor del pueblo*, a government posting that had been established ten years earlier when he was still president of CREDHOS. His understanding of the AUC's strategy is, not surprisingly, more complete than that offered by Castaño. As Gómez Lizarazo suggests, the paramilitary project that "took over" Barranca was built up through the progressive domination of drug trafficking and contraband, as well as local politics: "The paramilitary take control of territory militarily, but also from social, political, and economic points of view. So they begin to control the flow of gasoline, they start to control drug trafficking, they control the selling of coca paste coming out of the south of the department of Bolívar, they begin extorting businesses and industries, they extort contract workers for the city and for Ecopetrol, and they create in this way an economic empire of great proportions. Their project also entails control over the political sphere, financing political campaigns."[29] The paramilitaries achieved their goal of seizing control over Barranca and forcing the guerrillas into retreat by late 2000. What followed was a "*limpieza*" or political cleansing of the city. Municipal officials would become directly involved in paramilitary crimes during this time. In 2003 Mayor Julio César Ardila Torres (2002–2005) paid paramilitaries $150 million pesos ($52,000 U.S.) to assassinate the local radio journalist Emeterio Rivas.[30] Rivas had received numerous death threats prior to his murder for having denounced the alleged awarding of city contracts to paramilitary-connected businesses. Traditional popular support for the Liberal Party also eroded during this time, as evidenced by the high percentage of votes cast for Álvaro Uribe in 2006 presidential elections. The process of political extirpation—of leftists and social activists—is still being carried out.[31]

Social Movements Respond
to the Paramilitary Occupation

The paramilitarization of Barranca entailed disastrous consequences for social activists. In the words of Yolanda Becerra, longtime president
of the Organización Femenina Popular (OFP) and human rights activist: "In
this country, whoever has the power and the guns, has the people. We do not
have the guns or the people. We are in crisis. I would say that in Colombia
there really are no social movements left."[32] The last major *paro cívico* in
Barranca was the five-day protest organized in the aftermath of the May 16,
1998, massacre. In May 1999 an "International Opinion Tribunal" was organized by civil society groups and solidarity committees in Canada. Witnesses
to the massacre were flown from Barrancabermeja to Montreal and Toronto
to give testimony to the judges who volunteered to overhear the case.[33] In
2004 the legal case against the Colombian state for its complicity in the massacre
was submitted to the jurisdiction of the Inter-American Commission of Human
Rights, which declared the case admissible.[34] The Commission has yet to refer
the case to the Inter-American Court of Human Rights. Despite the concern
that the paramilitary takeover of Barranca has generated, it has been a major
challenge for social activists and victims of violence to maintain hope that
justice will be done.

To the extent that the level of popular participation in protests is an
important measure of the strength of the civic-popular movement, we can
speak of a period of contraction. As Yolanda Becerra's comments illustrate,
there were tremendous feelings of loss among many who had spent their entire
adult lives building organizational processes. The case of the OFP, which
Becerra led for more than two decades, is an important illustration. The OFP
is by far the largest social movement organization in Barrancabermeja. Established by the Pastoral Social of the Catholic diocese of Barrancabermeja in
1972 as Homemakers' Clubs, or Clubes de Amas de Casa, the OFP has been
independent since 1987. In the 1990s the OFP established community kitchens
and educational programs in several *municipios* along the Magdalena River,
as well as in the city's poor neighborhoods. Despite feeling threatened and
harassed by paramilitaries, the OFP initially continued to expand its activities
in the Magdalena Medio region. At one point in the late 1990s they had four
Casas de la Mujer community centers in Barrancabermeja, in the center, north,
northeast, and southeast. They even established a center in Bogotá to work
with displaced women in the Colombian capital. Becerra herself has survived
numerous threats, and in 2007 she was obliged to relocate temporarily to
Bucaramanga for the safety of herself and her family.[35]

The persistence of politically motivated violence in Barrancabermeja, years after paramilitaries allegedly pacified the city, suggests that the battle of Barranca did not end quickly or cleanly. David Ravelo, the imprisoned president of CREDHOS and former municipal councillor on behalf of the Communist Party (PCC), tried to strike a hopeful note during our interview in 2005: "Here in the city we have a long and important accumulated history and important democratic reserves."[36] The ethos and discourse of defiance is indeed still very much in evidence in the city and the Magdalena Medio. Marco Tulio Torres, a physical education teacher who represented CREDHOS in the small town of San Pablo, in the department of Bolívar, was interviewed by Canadian documentary filmmakers in December 1998, just a few weeks before he and the local parish priest had to leave town due to death threats: "I have not given up anything [to the paramilitaries]. I still have hope. . . . I have not given up anything."[37]

CREDHOS's entire staff and board of directors resigned following the organization's 2003 General Assembly, partly in response to the constant threats against veteran members of the organization, and partly out of internal disagreements about the surest way forward for the organization. As the former executive member Francisco Campos explains, CREDHOS entered a major crisis during the final paramilitary push into the city. A number of prominent individual members were displaced from Barranca due to threats, and debates emerged as to how to rebuild the organization. Campos recalls that some of the more experienced people within CREDHOS proposed undertaking a new kind of human rights work that was less focused on denouncing violence and more focused on promoting social justice. According to Campos, this shift signified an attempt to recognize the links between social movement activism and human rights. In his words, "making proposals" about ways to end the violence would be more productive than simply counting the dead. By Campos's account, it was an attempt to renew the spirit of the broad-based protest culture that flourished in the years prior to the dirty war. But to others, it seemed an overly cautious move. In any case, the adjustment proved too divisive, and a new group of people emerged who wanted to run the organization. Campos reflects: "There were internal problems and contradictions, which were resolved when we finally decided to leave CREDHOS."[38]

The Coordinadora Popular de Barrancabermeja also entered into crisis during the paramilitary siege of the city, and it was dissolved in 2003. In terms of major shifts in local social movement organizing, this has to be counted as the most significant change of the paramilitary era. For twenty years the Coordinadora Popular had served as a civil society coalition that grouped together all of the city's major unions and social movements. The Coordinadora Popular had what *barranqueños* call *capacidad de convocatoria*, or the power to call the local population to protests. As the former Coordinadora Popular spokesperson Evangelina Marín explained in an interview in 2004: "The Coordinadora Popular, all modesty aside, could convene popular assemblies, which meant 10,000 to 15,000 people in front of the USO [union building] or in the Parque Infantil."[39] The decision on the part of Coordinadora Popular members to turn the page meant that Barranca's social movements would have to create new mechanisms for sharing information.

In 2003 a new civil society coalition emerged that focused specifically on human rights. The Espacio de Trabajadores y Trabajadoras de Derechos Humanos del Magdalena Medio, or the Space of Magdalena Medio Human Rights Workers, was set up by a group of unions and social movements, including the Pastoral Social, CREDHOS, the oil workers' union, the OFP, and others. What is perhaps most significant about the Espacio is it recognizes that a diversity of groups have been working on human rights issues in the city.[40] Human rights protection is not just the role of CREDHOS but has become a mainstream aspect of the work of all social and labor organizations. The new human rights coalition differs from the Coordinadora Popular in that it is not dedicated to addressing a broad range of issues. The Espacio was conceived as a new point of convergence around human rights, understood mainly in terms of monitoring and denouncing political violence in the Magdalena Medio region. Unlike the Coordinadora Popular, the Espacio was not meant to be a vehicle for the organization of public protests.[41] Unlike CREDHOS, it did not offer legal representation to victims, or submit habeas corpus writs to judicial authorities. The major benefit of the Espacio was that individual organizations under pressure from paramilitaries in their daily activities would benefit from issuing joint statements and engaging collectively in public debate and would share information about the security concerns of people living in different parts of the region.

The social memory of Barranca's violent past has been kept alive through competing historical projects, one led by the national state and the other by its critics. The state-sponsored Reconciliation and Reparations Commission, a product of the Justice and Peace process initiated by President Uribe in 2005, has worked on Barrancabermeja-related cases. However, many local groups refused to collaborate. In 2006 the human rights organization Espacio formally distanced itself from the former CREDHOS president Régulo Madero's decision to participate in the government initiative.[42] One of the new projects assumed by CREDHOS is its work with the national Movement of Victims of State Crimes, or the Movimiento Nacional de Víctimas de Crímenes de Estado, established in 2004 by dissident activists in Bogotá to document and advocate on behalf of the victims of violence in opposition to government-led efforts, which were seen as linked to the ersatz demobilization of paramilitaries.[43] Since 2005 CREDHOS has hosted gatherings of victims of paramilitary violence attended by hundreds of people from around the Magdalena Medio.[44]

At the same time, security concerns persisted. CREDHOS moved its headquarters from a small, poorly ventilated office to a more secure location in a two-story house situated on a major avenue, complete with bright meeting spaces and a backyard garden. As of 2005, several members of the organization had bodyguards, often stationed in front of the office in armored vehicles. CREDHOS's vice president, Socorro Abril, denounced an attempt on her life on November 9, 2005. According to a *denuncia* published by the organization for displaced peasants that Abril also worked for, she had been receiving constant threats. The *denuncia* describes how several suspicious men appeared outside of her home, including three on the roof, and how she hid in her bathroom to call her bodyguards and the police to come to her assistance.[45]

Veterans of the city's social movements, those who have left Barranca and those who remain, found themselves in the position of reflecting on the personal and collective losses suffered during the previous decades. One such leader is Ángel Tolosa, former president of the Independent Sector of Colombia's National Association of Peasant Users (ANUC). Tolosa has lived in Bogotá since the late 1980s, although he remains in close contact with friends and family in Barranca. In his view, political violence has led to the depoliticization of the struggle for human rights. The human rights struggle is now narrowly defined in humanitarian terms, saving lives, rather than in terms of an agenda for social and political change. Tolosa explains:

> Before the work was more open. I think that there was also more extensive educational work. And then all of a sudden things got so much more specialized, more focused. I think it was broader before. Maybe a bit careless too. Now CREDHOS does the same kind of work that other human rights organizations do, which I question, because it is very much centered on humanitarian assistance; they do not go beyond condemnation and humanitarian assistance. It would be worthwhile if human rights organizations did more systematic work, confronting real problems. For example, one very serious problem in the Magdalena Medio that they could confront is the eviction [of peasants] from the land. People are saying that there are a lot of evictions occurring, but we do not know how many. What concrete actions are being taken to respond to these evictions? While it may seem contradictory, I believe that human rights organizations have to take on structural problems in some way. This kind of work that has to do with food security and sovereignty, the defense of

our collective community legacy. Maybe it seems like it does not have much to do with human rights, but deep down it does. Human rights should not only be contestatory and humanitarian but also preventative. They could be organizing more in terms of the themes that social organizations work on, thinking about the short, medium, and long-term.[46]

Human rights, says the former peasant leader, who now works for Planeta Paz, a high-profile national organization dedicated to training, research, and developing collaboration among different social movements, must be an "integral" struggle, where issues such as land rights and economic justice are all articulated, linked, and defended.

Ángel Tolosa's ideas for revitalizing human rights struggles in the Magdalena Medio coincide with the conception of human rights that was first espoused by CREDHOS in the late 1980s. Francisco Campos was among the activists who took up leadership positions within CREDHOS after the attempt to annihilate the organization by the Colombian navy in the early 1990s. Like Tolosa, Campos argues that what is needed is a return to a more comprehensive definition of human rights: "When you internalize human rights, you understand the comprehensive nature of human rights, and you promote them in that way. . . . When human rights are reduced to the simple defense of civil and political rights, then the critics are probably right. When human rights are just about the number of dead people, they remain at the level of the denunciation and not much more than that."[47] Francisco Campos's personal trajectory led him from the student movement in Barranca, to the National University in Bogotá, and back to Barranca. Before joining CREDHOS, he served as a municipal councillor in the neighboring *municipio* of Sabana de Torres. In the mid-1990s he was forced to leave Sabana de Torres when the mayor, a member of the Patriotic Union, was murdered.[48] Later on, Campos served as cochair of the Coordinadora Popular de Barrancabermeja. His understanding of the "comprehensive" or interconnected nature of human rights work and social activism is thus derived from his education in Barranca and his experiences of participation in popular protest and progressive political causes.

The idea of a return to the principles of openness and pluralism was repeated by many former CREDHOS members whom I interviewed for this book. Rafael Gómez, a former oil workers' union leader and one of the cofounders of CREDHOS, suggests that CREDHOS is simply no longer in a position to throw its doors open to the wider community. How can you create democratic spaces in the midst of pervasive paramilitary pressure? As Gómez explains, significant changes may have to be made to the way in which groups like CREDHOS are structured: "This is a twenty-year history. CREDHOS is in the hearts of many people; it is a name that remains in many people's hearts. In 1988 we were so democratic that we left a very wide opening. But now there are other people representing CREDHOS. The people in the *barrios* still speak about CREDHOS, many people ask me about CREDHOS. So I think that CREDHOS has to take the next step, look at its structure, to get back to the values we had at the time."[49] Partly nostalgic, this is a vision of social movement activism that has been reinforced by generations of *barranqueños*. Social memories of unity remain strong in Barranca for activists who lament the contraction of the civic-popular movement and regret the way in which armed groups have seized the agenda in recent years.

Can Human Rights Be Reclaimed?

One of the main issues being examined in retrospect by Barranca activists is the role that guerrilla groups in the city—namely the ELN and FARC—played in the closing down of political space. The final offensive undertaken by the paramilitaries and security forces seemed to push the guerrillas into a corner. Before they retreated from the city, the guerrillas became engaged in a war against *sapos*, or informants. The confidence that some *barranqueños* had previously felt in the guerrillas slowly drained away. It was a disastrous process of disarticulation of the guerrillas' urban militias, and stories abound of individual *milicianos* who changed sides and joined the paramilitaries. As the former CREDHOS member and high school teacher Irene Villamizar reflects: "The guerrillas lost their way. The guerrillas lost sight of the interests of the people . . . and their own interests. In the end, the guerrillas were very cruel. The only thing that they have done in this neighborhood is change their uniforms. The paramilitary occupation, it is a degenerated version of the guerrillas. Here it was not like in other parts of the country where outsiders came. No, here those who were guerrillas one day were paramilitaries the next. It is very sad."[50] During the final days of guerrilla influence in Barranca, insurgent organizations even attacked one another. For instance, in 1999, at the height of the violence, the FARC carried out a series of murders of urban members of the much-smaller, Maoist-inspired Ejército Popular de Liberación (EPL).[51]

The grassroots work done by social movements in Barranca had been under attack for more than a decade prior to the final paramilitary offensive. Thinking historically, we can suggest one of the factors that facilitated the paramilitary incursion into the city was the conflation of the guerrillas and the culture of

Figure 9. "We do not give birth or create life for war." Members of the Organización Femenina Popular protest violence in the Magdalena Medio, May 1998. Photo by the author.

popular protest. The decline of social processes relative to the armed power of guerrilla groups was a prelude to disorder. By the end of 2001 the guerrillas had no more armed presence in the city. For the first time since urban militia were established by the ELN in the 1980s, Colombian police and military personnel could patrol the streets of the *barrios orientales* on foot. In the very same *barrios*, the paramilitaries carried out killings in an attempt to reorder existing social networks. Régulo Madero reflects on the future of Barranca's social movements in a post-guerrilla scenario:

> In the year 2001 many social movement organizations were waiting for the guerrillas to return, and I think that some are still waiting. But what we need to do is build on the experiences of the 1970s and the early 1980s. . . . We need to develop our own organizational proposals, proposals for peace, citizenship, and human security. Social organizations today are in flux. . . . It is very important because public space has been affected, has been violated by armed actors, by the army, by the police, by the paramilitaries, and by all the guerrilla organizations.[52]

Just as the *paros cívicos* had become more spontaneous and disorganized, making room for the guerrillas to exert themselves publicly through *paros armados*, the paramilitaries took advantage of the confusing and paranoid environment in which the guerrillas operated. Paramilitary and military actions carried out against *barrio* residents and social leaders had provoked that confusion in the first place.

The OFP was one of the organizations most severely tested by the paramilitary siege of Barranca. Yolanda Becerra, president of the OFP, recalls the pain that brought people together. In the days following the May 16, 1998, massacre, a large public assembly was held at which local activists decided to build twenty-five coffins to dramatize the disappearance of twenty-five people. The coffins would be painted white and carefully marched through the streets, before being laid in front of the headquarters of the oil workers' union. The challenge, according to Becerra, has been to maintain the feelings of solidarity produced during such moments of crisis:

> We lived through some very hard times. . . . Remembering what happened on May 16 in Barranca is terrible, it was so hard, so hard, a crime against humanity, which targeted the most vulnerable. But we knew what to do. There was a *paro cívico*, a *paro cívico* with a lot of symbolism. I remember those empty boxes were something that had a big impact, that was an idea that came out of a meeting attended by fifty people, where we cried, but we also asked what could be done, how should we denounce the crime, so that it would not just be speeches, not just words, so that it would be a symbol that could impact and reflect what this meant to Barranca, and I think we achieved that.[53]

Every day for the five days that the *paro cívico* lasted, the bishop of Barranca presided over a Mass of mourning in front of the union headquarters, with the empty coffins on display in front of him. At the time of the massacre the OFP's youth movement, or *movimiento juvenil*, based in the poor *barrios* of the city, was one of the most dynamic initiatives within the city's wider popular movement. Attacking young people at a party in the heart of the neighborhood greatly diminished the *capacidad de convocatoria* of the OFP and led to the undoing of their *movimiento juvenil*. The loss of youth groups dedicated to art and music cost the OFP essential links to their bases.

While the OFP itself has never been in critical danger of disappearing, its modus operandi changed. Indeed, the survival of the OFP and other groups is far from unequivocal. Becerra observed a process of bureaucratization and professionalization in local organizations that parallels similar developments across the country. As Winifred Tate writes: "Throughout the 1990s human rights work became increasingly professionalized, and new institutional norms and practices developed. Solidarity groups staffed by volunteers were replaced by nongovernmental organizations staffed by well-trained, full-time paid professionals, often lawyers."[54] The attendant disaffection of grassroots members has been problematic for groups in Barranca, where there is a tradition of mass participation in social movement–led activities. While there are fewer lawyers and full-time professional activists in Barranca than in Bogotá or Medellín, Becerra argues that Barranca-based groups are equally dependent on financial assistance from international agencies. Ironically, groups such as the OFP must justify the foreign aid they receive on the basis that they can prove high levels of popular participation in meetings and workshops. As Becerra observes:

> I think that international assistance caused the institutionalization of popular work. This assistance was institutionalized so much that many professionals in Colombia were able to find work. . . . One has to recall that in the popular movements there were always professionals who had their own jobs, and dedicated some of their free time, part of their life, to social movements. It was more a question of political commitment, but later on there was a lot of unemployment, an economic crisis, and these professionals no longer had work, so they turned to social movements. . . . While this process of institutionalization proceeded we lost a political dimension to the social movements. So, now NGOs convene the people to participate in timely things. And so the people say, "Well, we have conditions, I will go to the workshop, but you have to provide transportation to the meeting, I'll go, but . . ." Know what I mean? It was not always like this. It used to be, "I *want* to go to the workshop, I *have* to go to the workshop, I *need* to go." We lost our strength, and we left the people behind.[55]

The transformation of some Colombian social movements into NGOs was abetted by the influx of European and North American financial assistance, and the associated expectations of proficient financial reporting, measureable outputs, and just remuneration for staff people, influences that have been the subject of tremendous debate in Colombia. Becerra says that her own process of disillusionment began early on, with the 1985 murder of Lara Parada, the near-decimation of CREDHOS, the retreat of ANUC from the region, and many other catastrophes. As she dryly observes, the conversion of Barranca-based groups' *capacidad de convocatoria* into an asset to secure funding was not anticipated.[56]

Other factors that weakened local social movements' determination were exogenous to Barranca. The end of the Cold War signaled a shift in the politics of the region. While Colombia's two main rebel groups, the ELN and the FARC, continued to expand during the 1990s, this was exceptional in Latin America. By the early 1990s most Latin American revolutionary movements withered on the vine. Many signed peace agreements and dedicated themselves to the much less glamorous task of contesting elections. Others were simply defeated. The fall of the Sandinista government in Nicaragua in 1990 was a historic setback for the Latin American left. The decision by the United States to support the Plan Colombia military aid package in 1999 ushered in a new era of urgency among popular movement activists. But urgency soon turned to despair. The total collapse of peace talks between the FARC guerrillas and the government of Andrés Pastrana in 2002 all but foreclosed prospects for peace in Colombia. Yolanda Becerra reflects on the effect of many years of struggle and the losses suffered during that time:

> As the years pass, you feel as if the utopia is moving further away, but that it is not impossible, so you continue doing the same things, in the same dynamic. Because we started to speak about . . . an evaluation of some of the mistakes, certain things. . . . Nicaragua was a key moment, when we started to rethink things . . . like power, what are we going to do with it? We started to think about many things, and one day we had to start all over again because we were no longer capable of continuing on as before. This is not to say we would stop working, but you have to begin, to begin again.[57]

Conclusion

To make sense of the history of human rights movements in areas of conflict like the oil refinery town of Barrancabermeja and the region of Magdalena Medio, an empirically grounded understanding of the relation between human rights and social change is necessary. We have to consider the specific effects that major shifts in social or political context have on human rights movements. This is because, at least in this place, the human rights movement is intimately connected to popular movements; it grew out of them in response to the counterinsurgency violence of the Colombian military and its paramilitary allies that targeted guerrillas and social movement activists alike. In this economically and strategically important oil center, the guerrillas sought to build bases of political and social influence. Legal activists from officially recognized movements that shared the guerrillas' revolutionary politics—such as the Communist Party, the Patriotic Union, and ¡A Luchar!—were among the first to be attacked by paramilitaries. But the hardest blows were dealt to ordinary citizens, most of whom had no political affiliation, but participated in popular forms of protest, including *paros cívicos* and *marchas campesinas*. Neither the guerrillas nor the paramilitaries ever had total control over the territories to which they laid claim, but their presence ultimately diminished civilian space for organizing.

The future of Barranca's movement for human rights is not clear. The former CREDHOS president Régulo Madero maintains that human rights activism in Barranca has been successful because it has contributed to the sustaining of alternative visions of "this utopia, this chance to continue dreaming."[58] Defending human rights in a conflict area requires total immersion in the social and political environment. Many of the people interviewed for this book insist that the movement for human rights will be considered relevant only if local social movements are able to recover. From inside conflict-affected communities it is of course a challenge to see the broader patterns of violence in perspective. But such a deep level of engagement is absolutely necessary in order to respond to daily events and also to major shifts in the political landscape. None of the people I spoke with said that they judged the effectiveness of human rights activism solely in terms of saving lives. Time and again, the impact of CREDHOS and human rights activists in the Magdalena Medio is measured in terms of the continued existence of popular social movements and the persistence of the spirit of irreverence that has made Barranca famous.

Conclusion

"This utopia, this chance to continue dreaming"

Human rights defenders in the Magdalena Medio are human rights defenders by conviction; they have to put themselves at risk in defending the lives of others. I know human rights defenders across the world who can teach us many things that we do not know, and they deserve all of our respect, our admiration. But the love that we have for what we do, the self-sacrifice, the *mística* . . . here human rights work is militant work.

Francisco Campos, human rights defender[1]

The Line of Fire

It is a special condition of frontline human rights work that by engaging in it, activists expose themselves to violence. Just as they seek to protect lives, they risk their own. According to Amnesty International, forty-five human rights defenders and twenty-nine trade unionists were killed in Colombia in 2011, making it the most dangerous place in the world to do this kind of work through the first decade of the twenty-first century.[2] When human rights groups such as CREDHOS called attention to themselves, they became targets. In this way, human rights activism draws out the perpetrators of violence. By standing in the line of fire, activists in Barranca helped to lay bare the links between counterinsurgent violence, wider political repression, and social justice claims. The decision by Barranca-based groups to take up human rights was thus both a refutation of violence and an attempt by a community of activists to defend their collective efforts to achieve social and economic justice.

CREDHOS maintained an important position within the city of Barranca despite a nearly constant barrage of attacks. Within its first five years of existence, six members of the organization were murdered. Three cofounders, including the organization's first president, then chose to leave Barranca in order to be able to continue working for human rights. The death or departure of many other Barranca-based activists occurred along the way. *Campesino* and trade union movements were hit particularly hard in this period and would continue to struggle for the next two decades. Not even the Catholic Church was impervious, as a number of activist priests and lay workers in the region were either killed or displaced. As paramilitary violence intensified in the 1990s, and the guerrillas stepped up their attacks, many social movements rallied around CREDHOS. Support came from local groups, as well as national and international ones, and the organization grew in size and influence. So too did other urban and rural popular movements in the region. By the late 1990s the Organización Femenina Popular (OFP) acquired new relevance as a grassroots voice against diverse forms of violence. Three massive *éxodos campesinos* in the late 1990s were led by a new generation of peasant leaders. CREDHOS was sustained through four different presidents, whose selection as spokespeople for the group corresponded with major ruptures in the history of Barranca: Jorge Gómez Lizarazo (1987–1993), Osiris Bayter (1993–1998), Régulo Madero (1998–2003), and David Ravelo (2003–2010). CREDHOS has continued to participate in, and guide, social processes around the defense of human rights.

Collective organization against political violence closely resembled historical struggles for labor, land, and social rights. In the history of Barranca there are several key moments of dramatic change corresponding to local, national, and international conjunctures. The first of these occurred following the nationalization of the refinery in Barranca in 1961, which coincided with the consolidation of the National Front government in Colombia and the onset of a Cold War counterinsurgency campaign against progressive social activists. Contrary to expectations, the nationalization of oil in Colombia occasioned a re-awakening of class conflict and social unrest. The Colombian national government was seen by union organizers as antagonistic to workers' interests. Barranca had developed largely outside of the patronage networks and battles between Liberals and Conservatives that structured social relations in many other regions of Colombia.[3] This was partly due to a long history of bipartisan national government support for the Tropical Oil Company and the government's tendency to favor the company's interests over workers' rights. As such, in the 1960s, the city was home to strong bases of support for political groupings that had been excluded from participation in the National Front, including the Communist Party of Colombia (PCC), the Liberal Revolutionary Movement (MRL), and the National Popular Alliance (ANAPO). Left-wing political parties were very influential within labor and social movements, including the oil workers' union, which was affiliated with a Communist-oriented labor federation, the Confederación Sindical de Trabajadores de Colombia (CSTC), from 1964 to 1970.

Colombia has been an oil-producing nation since the 1920s and a major net exporter of oil since the 1980s.[4] More than 70 percent of Colombia's crude oil is processed at the vast state-owned Ecopetrol complex that sits on the banks of the Magdalena River. The Magdalena Medio is known as a frontier area of homesteaders, migrant laborers, refugees from civil wars, and nonstate armed groups, including both left-wing guerrillas and right-wing paramilitaries. In Colombia, frontier areas are generally thought of as being beyond the reach of the state, yet in the Magdalena Medio a unique form of state presence has evolved, due to the strategic importance of oil to national development and the export economy. The local state, namely the municipal government and its agencies, stood alongside social and union movements through much of the city's history. The national state, represented in Barranca by Ecopetrol, the military, and judicial authorities, has played contradictory roles. At times, national government officials have interceded to resolve labor disputes. Significant investments were made in response to popular mobilization by oil workers and the wider community. The city and its region have also garnered an unusually high level of negative attention from the national government. The ways in which agents of the national state asserted themselves in the region would shape the histories of the social movements that emerged.

Stimulated by the Unión Sindical Obrera (USO), the oil workers' union, the city's labor and social movements have worked alongside and in coalition with one another. The oil wealth that flows through Barranca has made the city a pole of attraction for migrants from all over the country and beyond. But relatively few people benefited directly from living in the shadow of the Tropical Oil Company or the Colombian Petroleum Company, Ecopetrol. Oil and coal, two of the most capital-intensive industries in the world, create very few jobs relative to profits.[5] Oil economies have a tendency to boom and bust: as the life stories of itinerant wildcatters and roughnecks attest, wells are emptied and investments shifted, often leaving behind dramatically transformed human geographies, parched landscapes, and few economic prospects.[6] Barranca's relationship to oil is somewhat different and reveals a different dimension of the history of oil than that associated with drilling activities and their impact. The Tropical Oil Company built a refinery that has been in continuous operation since 1922, which has translated to several thousand relatively well-paid positions in Barranca for most of the past century. However, the overwhelming majority of migrants who traveled to Barranca did not find work with the oil company. And there were few guarantees for oil workers themselves, who were poorly housed and subject to arbitrary treatment by La Troco.

Social and political conflict in Barranca during the Tropical Oil Company era occurred within a volatile political context, regionally and nationally. In the 1920s, during the last decade of Conservative Party rule, there was growing frustration in Colombia over the exclusion of most citizens from meaningful participation in politics. Barranca's labor movement leveraged nationalist sentiment against transnational interests, offering an alternative to traditional politics through strikes and street protests and challenging the Colombian establishment to address issues of social justice. Barranca became a mecca for new socialist movements and, later, an important base of support for the progressive Liberal Party leader Jorge Eliécer Gaitán. At its peak in the late 1940s, in response to the murder of Gaitán, the popular movement in Barranca mounted an armed uprising, led by *gaitanista* and the future Liberal guerrilla leader Rafael Rangel.

Colombia's two largest guerrilla groups established themselves early in the Magdalena Medio region, exerting a powerful influence on Barranca. The guerrillas provided both a source of inspiration to progressive social movement organizers and a justification for increased state intervention in the lives of ordinary citizens. Established in the mountainous region of Santander near Barrancabermeja, the Ejército de Liberación Nacional (ELN) directly descended from the popular nationalist and radical fighters who had settled Magdalena Medio during the War of a Thousand Days (1898–1902) and La Violencia (1946–1958). During the early years, the ELN members Juan de Dios Aguilera and Victor Medina Morón helped the guerrillas to set up a network of support in Barranca. The presence of the Fuerzas Armadas Revolucionarias de Colombia (FARC) in the Magdalena Medio region is equally significant, though often overlooked. The PCC, which was aligned with the FARC for more than thirty years, was very influential among unionized workers in Barranca and in the port towns of Puerto Berrío and Puerto Boyacá.[7] Like the ELN, the regional branch of the FARC was established by peasants who had fought against the Conservative Party during La Violencia in the 1940s and 1950s.

The emergence of new social movements in Barranca during the 1970s took place at a time of another significant change in the character of the state presence, as the main forms and objectives of popular protest shifted from a

Figure 10. Serving *sancocho*, May 1, 1998. Photo by the author.

focus on working conditions in the oil industry to a focus on local development, symbolized by the fight for clean water. New avenues for social action and collaboration opened in response to restrictions placed on union activities. During the era of the Tropical Oil Company, oil workers used collective bargaining and work stoppages to demand improvements to health, education, and other services that touched the lives of all residents of Barrancabermeja. Following the departure of La Troco, the city grew dramatically through rural-urban migration, and *barranqueños* from all walks of life began to make demands directly to the national government through the advent of the *paro cívico*. The severe repression of the oil workers' union by the national government following strikes in 1971 and 1977 created opportunities for a broad-based popular movement composed mainly of peasants, urban squatters, Catholic Church activists, and community organizers from neighborhood Juntas de Acción Comunal. The *paro cívico* was a form of mass protest that involved the mobilization of the entire community, and was not limited to unionized workers.[8] The main goals of the *paros cívicos* in Barranca related to issues of local development, including demands that the national government upgrade social services and infrastructure.

The relationship between rural and urban social movements is critical to understanding the process of popular movement formation in Barranca. Peasants were the first to be impacted by political violence, and the first to take up the cause of human rights. Agrarian conflicts in the rural Magdalena Medio in the 1960s gave rise to strong peasant alliances, including the National Association of Peasant Users (ANUC). Beginning in the mid-1960s, peasant movement leaders denounced counterinsurgency measures implemented by the Colombian military, notably in terms of restrictions on freedom of movement. These groups led large-scale rural land invasions, protest marches, strikes, and mass migrations involving thousands of people, demanding the recognition of property rights. Internal refugees from paramilitary violence have played multiple roles in the construction of Barranca's civic identity. Barranca was literally built up as a result of violence, particularly in new eastern *barrios* settled by displaced peasants, which would become areas of social movement organizing and strong guerrilla influence. Internal refugees would bring their struggles to the urban environment, in the form of organized *éxodos* and land invasions. Urban squatters would then become targets of state and parastate repression, having been stigmatized as the "social bases of the insurgency." Peasant organizations described their members as being treated as delinquent elements that represented real threats to the police and army.[9]

The role of the institutional Catholic Church as a central force behind social movement organizing in Barranca is exceptional in the Colombian context.[10] The Catholic Church provided leadership on issues of social justice, developed a grassroots structure that allowed poor urban squatters to become involved in popular protests, and mediated rural and urban people's sense that they belonged to a distinct region.[11] The diocese of Barrancabermeja maintained a socially and politically progressive orientation that was, and remains, unique in Colombia.[12] As Daniel H. Levine has observed, the mainstream Colombian Catholic Church is very conservative, and apart from the participation of a few priests in leftist movements since the 1960s, there has been relatively little "explicitly political" community-based religious activism.[13] A number of young priests inspired by the teachings of Vatican II and liberation theology were assigned to Barrancabermeja when the diocese was created in 1963. The establishment of the Pastoral Social in 1970 as a community service branch of the diocese then offered priests, nuns, and lay missionaries opportunities to work among poor urban squatters. The Pastoral Social formed the backbone of community-based social movement organizing and helped to renew the culture of protest in Barranca.

Right-wing paramilitary groups linked to the Colombian military first emerged in the Magdalena Medio in the early 1980s, provoking the displacement of peasants to Barrancabermeja and awakening urban social activists to the problem of political violence and the idea of human rights. The rise and spread of paramilitarism in the region occurred earlier than anywhere else in

Colombia following the outbreak of guerrilla violence in the 1960s. Significantly, the direct ties between paramilitary and military forces is clearer here than in most other areas of Colombia. From the outset, paramilitary groups targeted left-wing political parties and social movements in areas of guerrilla influence, concentrating on the southern subregion of the Magdalena Medio around the strategic towns of Puerto Berrío and Puerto Boyacá and then proceeding north toward the radical center of Barrancabermeja. Later on, they would perceive human rights activists through the same Cold War lens.

Human Rights, Social Movements, and the State

While the Colombian armed forces have long treated social movements as antagonists, Colombian civilian government officials have been obliged to address the concerns of grassroots human rights activism. In January 1987 the Ministry of the Interior convened a group of some of the most eminent social scientists at Bogotá's National University to undertake a study on the origins of the current violence in Colombia as a guide to government policy on peace and human rights. The assembled scholars were specialists in the history of violence in Colombia, including the civil wars of the nineteenth century and La Violencia in the 1950s. Among the academics who took up the challenge were the anthropologist Jaime Arocha Rodríguez, the sociologist Eduardo Pizarro Leongómez, and the project director Gonzalo Sánchez Gómez, as well as Major General (retired) Luis Alberto Andrade Anaya, the former inspector general of the Colombian Armed Forces. They treated the question of violence as a broad set of social and political problems, tied to economic exclusion, underdevelopment, and inequality. They stated that while all forms of violence were linked, at least 90 percent of all killings in Colombia were the result of social and economic conflict, rather than the exchange of fire between the guerrillas and the military: "The violations that are killing us are street crimes, not those committed in the guerrilla conflict [del monte]."[14]

Overlooked in studies of Colombia's civil wars, Barranca has received special attention since the advent of human rights. Barranca is discussed in-depth in the report of the 1987 government-sponsored academic commission on violence, both because of the scale of the problem in the city and its evident political importance. The authors noted that illegal paramilitary groups like those in Barranca, dedicated to "the elimination of citizens for their activism in political parties and the simple suspicion that they collaborate with armed groups," represented a greater potential threat to the country than the army and guerrillas combined.[15] Barrancabermeja was described as being the main staging ground for politically motivated killings in the country. The report noted: "the growing recourse to the privatization of justice is very worrying. It not only represents a private method of settling accounts. . . . It also represents the privatization of the administration of the political and justice systems."[16] The state, the authors contended, was allowing paramilitaries to illegally prosecute a war on suspected guerrillas and proponents of social and political change. Barranca was already singled out as an egregious case study.

In the late 1980s, Colombian popular movements and concerned scholars embraced human rights as a precondition to social, economic, and political change. It was time to address political violence in its complexity, in contradistinction to the view that political violence occurred mainly as fighting between belligerent armies. In September 1987 Colombia's largest trade union federation, the Central Unitaria de Trabajadores (CUT), called a one-hour strike in support of human rights.[17] Then, in December 1987, a human rights forum was convened in Bogotá by faculty from the city's three top universities. As previously discussed, the forum brought together top researchers, journalists, and social activists, as well as the government's top human rights official, the inspector general. A joint declaration read as follows: "Now more than ever the crisis in the country has gone beyond the diagnoses and the proposals of those Colombians who work toward democracy. It is no longer about finding an adequate distribution of economic and cultural goods, or of providing access without exclusion to political representation, but rather, above all else, to safeguard the most basic human rights. Life is threatened. Those of us who hold the ideal that difference should not be persecuted are being treated as enemies to be exterminated."[18] In his address, the political scientist Francisco Leal Buitrago said that "political violence in Colombia has reached intolerable limits," taking care to mention both guerrillas and paramilitaries as perpetrators of terror.[19] The recommendations put forward by the forum included staging citizens' protests, human rights education, concerted government action to end impunity, the dismantling of paramilitary groups, and the promotion of civic values.

During the late 1980s the Colombian state began to adopt international human rights norms into law. The number of Colombian judges, lawyers, and other public officials assigned to monitor and protect human rights was impressive, yet most crimes would continue to go unreported. Most violations that were denounced would never be effectively investigated due to threats against judicial personnel, the imposition of "state of siege" legislation, and the increase in paramilitarism.[20] By 1991, with the approval of a new constitution, the offices of the human rights ombudsman and attorney general were created. And yet just as these advances came into being, propelled forward by high-level discussions around the causes of the current crisis, violence in Colombia reached new heights and spread to almost every corner of the national territory. Nonetheless, it is important to recognize that the sacrifices of grassroots activists in Colombia have helped to make advances around human rights possible at the national level.

Rethinking Advocacy Networks

Human rights represent an important and historically contingent field of social and political struggle for progressive social movements. For frontline activists working in a conflict area, where violence threatened to undo decades of social mobilization, it is hardly surprising that activists' concerns extended beyond civil and political rights. Francisco Campos, former member of CREDHOS and spokesperson for the Coordinadora Popular civil society coalition, says that human rights movements must encompass wider struggles for social and economic justice if they are to stay relevant: "I think that is a much distorted view, a narrow view of human rights. When one is able to understand the comprehensiveness of human rights, and fully commit oneself, ethically and morally, politically. . . . Because the comprehensive defense of human rights is the defense of life, of dignity, of development, and of democracy. I don't know what on earth could be more vanguardist than that."[21] In order to understand the impact of human rights movements, I have argued that it is essential to look into the local roots of human rights activism. Do human rights movements create new channels of popular participation? The history of the movement for human rights in the Magdalena Medio is a unique and illustrative case study that brings into clear focus the relationships that exist between social movements and human rights in a context of armed conflict.

CREDHOS encouraged solidarity between diverse social movements around the principles of basic human rights. During the first most difficult years of the dirty war in Barrancabermeja, CREDHOS helped to galvanize activists and ordinary citizens alike. Hundreds of people signed up to become members of CREDHOS, and individuals working with all of the main labor and social movement organizations in the region participated in CREDHOS assemblies. After 1987 human rights became the number one reason for social protest in Colombia. Nowhere was this dynamic more apparent than in Barrancabermeja, where politically motivated violence inspired local residents to take to the streets on a regular basis. However, this would never have been possible if not for the fact that the civic-popular movement in Barrancabermeja was reaching a peak in the late 1980s. When the Coordinadora Popular was created in 1983 as a means of carrying out joint work by activist groups on a permanent basis, it seemed as if forward momentum for social change had been achieved. Military-paramilitary repression then undermined the capacity of Barranca's civic-popular movement to influence the national government. Perhaps more significantly, direct attacks against activists in the 1980s constituted an existential threat to Barranca's deeply rooted popular radical political culture.

The potential effectiveness of the movement for human rights in the Magdalena Medio was demonstrated very early on. *Barranqueños* participated in protests and mass funerals for the victims of political violence on a scale that recalled the landmark *paros cívicos* of 1963, 1975, 1977, and 1983. During the first year of its existence, CREDHOS convened national government officials to Barranca to partake in regional meetings in which *campesinos* denounced abuses taking place in isolated rural areas, where the presence of the national civilian government was weak. Almost as quickly, the movement's capacity to staunch the violence was tested. In 1989 paramilitaries working with high-ranking regional militarily authorities struck a major blow against human rights by targeting the national government. The massacre of La Rochela demonstrated that social movements, not government officials, were going to have to take responsibility for monitoring and defending human rights. Soon thereafter came direct attacks on CREDHOS and other groups engaged in documenting and protesting rights abuses. Notwithstanding the many lives lost during the 1980s and 1990s in the Magdalena Medio, the civic-popular movement was able to reinvent itself, and carry on human rights work under different guises.

The most influential studies of the history of human rights activism in Latin America focus on popular responses to military dictatorships in the southern cone countries of Argentina and Chile, rather than on areas of armed conflict.[22] This has skewed the findings of political scientists and legal theorists toward readings of human rights that are mainly concerned with civil and political rights and transitions to formal democracy. The focus on dictatorships leaves out the complicated dimensions of state participation in simultaneously institutionalizing and undermining human rights, as has happened in Colombia. The focus on the achievement of political transitions also prevents us from seeing how human rights movements learn and adapt through crises. In Barrancabermeja, human rights activists aimed to save lives and protect spaces for civil society organizing and political debate. Groups such as CREDHOS, ANUC, the USO, and others worked on ensuring that their constituencies are not deprived of what Yolanda Becerra describes as the right to breathe: the human energy needed to assemble, protest, and engage in dialogue with government authorities on a range of social and economic issues.[23] Human rights activists in the Magdalena Medio focused on the reduction of violence in the context of advocating broader social change. In areas of armed conflict, human rights work is a necessary corollary and enabler of social activism, and many organizations in Barranca consider it to be a central aspect of their overall work.[24] If human rights activists in the Magdalena Medio were neutral or indifferent with respect to historical social struggles, they would invariably be less relevant, incapable of mobilizing public opinion, and therefore less effective.

In their highly influential work on transnational advocacy networks, Keck and Sikkink demonstrate that grassroots activists can be successful in shaping the behavior of states. The "naming and shaming" of human rights violators, when combined with economic and political pressure, has proven an effective strategy in some cases.[25] In their conception, human rights movements begin to effect change when local civil society activists alert the international community to human rights atrocities.[26] Governments that violate human rights typically deny allegations of abuse and counterattack. This is often followed by a back-and-forth debate between international organizations and specific states, until "norm-consistent behavior," or compliance with human rights law, is achieved and sustained. Argentina is considered by some scholars to be a successful case because of the way in which NGOs and foreign governments rallied to force an abusive military regime out of power. Between 1977 and 1982, local activists such as the Madres de la Plaza de Mayo and the Nobel Laureate Adolfo Pérez Esquivel, in cooperation with international NGOs, the UN, and the U.S. government, all acted in favor of a transition to formal democracy in Argentina.[27]

By telling the story of human rights in transnational perspective many authors overlook the specific forms and content of protest that constitute the main thrust of human rights activism. In this book I argue that if we look to local contexts, then we can develop new ways of thinking about the relationship between popular movements, human rights, and social change. To be sure, CREDHOS provided larger organizations such as the Colectivo de Abogados, Amnesty International, Human Rights Watch, and others with "a concrete picture" that helped make the experience of repression "real to an international public."[28] The dozens of reports and urgent actions published by CREDHOS in the first few years are replete with the type of fine-grained details that would put a human face to international human rights reports. Human rights activists in Barrancabermeja challenged U.S. military cooperation with Colombia directly, as evidenced by Jorge Gómez Lizarazo's lobbying work in Washington, DC. They developed synergies with groups such as

Amnesty International and Peace Brigades International and even received funding from the European Union. But the main functions of CREDHOS—popular education, documentation, and denunciation through judicial authorities, municipal government, and news media—all took place mainly within the local sphere. Even when the national government was involved, the actions undertaken by CREDHOS and others were local. And none of these actions would have been given credence if not for the mobilization of ordinary citizens, manifested by the *paro cívico*. The impetus behind these efforts was popular indignation about political violence.

One of the critiques leveled at human rights movements is that they are limited in their capacity to effect social change by virtue of being liberal and reformist, rather than radical and revolutionary. At stake in this critique is the very definition of human rights. As Winifred Tate observes, some Colombian leftists have argued that human rights were a "bourgeois concept, originating in the West to strengthen the hegemony of the United States."[29] This is a similar critique put forward by legal scholar Makau Mutua, who has argued persuasively that international human rights norms privileged individual rights over social and economic justice in the case of post-Apartheid South Africa.[30] This observation has important historical implications for global debates around human rights.[31] There are two main schools of thought on the issue of human rights ascendancy in the late Cold War period. Are human rights movements nonthreatening abrogations of the aim to effect real socio-economic and political change? Or are human rights simply a more realistic transformative praxis, a view promoted by a much larger group of scholars? As Samuel Moyn has written, "Human Rights emerged as a minimalist, hardy utopia that could survive in a harsh climate."[32] A third option opened up by the case of conflict areas such as Barranca is that human rights constitute a nonreducible field of policies and practices.

The broad-based popular social movements that organized around human rights principles in Barrancabermeja in the late 1980s were, in the words of the CREDHOS founding member Rafael Gómez, on the "threshold" of a historic struggle. But what exactly was the nature of that struggle? Left-wing political movements in the Magdalena Medio throughout the twentieth century bequeathed local activists a revolutionary vision and language. Yet, at the same time, activists in Barrancabermeja were engaged directly in processes of political negotiation with the state. From the perspective of the unionized oil workers, peasants, or urban squatters, there was no contradiction between negotiation and disruption, between reform and revolution.[33] The CREDHOS cofounder Jorge Gómez Lizarazo believed that the defense of human rights called for popular mobilization and that the legal defense of the victims of violence, in and of itself, was insufficient: "A series of assassinations took place in the region, and demands around economic and social issues turned into demands around human rights. During the struggles of the 1970s there had been some detentions and abuses, some torture, but these were things that you could challenge from a legal point of view. But death—that required a movement."[34]

Long before the term "human rights" entered the vernacular of social movement activists in Barranca, oil workers made rights claims on the Colombian state. Unionized workers withheld their labor and demanded recognition for freedom of association, representation, and collective bargaining. In the early twentieth century, Colombian workers did not have the legal right to strike, yet they were able to have a positive impact on national politics and expand the national social benefits regime.[35] Workers' claims on labor rights were expressed more fully in Colombian law in the 1930s during the moderate reformist governments led by the Liberal Party. Because Tropical Oil was foreign owned, strike actions had important international dimensions as well, and the union developed a strong nationalist ideology. While many labor leaders espoused radical leftist political beliefs, the battles fought during the era of Tropical Oil were mostly over basic civil rights. Similar dynamics continued through the era of national control. Acts of sabotage were carried out against oil pipelines beginning in the early 1960s, though never in the name of the union. When they were arrested and dragged into military courts, oil workers offered legal arguments to demonstrate their innocence and the illegitimacy of the proceedings.

The Legacy of Local Human Rights Movements

If the language of human rights displaced the discourses of socialism and revolution that were such important aspects of Latin American popular political culture in the late twentieth century, then what are the implications of such a change? Parsing the academic debate around what sort of social and political changes are set in motion by the advance of human rights, I argue that Latin American human rights activism viewed from the ground up is mainly about the persistence of previously existing projects for social change. The advent of human rights movements in the later half of the twentieth century in Latin America must be understood with respect to prior forms of social activism. When we do this, we see that human rights movements are heterodox, complex iterations of past struggles. These struggles are at once radical and reformist. This allows us to read human rights from the activists' point of view, as a paradigm of social protest and a field of politics. Human rights are not necessarily whatever we want them to be, but definitions are contingent on time and place.[36]

Human rights movements do not constitute simple humanitarian responses to violence, although this is the impression left by the work they are called on to carry out. As has already been stated, "human rights violation" is a category for making violence socially and politically legible, establishing legal account-ability, and locating specific acts in broader histories. Amnesty International, the UN, and the Department of State would have no analysis of the Colombian situation, or the situation in the Democratic Republic of Congo, or any-where else where armed conflict appears inscrutable, without the work of frontline human rights defenders. The contentious politics that give rise to rights movements—their social origins—are all too often eclipsed by violence, both discursively and literally. While the history of human rights activism cannot be decoupled from the narratives of atrocity that human rights move-ments themselves reproduce, we can take a critical look at why, how, and with what impact people organize collectively around human rights. To paraphrase the oral historian Alessandro Portelli, I have sought to understand what these pioneering human rights activists did, but also what they wanted to do, what they believed they were doing, and what they now think they did.[37] We have to see human rights defenders for who they really are: complex actors, with multiple identities, oftentimes working within deep currents of social activism, vulnerable, capable of making mistakes, and capable of self-criticism. In short, researchers need to resist universalizing human rights talk in favor of close contextual analysis.

Human rights activism in conflict areas reflects the pressures to which social movements in these areas are subject. Human rights activists in Barranca-bermeja have made enormously important contributions to interpretations of the Colombian conflict precisely because they understand the ways in which decisions are made by local actors. Their documentation of political violence has elucidated the phenomenon of paramilitarism and the relationship between the state and private armed groups in Colombia. The public *denuncias* or urgent actions issued by CREDHOS and other organizations in Barranca are also calibrated to have a positive impact on events at the local level. At the outset, this has meant framing violations of human rights in a social and political context. Later on, it meant exercising discretion. Yolanda Becerra of the OFP sums up this point eloquently:

> I think that in Barranca we have been specialists in the definition and defense of human rights, conceptually and in practice. We have been

quite creative, really, in the methods we have used to defend human rights; we have had tremendous debates, analysis, to find solutions that fit each political moment, to know how to make effective denunciations. . . . It used to be that our work was more political, more ideological, it reflected the way we thought, our analysis. Then we began working more on the basis of simply reporting the facts, so that it did not come across as biased. . . . It has been a process, a dynamic, but what is most important I think is that no political crisis or conjuncture can be an excuse for not acting, despite everything we have been through.[38]

It may be too early to judge the outcomes of armed conflict in Barrancabermeja. While the civic-popular movement was not able to stop the advance of paramilitarism, there are other ways in which its efforts have been effective. For more than two decades, social activists in the Magdalena Medio have been subject to constant pressure from armed groups, mostly by paramilitary forces closely linked to the Colombian military. Yet they have survived to tell the tale and engage in important debates, local and international, about the ways in which human rights issues can be addressed in areas affected by armed conflict and counterinsurgency repression. Popular mobilization has been their greatest strength and source of creative energy in the face of violence.

Notes

Preface

1. Santander, Cesar, Bolívar, Antioquia, Boyacá, Caldas, and Cundinamarca.

2. Miguel Barreto Henriques, "El Laboratorio de Paz en el Magdalena Medio: ¿Un verdadero 'laboratorio de paz'?," in *Guerra y violencia en Colombia: Herramientas e interpretaciones*, ed. Jorge A. Restrepo and David Aponte (Bogotá: Editorial Pontificia Universidad Javeriana, 2009), 504.

3. Liam Mahony and Luis Enrique Eguren, *Unarmed Bodyguards: International Accompaniment for the Protection of Human Rights* (West Hartford, CT: Kumarian Press, 1997).

4. Since 1994, Peace Brigades International has maintained teams of a half-dozen international observers in Barrancabermeja. In the following years, other international organizations, including Médecins Sans Frontières, Christian Peacemaker Teams, Amnesty International, Paz y Tercer Mundo, and others set up projects in the city. The city would become a reference point for many international activists. Amnesty published its first ever in-depth report on Barranca in May 1999. Amnesty International, *Barrancabermeja: A City under Siege* (London: Amnesty International Publications, 1999).

5. Adam Isacson, "The New Masters of Barranca: A Report from CIP's Trip to Barrancabermeja, Colombia, March 6–9, 2001" (Washington, DC: Center for International Policy, April 2001).

6. At U.S. Senate hearings evaluating the progress of Plan Colombia in October 2003, expert witnesses and legislators made the link between Plan Colombia, eradication of drug crops, and forced internal migration. According to expert witnesses, there were nearly 2.5 million internally displaced persons (IDPs) in Colombia at the time. Committee on Foreign Relations, U.S. Senate, "Challenges for U.S. Policy towards Colombia: Is Plan Colombia Working?" (Washington, DC: U.S. Department of State, October 29, 2003), 34.

7. I discuss the process of conducting oral history interviews in Barrancabermeja in the essay "The Heart of Activism in Colombia: Reflections on Activism and Oral History Research in a Conflict Area," in *Off the Record: Unspoken Negotiations in the Practice of Oral History*, ed. Stacey Zembrycki and Anna Sheftel (New York: Palgrave Macmillan, 2013), 239–254.

8. International Federation for Human Rights (FIDH), "Colombia: Caso de David Ravelo Crespo," Communiqué (November 4, 2014), https://www.fidh.org/es/americas/colombia/16400-colombia-caso-de-david-ravelo-crespo#nb1.

9. "¿Las mentiras de 'El Panadero'?," *El Espectador* (Bogotá), September 16, 2014; "'El Panadero,' a juicio por el caso de la periodista Jineth Bedoya," *El Tiempo* (Bogotá), September 30, 2014.

Introduction

1. Rafael Gómez Serrano, interview with author (Bogotá, September 27, 2005). Unless otherwise noted, all translations are mine.

2. "Asesinada menor que presenció atentado a miembros de la UP," *El Tiempo* (Bogotá), May 5, 1987.

3. "La desbarrancada," *Semana* (Bogotá), May 25, 1987.

4. The term "dirty war," used by Colombian activists since the mid-1980s to describe a pattern of terrorist actions targeting civilians, is a key concept in this book. A "dirty war" can be defined as a covert military campaign carried out by state forces or their proxies against political dissidents. Practices such as arbitrary detention, torture, enforced disappearance, and extrajudicial execution were employed by Colombian military and paramilitary forces against social and political activists, but also guerrillas, suspected guerrillas, or guerrilla sympathizers.

5. Mauricio Archila Neira, *Idas y venidas: Vueltas y revueltas; Protestas sociales en Colombia, 1958–1990* (Bogotá: Instituto Colombiano de Antropología e Historia, ICANH, y el Centro de Investigación y Educación Popular, CINEP, 2004), 149.

6. Ibid., 195.

7. Homicide rates in Colombia had been steadily rising since the mid-1970s. The most dramatic increases occurred between 1984 and 1987. There were 9,969 homicides in 1984, 12,922 in 1985, 15,735 in 1986 and 17,447 in 1987. Ibid., 237.

8. "1987, el año de la 'guerra sucia': Más de 2.500 muertos," *El Mundo* (Medellín, Antioquia), December 28, 1987.

9. CREDHOS, "Barrancabermeja y la impunidad en los delitos de lesa humanidad" (Barrancabermeja, November 1989), 24, CREDHOS Archives, Barrancabermeja.

10. Mauricio Archila Neira, *Aquí nadie es forastero: Testimonios sobre la formación de una cultura radical Barrancabermeja, 1920–1950* (Bogotá: Centro de Investigación y Educación Popular, 1978), 199.

11. Leon Zamosc, "The Political Crisis and the Prospects for Rural Democracy in Colombia," *Journal of Development Studies* 25, no. 4 (1990): 48.

12. "Incidentes en paro de Barranca," *El Tiempo* (Bogotá), May 7, 1987.

13. Francisco Campos, interview with author (Barrancabermeja, September 20, 2005).

14. "Jornada ejemplar: El segundo paro cívico en Barrancabermeja," *Voz Proletaria* (Bogotá), May 14, 1987.

15. It is impossible to calculate the political homicide rate for Barrancabermeja during the 1980–2010 period with total accuracy. Based on government and non-governmental sources, we can estimate that there were between 3,000 and 5,000 murders committed in Barranca between 1982 and 2002. Another 1,000 homicides were committed in Barrancabermeja between 2003 and 2009. The human rights group Corporación Regional para la Defensa de los Derechos Humanos (CREDHOS) documented 902 homicides between 1988 and 1990 alone. CREDHOS, "La complicidad de la indiferencia" (Barrancabermeja, April 1991), 19, CREDHOS Archives, Barrancabermeja. The Colombian government's National Department of Statistics (DANE) recorded 331 homicides for the year 1991. Vicepresidencia de la República de Colombia, *Panorama actual de Barrancabermeja* (Bogotá: Observatorio del Programa Presidencial de Derechos Humanos y Derecho Internacional Humanitario, 2001), 8. The Coroner's Office in Barrancabermeja documented 1,307 homicides between 1999 and 2003. The Coroner's Office concluded that 84–89 percent of the homicides committed in 2000 (429 of 480) and 2001 (325 of 383) were politically motivated. See reports by Centro de Referencia Nacional Sobre la Violencia, "Lesiones infligidas por otros," http://www.medicinalegal.gov.co/.

16. Mauricio García Villegas and Rodrigo Uprimny Yepes, "La normalisation de l'exceptionnel sur le contrôle juridictionnel des états d'urgence en Colombie," in *Justice et démocratie en Amérique Latine*, ed. Marie-Julie Bernard and Michel Carraud (Grenoble: Presses Universitaires de Grenoble, 2005), 117–144.

17. John Ledy Phelan, *The People and the King: The Comunero Revolution in Colombia, 1781* (Madison: University of Wisconsin Press, 1978).

18. Winifred Tate, *Counting the Dead: The Culture and Politics of Human Rights Activism in Colombia* (Berkeley: University of California Press, 2007), 4.

19. UN Human Rights Commission, Report of the United Nations High Commissioner for Human Rights on the Human Rights Situation in Colombia, 58th session of the UN Human Rights Commission, Geneva, March 13, 2002.

20. van Isschot, "The Heart of Activism in Colombia," 241.

21. Irene Villamizar, interview with author (Barrancabermeja, March 8, 2006).

22. Tate, *Counting the Dead*, 50.

23. Liga Internacional por los Derechos y la Liberación de los Pueblos, *El camino de la niebla*, vol. 3, *Masacres en Colombia y su impunidad* (Bogotá: Liga Internacional por los Derechos y la Liberación de los Pueblos, Sección Colombiana, 1990), 444.

24. "Grupos identificaods y áreas de asentamientos," *El Tiempo* (Bogotá), October 1, 1987.

25. Tate, *Counting the Dead*, 51.

26. See Article 3, "Permiso del Estado," of the decree creating these private security units. Presidencia de la República, Julio César Trujillo, Ministerio de Defensa Nacional,

Rafael Pardo Rueda, Decreto número 356 de 1994 (febrero 11), "Por el cual se expide el Estatuto de Vigilancia y Seguridad Privada."

27. See Carlos Medina Gallego, *Autodefensas, paramilitares y narcotráfico en Colombia: Origen, desarrollo y consolidación, el caso "Puerto Boyacá"* (Bogotá: Editorial Documentos Periodísticos, 1990), and Mauricio Romero, *Paramilitares y autodefensas: 1982–2003* (Bogotá: Editorial Planeta Colombiana, S.A., Instituto de Estudios Políticos y Relaciones Internacionales, 2003).

28. In the middle of the first decade of the twenty-first century, a political scandal rocked Colombia, based on revelations that leading members of the Colombian Congress and the government of Álvaro Uribe were involved in the financing and organizing of right-wing paramilitary groups. Mauricio Romero, ed., *Parapolítica: La ruta de la expansión paramilitar y los acuerdos políticos* (Bogotá: Corporación Nuevo Arco Iris, 2007), and Jasmin Hristov, *Blood and Capital: The Paramilitarization of Colombia* (Athens: Ohio University Press, 2009).

29. Germán Guzmán Campos, Orlando Fals Borda, and Eduardo Umaña Luna, *La Violencia en Colombia*, 2 vols. (reprint, Bogotá: Taurus Historia, 2005).

30. The term *violentología* came into common usage among Colombian academics in the late 1980s, at a time when explanations of violence in Colombia that went beyond the hypothesis of competition between Liberals and Conservatives gained mainstream recognition. Comisión de Estudios sobre la Violencia, *Colombia: Violencia y democracia; Informe presentado al Ministerio de Gobierno* (Bogotá: Universidad Nacional de Colombia, 1987). For a review of the literature produced during this period, see Catherine C. LeGrand, "La política y la violencia en Colombia (1946–1965): Interpretaciones en la década de los ochenta," *Memoria y sociedad* 2, no. 4 (November 1997): 79–110.

31. Alejandro Reyes Posada, ed., *Pacificar la paz: Lo que no se ha negociado en los acuerdos de paz* (Bogotá: Comisión de Superación de La Violencia, 1992).

32. Several human rights activists from Barranca have written undergraduate or graduate theses reflecting on local social, economic, and political circumstances. See Juan de Dios Castilla Amell, "Participación popular y movimiento social: Barrancabermeja 1971–1985" (master's thesis, Universidad de los Andes, 1989); Ubencel Duque Rojas, "Conflictos y paz, realidad y aprendizajes significativos en la Región del Magdalena Medio" (master's thesis, Universidad Pedagógica Nacional, 2004); Jhon Jairo Londoño et al., "Estudio económico-social de Barrancabermeja 1977–1988" (undergraduate thesis, Universidad Cooperativa de Colombia, 1991).

33. Archila, *Idas y venidas*, 235.

34. Edward L. Cleary, *The Struggle for Human Rights in Latin America* (Westport, CT: Praeger, 1997), 63.

35. Several Colombian groups have undertaken major historical memory and archival projects in the past decade. Colombia's Association of Families of the Detained and Disappeared (ASFADDES) published a book on its twenty-five-year history. Asociación de Familiares de Detenidos-Desaparecidos, *Veinte años de historia y lucha: ASFADDES con todo el derecho* (Bogotá: ASFADDES, 2003).

36. Important studies include Flor Alba Romero, "El movimiento de derechos humanos en Colombia," in *Movimientos sociales, estado y democracia en Colombia*, ed. Mauricio Archila and Mauricio Pardo (Bogotá: Centro de Estudios Sociales, Facultad de Ciencias Humanas, Universidad Nacional de Colombia, 2001); Sophie Daviaud, "Las ONG colombianas de defensa de los DD HH de cara a las violencias," in *Violencias y estrategias colectivas en la región andina: Bolivia, Colombia, Ecuador, Perú y Venezuela*, ed. Eric Lair and Gonzalo Sánchez (Bogotá: Grupo Editorial Norma, 2004); Robin Kirk, *More Terrible than Death: Violence, Drugs, and America's War in Colombia* (New York: Public Affairs, 2003); Christopher Welna and Gustavo Gallón, eds., *Peace, Democracy, and Human Rights in Colombia* (Notre Dame, IN: University of Notre Dame Press, 2007).

37. Tate, *Counting the Dead*, 71.

38. Upendra Baxi, *The Future of Human Rights* (Oxford: Oxford University Press, 2002), xi.

39. Richard A. Wilson, "Afterword to 'Anthropology and Human Rights in a New Key': The Social Life of Human Rights," *American Anthropologist* 108, no. 1 (March 2006): 77–83.

40. Margaret Keck and Kathryn Sikkink, *Activists beyond Borders: Advocacy Networks in International Politics* (Ithaca, NY: Cornell University Press, 1998).

41. CREDHOS, "Estatutos de constitución" (Barrancabermeja, April 1989), 2, CREDHOS Archives, Barrancabermeja.

42. Progressive Catholic priests play a particularly important role in laying the groundwork for community-based organizing in favor of human rights. Such clerical activism was rare in Colombia, but not unheard of. See Grupo de Memoria Histórica de la Comisión Nacional de Reparación y Reconciliación, *Trujillo, una tragedia que no cesa: Primer informe de memoria histórica de la Comisión Nacional de Reparación y Reconciliación*, 2nd ed. (Bogotá: Editorial Planeta Colombiana, 2008).

Chapter 1. Oil Workers, *Colonos*, and the Roots of Popular Radicalism

1. Originally published in the oil workers' union newspaper *El Frente Obrero*. Aristóbulo Quiroga, "El Pito de la Troco," in *Barrancabermeja en textos e imágenes*, ed. Alfonso Torres Duarte (Barrancabermeja: Alcaldía de Barrancabermeja, 1997), 69.

2. Laura Restrepo, *The Dark Bride*, trans. Stephen Lytle (Toronto: Harper Flamingo Canada, 2002), 2.

3. Jacques Aprile-Gniset, *Génesis de Barrancabermeja: Ensayo* (Bucaramanga: Instituto Universitario de la Paz, Departamento de Ciencias Políticas, 1997), 215.

4. Alfredo Molano, *Los años del tropel* (Bogotá: Fondo Editorial CEREC, 1985).

5. Archila, *Aquí nadie es forastero*, 109.

6. Migrants from Santander, the department where Barranca is located, are a major influence in Barranca's origins, but the city is also strongly identified with its Caribbean roots. For further reading on music and popular culture of the Caribbean

coast and Magdalena River, see Peter Wade, *Music, Race, and Nation: Música Tropical in Colombia* (Chicago: University of Chicago Press, 2000).

7. Benedict Anderson, *Imagined Communities: Reflections on the Origin and Spread of Nationalism* (New York: Verso, 1991).

8. The current borders of the departments of Santander and Norte de Santander were drawn in 1910. From 1857 to 1886 the territory was known as the Estado de Santander and from 1886 to 1910 as El Gran Santander.

9. J. Michael Francis, ed., *Invading Colombia: Spanish Accounts of the Gonzalo Jiménez de Quesada Expedition of Conquest* (University Park: Pennsylvania State University Press, 2007), 35.

10. Colombian novelist Gabriel García Márquez has recounted harrowing journeys across the wide mouth of the Magdalena River, which he describes as having "an oceanic temperament." Gabriel García Márquez, *Living to Tell the Tale*, trans. Edith Grossman (New York: Vintage International, 2003), 7.

11. Ibid., 36.

12. The historical place-names attributed to Barrancabermeja require some clarification. "La Tora" is said to be the original name given by local Yareguíes native peoples to the small village located on the site where Barrancabermeja is located. In the historiography of the conquest, the names "Cuatro Bocas," "Barranca Bermeja," and "Infantas" are also used. The name "Infantas" is said to have been Jiménez's tribute to María and Juana, the daughters of Carlos I of Spain. In 1868 Barranca would be officially renamed Puerto Santander, after the Colombian leader of the war of independence against Spain. Throughout this book I use the name Barrancabermeja, or simply Barranca.

13. As quoted in Rafael Gómez Picón, *Magdalena, río de Colombia*, 7th ed. (Bogotá: Ediciones Tercer Mundo, 1983), 213.

14. Francis, *Invading Colombia*, 84.

15. Years later Jimémez de Quesada would lead another expedition into the interior, reaching the Orinoco River before being forced to turn back. Ibid.

16. For further information, see Gustavo Bell Lemus, "El canal del Dique, 1810–1840: El viacrusis de Cartagena," *Boletín Cultural y Geográfico* 26, no. 21 (1989): 15–23.

17. Tagua, also known as vegetable ivory, is the seed of a palm species used in the making of buttons and jewelry. Quina, also known as cinchona, is the bark of a plant from which the alkaloid quinine is derived, for treatment of malaria. See Frank R. Safford, "Commerce and Enterprise in Central Colombia, 1821–1870" (PhD diss., Columbia University, 1965), 270.

18. "Letter from Mr. Weir the Collector in New Grenada," *Proceedings of the Royal Horticultural Society, from January 1 to December 31, 1964* (London: Spottiswoode, 1964), 109.

19. Ibid.

20. Catherine LeGrand, *Frontier Expansion and Peasant Protest in Colombia, 1850–1936* (Albuquerque: University of New Mexico Press, 1986).

21. In 1824 German investor Johan Bernard Elbers was granted a twenty-year monopoly on steam navigation. Roland E. Duncan, "William Wheelwright and Early Steam Navigation in the Pacific, 1820–1840," *Americas* 32, no. 2 (October 1975): 261.

22. Alejo Vargas Veláquez, *Magdalena Medio Santandereano: Colonización y conflicto armado* (Bogotá: Centro de Investigación y Educación Popular, CINEP, 1992), 31.

23. Aprile-Gniset, *Génesis de Barrancabermeja*, 48.

24. Rafael Antonio Velásquez Rodríguez and Victor Julio Castillo León, *Los Yareguíes: Resistencia y exterminio* (Barrancabermeja: Corporación Memoria y Patrimonio, 2011).

25. The Colombian national territory is divided into large political jurisdictions known as *departamentos*, analogous to U.S. states. The designation *departamento* has been used since the adoption of the 1886 Constitution. *Departamentos* are represented by a governor and departmental assembly. *Muncipios* are subdivisions of *departamentos* analogous to U.S. counties. *Municipios* are represented by mayors and municipal councils and may include large cities, but many are mostly rural. *Corregimientos* are rural subdivisions of *municipios*. *Corregimientos* may include villages. Smaller rural settlements are known as *veredas*. Aprile-Gniset, *Génesis de Barrancabermeja*, 47.

26. Marco Palacios, *Coffee in Colombia: 1850–1970* (Cambridge: Cambridge University Press, 1980), 23.

27. LeGrand, *Frontier Expansion and Peasant Protest*, 41.

28. Rafael Antonio Velásquez Rodríguez and Victor Julio Castillo L., "Resistencia de la etnia Yareguíes a las políticas de reducción y 'civilización' en el siglo XIX," *Historia y Sociedad* 12 (November 2006): 313.

29. Velásquez and Castillo, *Los Yareguíes*, 45.

30. Phelan, *The People and the King*, 52.

31. Rafael Velásquez, "El proceso de exterminio definitivo de los Yareguíes," *Vanguardia Liberal* (Bucaramanga), April 26, 2006.

32. Velásquez and Castillo, *Los Yareguíes*, 218–220.

33. Vargas Velásquez, *Magdalena Medio Santandereano*, 35. For further reading on the Thousand Days' War, see Gonzalo Sánchez and Mario Aguilera, eds., *Memoria de un país en Guerra: Los mil días, 1899–1902* (Bogotá: Planeta, 2001).

34. David Bushnell, *The Making of Modern Colombia: A Nation in Spite of Itself* (Berkeley: University of California Press, 1993), 150.

35. Vargas Velásquez, *Magdalena Medio Santandereano*, 35.

36. David Church Johnson, "Social and Economic Change in Nineteenth-Century Santander, Colombia" (PhD diss., University of California, Berkeley, 1975).

37. Archivo General de la Nación (AGN), Ministerio de Industrias, Departamento de Baldíos, tomo 33, folios 156–159, Petition: Colonos to Ministerio de Obras Públicas (August 6, 1910).

38. Ibid.

39. Velásquez and Castillo, "Resistencia de la etnia Yareguíes," 315.

40. The Irish Republican Roger Casement documented the abuses imposed on native Huitoto people by rubber traders in the Putumayo in the 1900–1920 period. For a compilation of Casement's writings on the Putumayo, see Angus Mitchel, ed., *The Amazon Journal of Roger Casement* (London: Anaconda Editions, 1997).

41. "The Reward of a Petroleum Adventure," *Lamp* (New York), August 1926.

42. The same year another oil concession was purchased in northeastern Colombia by General Virgilio Barco, but these lands were even more isolated than Barranca and would remain undeveloped for more than fifty years.

43. Amanda Romero, *Magdalena Medio: Luchas sociales y violaciones de derechos humanos, 1980–1992* (Bogotá: Corporación Avre, 1992), 41.

44. "Vision, courage and capital required to create an oil field in the toughest wilderness ever tackled by the driller," from "The Reward of a Petroleum Adventure," *Lamp* (New York), August 1926.

45. Law 30 of 1903 specified that all subsoil rights pertaining to coal and oil exploitation had to be approved by Congress. See Jorge Villegas, *Petróleo, oligarquía e imperio* (Bogotá: El Áncora Editores, 1982), 16.

46. Bushnell, *The Making of Modern Colombia*, 102.

47. Marcelo Bucheli, *Bananas and Business: The United Fruit Company in Colombia, 1899–2000* (New York: New York University Press, 2005), 88.

48. Humberto Vélez, "Rafael Reyes: Quinquenio, régimen político y capitalismo," in *Nueva historia de Colombia*, vol. 1, ed. Álvaro Tirado Mejía (Bogotá: Planeta Colombiana, 1989), 199.

49. Jonathan C. Brown, *Oil and Revolution in Mexico* (Berkeley: University of California Press, 1993), 239.

50. Pearson owned the subsoil rights to what was at the time recognized as one of the world's largest oilfields, Mexico's Potrero del Llano. Marcelo Bucheli, "Negotiating under the Monroe Doctrine: Weetman Pearson and the Origins of U.S. Control of Colombian Oil," *Business History Review* 82, no. 3 (Autumn 2008): 529–557.

51. AGN, Ministerio de Minas y Energía, Fondo Minas y Energía, libro 153, tomos 212–214.

52. AGN, Ministerio de Minas y Energía, Fondo Minas y Energía, libro 153, tomo 220.

53. George S. Gibb and Evelyn H. Knowlton, *The Resurgent Years, 1911–1927: History of Standard Oil Company (New Jersey)* (New York: Harper and Brothers, 1956), 369–370.

54. "The oil that had been waiting for so many years seemed impatient to be found. At 80 feet, the first barrel started to flow 50 barrels a day. When it was deepened to 2,260 feet it gushed 5,000 barrels. Two more wells flowed even more prolifically." Ruth Sheldon Knowles, *The Greatest Gamblers: The Epic of American Oil Exploration*, 2nd ed. (Norman: University of Oklahoma Press, 1959), 168.

55. Gibb and Knowlton, *The Resurgent Years*, 371.

56. AGN, Ministerio de Industrias, *Memoria presentada al congreso de 1924* (Bogotá: República de Colombia, 1924), 21.

57. Aprile-Gniset, *Génesis de Barrancabermeja*, 150.

58. Pamela Murray, "Know-How and Nationalism: Colombia's First Geological and Petroleum Experts, c. 1940–1970," *Americas* 52, no. 2 (October 1995): 213.

59. Ministerio de Industrias, *Memoria de 1924*, 15.

60. Ibid., 16.

61. In a landmark antitrust decision in 1911 the U.S. Supreme Court found Standard Oil to be monopolizing the oil business. John D. Rockefeller was then forced to dismember Standard Oil into dozens of smaller companies. Standard Oil of New Jersey remained the largest of these.

62. H. M. Grant, "Solving the Labor Problem at Imperial Oil," in *Canadian Working-Class History: Selected Readings*, 3rd ed., ed. Laurel Sefton MacDowell and Ian Radforth (Toronto: Canadian Scholars Press, 2006), 232–252.

63. In 1921 the Colombian government recognized its former territory of Panama as an independent country in exchange for a $25 million U.S. payout by the U.S. government. Some Colombians accused the United States of utilizing negotiations around indemnization for Panama as leverage to open Colombia to U.S. investors.

64. "Canadians Conquer Tropical Obstacles to Secure Crude Oil," *Globe and Mail* (Toronto), August 9, 1926.

65. Ibid.

66. William Paul McGreevey, *An Economic History of Colombia, 1845–1930* (Cambridge: Cambridge University Press, 1971), 207; Ann Farnsworth-Alvear, *Dulcinea in the Factory: Myths, Morals, Men and Women in Colombia's Industrial Experiment, 1905–1960* (Durham, NC: Duke University Press, 2003), 47.

67. The initial contract between Colombian-French engineer Roberto De Mares and the Colombian government stipulated that the state would receive 15 percent of total production. The amount was changed to 10 percent when the Colombian government signed a contract with the newly incorporated Tropical Oil Company in 1916. In 1919 the Colombian government passed legislation declaring all subsoil resources the property of the Colombian state but quickly reversed this decision upon receiving negative feedback from foreign investors. The Colombian government attempted to increase the percentage of royalties paid to the state in 1927 but was again rebuffed. See John D. Wirth, ed., *The Oil Business in Latin America: The Early Years* (Lincoln: University of Nebraska Press, 1985), 28.

68. Ibid.

69. Greg Grandin, *Fordlandia: The Rise and Fall of Henry Ford's Forgotten Jungle City* (New York: Metropolitan Books, 2009), 319.

70. Aprile-Gniset, *Génesis de Barrancabermeja*, 257.

71. Ibid., 57.

72. Guillermo Serrano Carranza, "Barrancabermeja; fragmentos y territorios: Procesos compositivos del área urbana" (master's thesis, Universidad Nacional de Colombia, 2001), 70.

73. Renán Vega Cantor, Luz Ángela Núñez Espinel, and Alexander Pereira Fernández, *Petróleo y protesta obrera: La USO y los trabajadores petroleros en Colombia*,

vol. 1, *En tiempos de la Tropical* (Bogotá: Corporación Aury Sará Marrugo, 2009), 120.

74. Ibid., 126–128.

75. Jairo Ernesto Luna García, "La salud de los trabajadores y el Tropical Oil Company," conference paper delivered at XIII Congreso Colombiano de Historia (Bucaramanga, August 22–26, 2006), 6.

76. Aprile-Gniset, *Génesis de Barrancabermeja*, 193.

77. Vega Cantor, Núñez Espinel, and Pereira Fernández, *Petróleo y protesta*, 1:128.

78. In exchange for a job and a place to live, young men from across Colombia agreed to indebt themselves to agents acting on behalf of Tropical Oil. Later, recruitment though the *enganche* system coincided with labor unrest, as was the case in 1927 when nearly two thousand men were brought in following a labor stoppage that had resulted in the summary dismissal of half the labor force. See Serrano Carranza, "Barrancabermeja; fragmentos y territorios," 33.

79. Álvaro Valencia Tovar, ed., *Historia de la policía nacional de Colombia* (Bogotá: Planeta, 1993).

80. Aprile-Gniset, *Génesis de Barrancabermeja*, 190.

81. Ibid., 167.

82. Christopher Michael Cardona, "Politicians, Soldiers, and Cops: Colombia's La Violencia in Comparative Perspective" (PhD diss., University of California, Berkeley, 2008).

83. Serrano, "Barrancabermeja; fragmentos y territorios," 6.

84. W. O. Durham, *From Kittyhawk to the Moon: The Life, Times and Heritage of a Texas Oilman* (New York: Vantage Press, 2007).

85. P. Appelbaum and L. Appelbaum, "Barrancabermeja or Bust: Looking for Daddy's Oil Well," *New York Times*, October 28, 1973, 7.

86. Ibid.

87. Gonzalo Buenahora, *Sangre y petróleo*, 2nd ed. (Bogotá: Fotolito Inter, 2000), 29.

88. See Guansú Sohn, "La novela colombiana de protesta social: 1924–1948" (PhD diss., University of Oklahoma, 1976), and Luis Guillermo Romero García, *Sueños de río: Inventario breve de la literatura en Barrancabermeja* (Bogotá: Fundación Somos, 2005).

89. Rafael Jaramillo Arango, *Barrancabermeja: Novela de proxenetas, rufianes, obreros y petroleros* (Bogotá: Editorial E.S.B., 1934).

90. Sohn, "La novela colombiana," 57.

91. Buenahora, *Sangre y petróleo*.

92. There is important and growing body of academic literature on the connections between oil and armed conflict globally, particularly since the United States–led invasion of Iraq in 2003. For work on oil, war, and conflict, see Mary Kaldor, Terry Lynn Karl, and Yahia Said, eds., *Oil Wars* (London: Pluto Press, 2007), and Philippe le Bion, ed., *The Geopolitics of Resource Wars: Resource Dependence, Governance and Violence* (New York: Frank Cass, 2005).

93. Miguel Tinker Salas, *The Enduring Legacy: Oil, Culture, and Society in Venezuela* (Durham, NC: Duke University Press, 2009), 75.

94. Ibid., 116.

95. Gibb and Knowlton, *The Resurgent Years*, 374.

96. Ibid., 376.

97. Luna García, "La salud de los trabajadores," 15.

98. Medófilo Medina, *Historia del Partido Comunista de Colombia*, vol. 1 (Bogotá: Editorial Colombia Nueva, 1980).

99. Bucheli, *Bananas and Business*, 88.

100. Mauricio Archila Neira, "Barranquilla y el Río: Una historia social de sus trabajadores," *Controversia* 142 (November 1987): 46; Sergio Paolo Solano de las Aguas, *Puertos, sociedad y conflictos en el Caribe colombiano, 1850–1930* (Cartagena: Observatorio del Caribe Colombiano, Universidad de Cartagena, 2001), 29.

101. Bucheli, *Bananas and Business*, 122.

102. Mauricio Archila Neira, "La clase obrera colombiana (1886–1930)," in *Nueva Historia de Colombia*, vol. 3, ed. Mauricio Archila Neira (Bogotá: Editorial Planeta, 1989), 223.

103. Ignacio Torres Girado, *María Cano, mujer rebelde* (Bogotá: Publicaciones de la Rosca, 1972), 88. Publication of *Vanguardia Obrera* was suspended during Mahecha's imprisonment in 1924. It was revived in 1926 and published for two more years. The *Vanguardia Obrera* was revived again during the 1930s by a group of left-wing intellectuals in Barranca known as Los Saturnales. Gonzalo Buenahora, *La comuna de Barranca: 9 de abril de 1948* (Bogotá: Gráfica Leipzig, 1971).

104. Renán Vega Cantor, *Gente muy rebelde*, vol. 1, *Enclaves, transportes y protestas obreras* (Bogotá: Ediciones pensamiento crítico, 2002), 270.

105. Ibid., 1:139.

106. Ministerio de Industrias, *Memoria de 1924*, 24.

107. Ibid.

108. Vega Cantor, *Gente muy rebelde*, 1:138.

109. Geo C. Shgweickert, "Informe de un funcionario norteamericano sobre la huelga de Barrancabermeja 1924," *Anuario colombiano de historia social y de la cultura* 13–14 (1985–1986): 319–333.

110. Vega Cantor, *Gente muy rebelde*, 1:234.

111. "The Reward of a Petroleum Adventure," *Lamp*, August 1926.

112. Miguel Escobar Calle, *Apuntes para una cronología de la fotografíía en Antioquia* (Medellín: Biblioteca Pública Piloto de Medellín, Archivos Fotográficos, Memoria Visual de Antioquia y del País, 2001).

113. The term "Flower of Labor" is derived from the title bestowed on women workers who won factory beauty pageants or *reinados*. For more on women's labor in Colombia and the special significance of María Cano, see Farnsworth-Alvear, *Dulcinea in the Factory*, 173.

114. María Cano Márquez, *Escritos*, comp. Miguel Escobar Calle (Medellín: Extensión Cultural Departamental, 1985), 109.

115. Torres Giraldo, *María Cano, mujer rebelde*, 88.

116. AGN, Ministerio de Industrias, *Memoria presentada al congreso de 1927* (Bogotá: República de Colombia, 1927), 49.

117. Ministerio de Industrias, *Memoria de 1927*, 49–51.

118. The term *estado de sitio*, or "state of siege," used in Colombia and throughout Latin America, is derived from French revolutionary law. The term was first used in a decree of the French Constituent Assembly in 1791 granting civilian political authority to the military. In Anglo-Saxon law the preferred terms are "state of emergency" or "martial law." I use the Colombian term *estado de sitio*. Giorgio Agamben, *States of Exception* (Chicago: University of Chicago Press, 2005), 4–5.

119. Richard Sharpless, *Gaitán of Colombia: A Political Biography* (Pittsburgh: University of Pittsburgh Press, 1978).

120. Herbert Braun, *The Assassination of Gaitán: Public Life and Urban Violence in Colombia* (Madison: University of Wisconsin Press, 1985).

121. John W. Green, *Gaitanismo, Left Liberalism, and Popular Mobilization in Colombia* (Gainesville: University Press of Florida, 2003), 330.

122. Ibid., 61.

123. John W. Green, "'Vibrations of the Collective': The Popular Ideology of Gaitanismo on Colombia's Atlantic Coast, 1944–1948," *Hispanic American Historical Review* 76, no. 2 (1996): 287.

124. Gonzalo Sánchez, *1929, los bolcheviques del Líbano* (Bogotá: El Mohan Editores, 1976).

125. Alejo Vargas Velásquez, "Tres momentos de la violencía política en San Vicente Chucurí (de los bolcheviques del año 29 a la fundación del ELN)," *Análisis Político* 8 (September–December 1988): 33–47.

126. Renán Vega Cantor, *Gente muy rebelde*, vol. 4, *Socialismo, cultura y protesta popular* (Bogotá: Ediciones Pensamiento Crítico, 2002), 270.

127. Sánchez, *1929, los bolcheviques del Líbano*, 97.

128. "Red Risings Alarm Colombia, with 10 Dead; Cavalry Involved, Reserves May Be Called," *New York Times*, August 6, 1929.

129. The only killing of a foreign national working for Tropical Oil was the robbery and shooting of paymaster Paul Leroy Keating on May 9, 1930. U.S. Department of State, "Colombia: Murder of American Citizen," *Press Releases* 32 (May 10, 1930): 245.

130. For a discussion of radical Liberalism and its outcomes in a Colombian coffee-growing region, see Michael F. Jiménez, "The Limits of Export Capitalism: Economic Structure, Class and Politics in a Colombian Coffee Municipality, 1900–1930" (PhD diss., Harvard University, 1985).

131. Eric Hobsbawm and Terence Ranger, eds., *The Invention of Tradition* (Cambridge: Cambridge University Press, 1983).

132. Apolinar Díaz Callejas, *Diez días de poder popular: El 9 de abril en Barranca-bermeja* (Bogotá: Editorial el Labrador, 1988), 101.

133. Gonzalo Sánchez, *Los días de la revolución: Gaitanismo y 9 de abril en provincia* (Bogotá: Centro Cultural Jorge Eliécer Gaitán, 1983).

134. Jorge Villegas, *Petróleo colombiano, ganancia gringa*, 2nd ed. (Bogotá: El Áncora Editores, 1998).

135. Murray, "Know-How and Nationalism," 216.

136. In 1945 taxes and royalties earned from oil production represented 7.3 percent of state revenues. Nearly fifteen thousand Colombians were directly employed by the oil industry. The coffee industry's total economic output was double that of oil, and coffee employed hundreds of thousands of Colombians. By 1955 there were 212,970 coffee farms in Colombia, most of which were small owner-administered businesses. Charles Bergquist, *Labor in Latin America: Comparative Essays on Chile, Argentina, Venezuela, and Colombia* (Stanford: Stanford University Press, 1986), 302.

137. Archila, *Aquí, nadie es forestero*, 143.

138. "In 1951 Tropical Oil Company Concession of 30 Years Comes to End: Present Government Seeks Expert Aid from U.S. to Guide Later Acts," *Globe and Mail* (Toronto), August 6, 1948.

139. John Edgar Hicks, personal correspondence, March 21, 1946 (El Centro, Colombia), personal papers and correspondence of John Hicks, Vancouver Island, British Columbia.

140. John Edgar Hicks, personal correspondence, December 29, 1946 (El Centro, Colombia).

141. John Edgar Hicks, personal correspondence, November 3, 1947 (El Centro, Colombia).

142. John Edgar Hicks, personal correspondence, November 17, 1947 (El Centro, Colombia).

143. Vega Cantor, Núñez Espinel, and Pereira Fernández, *Petróleo y protesta*, 1:310.

144. Archila, *Aquí, nadie es forestero*, 144.

145. For further reading on La Violencia, see Paul Oquist, *Violence, Conflict, and Politics in Colombia* (New York: Academic Press, 1980); Mary Roldán, *Blood and Fire: La Violencia in Antioquia, 1946–1963* (Durham, NC: Duke University Press, 2002); Gonzalo Sánchez Gómez and Donny Meertens, *Bandits, Peasants and Politics: The Case of La Violencia in Colombia*, trans. Alan Hynds (Austin: University of Texas Press, 2001); Daniel Pécaut, *L'ordre et la violence: Évolution socio-politique de la Colombie entre 1930 et 1953* (Paris: Editions de l'Ecole des Hautes Etudes en Sciences Sociales, 1987).

146. Robert Karl, "State Formation, Violence, and Cold War in Colombia, 1957–1966" (PhD diss., Harvard University, 2009), 5.

147. Buenahora, *La comuna de Barranca*.

148. Díaz Callejas, *Diez días de poder popular*, 101.

149. Ibid., 144.

150. Guzmán, Fals, and Umaña, *La Violencia en Colombia*, 1:213.

151. Vargas Velásquez, *Magdalena Medio Santandereano*, 214.

152. Guzmán, Fals, and Umaña, *La Violencia en Colombia*, 1:214.

153. Gabriel Ricardo Nemogá, "Contexto social y político de las transformaciones institucionales de la administración de justicia en Colombia," in *El caleidoscopio de las*

justicias en Colombia, vol. 1, ed. Boaventura de Sousa Santos and Mauricio García Villegas (Bogotá: Siglo del Hombre Editores, 2001), 215–260.

154. Luisa Serrano, "Barrancabermeja Ciudad-Región" (paper presented at III Congreso de la Asociación de Historiadores Latinoamericanos y del Caribe, Pontevedra, Spain, October 2001), 10.

155. "De Mares Concession Reverts to Colombia," *Globe and Mail* (Toronto), August 27, 1951.

156. Roldán, *Blood and Fire*, 106.

157. Oquist, *Violence, Conflict, and Politics*, 235.

158. Alberto Flórez-Malagón, *Una isla en un mar de sangre: El Valle de Ubaté durante La Violencia, 1946–1958* (Bogotá: Centro Editorial Javeriano, La Carreta Ediciones, 2005).

159. Roldán, *Blood and Fire*, 145.

160. Bergquist, *Labor in Latin America*, 268.

161. Catherine C. LeGrand, "Historias transnacionales: Nuevas interpretaciones de los enclaves en América Latina," *Nómadas* 25 (October 2006): 144–154.

162. Archila, *Idas y venidas*, 20.

163. Ibid., 177.

Chapter 2. Oil and Water

1. Archila, *Aquí nadie es forastero*, 50.

2. "El gobierno impedirá mas desordenes," *El Espectador* (Bogotá), August 16, 1971.

3. Ejército de Liberación Nacional (ELN), Fuerzas Armadas Revolucionarias de Colombia (FARC), the Movimiento 19 de Abril (M-19), and the Ejército Popular de Liberación (EPL).

4. The state of siege order was signed on February 26, 1971, on the day of a large student protest at the Universidad del Valle, in Cali, which ended in violence, and the deaths of twenty student protestors. Presidente de la República de Colombia, Decreto Legislativo 260 de 1971, *Diario Oficial* No. 33.257 (March 3, 1971).

5. Vega Cantor, Núñez Espinel, and Pereira Fernández, *Petróleo y protesta*, 2:189.

6. For further reading on Colombian expertise in the oil, gas, and coal sectors, see Pamela Murray, *Dreams of Development: Colombia's National School of Mines and Its Engineers, 1887–1970* (Tuscaloosa: University of Alabama Press, 1997), and Frank Safford, *The Ideal of the Practical: Colombia's Struggle to Form a Technical Elite* (Austin: University of Texas Press, 1976).

7. Carlos A. Flórez López and Luisa Castañeda Rueda, *Así se pobló la ciudad: Crecimiento urbano en Barrancabermeja, 1970–1990* (Barrancabermeja: Alcaldía Municipal de Barrancabermeja, 1997), 48.

8. Universidad de los Andes, *Barrancabermeja: Plan de ordenamiento urbano* (Bogotá: Centro de planificación y urbanismo, Centro de estudios sobre el desarrollo económico, sección de sociología, Facultad de artes y ciencias, 1979), 24.

9. Archila, *Idas y venidas*, 67.

10. Vargas Velásquez, *Magdalena Medio Santandereano*, 151.

11. Archila, *Idas y venidas*, 157.

12. Equipo de Trabajo Popular, "El Movimiento Popular en Barrancabermeja," in *Los movimientos cívicos*, ed. Álvaro Cabrera et al. (Bogotá: Centro de Investigación y Educación Popular, CINEP, 1986), 76.b.

13. Francisco Leal Buitrago, *La seguridad nacional a la deriva: Del frente nacional a la posguerra fría* (Mexico City: Alfaomega Grupo Editor, 2002), 39.

14. A. Eugene Havens and Michel Romieux, *Barrancabermeja: Conflictos sociales en torno a un centro petrolero* (Bogotá: Ediciones Tercer Mundo y Facultad de Sociología, Universidad Nacional de Colombia, 1966), 11.

15. "Institutions," *Current Anthropology* 5, no. 2 (April 1964): 118.

16. Havens and Romieux, *Barrancabermeja*, 18.

17. Jaime Carrillo Bedoya, *Los paros cívicos en Colombia* (Bogotá: La Oveja Negra, 1981), 137.

18. Ibid.

19. Sonia M. Rodríguez Reinel, "Barrancabermeja, manifestaciones culturales radicales 1945–1990" (undergraduate thesis, Universidad Nacional de Colombia, Bogotá, 1992).

20. Jairo Chaparro, *Recuerdos de un tropelero* (Bogotá: Centro de Investigación y Educación Popular, CINEP, 1991), 12.

21. Archivo General de la Nación (AGN), Ministerio de Minas y Petróleos, *Memoria presentada al congreso de 1965* (Bogotá: República de Colombia, 1966), 282.

22. AGN, Ministerio de Minas y Petróleos, *Memoria presentada al congreso de 1965, Separata* (Bogotá: República de Colombia, 1966).

23. Vega Cantor, Núñez Espinel, and Pereira Fernández, *Petróleo y protesta*, 2:232–233.

24. "Delicada situación entre los trabajadores de la 'Ecopetrol,'" *Vanguardia Liberal* (Bucaramanga, Santander), July 19, 1963, 3.

25. Ibid.

26. "Paro en Barrancabermeja," *Vanguardia Liberal* (Bucaramanga, Santander), July 21, 1963, 1.

27. "El Comunismo responsable de los hechos en Barranca," *Vanguardia Liberal* (Bucaramanga, Santander), August 18, 1963, 1.

28. Sindicato de Trabajadores de la Shell Condor, Resolución No. 0032, signed by Angel G. Corena Salcedo (July 26, 1963), Ministerio de Minas y Energía.

29. Vargas Velásquez, *Magdalena Medio Santandereano*, 169.

30. Ibid.

31. "El 50% de los Trabajadores de Ecopetrol se hallan laborando," *Vanguardia Liberal* (Bucaramanga, Santander), July 23, 1963.

32. Amanda Romero, *Magdalena Medio*, 59.

33. "7 líderes huelguistas fueron destituidos," *Vanguardia Liberal* (Bucaramanga, Santander), August 17, 1963.

34. "Comisión parlamentaria mediadora a Barranca," *Vanguardia Liberal* (Bucara-manga, Santander), August 28, 1963.

35. AGN, Ministerio de Minas y Petróleos, *Memoria presentada al congreso de 1964* (Bogotá: República de Colombia, 1965), 309–310.

36. In a declaration published in the union newspaper *El Petrolero* in February 1959, the national Federation of Petroleum Workers Unions wrote: "We support the National Front as a formula for undoing political sectarianism and reclaiming the rule of law and democratic freedoms." As quoted in Vega Cantor, Núñez Espinel, and Pereira Fernández, *Petróleo y protesta*, 2:253.

37. Álvaro Zapata-Domínguez, "Etnografía e interpretación interdisciplinaria de la negociación de una convención colectiva en Ecopetrol, Colombia" (PhD diss., Université de Montréal, 2002), 158.

38. Vargas Velásquez, *Magdalena Medio Santandereano*, 194.

39. Zapata-Domínguez, "Etnografía e interpretación interdisciplinaria," 156.

40. Pastoral Social, "Experiencia de trabajo: Período de 1971 a 1986" (Barrancaber-meja: Diócesis de Barrancabermeja, August 1986), 58.

41. Conferencia Episcopal de Colombia, "Diócesis de Barrancabermeja" Conferen-cia Episcopal de Colombia, http://www.cec.org.co/?apc=ba1;002;;-&x=4743.

42. Memorias Primer Congreso Juvenil Diocesano, "Ponencia del eje fe e iglesia: P. Eduardo Díaz Ardila" (Barrancabermeja: Diócesis de Barrancabermeja, 2004), 45.

43. Ibid.

44. On 1961 agrarian reform, see Bruce Michael Bagley, "Political Power, Public Policy and the State in Colombia: Case Studies of the Urban and Agrarian Reforms during the National Front, 1958–1974" (PhD diss., University of California, Los Angeles, 1979).

45. Leopoldo Múnera Ruíz, *Rupturas y continuidades: Poder y movimiento popular en Colombia, 1968–1988* (Bogotá: Universidad Nacional de Colombia, 1998), 243.

46. Vargas Velásquez, *Magdalena Medio Santandereano*, 180.

47. Leon Zamosc, *The Agrarian Question and the Peasant Movement in Colombia: Struggles of the National Peasant Association, 1967–1981* (Cambridge: Cambridge University Press, 1986), 25.

48. Bettina Ng'weno, *Turf Wars: Territory and Citizenship in the Contemporary State* (Stanford: Stanford University Press, 2007), 78.

49. Jonathan Hartlyn, *The Politics of Coalition Rule in Colombia* (Cambridge: Cambridge University Press, 1988), 168.

50. Ng'weno, *Turf Wars*, 78.

51. Archila, *Idas y venidas*, 142.

52. Vargas Velásquez, *Magdalena Medio Santandereano*, 215.

53. Stephen J. Randall, *Alfonso López Michelsen: Su vida, su época*, trans. Paulina Gómez (Bogotá: Villegas Editores, 2008), 203–227.

54. Sánchez Gómez and Meertens, *Bandits, Peasants, and Politics*, 152.

55. Kenneth F. Johnson, "Political Radicalism in Colombia: Electoral Dynamics of 1962 and 1964," *Journal of Inter-American Studies* 7, no. 1 (January 1965): 15–26.

56. Ibid.

57. Vargas Velásquez, *Magdalena Medio Santandereano*, 224.

58. Ibid., 184.

59. Ibid., 189.

60. Ricardo Lara Parada, *El guerrillero y el político: Conversación con Óscar Castaño* (Bogotá: Editorial Oveja Negra, 1984).

61. Libardo Vargas Díaz, *Expresiones políticas del movimiento estudiantil AUDESA, 1960–1980* (Bucaramanga: Ediciones UIS, Escuela de Historia, Universidad Industrial de Santander, 1996).

62. Vargas Velásquez, *Magdalena Medio Santandereano*, 202–203.

63. *Crisis universitaria colombiana 1971: Itinerario y documentos* (Medellín: Ediciones El Tigre de Papel, 1971), 18.

64. Vargas Díaz, *Expresiones políticas del movimiento estudiantil.*

65. In the 1960s the first generation of leaders of the ELN guerrillas had been student activists at the UIS. Vargas Días, *Expresiones políticas del movimiento estudiantil*, 63.

66. In the 1960s the United States provided more than $4 million to fund a reform program at the UIS. For a detailed report on the project, see Programa de las Naciones Unidas para el Desarrollo, "Informe preparado para el gobierno de Colombia por la Organización de las Naciones Unidas para la Educación, la Ciencia y la Cultura, como organismo participante y de ejecución del Programa de las Naciones Unidas para el Desarrollo correspondiente al periodo 1962–1968" (Bucaramanga: Universidad Industrial de Santander, 1968).

67. Vargas Díaz, *Expresiones políticas del movimiento estudiantil*, 64.

68. Juan de Dios Castilla Amell, interview with author (Barrancabermeja, October 26, 2006).

69. Spanish priests and the ELN guerrillas Jose Antonio Jiménez, Domingo Laín, and Manuel Pérez were all members of the Golconda Group. Joseph Novistski, "Radical Priests in Colombia, Heirs to Slain Guerrilla, Have Forged an Open Marxist-Catholic Alliance," *New York Times*, February 16, 1970.

70. Dios Castilla, interview with author.

71. Ibid.

72. Universidad de los Andes, *Barrancabermeja*, 9.

73. Dios Castilla, interview with author.

74. Universidad de los Andes, *Barrancabermeja*, 21.

75. Colombian mayors were named by departmental governors until 1986, after which mayors were elected by popular vote. See María Emma Wills Obregón, *La democracia: Un camino por recorrer; La reforma política en Barrancabermeja de 1986–1988* (Bogotá: Centro de Investigación y Educación Popular, 1989).

76. Luis Pinilla Pinilla, *Horacio Serpa Uribe: Una experiencia, un futuro* (Bogotá: Alfomega, 2002), 25.

77. Ibid., 26.

78. During the 1998 presidential elections, Horacio Serpa was the candidate for the Liberal Party. His campaign rally in Barranca attracted a huge crowd. During his

speech, Serpa declared himself the "revolutionary candidate" and even evoked the name of the radical priest Camilo Torres Restrepo.

79. Álvaro Valencia Tovar, *El final de Camilo* (Bogotá: Tercer Mundo, 1976), 257.

80. Barrancabermeja Municipal Council Minutes, No. 016 (April 28, 1970), Archivo del Concejo Municipal de Barrancabermeja, Barrancabermeja, Colombia.

81. Pastoral Social, "Experiencia de trabajo," 46.

82. Ibid., 49.

83. Luis Pinilla Pinilla, interview with author (Bogotá, December 22, 2007).

84. Salomón Kalmanovitz Krauter, *Economía y nación: Una breve historia de Colombia*, 2nd ed. (Bogotá: Editorial Norma, 2003), 249.

85. C. H. Neff, "Review of 1970s Petroleum Developments in South America, Central America and Caribbean Area," *American Association of Petroleum Biologists Bulletin* 55, no. 9 (September 1971): 1418–1492.

86. AGN, *Memoria del Ministro de Minas y Petróleos al Congreso de 1965, Separata* (1966), 40–41.

87. "Ecopetrol inicia investigación: Sigue paro de 'brazos caídos,'" *Vanguardia Liberal* (Bucaramanga, Santander), July 28, 1971.

88. "Carta blanca a 'USO' para decretar huelga," *Vanguardia Liberal* (Bucaramanga, Santander), July 30, 1971.

89. "Normalidad en Barranca; no se justifica un paro," *El Tiempo* (Bogotá), July 30, 1971.

90. "Explusados 4 obreros de Ecopetrol," *El Tiempo* (Bogotá), August 1, 1971.

91. Ibid.

92. The strike at the pumping station at Puerto Salgar threatened to shut down the flow of gasoline to Bogotá and thus helped Barranca's oil workers get the attention of Bogotá. The army was sent to Puerto Salgar, and local union leader Ricardo Álvarez was arrested. "Trabajadores ocuparon refinería de Ecopetrol," *El Tiempo* (Bogotá), August 6, 1971, 6.

93. "Paro petrolero se inició ayer," *Vanguardia Liberal* (Bucaramanga, Santander), August 6, 1971.

94. Leal, *Seguridad nacional a la deriva*, 75.

95. "Paro petrolero se inició ayer," *Vanguardia Liberal* (Bucaramanga, Santander), August 6, 1971.

96. "Ley marcial contra obreros petroleros aplica Pastrana," *Voz Proletaria* (Bogotá), August 12, 1971.

97. Ibid.

98. "Consejo de guerra a 23 saboteadores," *Vanguardia Liberal* (Bucaramanga, Santander), August 10, 1971.

99. "Daños por varios millones en refinería de Barranca," *Vanguardia Liberal* (Bucaramanga, Santander), August 8, 1971.

100. "Torturados los técnicos en refinería," *El Tiempo* (Bogotá), August 7, 1971.

101. "Amenaza de horca en Barranca," *El Espectador* (Bogotá), August 11, 1971.

102. "'Aterrado' llegó el gobernador," *El Tiempo* (Bogotá), August 10, 1971.

103. The Bogotá-based newspaper *El Tiempo* published no fewer than fifty articles between May and October of 1971, covering all of the events of the strike and military trial.

104. "Con gran tensión se inició el consejo de guerra en Barranca," *El Tiempo* (Bogotá), August 19, 1971.

105. "Normalidad al iniciarse labor en Barrancabermeja," *El Tiempo* (Bogotá), August 24, 1971.

106. Gilberto Chinome was assassinated on July 28, 2005, on the streets of Bogotá. Chinome had received threats thought to be linked to his lawsuit against Ecopetrol for restitution related to the 1971 trial. Public Statement, Unión Sindical Obrera, Comisión Nacional de Derechos Humanos y Junta Directiva Nacional, July 29, 2005, CREDHOS Archives, Barrancabermeja.

107. "El consejo es nulo y debe ser reparada la enorme injusticia," *Voz Proletaria* (Bogotá), November 4–10, 1971.

108. In 1972 the Colombian Supreme Court reached a decision that forced all of the workers sentenced in the case to never return to Barranca.

109. On the second day, the trial was suspended because two of the accused, Julio González Ríos and Francisco Martínez, had given themselves up to the army.

110. "286 años de presidio para 36 ex-trabajadores de Ecoperol," *Vanguardia Liberal* (Bucaramanga, Santander), October 24, 1971.

111. Chaparro, *Recuerdos de un tropelero*, 13.

112. "Gobierno pide amnistía para presos de Barranca," *El Tiempo* (Bogotá), August 1, 1973.

113. "Creado comité de presos políticos," *El Tiempo* (Bogotá), August 22, 1973.

114. "5 bombas en zona petrolera," *El Tiempo* (Bogotá), October 9, 1971.

115. "Calma en Barrancabermeja," *El Tiempo* (Bogotá), October 10, 1971.

116. "Cayó red del ELN: Más de 100 detenidos en Bogotá y Barranca," *El Espectador* (Bogotá), July 9, 1972.

117. Aponte would continue to work in defense of labor and peasant movement members and was the victim of death threats issued in the name of paramilitary groups in Barrancabermeja in 1983 and 1987.

118. Marta Harnecker, *Unidad que multiplica: Entrevista a dirigentes máximos de la Unión Camilista Ejército de Liberación Nacional sobre la historia del ELN, y una reflexión sobre la situación de las guerrillas en ese momento* (Managua: Centro de Documentación y Ediciones Latinoamericanas, 1988), 49.

119. Colonel Hernán Hurtado Vallejo as quoted in María Elvira Bonilla, *Hablan los generales: Las grandes batallas del conflicto colombiano contadas por sus protagonistas* (Bogotá: Editorial Norma, 2005), 147.

120. Harnecker, *Unidad que multipica*, 51.

121. Alfredo Molano, "La justicia guerrillera," in *El caleidoscopio de las justicias en Colombia*, vol. 2, ed. Boaventura de Sousa Santos and Mauricio García Villegas (Bogotá: Siglo del Hombre Editores, 2001), 332.

122. Fabio Vásquez continues to live in Cuba and has never spoken on record about his time with the ELN.

123. Milton Hernández, *Rojo y negro: Historia del ELN* (Tafalla: Txalaparta, 2006), 265.

124. Anonymous interview (Bogotá, 2004), CINEP Archives, Bogotá.

125. Rafael Gómez Serrano, interview with author (Bogotá, September 27, 2005).

126. Pastoral Social, "Experiencia de trabajo," 35.

127. "En forma total la ciudad respondío al paro cívico," *El Sideral* (Barrancabermeja, Santander), January 26, 1975.

128. "El gobierno rechaza amenazas de paro y motines en Barranca," *El Tiempo* (Bogotá), January 29, 1975.

129. "Se enfrentan arzobispo y gobernador en Santander," *El Tiempo* (Bogotá), February 1, 1975.

130. "Comunicado del gobierno," *El Sideral* (Barrancabermeja, Santander), February 16, 1975.

131. "Violencia en Barranca," *El Tiempo* (Bogotá), February 11, 1975.

132. Memorandum to Secretary of State, United States Embassy, Bogotá, February 30, 1975, National Archives, Washington, DC.

133. Pastoral Social, "Experiencia de trabajo," 35.

134. "De militar a civil: Leonel León Gamarra alcalde de Barranca," *El Sideral* (Barrancabermeja, Santander), June 29, 1975.

135. William Fredy Pérez T., "El sistema penal y la emergencia en Colombia," *Scripta Nova: Revista Electrónica de Geografía y Ciencias Sociales* 45, no. 24 (Universidad de Barcelona, August 1, 1999).

136. "Comité de Solidaridad con los Detenidos Políticos," *El Sideral* (Barrancabermeja, Santander), June 6, 1976.

137. In 2003 a compendium of all of the bulletins, press releases, newspaper clippings, and public documents pertaining to the 1977 strike was published under the pseudonym Paul French. Paul French, *No fue una huelga . . . fue una guerra . . . !! Conflicto laboral en Ecopetrol* (Bogotá: Mundo Gráfico Editores, 2003).

138. "El Alcalde Bonilla López no permitirá: 'Los Zánganos no los funcionarios deshonestos,'" *El Sideral* (Barrancabermeja, Santander), October 25, 1976.

139. In its first fifty-five years Barranca was governed by seventy different mayors. See the compilation of municipal government documents published by the mayor's office: Yolanda Sandino de Hoyos, ed., *Informe de actividades 1977* (Barrancabermeja: Alcaldía Municipal de Barrancabermeja, 1997), 127.

140. Alfonso Torres Duarte, ed. *Barrancabermeja en textos e imágenes* (Barrancabermeja: Alcaldía Municipal Barrancabermeja, April 1997), 72.

141. Sandino, *Informe de actividades*, 16.

142. The *Vanguardia Liberal* estimated that more than five thousand women worked as prostitutes in more than three hundred bars and *cantinas* in the city. According to the city's director of health, the women of Barranca suffered high rates of spousal abandonment, unwanted pregnancies, venereal diseases, and tuberculosis. Sandino, *Informe de actividades*, 37.

143. Ibid.

144. Ibid., 44.

145. Vega Cantor, Núñez Espinel, and Pereira Fernández, *Petróleo y protesta*, 2:327.

146. French, *No fue una huelga*, 14.

147. Presidencia de la República, Decreto 2004 de 1977 (agosto 26), *Diario Oficial* No. 34.873 del 22 de septiembre 1977.

148. Vega Cantor, Núñez Espinel, and Pereira Fernández, *Petróleo y protesta*, 2:327.

149. Sandino, *Informe de actividades*, 133.

150. Ibid., 155.

151. Ibid., 138.

152. Ibid., 145.

153. Equipo de Trabajo Popular, "El Movimiento Popular en Barrancabermeja," 86.

154. The practice of throwing tacks onto the streets during *paros cívicos* or strikes was common across Colombia. For a detailed discussion of the tactics employed by oil workers in 1977, see Vega Cantor, Núñez Espinel, and Pereira Fernández, *Petróleo y protesta*, 2:324–346.

155. Pablo Elías González Mongui, *Derechos penal en la relaciones laborales públicas y privadas* (Madrid: Universidad de Jaen, CIVITAS, 1998), 30.

156. Presidencia de la República, Decreto legislative 1923 de 1978 (Septiembre 6), *Diario Oficial* No. 35.101 de 21 de septiembre de 1978.

157. Pastoral Social, "Experiencia de trabajo," 32.

158. Foro Nacional por Colombia, *Primer congreso nacional de movimientos cívicos: Memoria, octubre de 1983* (Bogotá: Foro Nacional por Colombia, 1983).

Chapter 3. War in the Countryside and the Transformation of a Company Town

1. Martha Arenas Obregón, *Cerrando fronteras: Historias contadas del Magdalena Medio* (Barrancabermeja: Programa de Desarrollo y Paz del Magdalena Medio, 1999), 54.

2. Paramilitary organizing by political party bosses and large landholders had been a major factor in the Magdalena Medio during La Violencia. Conservative para militaries called *contrachusmas* carried out assassinations and massacres. See Darío Betancourt and Martha L. García, *Matones y cuadrilleros: Origen y evolución de la violencia en el occidente colombiano* (Bogotá: Tercer Mundo Editores e Instituto de Estudios Políticos y Relaciones Internacionales, Universidad Nacional de Colombia, 1990).

3. "Nuevo éxodo campesino y jornada por la vida: Defender la paz en la región," *La Opinión del Magdalena Medio* 1, no. 4 (1988): 1.

4. Some of the best research into the development of paramilitarism looks at regional dynamics within the wider context of political violence in Colombia. See

Carlos Medina Gallego and Mireya Téllez Ardila, *La violencia parainstitucional: paramilitar y parapolicial en Colombia* (Bogotá: Rodríguez Quito Editores, 1994); Carlos Medina Gallego, *Autodefensas, paramilitares y narcotráfico en Colombia: Origen, desarrollo y consolidación, el caso "Puerto Boyacá"* (Bogotá: Editorial Documentos Periodísticos, 1990); Mauricio Romero, "Changing Identities and Contested Setting: Regional Elites and the Paramilitaries in Colombia," *International Journal of Politics, Culture and Society* 14, no. 1 (2000): 51–70; Mauricio Romero, *Paramilitares y autodefensas: 1982–2003* (Bogotá: Editorial Planeta Columbiana, S.A., Instituto de Estudios Políticos y Relaciones Internacionales, 2003); Nazih Richani, *Systems of Violence: The Political Economy of War and Peace in Colombia* (Albany: State University of New York Press, 2002).

5. According to the United Nations Guiding Principles on Internal Displacement, presented to the UN Commission on Human Rights by Sudanese diplomat and academic Frances M. Deng: "internally displaced persons are persons or groups of persons who have been forced or obliged to flee or to leave their homes or places of habitual residence, in particular as a result of or in order to avoid the effects of armed conflict, situations of generalized violence, violations of human rights or natural or human-made disasters, and who have not crossed an internationally recognized State border." Francis Deng, "The Guiding Principles on Internal Displacement," E/CN.4/1998/53/Add.l, February 11 (New York: United Nations, 1998).

6. Internal displacement due to political violence dates back to the Spanish conquest but was not formally recognized as a major crisis until the 1990s. According to the leading nongovernmental authority on internal displacement in Colombia, the Consultancy on Human Rights and Displacement (CODHES), which was founded in 1992, some 380,863 Colombians were forced from their homes in 2008 (an increase of nearly 25 percent from 2007, and the highest level since 2002, when the number of displaced was greater than 400,000). Consultoría para los derechos humanos y el desplazamiento, "Víctimas emergentes," *Codhes Informa* 75 (April 22, 2009).

7. Vega Cantor, Núñez Espinel, and Pereira Fernández, *Petróleo y protesta*, 2:352.

8. Serrano Carranza, "Barrancabermeja," 33.

9. Ibid., 73.

10. Yolanda Becerra, interview with author (Barrancabermeja, March 10, 2006).

11. Tate, *Counting the Dead*, 80.

12. Jorge Villegas Arango, *Libro negro de la represión: Frente Nacional, 1958–1974* (Bogotá: Comité de Solidaridad con los Presos Políticos, 1974).

13. More than fifty individuals involved in diverse social and labor organizations participated in the formation of the Permanent Committee for the Defense of Human Rights. Dozens of members of the Permanent Committee were killed during the 1980s and 1990s, including four from the Magdalena Medio region. Comité Permanente por la Defensa de los Derechos Humanos, *Derechos humanos en Colombia: Veinticinco años; Itinerario de una historia* (Bogotá: Panamericana Formas e Impresos S.A., 2004), 31, 41.

14. Consuelo Salgar de Montejo, "Observaciones del Comité de Derechos Humanos," Comunicación 64 (Organización de Naciones Unidas, Comité de Derechos Humanos, December 18, 1979).

15. Amnesty International was established in 1961 as a volunteer-driven activist organization that reports on states' compliance with international human rights norms and advocates on behalf of individual human rights defenders. For background on Amnesty International, see Stephen Hopgood, *Keepers of the Flame: Understanding Amnesty International* (Ithaca, NY: Cornell University Press, 2006).

16. Amnesty International, *Violación de los derechos humanos en Colombia: Informe de Amnistía Internacional* (Bogotá: Comité de Solidaridad con los Presos Políticos, 1980).

17. Amnesty International, *Amnesty International Report 1981* (London: Amnesty International Publications, 1981), 129.

18. The Inter-American Commission on Human Rights and the Inter-American Court of Human Rights constitute the investigative and deliberative branches of a regional justice system with jurisdiction in the thirty-five member states of the Organization of American States (OAS). Together they have delivered hundreds of judgments and undertaken dozens of on-site investigations since the OAS was created in 1948.

19. Tate, *Counting the Dead*, 190.

20. At the time, Guatemala, Honduras, Argentina, El Salvador, Uruguay, Chile, Brazil, Haiti, Nicaragua, Paraguay, and Bolivia were governed by military dictatorships. Peru was just emerging from military rule.

21. Americas Watch, *The Central-Americanization of Colombia? Human Rights and the Peace Process* (New York: Americas Watch, January 1986), 17.

22. Gerardo L. Munk, *Authoritarianism and Democratization: Soldiers and Workers in Argentina, 1976–1983* (University Park: Pennsylvania State University Press, 1998), 53.

23. In 1994 several founding members of MAS would establish the Peasant Self-Defense Forces of Córdoba and Urabá (ACCU). In 1997 the leaders of the ACCU would establish the United Self-Defense Forces of Colombia (AUC), a national paramilitary movement that claimed to have thousands of men at arms. For in-depth reading on the origins of the AUC, see Carlos Castaño, *Mi confesión: Carlos Castaño revela sus secretos*, interview by Mauricio Aranguren Molina (Bogotá: Oveja Negra, 2001).

24. Medina, *Autodefensas, paramilitares y narcotráfico*, 120.

25. Amanda Romero, *Magdalena Medio*, 108.

26. Vargas Velásquez, *Magdalena Medio Santandereano*, 245.

27. Puerto Boyacá competes with Puerto Berrío for the title "counterinsurgency capital of Colombia," as declared on billboards at the entrances to both towns.

28. Vargas Velásquez, *Magdalena Medio Santandereano*, 300.

29. Rafael Gómez, interview with author (Bogotá, September 27, 2005).

30. Amnesty International's second visit to Colombia was carried out in 1981.

31. Mario Calderón held a PhD in sociology and was a pioneering human rights organizer. In the late 1980s he would spend time in the paramilitary stronghold of Tierralta, Córdoba. Calderón left the priesthood several years later and married fellow activist-researcher Elsa Alvarado. They would be murdered by paramilitaries in their apartment in Bogotá's Chapinero neighborhood on May 19, 1997.

32. Medina, *Autodefensas, paramilitares y narcotráfico*, 152.

33. Ibid., 156.

34. Ibid.

35. Asociación Nacional de Usuarios Campesinos (ANUC) — Magdalena Medio, "Posición de la ANUC Magdalena Medio Frente a los Problemas de Inseguridad, Tenencia de Tierra y Fomento Agropecuario," Primer Foro Agropecuario de la Zona del Magdalena Medio (Barrancabermeja, July 23, 1983), CREDHOS Archives, Barrancabermeja.

36. Ibid.

37. ANUC — Sector Independiente, "Conclusiones de la Junta Nacional Ampliada" (Barrancabermeja, April 4, 1984), CREDHOS Archives, Barrancabermeja.

38. ANUC — Sector Independiente, "Origen de la Violencia y la Violencia en sí en el Magdalena Medio," I Simposio Internacional y II Seminario sobre Movimientos Sociales en Colombia (Bogotá, July 24–30, 1984), CREDHOS Archives, Barrancabermeja.

39. Richani, *Systems of Violence*, 117–118.

40. Ibid.

41. Álvaro Camacho Guizado, "De narcos, paracracias y mafias," in *En la encrucijada: Colombia en el siglo XXI*, ed. Francisco Leal Buitrago (Bogotá: Editorial Norma, 2006), 394–395.

42. Olga Behar and Carolina Ardila, *El caso Klein: El origen del paramilitarismo* (Bogotá: Icono, 2012).

43. ANUC — Sector Independiente, "Origen de la Violencia," CREDHOS Archives, Barrancabermeja.

44. Kirk, *More Terrible than Death*, 106, 108.

45. Eduardo Pizarro Leongómez, *Una democracia asediada: Balance y perspectiva del conflicto armado en Colombia* (Bogotá: Editorial Norma, 2004), 94.

46. Ibid., 146.

47. Revolutionary Armed Forces of Colombia–People's Army, *FARC-EP: Historical Outline* (Toronto: International Commission, Revolutionary Armed Forces of Colombia-People's Army, 2001), 26.

48. Michael Shifter and Jennifer Stillerman, "U.S. Human Rights Policy toward Colombia," in *Implementing U.S. Human Rights Policy*, ed. Debra Liang-Fenton (Washington, DC: United States Institute of Peace, 2004), 336.

49. Ibid., 335.

50. In 1983 the Batallón Bomboná was one of five battalions in the area reorganized for counterinsurgency purposes under the command of the Fourth Brigade of the Colombian army, based in Medellín. The battalion was closely associated with the rise of paramilitarism in the region. See Proyecto Nunca Más, *Crimenes de lesa humanidad: Zona 14a 1996* (Bogotá: Colombia Nunca Más, 2000), 383.

51. Medina Gallego, *Autodefensas, paramilitares y narcotráfico*, 147.

52. Carlos Miguel Ortiz, "Magdalena Medio," in *La violencia y el municipio colombiano*, ed. Fernando Cubides, Ana Cecilia Olaya, and Carlos Miguel Ortiz (Bogotá: Centro de Estudios Sociales, Universidad Nacional de Colombia, 1998), 82–83.

53. Carlos Salgado and Esmeralda Prada, *Campesinado y protesta social en Colombia, 1980–1995* (Bogotá: Centro de Investigación y Educación Popular, CINEP, 2000), 162.

54. Proyecto Nunca Más, *Crimenes de lesa humanidad*, 296.

55. Ibid., 202.

56. Daniel Pécaut, *Crónica de cuatro décadas de política colombiana* (Bogotá: Editorial Norma, 2006), 304. For detailed commentary on the legacy of Belisario Betancur, see the collection of essays by former ministers and advisers who served during the Betancur administration: Diego Pizano, ed., *La penitencia del poder: Lecciones de la administración del presidente Belisario Betancur, 1982–1986* (Bogotá: Universidad de los Andes, 2009).

57. As quoted in Medina Gallego, *Autodefensas, paramilitares y narcotráfico*, 189.

58. Shifter and Stillerman, "U.S. Human Rights Policy," 336.

59. Proyecto Nunca Más, *Crimenes de lesa humanidad*, 296.

60. The killing of between three thousand and five thousand members of the UP between the creation of the party in 1985 and its official demise in 2002 has been described by some human rights scholars as a political genocide. See Steven Dudley, *Walking Ghosts: Murder and Guerrilla Politics in Colombia* (London: Routledge, 2004); Leah Carroll, *Violent Democratization: Social Movements, Elites, and Politics in Colombia's Rural War Zones, 1984–2008* (Notre Dame, IN: University of Notre Dame Press, 2011); Andrei Gómez-Suárez, "Perpetrator Blocs, Genocidal Mentalities, and Geographies: The Destruction of the Unión Patriótica in Colombia and Its Lessons for Genocide Studies," *Journal of Genocide Research* 9, no. 4 (December 2009): 637–660; Anniseh Van Engeland, "Failed Attempts: The Fuerzas Armadas Revolucionarias de Colombia and the Unión Patriótica," in *From Terrorism to Politics*, ed. Anniseh Van Engeland and Rachael M. Rudolph (Hampshire, England: Ashgate, 2008); Suzanne Wilson and Leah A. Carroll, "The Colombian Contradiction: Lessons Drawn from Guerrilla Experiments in Demobilization and Electoralism," in *From Revolutionary Movements to Political Parties*, ed. Kalowatie Deonandan, David Close, and Gary Prevost (New York: Palgrave Macmillan, 2007).

61. General Yanine Díaz was born in Gramalote, a small town in the mountains of the department of Norte de Santander in 1937. He died in Bogotá of cancer on August 28, 2009, at age seventy-two. At the time of his death, he was facing charges for having ordered paramilitary massacres in the Magdalena Medio in the late 1980s. Presidencia de la República, Secretaría de Prensa, "Presidente Uribe lamenta fallecimientos de Monseñor Gustavo Martínez y del general (r) Yanine Díaz" (August 29, 2009), http://historico.presidencia.gov.co/sp/2009/agosto/29/05292009_i.html.

62. Medina Gallego, *Autodefensas, paramilitares y narcotráfico*, 165.

63. Ibid.

64. Grupo de Memoria Histórica, Comisión Nacional de Reparación y Reconciliación, *La Rochela: Memorías de un crímen contra la justicia* (Bogotá: Ediciones Semana, 2010), 59.

65. Jenny Pearce, *Colombia: Inside the Labyrinth* (London: Latin American Bureau, 1990), 247.

66. Dudley, *Walking Ghosts*, 68.

67. ACDEGAM leaders were named by the Inter-American Court of Human Rights as being among the "intellectual authors" or planners of the 1987 forced disappearance of nineteen tradesmen from the Bucaramanga area as they traveled

through the Magdalena Medio en route to Medellín, in the department of Antioquia. ACDEGAM is also named as having helped plan the La Rochela massacre in 1989. See Inter-American Court of Human Rights, *Case of the Rochela Massacre v. Colombia*, Series C No. 163, Merits, Reparations, and Costs, Judgment of May 11, 2007, 28.

68. Grupo de Memoria Histórica, *La Rochela*, 62–63.

69. Dudley, *Walking Ghosts*, 68.

70. Gómez, interview with author (Bogotá, September 27, 2005).

71. Amanda Romero, *Magdalena Medio*, 108.

72. Ibid.

73. The Juntas de Acción Comunal (JACs) were created in 1958 by the first National Front president, Alberto Lleras Camargo, to administer small development projects in poor rural areas and urban barrios. Intended as a clientelist network to serve the interests of the state, many JACs became bases of independent social organization. See Rodrigo Villar, *El tercer sector en Colombia* (Bogotá: Confederación Colombiana de Organizaciones No Gubernamentales, 2001), 13. As the political scientist Jenny Pearce writes: "In the wake of La Violencia, the National Front government attempted to construct its own communication channels with the people. One of the first laws of the 1958 government was to create Juntas de Acción Comunal (Community Action Committees)." See Pearce, *Colombia*, 148.

74. Castilla, "Participación popular y movimiento social," 102–103.

75. Equipo de Trabajo Popular, "El movimiento popular en Barrancabermeja," 87.

76. Londoño et al., "Estudio económico-social de Barrancabermeja."

77. "Aprueban paro en Barrancabermeja," *Vanguardia Liberal* (Bucaramanga, Santander), April 8, 1983.

78. "Hoy definen fecha del paro cívico," *Vanguardia Liberal* (Bucaramanga, Santander), April 7, 1983.

79. "Usitrás apoya paro cívico en Barrancabermeja," *Vanguardia Liberal* (Bucaramanga, Santander), April 12, 1983.

80. Jaime Barba Rincón, interview with author (Barrancabermeja, October 25, 2006).

81. "Hoy, paro cívico," *Vanguardia Liberal* (Bucaramanga, Santander), April 12, 1983.

82. "Vendrá comisión de alto nivel para estudiar los problemas," *Vanguardia Liberal* (Bucaramanga, Santander), April 27, 1983.

83. Chaparro, *Recuerdos de un tropelero*, 25.

84. Ibid., 26.

85. "Toque de queda en Barranca," *Vanguardia Liberal* (Bucaramanga, Santander), May 3, 1983.

86. "Ley seca y toque de queda en Barranca," *El Tiempo* (Bogotá), May 3, 1983.

87. The first student strike in the history of Barranca was organized at the Colegio Diego Hernández de Gallegos in 1957. The strike established in Barranca a tradition of high school student radicalism that encouraged and replenished the ranks of the

city's broader civic-popular movement. Rafael Antonio Velásquez Rodríguez, "Primera huelga estudiantil en Barrancabermeja, Junio de 1957," unpublished document, 2006.

88. "Aprobado paro cívico," *Vanguardia Liberal* (Bucaramanga, Santander), May 19, 1983.

89. "Comité cívico dialogará con Belisario Betancur," *Vanguardia Liberal* (Bucaramanga, Santander), May 25, 1983.

90. Ibid.

91. "Dice el Gobernador: El acueducto de Barranca, preocupación prioritaria," *Vanguardia Liberal* (Bucaramanga, Santander), May 28, 1983.

92. José Manuel Bonnet would be promoted to general following his stint in Barranca and would eventually serve as top commander of Colombia's armed forces. "Expectativa por la situación en Barranca," *Vanguardia Liberal* (Bucaramanga, Santander), May 15, 1983.

93. Barba Rincón, interview with author (Barrancabermeja, October 25, 2006).

94. Forest Hylton, *Evil Hour in Colombia* (New York: Verso, 2006), 70.

95. "Abatidos ocho guerrilleros," *Vanguardia Liberal* (Bucaramanga, Santander), January 14, 1984.

96. "500 campesinos se tomaron el Palacio de Justicia," *Vanguardia Liberal* (Bucaramanga, Santander), January 30, 1984.

97. The parish priest Nel Beltrán became director of the office of the Pastoral Social in Barranca in 1987 and the bishop of Sincelejo, Córdoba, in 2000. In 2005 he was appointed to the committee overseeing negotiations between the government of the Conservative president Álvaro Uribe Vélez and the paramilitary Autodefensas Unidas de Colombia (AUC).

98. Jael Quiroga, interview with author (Bogotá, September 27, 2005).

99. Marbel Sandoval Ordóñez is a Bogotá-based journalist and novelist who spent time in Barrancabermeja in the 1990s working for the *Vanguardia Liberal* daily newspaper.

100. Marbel Sandoval Ordóñez, *En el brazo del río* (Bogotá: Hombre Nuevo Editores, 2006), 121.

101. The Colombian Ministry of Defense has estimated that the FARC expansion accelerated significantly after 1984, nearly doubling in size between 1985 and 1988. As quoted by Carlo Nasi in Virginia M. Bouvier, ed., *Colombia: Building Peace in a Time of War* (Washington, DC: United States Institute for Peace, 2009), 44.

102. David Ravelo, interview with author (Barrancabermeja, March 10, 2006).

Chapter 4. Popular Protest and Human Rights Activism

1. Yolanda Becerra, interview with author (Barrancabermeja, March 10, 2006).

2. Carlos Basombrio Iglesias, "Sendero Luminoso and Human Rights: A Perverse Logic that Captured the Country," in *Shining and Other Paths: War and Society*

in Peru, 1980–1995, ed. Steve J. Stern (Durham, NC: Duke University Press, 1998), 426.

3. As cited in Santos and García, *El caleidoscopio de las justicias*, 2:322.

4. Archila, *Idas y venidas*, 241.

5. To Latin Americanists, the term "dirty war" is most frequently associated with the Argentinian junta, but it has a longer etymology. The term "dirty war" was popularized in the 1950s by French activists protesting colonial repression in Indochina. A January 1948 essay by *Le Monde* publisher Hubert Beuve-Méry accused French officials of carrying out a dirty war in Vietnam. The term was then used regularly by the French Communist Party newspaper *L'Humanité*, notably following the arrest and imprisonment of the sailor and anticolonial organizer Henri Martin. Hubert Beuve-Méry, "Une guerre sale," *Une Semaine dans le Monde*, January 17, 1948; Marcel Cachin, "La guerre du Vietnam, une sale guerre," *L'Humanité*, January 21, 1948. The most famous expression of protest against French policies in Vietnam at the time came with the publication of *L'affaire Henri Martin* (Paris: Gallimard, 1953) by a group of leading French intellectuals, including Jean-Paul Sartre, Jean Cocteau, and others.

6. M. L. R. Smith and Sophie Roberts, "War in the Gray: Exploring the Concept of Dirty War," *Studies in Conflict and Terrorism* 31, no. 5 (2008): 377–398.

7. The use of the term "dirty war" by Argentinian military leaders has been explained as a translation of a counterinsurgency approach utilized by the French in Algeria and described by President Charles de Gaulle as "la sale de guerre," or "the dirty side of war." Marguerite Feitlowitz, *A Lexicon of Terror: Argentina and the Legacies of Torture* (New York: Oxford University Press, 1988), 12.

8. Comisión Andina de Juristas, Seccional Colombia, *Guerra sucia y estado de sitio en Colombia* (Bogotá, November 30, 1988).

9. Americas Watch, *The Killings in Colombia: An Americas Watch Report* (New York: Americas Watch, April 1989), 60.

10. Régulo Madero, interview with author (Barrancabermeja, March 8, 2006).

11. Juan de Dios Castilla Amell, "Participación popular y movimiento social: Barrancabermeja 1971–1985" (master's thesis, Universidad de los Andes, 1989), 25.

12. Tate, *Counting the Dead*, 26.

13. The term *sapo*—literally "toad"—is used to refer to people who work as spies on behalf of the police or military. An English equivalent might be "informer" or "snitch." The former guerrilla Jaime Arenas Reyes deserted the ELN in 1969 and was assassinated in Bogotá by his former comrades on March 28, 1971. While a student in Bogotá, Arenas became a close confidant of the chaplain of the National University, the sociologist and Jesuit priest Camilo Torres. To some, Arenas was one of the bright lights of the movement. Like Torres, who died in 1965 fighting for the ELN, Arenas was admired by urban activists and intellectuals for giving up civilian life to join the rebel cause. To the ELN, Arenas was a turncoat who had revealed secrets to the Colombian state. In his memoir of life inside the ELN, *La guerrilla por dentro*, Arenas accused social activists, including oil workers' union leaders, of actively supporting the ELN. Pécaut, *Crónica de cuatro décadas*, 97.

14. Jorge Eduardo Nuñez H., *Crónicas de lucha por el poder local* (Barrancabermeja: Alcaldía Municipal de Barrancabermeja, 1997), 28.

15. Arenas Obregón, *Cerrando fronteras*, 118.

16. For a discussion of important works on the Comuneros revolt and other late colonial social and popular political movements, see Bernardo Tovar Zambrano, "La historiografía colonial," and Fabio Zambrano Pantoja, "Historiografía sobre los movimientos sociales en Colombia: Siglo XIX," in *La historia al final del milenio: ensayos de historiografía colombiana y latinoamericana*, vol. 1, ed. Bernardo Tovar Zambrano (Bogotá: Editorial Universidad Nacional, Facultad de Ciencias Humanas, 1994).

17. Hernández, *Rojo y negro*, 31.

18. Memorandum, United States Consulate–Medellín, cable to United States Secretary of State (November 30, 1973), National Security Archive, George Washington University, Washington, DC.

19. For further reading on the negotiation process, see Mark Chernick, "Negotiating Peace amid Multiple Forms of Violence: The Protracted Search for a Settlement to the Armed Conflicts in Colombia," in *Comparative Peace Processes in Latin America*, ed. Cynthia J. Aronson (Washington, DC: Woodrow Wilson Press; Stanford: Stanford University Press, 1999), 159–196.

20. Frente Amplio del Magdalena Medio, "En el F.A.M. no inventamos una plataforma de lucha!!!," *Alternativa de cambio* (pamphlet, 1984), CREDHOS Archives.

21. Ibid., 14.

22. Harnecker, *Unidad que multiplica*, 56.

23. Hernández, *Rojo y negro*, 247.

24. In 2008 the one-time FARC *miliciano* and confessed paramilitary Mario Jaimes Mejía, alias *"el panadero,"* confessed his involvement in massacres that took place in Barranca on May 16, 1998, and February 28, 1999. In his statements, which were filmed and simulcast to an audience in Barranca, *"el panadero"* claimed that he had been recruited to the FARC by a former FAM leader. As quoted in Estefanía González Vélez and Orián Jiménez Meneses, *Las guerras del Magdalena Medio* (Bogotá: Intermedio, 2008), 237.

25. Irene Villamizar, interview with author (Barrancabermeja, March 8, 2006).

26. Vargas Velásquez, *Magdalena Medio Santandereano*, 258.

27. van Isschot, "The Heart of Activism in Colombia," 246.

28. Anonymous interview with author (Bogotá, October 28, 2006).

29. Marta Harnecker, *Entrevista con la nueva izquierda: Entrevista a Bernardo Jaramillo, de la Unión Patriótica, y Nelson Berríos, de A Luchar, sobre los desafíos que enfrentan los cuadros públicos en un país en que existe una guerra de guerrillas* (Managua: Centro de Documentación y Ediciones Latinoamericanas, 1989).

30. Arenas Obregón, *Cerrando fronteras*, 119.

31. Duque, "Conflictos y paz," 65.

32. Leonardo Posada was one of nine members of the Colombian House of Representatives and five members of the Senate elected on behalf of the Patriotic Union in 1986, one year after the founding of the party.

33. "La calle 10 ahora se llama Avenida Leonardo Posada," *La Opinión del Magdalena Medio* (Barranabermeja), September 1987, 3.

34. Anonymous, "Leonardo Posada, historia de vida," unpublished document, December 10, 1998.

35. "Primer aniversario de Leonardo Posada: Un mártir con los ojos abiertos," *La Opinión del Magdalena Medio* (Barrancabermeja, Santander), September 1987.

36. Ibid.

37. Ibid.

38. "Ley seca por disturbios en Barrancabermeja," *El Tiempo* (Bogotá), April, 24 1987.

39. David Ravelo, interview with author (Barrancabermeja, March 10, 2006).

40. At the time, the UP was a major force in Barranca and throughout the region. The mayors of the largely rural municipalities of El Carmen and Sabana de Torres (Santander), Yondó (Antioquia), and San Pablo (Bolívar) were all members of the UP, as were three Barranca city councillors. "Los alcaldes de la UP en el Magdalena Medio," *La Opinión del Magdalena Medio* (Barrancabermeja, Santander), April 1987.

41. "Ley seca por disturbios en Barrancabermeja," *El Tiempo* (Bogotá), April, 24 1987.

42. "Ley seca y toque de queda en Barrancabermeja," *El Tiempo* (Bogotá), May 3, 1987.

43. Vargas Velásquez, *Magdalena Medio Santandereano*, 238.

44. Attempts have been made to calculate levels of impunity vis-à-vis the justice system in Colombia. For the purposes of this study, a useful formulation is to simply look at the total number of homicides and the number of convictions that result. This formulation cannot account for the quality of the convictions. However, it does help to explain the frustration felt by victims of violence. In 1994, for instance, only 0.8 percent of homicides led to convictions. Hernando Gómez Buendía, ed., *El conflicto, callejón con salida: Informe nacional de desarollo para Colombia—2003* (Bogotá: Programa de las Naciones Unidas para el Desarrollo, PNUD, September 2003), 167.

45. Alonso Heredia Durán, "Con nutrida manifestación terminó el paro cívico en Barrancabermeja," *El Espectador* (Bogotá), May 8, 1987.

46. Chaparro, *Recuerdos de un tropelero*, 32.

47. Inaugurated in 1983, the Parque Camilo Torres Restrepo commemorates the Jesuit priest and iconic member of the ELN who died in combat near Barranca in 1966. On several occasions in the early 1990s the bust of Camilo Torres that was placed on a monument at the center of the small concrete plaza was decapitated. For many years afterward the park was referred to locally as "El descabezado," or "the headless man." Arenas Obregón, *Cerrando fronteras*, 77. For an interpretation of a similar desecration of a public memorial in Colombia, see Comisión Nacional de Reparación y Reconciliación (Colombia), "Amenazas y ataques a la memoria y sus símbolos," in *Trujillo, una tragedia que no cesa: Primer informe de memoria histórica de la Comisión Nacional de Reparación y Reconciliación* (Bogotá: Planeta, 2008), 211–213.

48. Isamel Jaimes, "El Frente Comun: Une reto y una esperanza," *La Opinión del Magdalena Medio*, December 1988, 3.

49. "Nadie se salva," *Semana* (Bogotá), May 12, 1987.

50. Tate, *Counting the Dead*, 256.

51. Ibid., 40.

52. "Dirección Liberal condena el paro del nororiente," *El Tiempo* (Bogotá), June 7, 1987.

53. Chaparro, *Recuerdos de un tropelero*, 35–36.

54. "Disturbios en Barrancabermeja," *El Tiempo* (Bogotá), June 10, 1987.

55. "El Padre Eduardo Díaz," *Familia Diocesana* 16 (May 1987), 5.

56. Memorias Primer Congreso Juvenil Diocesano, "Ponencia del eje fe e iglesia," 48.

57. In 1985 Brother Álvarez was recognized by the Medellín newspaper *El Colombiano* with an award for his humanitarian work. "Muerte del hermano Javier Álvarez, F.S.C.," *Familia Diocesana* 16 (May 1987), 7.

58. "Del Pastor," *Familia Diocesana* 17 (June 1987), 1.

59. Javier Giraldo, *Colombia: The Genocidal Democracy* (Monroe, ME: Common Courage Press, 1996), 45.

60. Father Eduardo Díaz went to Vancouver, Canada, where he spent several years working as a priest among Latin American immigrants and teaching at the Vancouver School of Theology. He would return to Colombia years later to teach at La Javeriana, the city's Jesuit university.

61. Dudley, *Walking Ghosts*, 104.

62. Chaparro, *Recuerdos de un tropelero*, 39.

63. In September 1987 the ELN, FARC, and other guerrilla groups entered into a cooperation agreement for the first time in their more than twenty years of coexistence, creating the Coordinadora Guerrillera Simón Bolívar. See Harnecker, *Unidad que multiplica*, 107.

64. Anonymous interview (Barrancabermeja, September 2004), CINEP Archives, Bogotá.

65. Vargas, Velásquez *Magdalena Medio Santandereano*, 152.

66. Chaparro, *Recuerdos de un tropelero*, 27.

Chapter 5. Biography of a Movement

1. Yolanda Becerra, interview with author (Barrancabermeja, March 10, 2006).

2. CREDHOS was incorporated on July 7, 1988. But in all documents recounting the history of the organization, December 10, 1987, is given as the founding date. Not coincidentally, December 10 is International Human Rights Day, marking the date that the Universal Declaration of Human Rights was adopted by the United Nations.

3. CREDHOS, *Estatutos de Constitución*, 1, CREDHOS Archives, Barrancabermeja.

4. Archila, *Idas y venidas*, 235.

5. Marcelo M. Giugale, Olivier Lafourcade, and Connie Luff, eds., *Colombia: The Economic Foundation of Peace* (Washington, DC: World Bank, 2003), 92.

6. Tate, *Counting the Dead*, 222.

7. Álvaro Tirado Mejía, "Derechos humanos y democracia en Colombia," *Análisis Político* 2 (September–December 1987): 50.

8. Sikkink, *Mixed Signals*, 47.

9. These included the Committee for Solidarity with Political Prisoners (est. 1973), the Permanent Committee for the Defense of Human Rights (est. 1979), the "José Alvear Restrepo" Lawyers Collective (est. 1980), and the Association of Families of the Detained and Disappeared (est. 1982). Attorney General Carlos Mauro Hoyos was killed in Medellín on January 25, 1988, by gunmen assumed to be acting on behalf of *los extraditibles*, narcotraffickers upset with the policy of extraditing accused drug dealers to the United States. He was replaced by the former Barranca mayor Horacio Serpa.

10. Tate, *Counting the Dead*, 215.

11. Martha Finnemore and Kathryn Sikkink, "International Norms and Political Change," *International Organization* 52, no. 4 (Autumn 1998), 887–917.

12. Alfredo Molano, *The Dispossessed: Chronicles of the Desterrados of Colombia*, trans. Daniel Bland (Chicago: Haymarket Books, 2005), 25.

13. Ibid., 26.

14. Human Rights Watch, *Colombia's Killer Networks: The Military-Paramilitary Partnership and the United States* (New York: Human Rights Watch, November 1996).

15. Mahony and Eguren, *Unarmed Bodyguards*, 85.

16. "Barrancabermeja, florida Barranca, te quiero por libre, por recia y por franca," *Opción* (Bogotá), May 1988, 7.

17. Archila, *Idas y venidas*, 74.

18. Charles Tilly and Sidney Tarrow, *Contentious Politics* (Boulder, CO: Paradigm, 2007), 111.

19. Joe Foweraker, *Theorizing Social Movements* (London: Pluto Press, 1995), 23.

20. This was a play on the name of the surreal goings-on in the town of Macondo, as imagined by Gabriel García Márquez in *One Hundred Years of Solitude* and has since become a synonym for anything outlandish or bizarre, as in: "Did you hear about what happened last night? *Era macondiano.*"

21. The original Spanish is worth quoting directly: "1. *Por la vida, p'alante con todo*, 2. *Prohibido prohibir los amores de barricada*, 3. *Prohibido prohibir la rumba . . . Por el derecho a inventar cosas, ser creativos y darle rueda suelta a la fantasia, p'adelante.*" "El Frente Único de Macondo: Capítulo del Magdalena Medio decreta," *La Opinión del Magdalena Medio* (Barrancabermeja, Santander), July 1987.

22. "Barrancabermeja, florida Barranca," *Opción* (Bogotá), May 1988, 7.

23. Francisco Campos, interview with author (Barrancabermeja, September 20, 2005).

24. In the original interview in Spanish, Luisa Castro uses the term *encoñe*, which has an explicit sexual meaning. Anonymous interview with author (Bogotá, March 14, 2006).

25. Subsequent financial support came from a Jesuit-run organization called Programa Caminos por la Paz. CREDHOS, "Creación de la Regional de Derechos Humanos del Magdalena Medio" (February 1990), 2, CREHDOS Archives, Barrancabermeja.

26. Jorge Enrique Gómez Lizarazo, Hoja de Vida, CREDHOS Archives, Barrancabermeja.

27. Irene Villamizar, interview with author (Barrancabermeja, March 8, 2006).

28. Jael Quiroga, interview with author (Bogotá, September 27, 2005).

29. Jorge Gómez Lizarazo, interview with author (Barrancabermeja, March 8, 2006).

30. Ibid.

31. Corporación Regional para la Defensa de los Derechos Humanos (CREDHOS), "Informe del Encuentro Regional," 57, CREDHOS Archives, Barrancabermeja.

32. Ibid., emphasis in the original text.

33. "Los derechos humanos," *La Opinión del Magdalena Medio* (Barrancabermeja, Santander), January 1988.

34. CREDHOS, "Estatutos del Comité Regional para la Defensa de los Derechos Humanos" (Barrancabermeja, April 26, 1989), 2–3, CREDHOS Archives, Barrancabermeja.

35. In 2002 the Plazoleta de Ecopetrol, the small plaza in front of the national headquarters of Ecopetrol in Bogotá, was named after Manuel Gustavo Chacón.

36. Declaración de Luis Eduardo Galindo Saavedra, January 21, 1988, 1, CREDHOS Archives, Barrancabermeja.

37. Ibid., 3.

38. Diligencia de Declaración de Agente César Julio Mora, January 16, 1988, 2, CREDHOS Archives, Barrancabermeja.

39. Declaración de María Elba [*sic*] Uribe de Chacón, January 21, 1988, CREDHOS Archives, Barrancabermeja.

40. "MAS" letter to Fernando Acuña, January 23, 1988, CREDHOS Archives, Barrancabermeja.

41. Washington Office on Latin America (WOLA), *Colombia Besieged: Political Violence and State Responsibility* (Washington, DC: WOLA, 1989), 33.

42. Colombia Nunca Más: Memoria de Crímenes de Lesa Humanidad, "Crímenes de lesa humanidad en la zona 5a: Barrancabermeja" (Bogotá, 2008).

43. "Prolongan paro cívico," *Vanguardia Liberal* (Barrancabermeja, Santander), May 27, 1988.

44. CREDHOS, Urgent Action (June 28, 1991), CREDHOS Archives, Barrancabermeja.

45. "Dice Ángel Tolosa: 'Es difícil atajar goles,'" *Opción* 2 (July 1988), 19.

46. Comisión Intercongregacional de Justicia y Paz, "Informe de la Comisión Intercongregacional de Justicia y Paz sobre la situación de violencia que se vive en los municipios de El Carmen y San Vicente de Chucurí (Santander), debida a la acción de grupos paramilitares" (Bogotá: Justicia y Paz, August 1990), 5.

47. Giraldo, *The Genocidal Democracy*, 96.

48. Liga Internacional por los Derechos y la Liberación de los Pueblos, *El camino de la niebla*, vol. 2, *El asesinato político en Colombia y su Impunidad* (Bogotá: Liga Internacional por los Derechos y la Liberación de los Pueblos, Sección Colombiana, 1990), 291.

49. "La balacera duró hora y media," *Colombia Hoy Informa* 9, no. 58 (1988): 27.

50. Justicia y Paz, "Informe de la comisión intercongregacional," 32.

51. National Police Commander Major Guillermo Vélez Botero, Barrancabermeja Municipal Council Minutes, No. 042 (November 22, 1988), Barrancabermeja Municipal Archives, Barrancabermeja.

52. CREDHOS president Jorge Gómez Lizarazo, Barrancabermeja Municipal Council Minutes, No. 042 (November 22, 1988), Barrancabermeja Municipal Archives, Barrancabermeja.

53. Wills, *La democracia*, 98.

54. Ibid.

55. Municipal councillor Orlando Higuita, Barrancabermeja Municipal Council Minutes, No. 023 (August 5, 1988).

56. Villamizar, interview with author (Barrancabermeja, March 8, 2006).

57. Torres Duarte, *Barrancabermeja en textos e imágenes*, 90.

58. Ibid.

59. Gómez Lizarazo, interview with author (Barrancabermeja, March 8, 2006).

Chapter 6. The War on Human Rights Defenders

1. Jael Quiroga, interview with author (Bogotá, September 27, 2005).

2. Two minsters of justice (Rodrigo Lara Bonilla in 1984 and Enrique Low Murta in 1991) and one attorney general (Carlos Mauro Hoyos in 1988) were killed by drug traffickers. Eleven Supreme Court justices were killed in 1985 during the Colombian armed forces' assault on the Palace of Justice in Bogotá after it had been occupied by M-19 guerrillas. Inter-American Court of Human Rights, *Case of the Rochela Massacre v. Colombia*, Series C No. 163, Merits, Reparations, and Costs, Judgment of May 11, 2007.

3. Those murdered at La Rochela include Mariela Morales Caro, Pablo Antonio Beltrán Palomino, Virgilio Hernández Serrano, Carlos Fernando Castillo Zapata, Luis Orlando Hernández Muñoz, Yul Germán Monroy Ramírez, Gabriel Enrique Vega Fonseca, Benhur Iván Guasca Castro, Orlando Morales Cárdenas, César Augusto Morales Cepeda, Arnulfo Mejía Duarte, and Samuel Vargas Páez. Grupo de Memoria Histórica, *La Rochela*.

4. Tate, *Counting the Dead*, 218.

5. The Revolutionary Armed Forces of Colombia (FARC), the National Liberation Army (ELN), the Popular Liberation Army (EPL), and the April 19 Movement (M-19).

6. Corporación Regional para la Defensa de los Derechos Humanos (CREDHOS), "Encuentro regional sobre la situación de los Derechos Humanos en Colombia: testimonios, ponencias, conclusiones" (1989), 12, CREDHOS Archives, Barrancabermeja.

7. Ibid., 49.

8. Peace negotiations between insurgent groups and the Colombian government in the 1980s created the conditions that allowed guerrilla spokespeople to attend public meetings in certain areas of the country. Leah Carroll, "The Patriotic Union and Its Successors in Arauca, 1984–2007: From Electoral Power to Leadership in the Struggle Against Impunity," paper presented at International Congress of Latin American Studies Association, October 6–9, 2010, Toronto.

9. CREDHOS, "Encuentro regional," 55.

10. Quiroga, interview with author (Bogotá, September 27, 2005).

11. "Ecopetrol: Asesinado jefe de producción," *El Tiempo* (Bogotá), April 5, 1993.

12. "Capturadas 270 personas ayer en Barranacbermeja," *El Tiempo* (Bogotá), April 8, 1991.

13. "Asesinadas 9 personas en Barranca," *El Tiempo* (Bogotá), October 20, 1992; "Muertos en combate," *El Tiempo* (Bogotá), February 4, 1992.

14. Tate, *Counting the Dead*, 199.

15. They were accompanied by a congressional Appropriations Committee staffer, one U.S. Army general, and two lieutenant-colonels.

16. Memorandum, United States Embassy, Bogotá, "Murtha and Marsh Visit Concentrates on Narco Power and Insurgency" (Bogotá, May 24, 1988), National Security Archive, George Washington University, Washington, DC.

17. Ibid.

18. Memorandum, United States Embassy, "Government Responds to Continued Guerrilla Violence" (Bogotá, February 22, 1988), National Security Archive, George Washington University, Washington, DC.

19. WOLA, *Colombia Besieged*, 109.

20. Donna Lee Van Cott, *The Friendly Liquidation of the Past: The Politics of Diversity in Latin America* (Pittsburgh: University of Pittsburgh Press, 2000); Ana María Bejarano, "Perverse Democratization: Pacts, Institutions and Problematic Consolidations in Colombia and Venezuela" (PhD diss., Columbia University, 2000).

21. Tate, *Counting the Dead*, 226.

22. Corporación Regional para la Defensa de los Derechos Humanos (CREDHOS), *Boletín*, August–September 1991, CREDHOS Archives, Barrancabermeja.

23. Richani, *Systems of Violence*.

24. Jorge Gómez Lizarazo, interview with author (Barrancabermeja, March 8, 2006).

25. Definitions of militarization generally take into account two main variables: the size of the military and the "political influence and prerogatives" of the military. The number of troops per capita and the level of encroachment of the military into civilian functions of the state therefore become the measures of militarization. See Kirk S. Bowman, *Militarization, Democracy, and Development: The Perils of Praetorianism in Latin America* (University Park: Pennsylvania State University Press, 2002), 20.

26. The Batallón de Artillería y defensa antiaérea Número 02, "Nueva Granada," Batallón Contraguerrilla 45, "Héroes de Majagual," National Police, the Ejército de

Liberación Nacional (ELN), Fuerzas Armadas Revolucionarias de Colombia (FARC), and Ejército de Liberación Popular (EPL).

27. Medina Gallego, *Autodefensas, paramilitares y narcotráfico*; Vargas Velásquez, *Magdalena Medio Santandereano*; Comisión de Estudios sobre la Violencia, *Colombia*.

28. In addition to reports published regularly by CREDHOS, see Comisión Intercongregacional de Justicia y Paz, "Informe de la Comisión Intercongregacional de Justicia y Paz"; Liga Internacional, *El camino de la niebla*, vol. 2.

29. Corporación Regional para la Defensa de los Derechos Humanos (CREDHOS), "Sobre la situación de los Derechos Humanos en el Magdalena Medio" (Barranca, March 13, 1992), CREDHOS Archives, Barrancabermeja.

30. The military is said to have provided "subtle backing" to paramilitaries against leftist guerrillas in the department of Córdoba in the 1990s. Mauricio Romero, "Changing Identities," 52.

31. Anonymous interview (Barrancabermeja, 2004), CINEP Archives.

32. On May 11, 2007, the Inter-American Court of Human Rights held the Colombian state responsible for the La Rochela massacre.

33. In February 1989 local social and political activists submitted reports to the regional branch of the Office of the Inspector General concerning the participation of high-ranking military officials in the La Rochela massacre. See Inter-American Court of Human Rights, *Case of the Rochela Massacre v. Colombia*, 48.

34. Inter-American Court of Human Rights, *Case of the 19 Merchants v. Colombia*, Series C No. 93, Preliminary Objection, Judgment of June 12, 2002.

35. Liga Internacional, *El camino de la niebla*, 2:386.

36. Ibid.

37. Ibid., 2:387.

38. The commission was headed by two judges assigned to the *municipio* of San Gil, located near the city of Bucaramanga. The other commissioners included judicial and police investigators from San Gil, Bucaramanga, and Barrancabermeja. Inter-American Court of Human Rights, *Case of the Rochela Massacre v. Colombia*, 22.

39. The police inspector is a civilian municipal official who fulfills the basic duties of a regular police officer in smaller communities where there is no national police presence.

40. Grupo de Memoria Histórica, *La Rochela*.

41. Inter-American Court of Human Rights, *Case of the Rochela Massacre v. Colombia*, 43.

42. "Colombia Ordered to Pay $7.8 Million in Paramilitary Massacre of 12 Judicial Workers," Associated Press (June 9, 2007).

43. "Colombia Ordered to Pay $7.8m to Relatives of Massacred Victims," Associated Press (June 10, 2007).

44. Asociación Nacional de Usuarios Campesinos (ANUC), "El avance de la guerra sucia en Colombia: El caso del Magdalena Medio" (Barrancabermeja, 1988), CREDHOS Archives, Barrancabermeja.

45. Comisión Intercongregacional de Justicia y Paz, "Informe de la Comisión Intercongregacional de Justicia y Paz."

46. Comisión Andina de Juristas, Seccional Colombiana, *Nordeste Antioqueño y Magdalena Medio*, Serie Informes Regionales de Derechos Humanos (Bogotá, January 1, 1993).

47. CREDHOS, "Inauguración de albergue," Bulletin (June 1989), CREDHOS Archives, Barrancabermeja.

48. Father Giraldo is a prolific observer of human rights and social justice issues in Colombia. His frequently updated website is entitled *Desde los márgenes* (From the Margins). http://www.javiergiraldo.org.

49. Albergue Campesino, "Informe Albergue de Campesinos Damnificados por la Guerra Sucia Magdalena Medio" (January 1990), CREDHOS Archives, Barrancabermeja.

50. Including Carmen de Chucurí, San Vicente de Chucurí, San Pablo, and Puerto Wilches. See Albergue Campesino, "Experiencia de derechos humanos en la región del Magdalena Medio (Proyecto Albergue Campesino)" (no date), CREDHOS Archives, Barrancabermeja.

51. Flor Castro, interview with author (Bogotá, March 14, 2006).

52. Proyecto Albergue Campesino, "Experiencia de derechos humanos en la región del Magdalena Medio" (no date), CREDHOS Archives, Barrancabermeja.

53. Anonymous interview with author (Bogotá, October 28, 2006).

54. "Comisión de la OEA escuchó quejas," *Vanguardia Liberal* (Barrancabermeja), July 5, 1992.

55. As quoted in Mahony and Eguren, *Unarmed Bodyguards*, 231.

56. Castro, interview with author (Bogotá, March 14, 2006).

57. In an internal evaluation conducted by members of the Albergue Campesino, a number of "alternative proposals" were generated as suggestions for continued advocacy work on behalf of displaced people in Barranca. Tellingly, several of these focused on the settlement and integration of migrants within the city itself. Proyecto Albergue Campesino, "Experiencia del albergue campesino de Barrancabermeja" (no date), CREDHOS Archives, Barrancabermeja.

58. "Violence Takes Over a Colombian City," *New York Times*, March 1, 1987.

59. Ibid.

60. There is a significant literature on the *sicarios* of Medellín that runs the gamut from serious academic inquiry to human rights reports, poetry, film, music, and novels. Some of the best known examples include Alonso Salazar's ethnography of violence, *No nacimos pa' semilla* (1990); novels by Fernando Vallejo, *La vírgen de los sicarios* (1994), and Jorge Franco Ramos, *Rosario Tijeras* (1999); and Víctor Gaviria's cinéma vérité film *Rodrigo D: No futuro* (2005). Pathbreaking academic work on violence in Medellín has been done by the anthropologist Pilar Riaño-Alcalá, *Dwellers of Memory: Youth and Violence in Medellín, Colombia* (New Brunswick, NJ: Transaction, 2006). See also original research into the emergence of a model of enforced protection, or protection racketeering, by organized criminal groups in an urban setting by the former director of the human rights research institute Instituto Popular de Capacitación (IPC) in Medellín. See Jairo Bedoya, *La protección violenta en Colombia: El caso de*

Medellín desde los años noventa (Medellín: IPC-Confiar, 2010), and John J. Bedoya, "Seguridad y ciudadanía en los 90s en Medellín: El surgimiento de las empresas colombianas de protección violenta," *Canadian Journal of Latin American and Caribbean Studies* 31, no. 62 (2006): 87–130.

61. "Concejal muerto era trabajador de Ecopetrol," *El Tiempo* (Bogotá), February 9, 1991.

62. CREDHOS, "Relación de casos: Víctimas de homocidios miembros de CREDHOS" (1994), CREDHOS Archives, Barrancabermeja.

63. "Asesinado exdirigente de la USO," *Vanguardia Liberal* (Bucaramanga, Santander), March 20, 1991.

64. CREDHOS, "H.H. Viejo Querido" (April 19, 1991), CREDHOS Archives, Barrancabermeja.

65. CREDHOS and Corporación Colectivo de Abogados José Alvear Restrepo (CAJAR), *Hoy como ayer, persistiendo por la vida: Redes de inteligencia y exterminio en Barrancabermeja* (Bogotá: CREDHOS, CAJAR, 1999).

66. In 1994 four officers and three noncommissioned officers, including the marine lieutenant colonel Rodrigo Quiñónez Cárdenas, were "severely reprimanded" for conspiring to form paramilitary groups in the port city of Barrancabermeja. Five years later, the then rear admiral Rodrigo Quiñónez was "administratively sanctioned" for "failing to prevent" the massacre of twenty-seven unarmed civilians in Chengue, Sucre. U.S. Department of State, "Country Reports on Human Rights Practices—2003," Bureau of Democracy, Human Rights, and Labor (Washington, DC: February 25, 2004), National Security Archive, George Washington University, Washington, DC.

67. Human Rights Watch, *Colombia's Killer Networks*, 36.

68. The Institute for Policy Studies (IPS) is a Washington-based think tank that every year recognizes a human rights defender with an award named after the exiled Chilean diplomat Orlando Letelier and the U.S. activist Ronni Karpen Moffitt, killed in 1976 by a car bomb in Washington, DC. Letelier and Moffitt were killed by Chilean secret service agents, under orders from the government of Augusto Pinochet.

69. Washington Office on Latin America letter to United States Congressional Offices, Re: Appeal for Response to killing in Colombia, January 30, 1992, CREDHOS Archive, Barrancabermeja.

70. "Asesinada secretaria de Derechos Humanos," *Vanguardia Liberal* (Bucaramanga, Santander), January 30, 1992.

71. "Sin transporte Barrancabermeja," *Vanguardia Liberal* (Bucaramanga, Santander), January 31, 1992.

72. Letter to Colombian president César Gaviria Trujillo from United States senator Alan Cranston et al., January 31, 1992, CREDHOS Archives.

73. Marco Tulio Bruni Cellis, president of the Inter-American Commission on Human Rights, letter to Nohemí Sanín Posada de Rubio, Colombian minister of foreign affairs, February 5, 1992, CREDHOS Archives, Barrancabermeja.

74. The first hearings on human rights by the House Subcommittee on International Organizations of the U.S. Congress were held from August to December

1973. Brazil and Chile were the only two Latin American cases discussed in detail at these inaugural hearings. Kathryn Sikkink, *Mixed Signals: U.S. Human Rights Policy and Latin America* (Ithaca, NY: Cornell University Press, 2004), 66.

75. Jorge Gómez Lizarazo, "Colombian Blood, U.S. Guns," *New York Times*, January 28, 1992.

76. Ibid.

77. "Se calló *La Opinión*," *Vanguardia Liberal* (Bucaramanga, Santander), May 7, 1992.

78. "Ismael Jaimes Cortés," *Vanguardia Liberal* (Bucaramanga, Santander), May 8, 1992.

79. Human Rights Watch, *Colombia's Killer Networks*, 35.

80. "Homocidio," *Vanguardia Liberal* (Bucaramanga, Santander), June 30, 1992.

81. Ibid.

82. "Quieren sacarnos de Barranca," *Vanguardia Liberal* (Bucaramanga, Santander), June 30, 1992.

83. CREDHOS, "Relación de casos: Víctimas de homocidios miembros de CREDHOS" (1994), CREDHOS Archives, Barrancabermeja.

84. Subsequently, Ancizar Castaño Buitrago was arrested and investigated by Colombian judicial authorities for his involvement in various political murders in Barranca. On February 24, 1998, Castaño was sentenced to thirty years in prison on charges of homicide and terrorism. CREDHOS and CAJAR, *Hoy como ayer*, 180.

85. "Sin transporte Barrancabermeja," *Vanguardia Liberal* (Bucaramanga, Santander), January 31, 1992.

86. CREDHOS and CAJAR, *Hoy como ayer*, 93–95.

87. "Derechos abren sus puertas," *Vangaurdia Liberal* (Barrancabermeja), June 16, 1993.

88. CREDHOS, "III Asamblea General de Socios de CREDHOS," Acta 001 de 1993, Barrancabermeja, Colombia (June 17, 1993), CREDHOS Archives, Barrancabermeja.

89. "En Santander, inversiones contra pobreza y violencia," *El Tiempo* (Bogotá), July 7, 1993.

90. "Gaviria dejó más de una obra pendiente a lo largo del país," *El Tiempo* (Bogotá), August 6, 1994.

91. Corporación Regional para la Defensa de los Derechos Humanos, "Informe Presentado por la Corporación Regional para la Defensa de los Derechos Humanos sobre la Situación de los Derechos Humanos en el Magdalena Medio" (March 13, 1992), CREDHOS Archives, Barrancabermeja, 1992.

92. Bushnell, *The Making of Modern Colombia*, 251.

93. CREDHOS, "Informe Presentado por la Corporación Regional."

94. "La guerra es entre milicias," *El Tiempo* (Bogotá), September 2, 1992; "Barranca vive una guerra de milicias," *El Tiempo* (Bogotá), January 31, 1994.

95. Arenas, *La guerrilla por dentro*, 160.

96. Wills, *La democracia*, 43.

97. Human Rights Watch, *State of War: Political Violence and Counterinsurgency in Colombia* (New York: Human Rights Watch, 1993), 49.

98. Ibid.

99. Francisco Campos, interview with author (Barrancabermeja, September 20, 2005).

100. Russell Crandall, *Driven by Drugs: U.S. Policy toward Colombia* (Boulder, CO: Lynne Reiner, 2002), 35.

101. Francisco E. Thoumi, *Illegal Drugs, Economy, and Society in the Andes* (Washington, DC: Johns Hopkins University Press, 2003), 215.

102. In 1992 the commission was fused with the National Security Council, over which the president of Colombia presides. Departamento Administrativo de la Presidencia de la República, Decreto 2134 DE 1992 (Diciembre 30), *Diario Oficial* No 40.703 (December 31, 1992).

103. Leal, *La seguridad nacional a la deriva*, 41.

104. Mauricio Archila Neira et al., eds., *Conflictos, poderes e identitades en el Magdalena Medio, 1990–2001* (Bogotá: COLCIENCIAS, CINEP, 2006), 333.

105. Tate, *Counting the Dead*, 293.

Chapter 7. Social Movements Respond to Catastrophic Change

1. Régulo Madero, interview with author (Barrancabermeja, March 8, 2006).

2. Cynthia J. Arnson, ed., *The Peace Process in Colombia with the Autodefensas Unidas de Colombia–AUC* (Washington, DC: Woodrow Wilson Center for Scholars, 2005).

3. "Aguila Negra," or Black Eagle, was an alias used by paramilitary fighters during La Violencia. Sánchez and Meertens, *Bandits, Peasants and Politics*, 85.

4. Thad Dunning and Leslie Wirpsa, "Oil and the Political Economy of Conflict in Colombia and Beyond: A Linkages Approach," *Geopolitics* 9, no. 4 (2004): 81–108.

5. Lesley Gill, "The Parastate in Colombia: Political Violence and the Restructuring of Barrancabermeja," *Anthropologica* 51 (2009): 9.

6. As cited in Elkin Bueno Altahona, *Plan de desarrollo municipio de Barrancabermeja, 2012–2015: Documento técnico de trabajo; Versión para discusión* (Barrancabermeja: Alcalde de Barrancabermeja, February 2012).

7. These findings are based on a qualitative analysis completed of all cases of human rights violations in the *municipio* of Barrancabermeja for the 1991–2012 period, as recorded by the research institute CINEP, available through the Banco de Datos: Derechos Humanos y Violencia Política project. See http://www.nocheyniebla.org.

8. Banco de Datos de Violencia Política, Centro de Investigación y Educación Popular (CINEP) and Corporación Regional para la Defensa de los Derechos Humanos (CREDHOS), "Barrancabermeja, la otra versión: Paramilitarismo, control social y

desaparición forzada, 2000–2003," *Noche y Niebla Caso Tipo No. 3* (Bogotá: CINEP/CREDHOS, 2004).

9. Michael Taussig, *Law in a Lawless Land: Diary of a Limpieza* (Chicago: University of Chicago Press, 2005).

10. James C. Scott, *Domination and the Arts of Resistance: Hidden Transcripts* (New Haven, CT: Yale University Press, 1990).

11. Martha Cecilia García V., "Barrancabermeja: Ciudad en permanente disputa," in Archila et al., *Conflictos, poderes e identidades*, 297.

12. Gill, "The Parastate in Colombia," 8.

13. The most recent scholarship on events in the Magdalena Medio can be found in Archila et al., *Conflictos, poderes e identidades*. See also Banco de Datos de Violencia Política, Centro de Investigación y Educación Popular, and Corporación Regional para la Defensa de los Derechos Humanos, "Barrancabermeja, la otra versión: Paramilitarismo, control social y desaparición forzada, 2000–2003," *Noche y Niebla Caso Tipo No. 3* (Bogotá: CINEP/CREDHOS, 2004). Of special interest is the work of Franciscan priest Mario Rafael Toro Puerta, who spent several years in Barrio Boston, one of the poorest and most violent neighborhoods in Barranca. Mario Rafael Toro Puerta, O.F.M., *Pendientes de un hilo: El proceso de desafiliación en un sector de Barrancabermeja* (Bogotá: Editorial Bonaventuriana, 2004).

14. The practice of using *informantes encapuchados*, or hooded informants, was also used by the Colombian military during the 2002 assault on the Comuna 13 neighborhood in Medellín. The Comuna 13 was considered one of the last bastions of leftist militia influence in Colombia's second largest city. Banco de Datos de Violencia Política, Centro de Investigación y Educación Popular, and Justicia y Paz, "La comuna 13: La otra versión," *Noche y Niebla Caso Tipo No. 2* (Bogotá: CINEP/Justicia y Paz, 2003), 20.

15. According to the Consultancy on Human Rights and Displacement (CODHES), 1,195 people were displaced from Barrancabermeja in 2002. As cited in Felipe Osorio Viera and Fabián Ramírez Villarreal, "Barrancabermeja: Configuración territorial y conflicto social" (master's thesis, Universidad Nacional de Colombia, Bogotá, 2004).

16. Comisión Especial Disciplinaria, Procuraduría de la Nación, Bogotá (December 7, 1998), 47, CEJIL Archives, Washington, DC.

17. Ibid., 52.

18. Ibid.

19. Ibid., 34–35.

20. Jael Quiroga, interview with author (Bogotá, September 27, 2005).

21. As quoted in Amnesty International, *Barrancabermeja*, 20.

22. According to political scientist Mauricio Romero, the AUSAC was formed around 1995 in response to FARC activities northeast of Barrancabermeja. Romero, *Parapolítica*, 357, 363.

23. Ten years after the massacre, details about the fate of the twenty-five people disappeared from Barranca are starting to emerge. In May 2008 the remains of six of

the victims were found in a rural area of San Rafael de Lebrija, in the department of Santander near Bucaramanga, by representatives of the Colombian attorney general's office. Manuel Navarro, "Hallan primeros rastros de desaparecidos en masacre de desde hace 10 años en Barrancabermeja," *Vanguardia Liberal* (Bucaramanga, Santander), May 15, 2008. In March 2009 a demobilized paramilitary known by the alias Picúa tearfully confessed to a hearing of the government-run Justice and Peace Tribunal in Bucaramanga to having participated in the killing of the six victims whose bodies were located in San Rafael de Lebrija, the only victims accounted for thus far. "Detalles nunca revelados de la massacre de 16 de mayo en Barrancabermeja," *Vanguardia Liberal* (Bucaramanga, Santander), March 22, 2009.

24. Isacson, "The New Masters of Barranca."

25. Castaño, *Mi confesión*, 256.

26. For a discussion of the concept of enforced protection, see John J. Bedoya, "Seguridad y ciudadanía en los 90 en Medellín," 90.

27. Ibid., 257.

28. Ibid.

29. Jorge Gómez Lizarazo, interview with author (Barrancabermeja, March 8, 2006).

30. "Como avance contra la impunidad calificó la SIP condena por crimen de periodista en Barrancabermeja," *El Tiempo* (Bogotá), March 20, 2009.

31. In November 2009 Amnesty International reported that a Barranca-based member of the the human rights group Association of Families of the Detained and Disappeared (ASFADDES) received a threatening text message on her mobile phone that read: "Ms. Luz Almanza this is to let you know that you as representative of the organization which you are leading are declared a military target, sincerely Self Defence Forces." Amnesty International, "Human Rights Defender's Life in Danger" (Colombia, November 27, 2009), Urgent Action: 319/09, Index: AMR 23/029/2009.

32. Yolanda Becerra, interview with author (Barrancabermeja, March 10, 2006).

33. Banco de Datos, "Barrancabermeja, la otra versión," 120.

34. Center for Justice and International Law, "Comisión Interamericana admite denuncia contra Colombia por la masacre del 16 de mayo de 1998 en Barrancabermeja," press release, Washington, DC (October 27, 2003), CEJIL Archives, Washington, DC.

35. Claudia Ruíz, "Yolanda Becerra, colombiana ganadora del Premio Ginetta Sagan, Amnistía Internacional, 2009," *El Tiempo* (Bogotá), March 27, 2009.

36. David Ravelo, interview with author (Barrancabermeja, March 10, 2006).

37. *In the Company of Fear*, DVD, directed by Velcrow Ripper (1999; Vancouver, Canada: Reel-Myth Productions, 2007).

38. Francisco Campos, interview with author (Barrancabermeja, September 20, 2005).

39. Vladimir Carrillo and Tom Kucharz, *Colombia: Terrorismo de estado; Testimonios de la guerra sucia contra los movimientos populares* (Barcelona: Icario Editorial, 2006), 352.

40. Among the founding members of the Espacio were a number of established groups, including the Pastoral Social—Diócesis de Barrancabermeja, Organización Femenina Popular (OFP), Corporación Regional para la Defensa de los Derechos Humanos (CREDHOS), Central Unitaria de Trabajadores (CUT), Asociación Campesina del Valle Cimitarra (ACVC), and the Unión Sindical Obrera (USO), as well as several relatively new groups, including the Asociación Regional de Víctimas de la Violencia del Magdalena Medio (ASORVIN), and Asociación de Desplazados del Municipio de Barrancabermeja (ASODESAMUBA).

41. Subsequently another civil society initiative was launched, under the rubric of the Foro Social de Barrancabermeja y el Magdalena Medio. Inspired by the global phenomenon known as the World Social Forum, the Foro Social brought all sectors of civil society together to share information, develop proposals for local development, comment on government policy, and coordinate protests and other public activities.

42. Espacio de Trabajadores y Trabajadoras de Derechos Humanos, "Comunicado," Urgent Action (March 13, 20006), CREDHOS Archives, Barrancabermeja.

43. An earlier iteration of an alternative memory project published its first reports under the name Nunca Más, or Never Again, starting in 2000. Both Nunca Más and the Movimiento Nacional de Víctimas were intended to be rejoinders to the official story of the Colombian conflict that focus on armed actors, rather than victims. Guillermo Hoyos Vásquez, *Las víctimas frente a la búsqueda de la verdad y la reparación en Colombia* (Bogotá: Editorial Pontificia Universidad Javeriana, Instituto Goethe, Instituto de Estudios Sociales y Culturales Pensar, 2007).

44. Agencia Prensa Rural, "Se realizó el encuentro regional del Movimiento de Víctimas del Terrorismo de Estado en el Magdalena Medio," December 19, 2005, Colectivo de Abogados, José Alvear Restrepo, http://www.colectivodeabogados.org /Se-realizo-el-encuentro-regional.

45. Asociación de Desplazados Asentados en el Municipio de Barrancabermeja (ASODESAMUBA), "Atentado de muerte contra la compañera Socorro Abril, líder de asociación de desplazados en Barrancabermeja," Urgent Action (Barrancabermeja, November 10, 2005).

46. Angel Tolosa Pontón, interview with author (Bogotá, September 27, 2005).

47. Campos, interview with author (Barrancabermeja, September 20, 2005).

48. Between 1992 and 1997 CREDHOS was represented in Sabana de Torres by Mireya and Mario Calixto, both schoolteachers and social activists. When paramilitaries issued death threats against Mario Calixto in 1997, he prepared to leave town. Mario's departure was hastened when in December 1997 two armed men tried to abduct him from his home. While the two men spoke with members of Peace Brigades International, a human rights organization whose foreign volunteers provided accompaniment to Mario and his family, Mario ran out the back door and hid. He left later that day for Barranca, a few days later for Bogotá, and soon thereafter for Spain. Peace Brigades International, "Attempted Assassination of Human Rights Defender Mario Calixto; PBI Volunteers at Risk," Urgent Action (December 24, 1997).

49. Rafael Gómez, interview with author (Bogotá, September 27, 2005).

50. Irene Villamizar, interview with author (Barrancabermeja, March 8, 2006).

51. González Vélez and Jiménez, *Las guerras del Magdalena*, 99.

52. Madero, interview with author (Barrancabermeja, March 8, 2006).

53. Becerra, interview with author (Barrancabermeja, March 10, 2006).

54. Tate, *Counting the Dead*, 107.

55. Becerra, interview with author (Barrancabermeja, March 10, 2006).

56. Ibid.

57. Ibid.

58. Madero, interview with author (Barrancabermeja, March 8, 2006).

Conclusion

1. Francisco Campos, interview with author (Barrancabermeja, September 20, 2005).

2. Amnesty International, "Transforming Pain into Hope: Human Rights Defenders in the Americas" (London: Amnesty International, 2012), 18.

3. Francisco Leal Buitrago, *Clientelismo: El sistema político y su expresión regional* (Bogotá: Tercer Mundo Editores SID, IEPRI Universidad Nacional de Colombia, 1991).

4. By 1999 oil accounted for 32 percent of the total value of exports. Jenny Pearce, "Beyond the Perimeter Fence: Oil and Armed Conflict in Casanare, Colombia" (occasional paper, Center for the Study of Global Governance, London School of Economics, June 2004), 8–11.

5. Terry Lynn Karl, *The Paradox of Plenty: Oil Booms and Petro-States* (Berkeley: University of California Press, 1997), 47.

6. Daniel Yergin, *The Prize: The Epic Quest for Oil, Money, and Power* (New York: Simon and Schuster, 1991).

7. Chernick, "Negotiating Peace amid Multiple Forms of Violence," 197.

8. For work on the *paro cívico* in Colombia, see Medófilo Medina, "Los paros cívicos en Colombia (1957–1977)," *Estudios Marxistas* 2, no. 14 (1977): 3–24; Jaime Carrilllo Bedoya, *Los paros cívicos en Colombia* (Bogotá: Oveja Negra, 1981); and Elizabeth Ungar, *Los paros cívicos en Colombia, 1977–1980* (Bogotá: Uniandes, 1981).

9. Asociación Nacional de Usuarios Campesinos—Sector Independiente, *A hacha y machete: Tierra pa'l que la trabaja* (Barrancabermeja, June 1984), 5.

10. There was also an interesting progressive priest-led social experiment in San Gil, Santander, for several decades, described in Marietta Bucheli G., *Curas, campesinos y laicos como gerentes del desarrollo: La construcción de un modelo de desarrollo emergente en Colombia* (San Gil, Colombia: Fundación Editora Social de San Gil, 2006).

11. The Catholic Church, the Colombian military, civil society groups, guerrillas, paramilitaries, and national judicial authorities all maintain regional structures that give shape to the physical territory known as the Magdalena Medio.

12. One noteworthy point of comparison is the rural diocese of Facatativá, Cundinamarca. Covering 6,788 square kilometers, with a population of nearly half a

million divided into thirty-two parishes, Facatativá borders the diocese of Barrancaber-meja to the south. The diocese of Facatativá was a rare center of Christian Base Community organizing in Colombia in the 1970s and 1980s. Under the leadership of Spanish priest Román Cortés and a young Bogotá-born vicar-general by the name of Jaime Prieto Amaya, the diocese of Facatativá built up a network of rural education programs, cooperatives, and small development projects. Prieto Amaya left the diocese of Facatativá in 1993 to become bishop of Barrancabermeja. For background on Facatativá and its uniqueness in Colombian history, see Daniel H. Levine, "Colombia: The Institutional Church and the Popular," in *Religion and Political Conflict in Latin America*, ed. Daniel H. Levine (Chapel Hill: University of North Carolina Press, 1986), 204.

13. Ibid., 190, 192.

14. Gonzalo Sánchez G., ed., *Colombia: Violencia y democracia: Informe presentado al Ministerio de Gobierno* (Bogotá: Universidad Nacional de Colombia, 1987), 18.

15. Ibid., 68.

16. Ibid.

17. Harnecker, *Unidad que multiplica*, 179.

18. Francisco Leal Buitrago, "Los derechos humanos en la actual situación co-lombiana," *Análisis Político* 2 (September–December 1987): 61–62.

19. Ibid., 58.

20. Elvira María Restrepo, *Colombian Criminal Justice in Crisis: Fear and Distrust* (London: Palgrave Macmillan, 2003), 169–170.

21. Campos, interview with author (Barrancabermeja, September 20, 2005).

22. For comparisons in terms of how human rights activists negotiate the rough terrain of armed conflict, see Coletta Youngers and Susan C. Peacock, "Peru's Coordinadora Nacional de Derechos Humanos: A Case Study of Coalition Building" (Washington, DC: Washington Office on Latin America, 2002).

23. Yolanda Becerra, interview with author (Barrancabermeja, March 10, 2006).

24. Ramón Rangel, interview with author (Barrancabermeja, December 18, 2006).

25. Keck and Sikkink, *Activists beyond Borders*, 107.

26. Sikkink and Risse, "The Socialization of International Human Rights Norms," 22–35.

27. Ibid., 131.

28. Keck and Sikkink, *Activists beyond Borders*, 141.

29. Tate, *Counting the Dead*, 101.

30. Makua Mutua, *Human Rights: A Political and Cultural Critique* (Philadelphia: University of Pennsylvania Press, 2002), 198.

31. As mentioned in the introduction to this book, the Algiers Declaration of the Rights of Peoples of 1976 was drafted by nongovernmental activists as an assertion of collective rights, with an important emphasis on the right to self-determination of colonized peoples. Historically, the assertion of collective rights has been strongest by aboriginal peoples and left-wing movements, and the assertion of the right to

self-determination has been strongest by ethnic minorities and in Africa. Issa G. Shivji, *The Concept of Human Rights in Africa* (London: Council for the Development of Economic and Social Research in Africa, CODESRIA, 1989), 99.

32. Samuel Moyn, *The Last Utopia: Human Rights in History* (Cambridge, MA: Belknap Press of Harvard University Press, 2010), 121.

33. Zamosc, "The Political Crisis," 48.

34. Jorge Gómez Lizarazo, interview with author (Barrancabermeja, March 8, 2006).

35. "Even during the Conservative government certain rights were created. . . . They created the first norms on workplace accidents (1915) and life insurance paid for by companies (1921 and 1922), established health assistance for official employees (1923) and Sundays off for all workers (1926) . . . and consecrated the first laws on child labor (1929)." José Antonio Ocampo, ed., *Historia económica de Colombia* (Bogotá: Siglo Veintiuno Editores, Fedesarrollo, 1987), 319.

36. Paola Cesarini and Shareen Hertel, "Interdisciplinary Approaches to Human Rights Scholarship in Latin America," *Journal of Latin American Studies* 37, no. 4 (November 2005): 793–809.

37. Alessandro Portelli, *The Death of Luigi Trastuli and Other Stories: Form and Meaning in Oral History* (Albany: State University of New York Press, 1991), 50.

38. Becerra, interview with author (Barrancabermeja, March 10, 2006).

References

Oral Interviews

Acuña, Fernando. October 27, 2006. Former president of FEDEPETROL, former member of CREDHOS, historian, oil worker dismissed following 1977 strike, longtime resident of Barranca.

Becerra, Yolanda. March 10, 2006. Long-standing president of OFP, active with the OFP since 1989, longtime resident of Barranca.

Campos, Francisco. September 20, 2005. Member of CREDHOS (1990–2005), secretary general of CREDHOS (1998–2005), former municipal councillor in the nearby town of Sabana de Torres, Santander, longtime resident of Barranca.

Castilla Amell, Juan de Dios. October 26, 2006. Employee of the diocese of Barranca, former lay missionary worker with Pastoral Social in poor barrios of Barranca, former public functionary and university instructor, longtime resident of Barranca.

Gómez Lizarazo, Jorge. March 8, 2006. Former defensor del pueblo for the Magdalena Medio region, founding member of CREDHOS, president of CREDHOS (1987–1993), human rights lawyer, longtime resident of Barranca.

Gómez Serrano, Rafael. September 27, 2005. Employed by national NGO Reiniciar, founding member of CREHDOS, member CREDHOS board of directors (1988–1993), former president of USO, longtime resident of Barranca.

Madero, Régulo. September 8, 2006. Member of Barranca NGO Corporación Nación, former CREDHOS president (1998–2005), former departmental deputy for Antioquia for UP, longtime resident of Magdalena Medio region.

Nuñez, Jorge. December 21, 2007. Historian, editor of several locally published books, including *Crónicas de luchas por el poder local* (1997), former municipal official, longtime resident of Barranca.

Pinilla Pinilla, Luis. December 22, 2007. Political science professor at a university in Bogotá, formerly mayor of Barranca (1970–1971), but left the city in the 1970s. Born in Barranca, son of Conservative politician from Barranca who was killed during the 1948 uprising in the city known as the Comuna de Barranca.

Quiroga, Jael. September 27, 2005. President of national NGO Reiniciar, founding member of CREDHOS, CREDHOS board of directors (1987–1993), former Barranca city councillor for Conservative Party, longtime resident of Barranca.

Rangel, Ramón. December 18, 2007. Director of the Human Rights Commission of the USO since it was established in 1988, member of CREDHOS's board of directors (1990–1999), longtime resident of Barranca.

Ravelo, David. March 10, 2006. Current president of CREDHOS, former Barranca municipal councillor on behalf of the PCC, longtime resident of Barranca.

Rincón, Padre Jaime Barba. October 25, 2006. Catholic priest, rector of Barranca's Cathedral, former mayor of Barranca (1983–1985), public official, longtime resident of Barranca.

Romero, Amanda. October 19, 2006. Human rights activist who served as adviser to Barranca-based organizations between 1977 and 1999, while working with CSPP, CINEP, and ILSA.

Tolosa Pontón, Ángel. September 27, 2005. Employed by national NGO Planeta Paz, former president of ANUC–Sector Independiente, longtime resident of Barranca.

Villamizar, Irene. March 8, 2006. Elementary schoolteacher and administrator, founding member of CREDHOS, member of CREDHOS board of directors (1987–1992), community-based organizer for the Pastoral Social, longtime resident of Barranca.

Anonymous Interviews

Several individuals interviewed for this book chose not to be named or cited directly. Pseudonyms are used where appropriate.

Eight anonymous interview transcripts with Barranca social movement leaders conducted in 2004 were provided by the Centro de Investigación y Educación Popular (CINEP) in Bogotá.

Archives

Archives of the Centre for Justice and International Law (CEJIL), Washington, DC.

Archives of the Diócesis de Barrancabermeja, Barrancabermeja, Colombia.

Archivo General de la Nación, Bogotá, Colombia.

Archives of the Corporación Regional para la Defensa de los Derechos Humanos (CREDHOS): Boletines, Correspondencia, Acciones Urgentes y Comunicados Públicos (1987–1998), Barrancabermeja, Colombia.

Archivo del Concejo Municipal de Barrancabermeja: Actas, Correspondencia y Acuerdos (1970–1991), Barrancabermeja, Colombia.

National Archives, Washington, DC.

National Security Archive, George Washington University, Washington, DC.

Personal papers and correspondence of John Hicks, Vancouver Island, British Columbia.

Newspapers and Magazines

Alternativa, Bogotá (1975–1990)
Colombia Hoy Informa, Bogotá (1985–1990)
Controversia, Bogotá (1970–2000)
El Espectador, Bogotá (1970–1990)
El Mundo, Medellín (1987–1988)
El Sideral, Barrancabermeja (1974–1976)
El Tiempo, Bogotá (1970–1991)
Familia Diocesana, Barrancabermeja (1987–1993)
Globe and Mail, Toronto (1920–1990)
Lamp, New York (1920–1950)
La Opinión del Magdalena Medio, Barrancabermeja (1987–1991)
New York Times, New York (1920–2005)
Opción, Bogotá (1985–1991)
Semana, Bogotá (1970–1990)
Vanguardia Liberal, Bucaramanga, Satander (1963, 1970–1992)
Voz Proletaria, Bogotá (1970–1990)

Published Government and Nongovernment Human Rights Reports

Americas Watch. *The Central-Americanization of Colombia? Human Rights and the Peace Process*. New York: Americas Watch, January 1986.
———. *The Killings in Colombia: An Americas Watch Report*. New York: Americas Watch, April 1989.
Amnesty International. *Amnesty International Report 1981*. London: Amnesty International Publications, 1981.
———. *Barrancabermeja: A City under Siege*. London: Amnesty International Publications, 1999.
———. *Transforming Pain into Hope: Human Rights Defenders in the Americas*. London: Amnesty International Publications, 2012.
———. *Violación de los derechos humanos en Colombia: Informe de Amnistía Internacional*. Bogotá: Comité de Solidaridad con los Presos Políticos, 1980.
Asociación de Familiares de Detenidos-Desaparecidos. *Veinte años de historia y lucha: ASFADDES con todo el derecho*. Bogotá: ASFADDES, 2003.
Asociación Nacional de Usuarios Campesinos—Sector Independiente. *A hacha y machete: Tierra pa'l que la trabaja*. Barrancabermeja, June 1984.
Banco de Datos de Violencia Política, Centro de Investigación y Educación Popular, and Corporación Regional para la Defensa de los Derechos Humanos. "Barrancabermeja, la otra versión: Paramilitarismo, control social y desaparición forzada, 2000–2003." *Noche y Niebla Caso Tipo No. 3*. Bogotá: CINEP/CREDHOS, 2004.

Banco de Datos de Violencia Política, Centro de Investigación y Educación Popular and Justicia y Paz. "La comuna 13: La otra versión." *Noche y Niebla Caso Tipo No. 2.* Bogotá: CINEP/Justicia y Paz, 2003.

Comisión Andina de Juristas, Seccional Colombiana. *Nordeste Antioqueño y Magdalena Medio.* Serie Informes Regionales de Derechos Humanos. Bogotá, January 1, 1993.

———. *Guerra sucia y estado de sitio en Colombia.* Bogotá, November 30, 1988.

Comisión de Estudios sobre la Violencia. *Colombia: Violencia y democracia; Informe presentado al Ministerio de Gobierno.* Bogotá: Universidad Nacional de Colombia, 1987.

Comisión Intercongregacional de Justicia y Paz. "Informe de la Comisión Intercongregacional de Justicia y Paz sobre la situación de violencia que se vive en los municipios de El Carmen y San Vicente de Chucurí (Santander), debida a la acción de grupos paramilitares." Bogotá: Justicia y Paz, August 1990.

Comisión Nacional de Reparación y Reconciliación (Colombia). "Amenazas y ataques a la memoria y sus símbolos." In *Trujillo, una tragedia que no cesa: Primer informe de memoria histórica de la Comisión Nacional de Reparación y Reconciliación.* Bogotá: Planeta, 2008.

Comité Permanente por la Defensa de los Derechos Humanos. *Derechos Humanos en Colombia: Veinticinco años; Itinerario de una historia.* Bogotá: Panamericana Formas e Impresos S.A., 2004.

Committee on Foreign Relations, U.S. Senate. "Challenges for U.S. Policy towards Colombia: Is Plan Colombia Working?" Washington, DC: U.S. Department of State, October 29, 2003.

Consultoría para los Derechos Humanos y el Desplazamiento. "Víctimas emergentes." *Codhes Informa* 75 (April 22, 2009).

Corporación Regional para la Defensa de los Derechos Humanos (CREDHOS) and Corporación Colectivo de Abogados José Alvear Restrepo (CAJAR). *Hoy como ayer, persistiendo por la vida: Redes de inteligencia y exterminio en Barrancabermeja.* Bogotá: CREDHOS and CAJAR, 1999.

Crisis universitaria colombiana 1971: Itinerario y documentos. Medellín: Ediciones El Tigre de Papel, 1971.

Equipo de Trabajo Popular. "El Movimiento Popular en Barrancabermeja." In *Los movimientos cívicos,* edited by Álvaro Cabrera et al., 000–000. Bogotá: Centro de Investigación y Educación Popular, CINEP, 1986.

Foro Nacional por Colombia. *Primer congreso nacional de movimientos cívicos: Memoria, octubre de 1983.* Bogotá: Foro Nacional por Colombia, 1983.

Human Rights Watch. *Breaking the Grip? Obstacles to Justice for Paramilitary Mafias in Colombia.* New York: Human Rights Watch, 2008.

———. *Colombia's Killer Networks: The Military-Paramilitary Partnership and the United States.* New York: Human Rights Watch, 1996.

———. *State of War: Political Violence and Counterinsurgency in Colombia.* New York: Human Rights Watch, 1993.

———. *War without Quarter: Colombia and International Humanitarian Law.* New York: Human Rights Watch, 1998.

Liga Internacional por los Derechos y la Liberación de los Pueblos. *El camino de la niebla.* Vol.1, *La desaparición forzada en Colombia y su impunidad.* Bogotá: Liga Internacional por los Derechos y la Liberación de los Pueblos, Sección Colombiana, 1990.

———. *El camino de la niebla.* Vol. 2, *El asesinato político en Colombia y su impunidad.* Bogotá: Liga Internacional por los Derechos y la Liberación de los Pueblos, Sección Colombiana, 1990.

———. *El camino de la niebla.* Vol. 3, *Masacres en Colombia y su impunidad.* Bogotá: Liga Internacional por los Derechos y la Liberación de los Pueblos, Sección Colombiana, 1990.

Pastoral Social. "Experiencia de trabajo: Período de 1971 a 1986." Barrancabermeja: Diócesis de Barrancabermeja, August 1986.

Programa de las Naciones Unidas para el Desarrollo. "Informe preparado para el gobierno de Colombia por la Organización de las Naciones Unidas para la Educación, la Ciencia y la Cultura, como organismo participante y de ejecución del Programa de las Naciones Unidas para el Desarrollo correspondiente al periodo 1962–1968." Bucaramanga: Universidad Industrial de Santander, 1968.

Proyecto Nunca Más. *Crimenes de lesa humanidad: Zona 14a 1996.* Bogotá: Colombia Nunca Más, 2000.

Revolutionary Armed Forces of Colombia–People's Army. *FARC-EP: Historical Outline.* Toronto: International Commission, Revolutionary Armed Forces of Colombia-People's Army, 2001.

Royal Horticultural Society. "Letter from Mr. Weir the Collector in New Grenada." In *Proceedings of the Royal Horticultural Society, from January 1 to December 31, 1964.* London: Spottiswoode, 1964.

UN Human Rights Commission. Report of the United Nations High Commissioner for Human Rights on the Human Rights Situation in Colombia, 58th session of the UN Human Rights Commission. Geneva, March 13, 2002.

U.S. Department of State. "Colombia: Murder of American Citizen." *Press Releases* 32 (May 10, 1930): 245.

Vicepresidencia de la República de Colombia. *Panorama actual de Barrancabermeja.* Bogotá: Observatorio del Programa Presidencial de Derechos Humanos y Derecho Internacional Humanitario, 2001.

Secondary Sources

Agamben, Giorgio. *States of Exception.* Chicago: University of Chicago Press, 2005.

Agosín, Marjorie. *Circles of Madness: Mothers of the Plaza de Mayo.* Fredonia, NY: White Pine Press, 1992.

Anderson, Benedict. *Imagined Communities: Reflections on the Origin and Spread of Nationalism.* New York: Verso, 1991.

An-Na'im, Abdullahi Ahmed, ed. *Human Rights in Cross-Cultural Perspectives: A Quest for Consensus.* Philadelphia: University of Pennsylvania Press, 1995.

Aprile-Gniset, Jacques. *Génesis de Barrancabermeja: Ensayo.* Bucaramanga: Instituto Universitario de la Paz, Departamento de Ciencias Políticas, 1997.

Archila Neira, Mauricio. *Aquí nadie es forastero: Testimonios sobre la formación de una cultura radical Barrancabermeja, 1920–1950.* Bogotá: Centro de Investigación y Educación Popular, 1978.

———. "Barranquilla y el Río: Una historia social de sus trabajadores." *Controversia* 142 (November 1987).

———. "La clase obrera colombiana (1886–1930)." In *Nueva Historia de Colombia*, vol. 3, edited by Álvaro Tirado Mejía, 219–244. Bogotá: Editorial Planeta, 1989.

———. *Idas y venidas: Vueltas y revueltas; Protestas sociales en Colombia, 1958–1990.* Bogotá: Instituto Colombiano de Antropología e Historia, ICANH, y el Centro de Investigación y Educación Popular, CINEP, 2004.

Archila Neira, Mauricio, et al., eds. *25 años de luchas sociales en Colombia 1975–2000.* Bogotá: Centro de Investigación y Educación Popular, CINEP, 2001.

———, eds. *Conflictos, poderes e identidades en el Magdalena Medio, 1990–2001.* Bogotá: COLCIENCIAS, CINEP, 2006.

Arenas, Jacobo. *Diario de la resistencia de Marquetalia.* Bogotá: Ediciones Abejón Mono, 1972.

Arenas Obregón, Martha. *Cerrando fronteras: Historias contadas del Magdalena Medio.* Barrancabermeja: Programa de Desarrollo y Paz del Magdalena Medio, 1999.

Arnson, Cynthia J., ed. *The Peace Process in Colombia with the Autodefensas Unidas de Colombia–AUC.* Washington, DC: Woodrow Wilson Center for Scholars, 2005.

Arendt, Hannah. *The Origins of Totalitarianism.* New York: Harcourt, Brace, 1951.

Arredondo, Leon. "Liberalism, Working-Class Formation and Historical Memory: Dockworkers in a Colombian Frontier." PhD diss., City University of New York, 2005.

Avilés, William. *Global Capitalism, Democracy, and Civil-Military Relations in Colombia.* Albany: State University of New York Press, 2007.

Báez Pimiento, Adriana. "El imaginario rojista y la beligerancia política en el proceso de fundación de la Alianza nacional popular en Santander (1953–1960)." *Anuario de Historia Regional y de Fronteras* 9 (2004): 137–171.

Bagley, Bruce Michael. "Political Power, Public Policy and the State in Colombia: Case Studies of the Urban and Agrarian Reforms during the National Front, 1958–1974." PhD diss., University of California, Los Angeles, 1979.

Barreto Henriques, Miguel. "El Laboratorio de Paz en el Magdalena Medio: ¿Un verdadero 'laboratorio de paz'?" In *Guerra y violencia en Colombia: Herramientas e interpretaciones*, edited by Jorge A. Restrepo and David Aponte. Bogotá: Editorial Pontificia Universidad Javeriana, 2009.

Basombrio Iglesias, Carlos. "Sendero Luminoso and Human Rights: A Perverse Logic that Captured the Country." In *Shining and Other Paths: War and Society in Peru, 1980–1995*, edited by Steve J. Stern, 425–446. Durham, NC: Duke University Press, 1998.

Baxi, Upendra. *The Future of Human Rights*. Oxford: Oxford University Press, 2002.

Bedoya, Jairo. *La protección violenta en Colombia: El caso de Medellín desde los años noventa*. Medellín: IPC-Confiar, 2010.

Bedoya, John J. "Seguridad y ciudadanía en los 90 en Medellín: El surgimiento de las empresas colombianas de protección violenta." *Canadian Journal of Latin American and Caribbean Studies* 31, no. 62 (2006): 87–130.

Behar, Olga, and Carolina Ardila. *El caso Klein: El origen del paramilitarismo*. Bogotá: Icono, 2012.

Bejarano, Ana María. "Perverse Democratization: Pacts, Institutions and Problematic Consolidations in Colombia and Venezuela." PhD diss., Columbia University, 2000.

Bell Lemus, Gustavo. "El canal del Dique, 1810–1840: El viacrusis de Cartagena." *Boletín Cultural y Geográfico* 26, no. 21 (1989): 15–23.

Bergquist, Charles. *Café y conflicto en Colombia, 1886–1910: La guerra de los mil días, sus antecedentes y consecuencias*. Medellín: Fondo Rotatorio de Publicaciones, FAES, 1981.

———. *Coffee and Conflict in Colombia, 1886–1910*. Durham, NC: Duke University Press, 1978.

———. *Labor in Latin America: Comparative Essays on Chile, Argentina, Venezuela, and Colombia*. Stanford: Stanford University Press, 1986.

Bergquist, Charles, Ricardo Peñaranda, and Gonzalo Sánchez, eds. *Violence in Colombia, 1990–2000: Waging War and Negotiating Peace*. Wilmington, DE: Scholarly Resources Books, 2001.

Berry, R. Albert, Ronald G. Hellman, and Mauricio Solaún, eds. *Politics of Compromise: Coalition Government in Colombia*. New Brunswick, NJ: Transaction Books, 1980.

Betancourt, Darío, and Martha L. García. *Matones y cuadrilleros: Origen y evolución de la violencia en el occidente colombiano*. Bogotá: Tercer Mundo Editores e Instituto de Estudios Políticos y Relaciones Internacionales, Universidad Nacional de Colombia, 1990.

Bolívar, Ingrid, Adriana Posada, and Renata Segura. "El papel de la ONGs en la sociedad civil: La construcción de lo público." *Controversia* 170 (1997): 57–97.

Bonilla, María Elvira. *Hablan los generales: Las grandes batallas del conflicto colombiano contadas por sus protagonistas*. Bogotá: Editorial Norma, 2005.

Borderick, Walter J. *El guerrillero invisible*. Bogotá: Intermedio, 2000.

Bouvier, Virginia M., ed. *Colombia: Building Peace in a Time of War*. Washington, DC: United States Institute for Peace, 2009.

Bowman, Kirk S. *Militarization, Democracy, and Development: The Perils of Praetorianism in Latin America*. University Park: Pennsylvania State University Press, 2002.

Braun, Herbert. *The Assassination of Gaitán: Public Life and Urban Violence in Colombia*. Madison: University of Wisconsin Press, 1985.

Brittain, James J. *Revolutionary Social Change in Colombia: The Origin and Direction of the FARC-EP*. London: Pluto Press, 2009.

Brown, Cynthia. *With Friends Like These: The Americas Watch Report on Human Rights and U.S. Policy in Latin America*. New York: Pantheon, 1985.

Brown, Jonathan C. *Oil and Revolution in Mexico*. Berkeley: University of California Press, 1993.

Brown, Jonathan C., and Alan Knight, eds. *The Mexican Petroleum Industry in the Twentieth Century*. Austin: University of Texas Press, 1992.

Bucheli, Marcelo. *Bananas and Business: The United Fruit Company in Colombia, 1899–2000*. New York: New York University Press, 2005.

———. "Multinational Oil Companies in Colombia and Mexico: Corporate Strategy, Nationalism, and Local Politics, 1900–1951." Paper presented at International Economic History Conference, Helsinki, Finland, 2006.

———. "Negotiating under the Monroe Doctrine: Weetman Pearson and the Origins of U.S. Control of Colombian Oil." *Business History Review* 82, no. 3 (Autumn 2008): 529–557.

Bucheli, Marcelo, and Ruth Aguilera. "Political Survival, Energy Policies, and Multinational Corporations: A Historical Study for Standard Oil of New Jersey in Colombia, Mexico, and Venezuela in the Twentieth Century." Working Paper 06-0101, University of Illinois College of Business, 2006.

Bucheli G., Marietta. *Curas, campesinos y laicos como gerentes del desarrollo: La construcción de un modelo de desarrollo emergente en Colombia*. San Gil, Colombia: Fundación Editora Social de San Gil, 2006.

Buenahora, Gonzalo. *La comuna de Barranca: 9 de abril de 1948*. Bogotá: Gráfica Leipzig, 1971.

———. *Sangre y petróleo*. 2nd ed. Bogotá: Fotolito Inter, 2000.

Bueno Altahona, Elkin. *Plan de desarrollo municipio de Barrancabermeja, 2012–2015: Documento técnico de trabajo; Versión para discusión*. Barrancabermeja: Alcalde de Barrancabermeja, February 2012.

Bushnell, David. *The Making of Modern Colombia: A Nation in Spite of Itself*. Berkeley: University of California Press, 1993.

Cabrera, Álvaro, et al., eds. *Los movimientos cívicos*. Bogotá: Editorial CINEP, 1986.

Camacho Guizado, Álvaro. "De narcos, paracracias y mafias." In *En la encrucijada: Colombia en el siglo XXI*, edited by Francisco Leal Buitrago, 394–395. Bogotá: Editorial Norma, 2006.

Cano Márquez, María. *Escritos*. Compiled by Miguel Escobar Calle. Medellín: Extensión cultural departamental, 1985.

Cardona, Christopher Michael. "Politicians, Soldiers, and Cops: Colombia's La Violencia in Comparative Perspective." PhD diss., University of California, Berkeley, 2008.

Carozza, Paolo G. "From Conquest to Constitutions: Retrieving a Latin American Tradition of the Idea of Human Rights." *Human Rights Quarterly* 25, no. 2 (May 2003): 281–313.

Carrigan, Ana. *The Palace of Justice: A Colombian Tragedy*. New York: Four Walls Eight Windows, 1993.

Carrillo, Vladimir, and Tom Kucharz. *Colombia: Terrorismo de estado; Testimonios de la guerra sucia contra los movimientos populares*. Barcelona: Icario Editorial, 2006.

Carrillo Bedoya, Jaime. *Los paros cívicos en Colombia*. Bogotá: La Oveja Negra, 1981.

Carroll, Leah. "The Patriotic Union and Its Successors in Arauca, 1984–2007: From Electoral Power to Leadership in the Struggle against Impunity." Paper presented at International Congress of Latin American Studies Association, October 6–9, 2010, Toronto.

———. *Violent Democratization: Social Movements, Elites, and Politics in Colombia's Rural War Zones, 1984–2008*. Notre Dame, IN: University of Notre Dame Press, 2011.

———. "Violent Democratization: The Effect of Political Reform on Rural Social Conflict in Colombia." PhD diss., University of California, Berkeley, 1989.

Castañeda, Jorge G. *Utopia Unarmed: The Latin American Left after the Cold War*. New York: Knopf, 1993.

Castaño, Carlos. *Mi confesión: Carlos Castaño revela sus secretos*. Interview by Mauricio Aranguren Molina. Bogotá: Oveja Negra, 2001.

Castilla Amell, Juan de Dios. "Participación popular y movimiento social: Barrancabermeja 1971–1985." Master's thesis, Universidad de los Andes, 1989.

Cesarini, Paola, and Shareen Hertel. "Interdisciplinary Approaches to Human Rights Scholarship in Latin America." *Journal of Latin American Studies* 37, no. 4 (November 2005): 793–809.

Chaparro, Jairo. *Recuerdos de un tropelero*. Bogotá: Centro de Investigación y Educación Popular, CINEP, 1991.

Chernick, Marc. "Negotiating Peace amid Multiple Forms of Violence: The Protracted Search for a Settlement to the Armed Conflicts in Colombia." In *Comparative Peace Processes in Latin America*, edited by Cynthia J. Aronson, 159–196. Washington, DC: Woodrow Wilson Press; Stanford: Stanford University Press, 1999.

Chomsky, Noam, and Edward Herman. *The Washington Connection and Third World Fascism: The Political Economy of Human Rights*. Vol. 1. Cambridge, MA: South End Press, 1979.

Church Johnson, David. "Social and Economic Change in Nineteenth-Century Santander, Colombia." PhD diss., University of California, Berkeley, 1975.

Cleary, Edward L. *The Struggle for Human Rights in Latin America*. Westport, CT: Praeger, 1997.

Climo, Jacob C., and Maria G. Catelli, eds. *Social History and Memory: Anthropological Perspectives*. London: Alta Mira Press, 2002.

Comité Central del Partido Comunista de Colombia. *Treinta años de lucha del Partido Comunista de Colombia*. Bogotá: Ediciones los Comuneros, 1960.

Contreras N., Víctor. *Barrancabermeja: Estudio socioeconómico y administrativo del municipio*. Bogotá: Centros de Estudios sobre Desarrollo Económico, CEDE, Universidad de los Andes, Abril 1970.

Crandall, Russell. *Driven by Drugs: U.S. Policy toward Colombia*. Boulder, CO: Lynne Reiner, 2002.

Crawford, James, ed. *The Rights of Peoples*. Oxford: Oxford University Press, 1988.

Cubides, Fernando, Ana Cecilia Olaya, and Carlos Miguel Ortiz, eds. *La violencia y el municipio colombiano*. Bogotá: Centro de Estudios Sociales, Universidad Nacional de Colombia, 1998.

Daviaud, Sophie. "Las ONG colombianas de defensa de los DD HH de cara a las violencias." In *Violencias y estrategias colectivas en la región andina: Bolivia, Colombia, Ecuador, Perú y Venezuela*, edited by Eric Lair and Gonzalo Sánchez, 199–228. Bogotá: Grupo Editorial Norma, 2004.

Deas, Malcolm. *Del poder y la gramática, y otros ensayos sobre historia, política y literatura colombianas*. Bogotá: Tercer Mundo Editores, 1993.

Díaz Callejas, Apolinar. *Diez días de poder popular: El 9 de abril en Barrancabermeja*. Bogotá: Editorial el Labrador, 1988.

Dudley, Steven. *Walking Ghosts: Murder and Guerrilla Politics in Colombia*. London: Routledge, 2004.

Duncan, Roland E. "William Wheelwright and Early Steam Navigation in the Pacific, 1820–1840." *Americas* 32, no. 2 (October 1975): 257–281.

Dunning, Thad, and Leslie Wirpsa. "Oil and the Political Economy of Conflict in Colombia and Beyond: A Linkages Approach." *Geopolitics* 9, no. 4 (2004): 81–108.

Duque Rojas, Ubencel. "Conflictos y paz, realidad y aprendizajes significativos en la región del Magdalena Medio." Master's thesis, Universidad Pedagógica Nacional, 2004.

Durham, W. O. *From Kittyhawk to the Moon: The Life, Times and Heritage of a Texas Oilman*. New York: Vantage Press, 2007.

Escobar Calle, Miguel. *Apuntes para una cronología de la fotografía en Antioquia*. Medellín: Biblioteca Pública Piloto de Medellín, Archivos Fotográficos, Memoria Visual de Antioquia y del País, 2001.

Farnsworth-Alvear, Anne. *Dulcinea in the Factory: Myths, Morals, Men and Women in Colombia's Industrial Experiment, 1905–1960*. Durham, NC: Duke University Press, 2003.

Feitlowitz, Marguerite. *A Lexicon of Terror: Argentina and the Legacies of Torture*. New York: Oxford University Press, 1988.

Fisher, Josephine. *Mothers of the Disappeared*. Boston: South End Press, 1989.

Flórez López, Carlos A., and Luisa Castañeda Rueda. *Así se pobló la ciudad: Crecimiento urbano en Barrancabermeja, 1970–1990*. Barrancabermeja: Alcaldía Municipal de Barrancabermeja, 1997.

Florez-Malagón, Alberto. *Una isla en un mar de sangre: El Valle de Ubaté durante La Violencia, 1946–1958*. Bogotá: Centro Editorial Javeriano, La Carreta Ediciones, 2005.

Foweraker, Joe. *Theorizing Social Movements*. London: Pluto Press, 1995.

Francis, J. Michael, ed. *Invading Colombia: Spanish Accounts of the Gonzalo Jiménez de Quesada Expedition of Conquest*. University Park, PA: Pennsylvania State University Press, 2007.

French, Paul. *No fue una huelga . . . fue una guerra . . . !! Conflicto laboral en Ecopetrol*. Bogotá: Mundo Gráfico Editores, 2003.

Gallardo, Helio. *Derechos humanos como movimiento social*. Bogotá: Ediciones Desde Abajo, 2006.

García Márquez, Gabriel. *Living to Tell the Tale*. Translated by Edith Grossman. New York: Vintage International, 2003.

García Villegas, Mauricio, and Rodrigo Uprimny Yepes. "La normalisation de l'exceptionnel sur le contrôle juridictionnel des états d'urgence en Colombie." In *Justice et démocratie en Amérique Latine*, edited by Marie-Julie Bernard and Michel Carraud, 117–144. Grenoble: Presses Universitaires de Grenoble, 2005.

Gibb, George S., and Evelyn H. Knowlton. *The Resurgent Years, 1911–1927: History of Standard Oil Company (New Jersey)*. New York: Harper and Brothers, 1956.

Gill, Lesley. "Durable Disorder: Parapolitics in Barrancabermeja." *North American Congress on Latin America Report* 42, no. 4 (July/August 2009): 20–24.

———. "The Parastate in Colombia: Political Violence and the Restructuring of Barrancabermeja." *Anthropologica* 51 (2009): 1–11.

Giraldo, Javier. *Colombia: The Genocidal Democracy*. Monroe, ME: Common Courage Press, 1996.

Giraldo, Javier, and Santiago Camargo. "Paros y movimientos cívicos en Colombia." *Controversía* 128 (1985).

Giugale, Marcelo M., Olivier Lafourcade, and Connie Luff, eds. *Colombia: The Economic Foundation of Peace*. Washington, DC: World Bank, 2003.

Glendon, Mary Ann. "The Forgotten Crucible: The Latin American Influence on the Universal Human Rights Idea." *Harvard Human Rights Journal* 16 (Spring 2003): 27–39.

Gómez Buendía, Hernando, ed. *El conflicto, callejón con salida: Informe nacional de desarollo para Colombia—2003*. Bogotá: Programa de las Naciones Unidas para el Desarrollo (PNUD), September 2003.

Gómez Pérez, Diana Marcela. "Petróleo y huelgas: El caso de Barrancabermeja en 1971." PhD diss., Pontificia Universidad Javeriana, Bogotá, 2000.

Gómez Picón, Rafael. *Magdalena, río de Colombia*. 7th ed. Bogotá: Ediciones Tercer Mundo, 1983.

Gómez-Suárez, Andrei. "Perpetrator Blocs, Genocidal Mentalities, and Geographies: The Destruction of the Unión Patriótica in Colombia and Its Lessons for Genocide Studies." *Journal of Genocide Research* 9, no. 4 (December 2009): 637–660.

González, Fernán E., Ingrid J. Bolívar, and Teófilo Vázquez. *Violencia política en Colombia: De la nación fragmentada a la construcción del estado*. Bogotá: CINEP, Centro de Investigación y Educación Popular, 2003.

González, Olga Lucía, and Daniel Ramos, eds. *Mujeres, hombres y cambio social*. Bogotá: Universidad Nacional de Colombia, 1998.

González Mongui, Pablo Elías. *Derechos penal en la relaciones laborales públicas y privadas*. Madrid: Universidad de Jaen, CIVITAS, 1998.

González Vélez, Estefanía, and Orián Jiménez Meneses. *Las guerras del Magdalena Medio*. Bogotá: Intermedio, 2008.

Grandin, Greg. *Fordlandia: The Rise and Fall of Henry Ford's Forgotten Jungle City.* New York: Metropolitan Books, 2009.

———. "Human Rights and Empire's Embrace: A Latin American Counterpoint." In *Human Rights and Revolutions,* 2nd ed., edited by Jeffrey N. Wasserstrom et al., 191–212. Lanham, MD: Rowman and Littlefield, 2007.

———. "The Instruction of Great Catastrophe: Truth Commissions, State Formation, and National Identity in Argentina, Chile, and Guatemala." *American Historical Review* 109, no. 1 (February 2005): 46–67.

———. *The Last Colonial Massacre: Latin America in the Cold War.* Chicago: University of Chicago Press, 2004.

Grandin, Greg, and Thomas Miller Klubock, eds. "Truth Commissions: State Terror, History, and Memory." Special issue, *Radical History Review* 97 (Winter 2007).

Grant, H. M. "Solving the Labor Problem at Imperial Oil." In *Canadian Working-Class History: Selected Readings,* 3rd ed., edited by Laurel Sefton MacDowell and Ian Radforth, 232–252. Toronto, Canadian Scholars Press, 2006.

Green, W. John. *Gaitanismo, Left Liberalism, and Popular Mobilization in Colombia.* Gainesville: University Press of Florida, 2003.

———. "'Vibrations of the Collective': The Popular Ideology of Gaitanismo on Colombia's Atlantic Coast, 1944–1948." *Hispanic American Historical Review* 76, no. 2 (1996): 283–311.

Grupo de Memoria Histórica, Comisión Nacional de Reparación y Reconciliación. *La Rochela: Memorías de un crímen contra la justicia.* Bogotá: Ediciones Semana, 2010.

Gutierréz Sanín, Francisco, María Emma Wills, and Gonzalo Sánchez, eds. *Nuestra guerra sin nombre: Transformaciones del conflicto en Colombia.* Bogotá: Editorial Norma, 2006.

Guzman Bouvard, Marguerite. *Revolutionizing Motherhood: The Mothers of the Plaza de Mayo.* Wilmington, DE: Scholarly Resources, 1994.

Guzmán Campos, Germán, Orlando Fals Borda, and Eduardo Umaña Luna. *La Violencia en Colombia.* 2 vols. Reprint. Bogotá: Taurus Historia, 2005.

Harnecker, Marta. *Entrevista con la nueva izquierda: Entrevista a Bernardo Jaramillo, de la Unión Patriótica, y Nelson Berríos, de A Luchar, sobre los desafíos que enfrentan los cuadros públicos en un país en que existe una guerra de guerrillas.* Managua: Centro de Documentación y Ediciones Latinoamericanas, 1989.

———. *Unidad que multiplica: Entrevista a dirigentes máximos de la Unión Camilista Ejército de Liberación Nacional sobre la historia del ELN, y una reflexión sobre la situación de las guerrillas en ese momento.* Managua: Centro de Documentación y Ediciones Latinoamericanas, 1988.

Hartlyn, Jonathan. *The Politics of Coalition Rule in Colombia.* Cambridge: Cambridge University Press, 1988.

Havens, A. Eugene, and Michel Romieux. *Barrancabermeja: Conflictos sociales en torno a un centro petrolero.* Bogotá: Ediciones Tercer Mundo y Facultad de Sociología, Universidad Nacional de Colombia, 1966.

Hernández, Milton. *Rojo y negro: Historia del ELN.* Tafalla: Txalaparta, 2006.

Hobsbawm, Eric, and Terence Ranger, eds. *The Invention of Tradition*. Cambridge: Cambridge University Press, 1983.

Hopgood, Stephen. *Keepers of the Flame: Understanding Amnesty International*. Ithaca, NY: Cornell University Press, 2006.

Horna, Hernán. *Transportation Modernization and Entrepreneurship in Nineteenth Century Colombia: Cisneros and Friends*. Studia Historica Upsaliensia 172. Uppsala: Acta Universitatis Upsaliensis, 1992.

Hoyos Vásquez, Guillermo. *Las víctimas frente a la búsqueda de la verdad y la reparación en Colombia*. Bogotá: Editorial Pontificia Universidad Javeriana, Instituto Goethe, Instituto de Estudios Sociales y Culturales Pensar, 2007.

Hristov, Jasmin. *Blood and Capital: The Paramilitarization of Colombia*. Athens: Ohio University Press, 2009.

Hylton, Forest. *Evil Hour in Colombia*. New York: Verso, 2006.

Irazábal, Clara, and John Foley. "Space, Revolution and Resistance: Ordinary Places and Extraordinary Events in Caracas." In *Ordinary Places, Extraordinary Events: Citizenship, Democracy, and Public Space in Latin America*, edited by Clara Irazábal, 144–169. New York: Routledge, 2008.

Isacson, Adam. "The New Masters of Barranca: A Report from CIP's Trip to Barrancabermeja, Colombia, March 6–9, 2001." Washington, DC: Center for International Policy, April 2001.

Iván, Jorge, et al. *Los discursos del conflicto: Espacio público, paros cívicos y prensa en Colombia*. Bogotá: Pontifica Universidad Javeriana, 1998.

Jameson, Frederic. *Marxism and Form: Twentieth-Century Dialectical Theories of Literature*. Princeton, NJ: Princeton University Press, 1974.

Jaramillo Arango, Rafael. *Barrancabermeja: Novela de proxenetas, rufianes, obreros y petroleros*. Bogotá: Editorial E.S.B., 1934.

Jaramillo Panesso, Jaime. *La espada de Bolívar: El M-19 narada; José Yamel Riaño en conversación con Jaime Jaramillo Panesso*. Medellín, Colombia: Fondo Editorial ITM, 2006.

Jaramillo Uribe, Jaime, and Frank Safford. "An Interview with Jaime Jaramillo Uribe." *Hispanic American Historic Review* 64, no. 1 (February 1984): 1–15.

Jiménez, Michael F. "The Limits of Export Capitalism: Economic Structure, Class and Politics in a Colombian Coffee Municipality, 1900–1930." PhD diss., Harvard University, 1985.

Johnson, Kenneth F. "Political Radicalism in Colombia: Electoral Dynamics of 1962 and 1964." *Journal of Inter-American Studies* 7, no. 1 (January 1965): 15–26.

Kaldor, Mary, Terry Lynn Karl, and Yahia Said, eds. *Oil Wars*. London: Pluto Press, 2007.

Kalmanovitz Krauter, Salomón. *Economía y nación: Una breve historia de Colombia*. 2nd ed. Bogotá: Editorial Norma, 2003.

Kaplan, Temma. "Uncommon Women and the Common Good: Women and Environmental Protest." In *Women Resist Globalization: Mobilizing for Livelihood and Rights*, edited by Sheila Rowbotham and Stephanie Linkogle, 28–45. London: ZED Books, 2002.

Karl, Robert Alexander. "State Formation, Violence, and Cold War in Colombia, 1957–1966." PhD diss., Harvard University, September 2009.

Karl, Terry Lynn. *The Paradox of Plenty: Oil Booms and Petro-States*. Berkeley: University of California Press, 1997.

Keck, Margaret, and Kathryn Sikkink. *Activists beyond Borders: Advocacy Networks in International Politics*. Ithaca, NY: Cornell University Press, 1998.

Kirk, Robin. *More Terrible than Death: Violence, Drugs, and America's War in Colombia*. New York: Public Affairs, 2003.

Lair, Eric, and Gonzalo Sánchez, eds. *Violencias y estrategias colectivas en la región andina: Bolivia, Colombia, Ecuador, Perú y Venezuela*. Bogotá: Grupo Editorial Norma, 2004.

Lara Parada, Ricardo. *El guerrillero y el político: Conversación con Óscar Castaño*. Bogotá: Editorial Oveja Negra, 1984.

Larson, Henrietta M., Evelyn H. Knowlton, and Charles S. Popple. *New Horizons, 1927–1950: History of Standard Oil Company (New Jersey)*. New York: Harper and Row, 1971.

Lawson, Steven F. "Freedom Then, Freedom Now: The Historiography of the Civil Rights Movement." *American Historical Review* 96, no. 2 (April 1991): 456–471.

Leal Buitrago, Francisco. *Clientelismo: El sistema político y su expresión regional*. Bogotá: Tercer Mundo Editores SID, IEPRI Universidad Nacional de Colombia, 1991.

———. *La seguridad nacional a la deriva: Del frente nacional a la posguerra fría*. Mexico City: Alfaomega Grupo Editor, 2002.

———. "Los derechos humanos en la actual situación colombiana." *Análisis Político* 2 (September–December 1987): 61–62.

le Bion, Philippe, ed. *The Geopolitics of Resource Wars: Resource Dependence, Governance and Violence*. New York: Frank Cass, 2005.

LeGrand, Catherine. "Colombian Transformations: Peasants and Wage-Laborers in the Santa Marta Banana Zone." *Journal of Peasant Studies* 11, no. 4 (1984): 178–200.

———. *Frontier Expansion and Peasant Protest in Colombia, 1830–1936*. Albuquerque: University of New Mexico Press, 1986.

———. "Historias transnacionales: Nuevas interpretaciones de los enclaves en América Latina." *Nómadas* 25 (October 2006): 144–154.

———. "La política y la violencia en Colombia (1946–1965): Interpretaciones en la década de los ochenta." *Memoria y Sociedad* 2, no. 4 (November 1997): 79–110.

Levine, Daniel H., ed. *Religion and Political Conflict in Latin America*. Chapel Hill: University of North Carolina Press, 1986.

Liang-Fenton, Debra, ed. *Implementing U.S. Human Rights Policy*. Washington, DC: United States Institute of Peace, 2004.

Londoño, Jhon Jairo, et al. "Estudio económico-social de Barrancabermeja 1977–1988." Undergraduate thesis, Universidad Cooperativa de Colombia, Barrancabermeja, 1991.

Luna García, Jairo Ernesto. "La salud de los trabajadores y el Tropical Oil Company." Conference paper delivered at XIII Congreso Colombiano de Historia, Bucaramanga, August 22–26, 2006.

Mahony, Liam, and Luis Enrique Eguren. *Unarmed Bodyguards: International Accompaniment for the Protection of Human Rights*. West Hartford, CT: Kumarian Press, 1997.

Margoth Pulido, Luz, Ana Luz Rodríguez, and Betty Pedraza, eds. *Entre el fuego: Tres experiencias de participación en zonas de conflicto armado*. Bogotá: Fundación para la Participación Comunitaria, ARCOMUN, and Acción Ecuménica Sueca, 2000.

Matthews, Jessica T. "Power Shift." *Foreign Affairs* 76, no. 1 (January/February 1997): 50–67.

McGreevey, William Paul. *An Economic History of Colombia, 1845–1930*. Cambridge: Cambridge University Press, 1971.

Medina, Medófilo. *Historia del Partido Comunista de Colombia*. Vol. 1. Bogotá: Editorial Colombia Nueva, 1980.

———. "Los paros cívicos en Colombia (1957–1977)." *Estudios Marxistas* 2, no. 14 (1977): 3–24.

———. *Protesta urbana en Colombia en el siglo veinte*. Bogotá: Ediciones Aurora, 1984.

Medina Franco, Gilberto. *Una historia de las milicias de Medellín*. Medellín: Instituto Popular de Capacitación, IPC, 2006.

Medina Gallego, Carlos. *Autodefensas, paramilitares y narcotráfico en Colombia: Origen, desarrollo y consolidación, el caso "Puerto Boyacá."* Bogotá: Editorial Documentos Periodísticos, 1990.

———. *ELN: Una historia contada a dos voces; Entrevista con "el cura" Manuel Pérez y Nicolás Rodríguez Bautista, "Gabino."* Bogotá: Rodríguez Quito Editores, 1996.

Medina Gallego, Carlos, and Mireya Téllez Ardila. *La violencia parainstitucional: Paramilitar y parapolicial en Colombia*. Bogotá: Rodríguez Quito Editores, 1994.

Mertus, Julie. *Bait and Switch: Human Rights and U.S. Foreign Policy*. 2nd ed. New York: Routledge, 2008.

Mitchel, Angus, ed. *The Amazon Journal of Roger Casement*. London: Anaconda Editions, 1997.

Molano, Alfredo. *The Dispossessed: Chronicles of the Desterrados of Colombia*. Translated by Daniel Bland. Chicago: Haymarket Books, 2005.

———. *Los años del tropel*. Bogotá: Fondo Editorial CEREC, 1985.

Molano, Alfredo, and Alejandro Rojas. "Los bombardeos en El Pato." *Controversia* 89 (September 1978).

Moyn, Samuel. *The Last Utopia: Human Rights in History*. Cambridge, MA: Belknap Press of Harvard University Press, 2010.

Múnera Ruíz, Leopoldo. *Rupturas y continuidades: Poder y movimiento popular en Colombia, 1968–1988*. Bogotá: Universidad Nacional de Colombia, 1998.

Munk, Gerardo L. *Authoritarianism and Democratization: Soldiers and Workers in Argentina, 1976–1983*. University Park: Pennsylvania State University Press, 1998.

Murillo Posada, Amparo, ed. *Un mundo que se mueve como el rió: Historia regional del Magdalena Medio*. Medellín: Instituto Colombiano de Antropología, 1993.

Murray, Pamela. *Dreams of Development: Colombia's National School of Mines and Its Engineers, 1887–1970*. Tuscaloosa: University of Alabama Press, 1997.

———. "Know-How and Nationalism: Colombia's First Geological and Petroleum Experts, c. 1940–1970." *Americas* 52, no. 2 (October 1995): 211–226.

Mutua, Makau. *Human Rights: A Political and Cultural Critique*. Philadelphia: University of Pennsylvania Press, 2002.

Neff, C. H. "Review of 1970s Petroleum Developments in South America, Central America and Caribbean Area." *American Association of Petroleum Biologists Bulletin* 55, no. 9 (September 1971): 1418–1492.

Ng'weno, Bettina. *Turf Wars: Territory and Citizenship in the Contemporary State*. Stanford: Stanford University Press, 2007.

Nuñez H., Jorge Eduardo, ed. *Crónicas de lucha por el poder local*. Barrancabermeja: Alcaldía Municipal de Barrancabermeja, 1997.

Ocampo, José Antonio, ed. *Historia económica de Colombia*. Bogotá: Siglo Veintiuno Editores, Fedesarrollo, 1987.

Olarte Carreño, Augusto. *La construcción del ferrocarril de Puerto Wilches a Bucaramanga 1870 a 1941: Síntesis de una obra discontinua y costosa*. Bucaramanga: Sic Editorial, 2006.

Oquist, Paul. *Violence, Conflict, and Politics in Colombia*. New York: Academic Press, 1980.

Orozco, Iván Abad. *Combatientes, rebeldes y terroristas: Guerra y derecho en Colombia*. Bogotá: Editorial Temis, 1992.

Osorio Viera, Felipe, and Fabián Ramírez Villarreal. "Barrancabermeja: Configuración territorial y conflcito social." Master's thesis, Universidad Nacional de Colombia, 2004.

Parkman, Patricia. *Insurrectionary Civic Strikes in Latin America, 1931–1961*. Cambridge, MA: Albert Einstein Institution, 1990.

Pearce, Jenny. "Beyond the Perimeter Fence: Oil and Armed Conflict in Casanare, Colombia." Occasional paper, Center for the Study of Global Governance, London School of Economics, 2004.

———. *Colombia: Inside the Labyrinth*. London: Latin American Bureau, 1990.

Pécaut, Daniel. *Crónica de cuatro décadas de política colombiana*. Bogotá: Editorial Norma, 2006.

———. *L'ordre et la violence: Évolution socio-politique de la Colombie entre 1930 et 1953*. Paris: Editions de l'Ecole des hautes études en sciences sociales, 1987.

Peralta, Victoria, and Michael LaRosa. *Los colombianistas: Una completa visión de los investigadores extranjeros que estudian a Colombia*. Bogotá: Planeta, 1997.

Pérez T., William Fredy. "El sistema penal y la emergencia en Colombia." *Scripta Nova: Revista Electrónica de Geografía y Ciencias Sociales* 45, no. 24 (August 1, 1999).

Phelan, John Ledy. *The People and the King: The Comunero Revolution in Colombia, 1781*. Madison: University of Wisconsin Press, 1978.

Pinilla Pinilla, Luis. *Horacio Serpa Uribe: Una experiencia, un futuro*. Bogotá: Alfomega, 2002.

Pizano, Diego, ed. *La penitencia del poder: Lecciones de la administración del presidente Belisario Betancur, 1982–1986*. Bogotá: Universidad de los Andes, 2009.

Pizarro Leongómez, Eduardo. *Una democracia asediada: Balance y perspectiva del conflito armado en Colombia*. Bogotá: Editorial Norma, 2004.

Portelli, Alessandro. *The Death of Luigi Trastuli and Other Stories: Form and Meaning in Oral History.* Albany: State University of New York Press, 1991.

Rajagopal, Balakrishnan. *International Law from Below: Development, Social Movements, and Third World Resistance.* Cambridge: Cambridge University Press, 2003.

Ramírez, María Clemencia. *Entre el estado y la guerrilla: Identidad y ciudadanía en el movimiento de los campesinos cocaleros del Putumayo.* Bogotá: Instituto Colombiano de Antropología e Historia, Colciencias, 2001.

Ramsey, Russell W. "The Colombia Battalion in Korea and Suez." *Journal of Inter-American Studies* 9, no. 4 (October 1967): 541–560.

Randall, Stephen J. *Alfonso López Michelsen: Su vida, su época.* Translated by Paulina Gómez. Bogotá: Villegas Editores, 2008.

Rappaport, Joanne. *The Politics of Memory: Native Historical Interpretation in the Colombian Andes.* 2nd ed. Durham, NC: Duke University Press, 1998.

Rempe, Dennis M. "Counterinsurgency in Colombia: A US National Security Perspective, 1958–1966." PhD diss., University of Miami, 2002.

Restrepo, Elvira María. *Colombian Criminal Justice in Crisis: Fear and Distrust.* London: Palgrave Macmillan, 2003.

Restrepo, Laura. *The Dark Bride.* Translated by Stephen Lytle. Toronto: Harper Flamingo Canada, 2002.

———. *La multitud errante.* Bogotá: Editorial Planeta Colombiana, 2001.

Reyes Posada, Alejandro, ed. *Pacificar la paz: Lo que no se ha negociado en los acuerdos de paz.* Bogotá: Comisión de Superación de La Violencia, 1992.

Riaño-Alcalá, Pilar. *Dwellers of Memory: Youth and Violence in Medellín, Colombia.* New Brunswick, NJ: Transaction, 2006.

Richani, Nazih. *Systems of Violence: The Political Economy of War and Peace in Colombia.* Albany: State University of New York Press, 2002.

Rippy, Fred. *El capital norteamericano y la penetración imperialista en Colombia.* Bogotá: Editorial Oveja Negra, 1970.

Rivera, Silvia. *Política e ideología en el movimiento campesino colombiano: El caso de la ANUC (Asociación nacional de usuarios campesinos).* Bogotá: Centro de Investigación y Educación Popular, 1982.

Rodríguez Reinel, Sonia M. "Barrancabermeja, manifestaciones culturales radicales 1945–1990." Undergraduate thesis, Universidad Nacional de Colombia, Bogotá, 1992.

Roldán, Mary. *Blood and Fire: La Violencia in Antioquia, 1946–1963.* Durham, NC: Duke University Press, 2002.

Romero, Amanda. *Magdalena Medio: Luchas sociales y violaciones de derechos humanos, 1980–1992.* Bogotá: Corporación Avre, 1992.

Romero, Flor Alba. "El movimiento de derechos humanos en Colombia." In *Movimientos sociales, estado y democracia en Colombia*, edited by Mauricio Archila and Mauricio Pardo, 441–472. Bogotá: Centro de Estudios Sociales, Facultad de Ciencias Humanas, Universidad Nacional de Colombia, 2001.

Romero, Mauricio. "Changing Identities and Contested Settings: Regional Elites and the Paramilitaries in Colombia." *International Journal of Politics, Culture and Society* 14, no. 1 (2000): 51–70.

———. *Paramilitares y autodefensas: 1982–2003*. Bogotá: Editorial Planeta Colombiana, S.A., Instituto de Estudios Políticos y Relaciones Internacionales, 2003.

———, ed. *Parapolítica: La ruta de la expansión paramilitar y los acuerdos políticos*. Bogotá: Corporación Nuevo Arco Iris, 2007.

Romero García, Luis Guillermo. *Sueños de río: Inventario breve de la literatura en Barrancabermeja*. Bogotá: Fundación Somos, 2005.

Ruíz Novoa, Alberto. *El Batallón Colombia en Korea, 1951–1954*. Bogotá: Empresa Nacional de Publicaciones, 1956.

Safford, Frank R. "Commerce and Enterprise in Central Colombia, 1821–1870." PhD diss., Columbia University, 1965.

———. *The Ideal of the Practical: Colombia's Struggle to Form a Technical Elite*. Austin: University of Texas Press, 1976.

Safford, Frank, and Marco Palacios. *Colombia: Fragmented Land, Divided Society*. Oxford: Oxford University Press, 2002.

Salgado, Carlos, and Esmeralda Prada. *Campesinado y protesta social en Colombia, 1980–1995*. Bogotá: Centro de Investigación y Educación Popular, CINEP, 2000.

Salomon, Frank, and Stuart B. Schwartz, eds. *The Cambridge History of the Native Peoples of the Americas*. Vol. 3, *South America, Part 2*. Cambridge: Cambridge University Press, 1999.

Sánchez, Gonzalo. *1929, los bolcheviques del Líbano*. Bogotá: El Mohan Editores, 1976.

———. *Los dias de la revolución: Gaitanismo y 9 de abril en provincia*. Bogotá: Centro Cultural Jorge Eliécer Gaitán, 1983.

Sánchez, Gonzalo, and Mario Aguilera, eds. *Memoria de un país en guerra: Los mil días, 1899–1902*. Bogotá: Planeta, 2001.

Sánchez G., Gonzalo, ed. *Colombia: Violencia y democracia; Informe presentado al Ministerio de Gobierno*. Bogotá: Universidad Nacional de Colombia, 1987.

Sánchez Gómez, Gonzalo, and Donny Meertens. *Bandits, Peasants and Politics: The Case of La Violencia in Colombia*. Translated by Alan Hynds. Austin: University of Texas Press, 2001.

Sandino de Hoyos, Yolanda, ed. *Informe de actividades 1977*. Barrancabermeja: Alcaldía Municipal de Barrancabermeja, 1997.

Sandoval Ordoñez, Marbel. *En el brazo del río*. Bogotá: Hombre Nuevo Editores, 2006.

Santiago, Myrna. *Ecology of Oil: Environment, Labor, and the Mexican Revolution, 1900–1938*. New York: Cambridge University Press, 2006.

Santos, Boaventura de Sousa. *Toward a New Legal Common Sense: Law, Globalization, and Emancipation*. 2nd ed. London: Butterworths LexisNexis, 2002.

———. "Towards a Multicultural Conception of Human Rights." In *Space of Culture: City, Nation, World*, 2nd ed., edited by Mike Featherstone and Scott Lash, 214–229. London: Sage, 1999.

Santos, Boaventura de Sousa, and Mauricio García Villegas, eds. *El caleidescopio de las justicias en Colombia*. 2 vols. Bogotá: Siglo del Hombre Editores, 2001.

———, eds. *Emancipación social y violencia en Colombia*. Bogotá: Grupo Editorial Norma, 2004.

Scott, James. *Domination and the Arts of Resistance: Hidden Transcripts*. New Haven, CT: Yale University Press, 1990.

Serrano, Luisa. "Barrancabermeja Ciudad-Región." Paper presented at III Congreso de la Asociación de Historiadores Latinoamericanos y del Caribe (ADHILAC), Pontevedra, Spain, October 2001.

Serrano Carranza, Guillermo. "Barrancabermeja; fragmentos y territorios: Procesos compositivos del área urbana." Master's thesis, Universidad Nacional de Colombia, 2001.

Sharpless, Richard. *Gaitán of Colombia: A Political Biography*. Pittsburgh: University of Pittsburgh Press, 1978.

Sheldon Knowles, Ruth. *The Greatest Gamblers: The Epic of American Oil Exploration*. 2nd ed. Norman: University of Oklahoma Press, 1959.

Shgweickert, Geo C. "Informe de un funcionario norteamericano sobre la huelga de Barrancabermeja 1924." *Anuario colombiano de historia social y de la cultura* 13–14 (1985–1986): 319–333.

Shivji, Issa G. *The Concept of Human Rights in Africa*. London: Council for the Development of Economic and Social Research in Africa, CODESRIA, 1989.

Sikkink, Kathryn. *Mixed Signals: U.S. Human Rights Policy and Latin America*. Ithaca, NY: Cornell University Press, 2004.

Sikkink, Kathryn, and Thomas Risse. "The Socialization of International Human Rights Norms into Domestic Practice." In *The Power of Human Rights: International Norms and Domestic Change*, edited by in Thomas Risse, Stephen Ropp, and Kathryn Sikkink, 22–35. Cambridge: Cambridge University Press, 1999.

Smith, M. L. R., and Sophie Roberts. "War in the Gray: Exploring the Concept of Dirty War." *Studies in Conflict and Terrorism* 31, no. 5 (2008): 377–398.

Sohn, Guansú. "La novela colombiana de protesta social: 1924–1948." PhD diss., University of Oklahoma, 1976.

Solano de las Aguas, Sergio Paolo. *Puertos, sociedad y conflictos en el Caribe colombiano, 1850–1930*. Cartagena: Observatorio del Caribe Colombiano, Universidad de Cartagena, 2001.

Stokes, Doug. *America's Other War: Terrorizing Colombia*. London: Zed Books, 2005.

Taffer, Jeffrey F. *Foreign Aid as Foreign Policy: The Alliance for Progress in Latin America*. New York: Routledge, 2007.

Tate, Winifred. "Counting the Dead: Human Rights Claims and Counter-Claims in Colombia." PhD diss., New York University, 2005.

———. *Counting the Dead: The Culture and Politics of Human Rights Activism in Colombia*. Berkeley: University of California Press, 2007.

Taussig, Michael. *Law in a Lawless Land: Diary of a Limpieza*. Chicago: University of Chicago Press, 2005.

———. "Terror as Usual: Walter Benjamin's Theory of History as a State of Siege." *Social Text* 23 (Fall/Winter 1989): 3–20.

Thoumi, Francisco E. *Illegal Drugs, Economy, and Society in the Andes.* Washington, DC: Johns Hopkins University Press, 2003.

Tilly, Charles, and Sidney Tarrow. *Contentious Politics.* Boulder, CO: Paradigm, 2007.

Tinker Salas, Miguel. *The Enduring Legacy: Oil, Culture, and Society in Venezuela.* Durham, NC: Duke University Press, 2009.

Tirado Mejía, Álvaro. "Derechos humanos y democracia en Colombia." *Análisis Político* 2 (September–December 1987): 50.

Toro Puerta, Mario Rafael, O.F.M. *Pendientes de un hilo: El proceso de desafiliación en un sector de Barrancabermeja.* Bogotá: Editorial Bonaventuriana, 2004.

Torres Duarte, Alfonso, ed. *Barrancabermeja en textos e imágenes.* Barrancabermeja: Alcaldía de Barrancabermeja, 1997.

Torres Girado, Ignacio. *María Cano, mujer rebelde.* Bogotá: Publicaciones de la Rosca, 1972.

Tovar Zambrano, Bernardo, ed. *La historia al final del milenio: Ensayos de historiografía colombiana y latinoamericana.* 2 vols. Bogotá: Editorial Universidad Nacional, Facultad de Ciencias Humanas, 1994.

Ungar, Elizabeth. *Los paros cívicos en Colombia, 1977–1980.* Bogotá: Uniandes, 1981.

Universidad de los Andes. *Barrancabermeja: Plan de ordenamiento urbano.* Bogotá: Centro de planificación y urbanismo, Centro de estudios sobre el desarrollo económico, sección de sociología, facultad de artes y ciencias, 1979.

Uribe, María Victoria. *Limpiar la tierra: Guerra y poder entre esmeralderos.* Bogotá: Centro de Investigación y Educación Popular, CINEP, 1992.

Valencia Tovar, Álvaro. *El final de Camilo.* Bogotá: Tercer Mundo, 1976.

———, ed. *Historia de la policía nacional de Colombia.* Bogotá: Planeta, 1993.

Valencia Villa, Alejandro. *La humanización de la guerra: Derecho internacional humanitario y conflicto armado en Colombia.* 2nd ed. Bogotá: Tercer Mundo Editores, Ediciones Uniandes, 1992.

Van Cott, Donna Lee. *The Friendly Liquidation of the Past: The Politics of Diversity in Latin America.* Pittsburgh: University of Pittsburgh Press, 2000.

Van Engeland, Anniseh. "Failed Attempts: The Fuerzas Armadas Revolucionarias de Colombia and the Unión Patriótica." In *From Terrorism to Politics,* edited by Anniseh Van Engeland and Rachael M. Rudolph. Hampshire, England: Ashgate, 2008.

Vargas Castillo, Andrés Ricardo. "Guerra civil y violencia de guerra civil contra las organizaciones sociales de Barrancabermeja." Working paper, Centro de Recursos para el Análisis de Conflictos, CERAC, Universidad Pontificia La Javeriana, December 2008.

Vargas Díaz, Librado, ed. *Expresiones políticas del movimiento estudiantil AUDESA, 1960–1980.* Bucaramanga: Ediciones UIS, Escuela de Historia, Universidad Industrial de Santander, 1996.

Vargas Velásquez, Alejo. *Magdalena Medio Santandereano: Colonización y conflicto armado*. Bogotá: Centro de Investigación y Educación Popular, CINEP, 1992.

———. *Política y armas al inicio del frente nacional*. 2nd ed. Bogotá: Universidad Nacional de Colombia, 1996.

———. "Tres momentos de la violencía política en San Vicente Chucurí (de los bolcheviques del año 29 a la fundación del ELN)." *Análisis Político* 8 (September–December 1988): 33–47.

Vásquez Perdomo, María Eugenia. *My Life as a Colombian Revolutionary: Reflections of a Former Guerrillera*. Translated by Lorena Terando. Philadelphia: Temple University Press, 2005.

Vega Cantor, Renán. *Gente muy rebelde*. Vol. 1, *Enclaves, transportes y protestas obreras*. Bogotá: Ediciones Pensamiento Crítico, 2002.

———. *Gente muy rebelde*. Vol. 4, *Socialismo, cultura y protesta popular*. Bogotá: Ediciones Pensamiento Crítico, 2002.

Vega Cantor, Renán, Luz Ángela Núñez Espinel, and Alexander Pereira Fernández. *Petróleo y protesta obrera: La USO y los trabajadores petroleros en Colombia*. Vol. 1, *En tiempos de la tropical*. Vol. 2, *En tiempos de ecopetrol*. Bogotá: Corporación Aury Sará Marrugo, 2009.

Velásquez Rodríguez, Rafael Antonio. "Primera huelga estudiantil en Barrancabermeja, Junio de 1957." Unpublished document, 2006.

Velásquez Rodríguez, Rafael Antonio, and Victor Julio Castillo León. "Resistencia de la etnia Yareguíes a las políticas de reducción y 'civilización' en el siglo XIX." *Historia y Sociedad* 12 (November 2006): 285–320.

———. *Los Yareguíes: Resistencia y exterminio*. Barrancabermeja: Corporación Memoria y Patrimonio, 2011.

Vélez, Humberto. "Rafael Reyes: Quinquenio, régimen político y capitalismo." In *Nueva historia de Colombia*, vol. 1, ed. Álvaro Tirado Mejía, 187–214. Bogotá: Planeta Colombiana, 1989.

Villamizar Herrera, Darío. *Jaime Bateman: Biografía de un revolucionario*. Bogotá: Editorial Planeta, 2002.

Villar, Rodrigo. *El tercer sector en Colombia*. Bogotá: Confederación colombiana de organizaciones no gubernamentales, 2001.

Villegas, Jorge. *Petróleo colombiano, ganancia gringa*. 2nd ed. Bogotá: El Áncora Editores, 1998.

———. *Petróleo, oligarquía e imperio*. Bogotá: El Áncora Editores, 1982.

Villegas Arango, Jorge. *Libro negro de la represion: Frente Nacional, 1958–1974*. Bogotá: Comité de Solidaridad con los Presos Políticos, 1974.

Wade, Peter. *Music, Race, and Nation: Música Tropical in Colombia*. Chicago: University of Chicago Press, 2000.

Waltz, Susan. "Rebuilding and Reclaiming the History of the Universal Declaration of Human Rights." *Third World Quarterly* 2, no. 3 (June 2002): 437–448.

Washington Office on Latin America (WOLA). *Colombia Besieged: Political Violence and State Responsibility*. Washington, DC: WOLA, 1989.

Welna, Christopher, and Gustavo Gallón, eds. *Peace, Democracy, and Human Rights in Colombia*. Notre Dame, IN: University of Notre Dame Press, 2007.

Wills Obregón, María Emma. *La democracia: Un camino por recorrer; La reforma política en Barrancabermeja de 1986–1988*. Bogotá: Centro de Investigación y Educación Popular, CINEP, December 1989.

Wilson, Richard A. "Afterword to 'Anthropology and Human Rights in a New Key': The Social Life of Human Rights." *American Anthropologist* 108, no. 1 (March 2006): 77–83.

Wilson, Suzanne, and Leah A. Carroll. "The Colombian Contradiction: Lessons Drawn from Guerrilla Experiments in Demobilization and Electoralism." In *From Revolutionary Movements to Political Parties*, edited by Kalowatie Deonandan, David Close, and Gary Prevost, 81–106. New York: Palgrave Macmillan, 2007.

Wirpsa, Leslie. "Oil Exploitation and Indigenous Rights: Global Regime Network Conflict in the Andes." PhD diss., University of Southern California, 2004.

Wirth, John D., ed. *The Oil Business in Latin America: The Early Years*. Lincoln: University of Nebraska Press, 1985.

Yergin, Daniel. *The Prize: The Epic Quest for Oil, Money, and Power*. New York: Simon and Schuster, 1991.

Youngers, Coletta, and Susan C. Peacock. "Peru's Coordinadora Nacional de Derechos Humanos: A Case Study of Coalition Building." Washington, DC: Washington Office on Latin America, 2002.

Yunis, José, and Carlos Nicolás Hernández. *Barrancabermeja: Nacimiento de la clase obrera*. Bogotá: Tres Culturas Editores, 1986.

Zembrycki, Stacey, and Anna Sheftel, eds. *Off the Record: Unspoken Negotiations in the Practice of Oral History*. New York: Palgrave Macmillan, 2013.

Zamosc, Leon. *The Agrarian Question and the Peasant Movement in Colombia: Struggles of the National Peasant Association, 1967–1981*. Cambridge: Cambridge University Press, 1986.

———. "The Political Crisis and the Prospects for Rural Democracy in Colombia." *Journal of Development Studies* 25, no. 4 (1990): 44–78.

Zapata-Domínguez, Álvaro. "Etnografía e interpretación interdisciplinaria de la negociación de una convención colectiva en Ecopetrol, Colombia." PhD diss., Université de Montréal, 2002.

———. "Negociación, conflicto, mitos y poder en la gestión de las relaciones laborales en Ecopetrol." Master's thesis, Universidad del Valle, 1999.

Index

Page numbers in italics indicate illustrations.

civic-popular movement (*continued*)
141–142; *paros cívicos* and, 4; peasants and, 123–124; political economy and, 108, 195–196; political violence and, 14; presidential decree against, 79–80; professionalization of, 191–192; public services and, 52–56, 66, 88, 95, 97–100, 198–199; scholarship on, 202; sharing information and, 186, 191–192, 253n41; social justice and, 10, 14, 195–196; student activism and, 50, 63–64, 77, 93, 100, 134, 224n4, 236n87; water supply and, 53, 55–56, 75–76, 97, 99–100. See also *paros cívicos* (citizen-led general strikes); social activism/movements

class segregation, 32, 34–36, 52

Clubes de Amas de Casa (Homemakers' Clubs), 184. *See also* OFP (Organización Femenina Popular; Popular Women's Organization)

Cold War: counterinsurgency in context of, 81, 141–142, 147–148, 196; human rights in context of, 14, 107–108, 201, 206; Latin America and, 107–108, 192; social movements in context of, 19, 48, 53, 59, 132

Colectivo de Abogados José Alvear Restrepo (CAJAR; José Alvear Restrepo Lawyers' Collective), 136, 152, 205, 242n9

Colombia: Constitution of, 130, 152, 169, 202–203; export economy of, 24–30, 40–41, 43, 218n40, 223n136; oil production and, 30, 43, 56–57, 65, 69, 218n50, 223n136; political jurisdictions in, 217n25; royalties from oil industry and, 21–22, 39, 219n67

Colombian armed forces: in Barranca, 10–11, 33, 47, 125, 152–153, 175, 190–191; *bolcheviques* uprising and, 41, 62; civic-popular movement repression by, 8; counterinsurgency operations and, 14; death threats and, 130; dirty war and, 107; disappeared and, 89, 212n4; drug traffickers and, 14; homicides and, 82–83, 101–103, 131, 141–143, 179–180; human rights violations and, 123, 151, 154, 175; informants for, 143, 157, 251n14; leftist guerrillas' allegations and, 167–168; leftist guerrillas'

conflicts with, 73, 111, 149; in Magdalena Medio, 33, 92–94, 103, 147–148, 234n50, 235n61; military rulers and, 46–47, 56, 77–80; navy and, 33, 41, 139, 154, 164, 166–167; oil industry security and, 33, 38–40, 70; paramilitarism's link with, xv, 14, 92–93, 130, 147–148, 151, 153–158, 164–167, 204, 234n50, 235n61, 235n67, 244nn2–3, 246nn32–33, 246n38, 248n66; *paros cívicos* and, 98–99, 98–100, 237n93; presidential decrees and, 80; provincial/rural elites and, 14; public order, 11, 54, 80, 86; rural violence and, 131, 141–143; social movements' repression by, 8, 14, 54; student activism repression by, 64; U.S. funds and, xv, 151, 166, 172, 193, 211n5. *See also* National Police

Colombian Supreme Court, 43, 122–123, 172, 229n108

Comisión Andina de Juristas (Comisión Colombiana de Juristas), 106–107

Comisión Intereclesial de Justicia y Paz (Justicia y Paz; Inter-Ecclesial Commission for Justice and Peace), 153, 158–160, 162

Comisión Nacional de Reparación y Reconciliación (National Reparation and Reconciliation Commission), 15, 157

Comité de Solidaridad con los Presos Políticos (CSPP; Committee for Solidarity with Political Prisoners), 69, 72, 78, 85, 136, 158, 242n9

El Comité Permanente por la Defensa de los Derechos Humanos (Permanent Committee for the Defense of Human Rights), 7, 85, 87, 136, 232n13, 242n9

Communism, in Latin America, 9, 41. *See also* PCC (Partido Comunista de Colombia; Communist Party of Colombia)

La Comuna de Barranca (Barrancabermeja Commune), 42, 45–46, 110, 122

Confederación Sindical de Trabajadores de Colombia (CSTC; National Union Federation of Colombia), 59, 197

Consejería Presidencial para los Derechos Humanos, 129–130

consejo verbal de guerra (military tribunal), 46, 63, 70–73, 229n103, 229n106, 229nn108–109

estado de sitio (state of siege). *See* state of siege (*estado de sitio*)
ethnicity, 32, 36, 52
ethnography, 16

Fals Borda, Orlando, 87
FAM (Frente Amplio del Magdalena Medio; Middle Magdalena Broad Front), 112–116, 170, 239n4
FARC (Fuerzas Armadas Revolucionarias de Colombia; Revolutionary Armed Forces of Colombia): armed conflict and, 125; in Barranca, 169; Communism and, 63, 91; cooperation agreement between ELN and, 125, 241n63; extortion and, 183; FAM and, 113, 239n4; FARC-EP or -Ejército Popular and, 91, 104; history of, 9, 64, 91, 104, 192, 195, 198, 237n101; homicides in Barranca by, 189, 239n24; informants and, 143; kidnappings by, 10, 149; in Magdalena Medio, 64, 90–91, 251n22; paramilitary groups allegations and, 156–157; paramilitary groups and, 251n22; peace negotiations with, 92–93, 101, 111, 193; social activism and, 63
FEDEPETROL (Federación de Trabajadores del Petróleo; Federation Petroleum Workers), 88, 95–96, 139–140
FILA (Frente de Izquierda Liberal Auténtico; Authentic Liberal Leftist Front), 67
fishermen, 61, 68, 82, 101, 168–169
Frente Amplio del Magdalena Medio (FAM; Middle Magdalena Broad Front), 112–116, 170, 239n4
Frente de Izquierda Liberal Auténtico (FILA; Authentic Liberal Leftist Front), 67
front-line activists (local approach), 16–17, 19, 205–206, 208–209
Fuerzas Armadas Revolucionarias de Colombia (FARC; Revolutionary Armed Forces of Colombia). *See* FARC (Fuerzas Armadas Revolucionarias de Colombia; Revolutionary Armed Forces of Colombia)
Fuerzas Armadas Revolucionarias de Colombia-Ejército Popular (FARC-EP; Popular Revolutionary Armed Forces of Colombia-People's Army), 91, 104

Fundación para la promoción de la Cultura y la Educación Popular (FUNPROCEP; Foundation for the Promotion of Popular Education and Culture), 134
FUNPROCEP (Fundación para la promoción de la Cultura y la Educación Popular; Foundation for the Promotion of Popular Education and Culture), 134

Gaitán, Jorge Eliécer, 9, 40–42, 45–46, 122
Galán Gómez, Mario, 58, 65, 69
García Márquez, Gabriel, 85, 87, 111, 216n10, 242n20
Gaviria Trujillo, César, 12, 166, 168–169
Gibb, George S., 30, 36
Giraldo, Javier, 159, 161, 247n48
Golconda Group, 65, 227n69
Gómez, Rafael, 87–88, 94–95, 163–164, 171, 188–189, 206
Gómez Lizarazo, Jorge: ANUC and, 131; awards and, 165, 247n68; biographical information about, 135–136; on civilian population security, 148; CREDHOS and, 134–137, 141, 196; in exile due to death threats, 161, 165–166, 170, 183; human rights activism and, 88, 134, 144, 206–207; as human rights ombudsman, 183; international support and, 161, 165–166, 205–206; on local administrative actions, 80; on national government's attacks on CREDHOS, 167; on natural resources in Magdalena Medio, 148; on paramilitarism link with Colombian armed forces, 166; on sociopolitical conflicts and CREDHOS, 152
Gómez Serrano, Rafael, 3, 75
Gómez Villamizar, Jorge, 136, 161
González, Martha, 62
guerrilla groups, 46. *See also* leftist guerrillas

Harnecker, Marta, 73
Havens, Eugene, 54
Hernández, Milton, 110–111
Hernández Gavanzo, José Humberto, 164
Hernández Pardo, Hernando, 180–181
Hicks, John Edgar, 43–44
Higuita, Orlando, 144–145

historical approach, 16–17, 21–22

Homemakers' Clubs (Clubes de Amas de Casa), 184. *See also* OFP (Organización Femenina Popular; Popular Women's Organization)

homicides and homicide statistics: armed conflict and, 129; in Barranca, 4–5, 8, 144–145, 162–169, 175–184, 189–190, 212n7, 213n15, 239n24, 251n23; Catholic Church and, 196; civic-popular movement and, 93, 125, 138, 140, 144–145, 154, 164, 166–167, 170; Colombian armed forces and, 82–83, 101–103, 131, 141–143, 179–180; leftist guerrillas and, 189, 239n24; in Magdalena Medio, 94–95; national government statistics and, 106, 213n14; oil workers/industry and, 138, 140, 170, 229n103; paramilitarism and, 139–140, 213n15; peasants and, 140; political violence and, 91, 125, 140, 144–145, 164, 166, 213n15; protests against, 165–167; reports on, 152, 213n15; trade unionists and, 195–196; UP and, 93, 125, 132, 144–145, 154, 164, 166, 188, 235n60; La Violencia and, 9, 45

human rights: Catholic Church and, 7, 18, 215n42; civic-popular movement and, 10, 18, 103, 126; commission officials as targets and, 147–148, 154–158, 204, 235n67, 244nn2–3, 246nn32–33, 246n38; international reports on, 18–19, 85–86; leftist politics and, 206; lived experiences in context of, 14, 108; local administration and, 144; national government's protection of, 11, 19, 83, 93, 129–130, 146, 152, 202–203; OFP and, 7, 15; organizations for, 16; *paro cívico por la vida* and, 3–4, 6–7, 121–123; *paros cívicos* and, 7; political prisoners and, 69, 72, 85, 136, 158; protection of, 128–129; scholarship on, 15, 214n30; social activism's link with, 5, 10–11, 15, 17–19, 85, 103, 120, 160, 193–194, 205; social justice in context of, 129, 185, 187–189, 203; as social protest, 15, 17–19, 85, 152, 172, 203–204; U.S. hearings on, 166, 248n74; USO and, 7, 15, 18, 28; utopian dream in context of, 174, 193–194, 206. *See also* human rights violations

human rights activism: ANUC and, 153; armed conflict zones and, 176, 194; autonomy of, 17–18; in Barranca, xiv, 8, 11, 83, 88, 108, 126–127, 206–207; coalitions and, 18–19, 96–98, 101, 160; Cold War in context of, 14, 107, 201, 206; CREDHOS and, 18, 108, 136, 153, 172; death threats and, xiv, xvi, 11, 252n31; dirty war and, 3–5, 15, 107–108, 120–121, 146; history in Colombia of, 5–7, 206–207; IDPs as activists and, 175, 179, 185, 251n15; international, 14, 17–19, 158–162, 172, 205–206, 211n4, 255n31; judicial system and, xiv; in Latin America, 8; legacy of, 207–209; local approach and, 16–17, 19, 205–206, 208–209; local context and, 203, 205–206, 208; local organizations and, 18, 158–162, 185, 192, 196; in Magdalena Medio, 84–88, 93, 95, 158–162, 185, 195, 204–205, 232n13; methodologies and, 15; national government accountability and, 11; national organizations and, 158–162; paramilitarism and, 11, 87–88, 147–148, 154–158, 183, 204, 235n67, 244nn2–3, 246nn32–33, 246n38, 252n31; paramilitary groups and, 12; peasants and, 95; pluralism and, 137, 146, 188; political economy and, 4, 10, 14, 109, 148–149; radical politics and, 120; as resistance to political violence, 10; scholarship on, 16, 201–202, 204, 214n35; social memory of, xix, 15–16, 157, 175–176, 186–189, 192–193, 214n35, 253n43; unions and, 15, 123, 134, 158; urban topography and, 4, 5–6, 6; USO and, 153

human rights ombudsman (*defensoría del pueblo*), 152, 183, 202–203

human rights violations: armed conflict in context of, 10, 108–109, 122, 130–131; Colombian armed forces and, 123, 151, 154, 175; CREDHOS and, 108, 172; dirty war and, 136–137; IDPs and, 82–83, 159–162, 167, 170, 247n57; leftist guerrillas and, 175; as legible, 10, 108–109, 122, 130–131, 173, 195, 205, 208; national government and, 11, 84, 130, 157; paramilitarism and, 11–12, 87, 120, 130, 175, 202; peasants and, 7, 18, 92, 95, 116–117; Tribunal

Especial de Instrucción and, 122–123. *See also* human rights
Human Rights Watch, xiv–xv, 205
Hurtado, Hernando, 7

IDPs (internally displaced persons). *See* internally displaced persons (IDPs)
ILSA (Instituto de Servicios Legales Alternativos; Institute for Alternative Legal Services), 158
Imperial Oil, 31
indigenous populations' rights, 22, 25–27, 175, 218n40
inequalities: in Barranca, 65–66; CREDHOS and, 108; in Magdalena Medio, 168; National Front and, 54–55; oil industry and, 32–34, 36; political violence link with, 8, 18, 129; politics and, 36, 41, 198; radical politics in context of, 36; social conflicts in context of, 8, 35–36; social movements and, 18. *See also* political economy
Instituto de Servicios Legales Alternativos (ILSA; Institute for Alternative Legal Services), 158
Inter-American Commission on Human Rights, 85–86, 161, 166, 184, 233n18. *See also* Organization of American States (OAS)
Inter-American Court of Human Rights, 130, 155, 157–158, 184, 233n18, 235n67, 246n32. *See also* Organization of American States (OAS)
Inter-Church Committee for Human Rights in Latin America, xiv–xv, 160
internally displaced persons (IDPs): from Barranca, 175, 179, 185, 196, 251n15; in Barranca, 82–83; Catholic Church and, 196; history and description of, 211nn5–6, 232n5; human rights activists as, 175, 179, 185, 251n15; human rights violations and, 82–83, 159–162, 167, 170, 247n57; OFP and, 184; rural violence and, 8, 82–83, 89–90, 102–103
international (transnational) organizations: civic-popular movement's support from, 17, 161, 192, 205–206; human rights activism and, 14–15, 18–19, 84–86, 158–162, 172, 205–206, 211n4, 255n31; in Latin

America, 8; local approach and, 205–206, 208; regional approach and, 18; reports on human rights and, 18–19, 85–86; unions and, 160. *See also* NGOs (nongovernmental organizations); *and specific organizations*
International Petroleum, 30, 47
Isaza Arango, Ramón, 157

JACs (Juntas de Acción Comunal; Community Action Councils), 96–97, 105, 136, 199, 236n73
Jaimes Cortés, Ismael, 119, 132–133, 166–167
Jaramillo Arango, Rafael, 35
Jersey Standard (Standard Oil of New Jersey), 28–32, 39–40, 47, 219n60, 219n61. *See also* Tropical Oil Company (La Troco)
Jiménez de Quesada, Gonzalo, 22–24, 30, 216n15
judicial system (legal system): coalitions and, xiv; Colombian Supreme Court and, 43, 122–123, 172, 229n108; death threats against judges and, 155, 202; human rights and, xiv, 18, 137, 141, 206–207; Justice and Peace process and, xvi, 174, 186, 251n23; military tribunal and, 46, 63, 70–73, 229n103, 229n106, 229nn108–109; Tribunal Especial de Instrucción and, 122–123; Tribunal Superior de Orden Público and, 157
Juntas de Acción Comunal (JACs; Community Action Councils), 96–97, 105, 136, 199, 236n73
Justice and Peace Law of 2005 process, xvi, 174, 186, 251n23
Justicia y Paz (Comisión Intereclesial de Justicia y Paz; Inter-Ecclesial Commission for Justice and Peace), 153, 158–160, 162

Keck, Margaret, 17, 205

labor movement: in Barranca, 38, 88; civil rights and, 10, 88; history of, 37–38; leftist support for, 37–38; in Magdalena Medio, 37–38; social activism and, 10; women domestic workers protests and, 43–44. *See also* oil workers and industry; *and specific unions* land invasions: rural, 62, 89–90, 98, 200; urban, 5, 62, 68, 77, 83–84, 132–133, 200

land rights, 26–27, 29, 188

Lara Parada, Ricardo, 63, 109–116, 130, 138, 192

Latin America: Cold War and, 107–108, 192; Communism in, 9, 41; dirty war as term of use in, 107, 238n4, 238n7; human rights in, 8, 14, 18, 85–86, 106–108, 172, 204, 207; human rights violations as legible in, 205; international reports in, 85–86; leftist guerrillas in, 60, 192–193; military rule in, 86, 106, 204, 233n20; national liberation movements in, 84; oil production and industries in, 28–29, 47–48; paramilitarism in, 11–12; private foreign-controlled development in, 32, 36; revolutionary movements in, 114–115, 192–193; scholarship on, 204; social activism and, 207; WOLA and, xiv–xv, 165

Leal Buitrago, Francisco, 54

leftist guerrillas: armed conflict and, 8, 10, 41, 182–183, 251n14; in Barranca, 148–149, 153, 189–190; Colombian armed forces' allegations and, 156–157, 167–168; Colombian armed forces' armed conflict with, 149; cooperation agreement between, 125, 241n63; disappeared and, 212n4; drug traffickers' conflation with, 146, 151; ethics and, 114, 130; extortion and, 182–183; history of, 8–9, 18, 60, 113, 193–194, 195; human rights and, 5; human rights violations and, 175; informants and, 109, 143, 189, 238n13; in Latin America, 60, 192–193; local administrators' armed conflict with, 149; in Magdalena Medio, 9, 62, 91; oil industry infrastructure and, 10; oil industry infrastructure attacks by, 149; paramilitary groups allegations and, 156–157; paramilitary groups' armed conflict with, 177, 179, 181–183, 189–191, 246n30; *paro cívico por la vida* and, 7; *paros armados* and, 125–126, 170–171, 190; peace negotiations with, 92–93, 101, 111, 245n8; public meetings participation by, 148,

245n8; social activism autonomy in context of, 10, 109, 114; social movements in context of, 10, 19; La Violencia and, 9. *See also* guerrilla groups; leftist politics/movements; paramilitarism; paramilitary groups; *and specific groups*

leftist politics/movements: armed conflict and, 114; armed conflict in Barranca and, 3; in Barranca, 3, 42, 45–46, 110, 114; La Comuna de Barranca and, 42, 45–46, 110; Coordinadora Popular de Barrancabermeja and, 98; disappeared and, 212n4; factions in, 113; history of, 28; human rights and, 206; Liberals and, 67; local administration and, 67–68, 227n78; in Magdalena Medio, 62; oil workers/industry and, 37–42, 221n113; paramilitarism and, 90, 164, 183; political violence against, 93, 164; rural violence and, 90; social activism and, 71–72. *See also* leftist guerrillas

legal approach, 16

legal system (judicial system). *See* judicial system (legal system)

Letelier-Moffitt Human Rights Award, 165, 248n68

Liberals/Liberal Party: ANUC and, 61; Coordinadora Popular de Barrancabermeja and, 98; ELN and, 63–64; guerrilla groups and, 46; leftist politics and, 67; local administration and, 67–68, 112; military rulers and, 79; oil worker's rights support from, 39; paramilitarism and, 183; *paros cívicos* and, 4; Thousand Days War veterans and, 26, 37, 41–42; USO and, 37, 40–41; La Violencia and, 47–48; youth movement and, 110. *See also* National Front

liberation theology, 60, 64, 88, 200

Llana Caliente massacre, 131, 141–143

Lleras Camargo, Alberto, 51, 236n61

Lleras Restrepo, Alberto, 61

local administration: activists in, 4, 7, 98, 108, 112, 117–119, 125, 164, 166, 188, 239n32, 240n40, 253n48; Communism and, 68, 116, 185; dirty war and, 144; extortion and, 183; guerrilla groups and, 149; history and influence of, 66–68, 227n75, 230n139; human rights and, 144; leftist politics and, 67–68, 227n78; Liberals and, 67–68, 112; military rulers and, 46–47, 78–80; paramilitarism and, 183; *paros cívicos* participation and, 55; political violence against activists in, 108, 117–119, 125, 164, 166, 239n32, 240n40; public order and, 80, 86, 99

local approach (front-line activists), 16–17, 19, 205–206, 208–209

local organizations, 18, 158–162, 185, 192, 196. *See also* civic-popular movement; international (transnational) organizations; national organizations; *and specific organizations*

López Michelsen, Alfonso, 62, 76–78, 80

López Pumarejo, Alfonso, 62

¡A Luchar!, 10, 115, 193

Madero, Régulo, 108, 174, 184, 186, 190, 194, 196

Magdalena Medio: armed conflict and, 26, 88–90; *bolcheviques* uprising in, 41, 62; Catholic Church in, 22, 59–61; civic-popular movement repression in, 8; Colombian armed forces in, 33, 92–94, 103, 147–148, 234n50, 235n61; colonial history of, 22–24; El Comité Permanente por la Defensa de los Derechos Humanos and, 85, 232n13; Communism in, 62–63, 87, 91, 93; counterinsurgency operations in, 72–74, 88, 92, 234n50; CREDHOS in, 181, 185; description and map of, xi, 12, *13*; disappeared in, 88, 103, 155, 235n67; drug traffickers in, 90–91; ELN in, 53, 62–63, 114; export of products from, 24–30, 218n40; FARC in, 64, 90–91, 251n22; fishermen and, 61, 68, 82, 101, 168–169; homicides in, 94–95; human rights activism and, 84–88, 93, 95, 158–162, 185, 195, 204–205, 232n13; human rights officials as targets in, 147–148, 154–158, 204, 235n67, 244nn2–3, 246nn32–33, 246n38; indigenous populations in, 22, 25–27, 175; inequalities in, 168; international support in, xv; labor movement in,

37–38; land rights and, 26–27, 29; leftist guerrillas in, 9, 62, 91; leftist politics in, 62; Liberals in, 26; local administration as weak in, 22; national government presence in, 24–27, 29–31, 217n21; National Police in, 33, 179; natural resources of, 24, 29, 137, 148; oil industry development in, 29–31, 218n54; paramilitarism in, 8, 12, 82, 87–95, 140–141, 147–148, 153–154, 163, 200–201, 231n2, 233n27, 235n61; political authority in, 25–26; political conflicts in, 26–27; political economy in, xi, 61, 98; political jurisdictions in, 25, 217n25; political violence in, 19, 91–93, 116, 168; population diversity in, 28; population statistics for, xi; private foreign-controlled development and, 24–32, 218n40; public services in, 168–169; radical politics and, 9, 26; regional approach and, 25, 59–60, 141, 198, 254n11; La Rochela massacre in, 147–148, 154–158, 235n67, 244nn2–3, 246nn32–33, 246n38; rural violence in, 131, 141–143; social conflicts in, 26–27; Vuelta Acuña massacre in, 82–83, 101–103. *See also* oil workers and industry; peasants (*campesinos*)

Magdalena River, 22, 23, 30, 216n10

Mahecha, Raúl Eduardo, 37–40, 63, 221n103

Mantilla, Ricardo, 69, 71

Marín, Evangelina, 168, 186

MAS (Muerte a Secuestradores; Death to Kidnappers), 12, 87, 90–92, 116–117, 124–125, 139–140, 154, 156, 233n23

May 16, 1998, massacre, xv, 178–181, 184, 251n23

May Day celebrations, 99, 119–120

Medellín, 39, 60–61, 72, 91, 101, 111, 163, 192

Medellín Cartel, 89–90

Medina Gallego, Carlos, 91

Mejía, Mario Jaimes "El Panadero," xvi, 239n24

memorials/memories, and human rights activism, xix, 15–16, 157, 175–176, 186–189, 214n35, 253n43

methodology and research, xiv–xvi, 16–18, 21–22, 176–177

migrant population: in Barranca, 5, 21–22, 33, 41, 65, 247n57; land invasions and, 83–84; in oil industry, 21–22, 27, 33, 41

military tribunal (*concejo verbal de guerra*), 46, 63, 70–73, 229n103, 229n106, 229nn108–109

Millán, Fernando, xiv

M-19 (Movimiento 19 de Abril; April 19 Movement), 90, 92, 111, 113, 130, 244n2

Montaña Cuellar, Diego, 59

Movimiento Nacional de Víctimas de Crímenes de Estado (National Movement of Victims of State Crimes), 186–187, 253n43

Movimiento Revolucionario Liberal (MRL; Liberal Revolutionary Movement), 62, 197

MRL (Movimiento Revolucionario Liberal; Liberal Revolutionary Movement), 62, 197

Muerte a Secuestradores (MAS; Death to Kidnappers), 12, 87, 90–92, 116–117, 124–125, 139–140, 154, 156, 233n23

National Front: civil rights suppression by, 51; description of, 48, 51; inequalities and, 54–55; oil workers and, 8, 51, 58–59, 226n36; partisan politics suppression by, 51, 54, 58–59, 226n36; peasant activism and, 61; political economy and, 54–55; social movements and, 8; strikes ban under, 51–52; two-party rule and, 8; USO ban under, 59

national government: activists as elected officials in, 117, 239n32; Barranca's relations with, 8, 19, 22, 34, 37, 152; decrees and orders from, 79–80, 84–85, 96–97, 106–107, 129, 164; homicide statistics and, 106; human rights protection and, 11, 19, 83, 93, 129–130, 146, 152, 202–203, 207, 256n35; human rights violations and, 11, 84, 130, 157; international reports on, 85–86; May 16, 1998, massacre and, 184; National Peace Commission and, 89, 93, 181; National Security Statute and, 80, 84–85, 96–97, 106–107, 129; Office of the Inspector General and, 92, 147, 152,

155, 179, 202, 246n33; oil workers' rights protection by, 28, 38, 45; paramilitarism reports by, 92–93, 124–125; paramilitarism's link with, 11, 12, 14, 147–148, 163, 214n28; paramilitary groups' demobilization and, xvi, 12, 129, 130, 172, 174–175, 186–187, 250n102, 251n23; peace negotiations with, 92–93, 101, 111, 130, 245n8; private foreign-controlled industry protection by, 29–32, 38–39, 41, 219n61; public meetings participation by, 148; public order in context of protests against, 54; radical politics versus, 8; social activism repression by, 10, 42, 47, 54; social justice and, 84, 89; social memory of human rights activism and, 15, 157, 186–187; student activism opposition and, 50; unions and, 47–48, 57, 61, 68, 81, 107, 166; Vuelta Acuña massacre commission and, 83, 102–103. *See also* counterinsurgency operations; National Front; state of siege (*estado de sitio*)

nationalism, 28, 31, 37–38, 42

National Movement of Victims of State Crimes (Movimiento Nacional de Víctimas de Crímenes de Estado), 186–187, 253n43

national organizations, 18, 84, 158–162. *See also* international (transnational) organizations; local organizations; *and specific organizations*

National Police: in Barranca, 33, 47, 114, 144, 190; as CREDHOS bodyguards, 161; garrisons for, 33–34; in Magdalena Medio, 33, 179; May 16, 1998, massacre and, 179–180; paramilitarism's link with, 130; private business development in oil industry and, 33–34; U.S. funds and, 172. *See also* Colombian armed forces

National Reparation and Reconciliation Commission (Comisión Nacional de Reparación y Reconciliación), 15, 157, 186

national security forces. *See* Colombian armed forces

Navarro Velásquez, Camilo, 155

Nevado, Jaime, 92

NGOs (nongovernmental organizations): demobilized paramilitary groups and, 175; history of, 72; homicide statistics and, 213n15; human rights activism in context of national, 17, 84–85, 129–130; human rights activists' reorganization and, 191–192; national government interactions with, 102–103, 129–130, 148. *See also* international (transnational) organizations; national organizations; *and specific NGOs*

OAS (Organization of American States), 17, 84, 155, 165–166, 169, 233n18. *See also* Inter-American Commission on Human Rights; Inter-American Court of Human Rights

OFP (Organización Femenina Popular; Popular Women's Organization): *capacidad de convocatoria* or "power to convene" and, 191; coalitions and, 145–146; Espacio and, 186, 253n40; history of, 75, 170, 184; human rights activism and, 7, 15, 161; paramilitarism and, 191–192, 196; *paro cívico por el agua* and, 75; political violence protests and, 191; youth movement and, 191

oil workers and industry: armed conflict and, 41, 48, 181–182, 222n129; challenges for, 28, 30; class segregation and, 34–36; coalitions and, 134, 139; collective bargaining with, 6, 38, 199, 207; Colombian armed forces in, 33, 38–40, 70; Communism and, 41–42; conflicts between, 28, 35–36; Conservatives' support of workers' rights and, 39; el Cristo Petrolero and, xi, *xiii*; death threats and, 229n103; De Mares Concession and, 28–30, 42–43, 47, 49, 54; drilling rights and, 51; ethnicity and, 36; foreign-controlled development of, 22; history of, 29, 196–199; homicides and, 138, 140, 170, 229n103; housing for, 65; inequalities and, 32–34, 36; infrastructure for, 29–30, 149; International Petroleum and, 30, 47; kidnappings and, 51, 57, 70–71, 149; labor force for, 33, 220n78; land rights and, 29; leftist politics

and, 37–42, 221n113; Liberals and, 40–42; Liberals' support of workers' rights and, 39; lived experiences for workers and, 32–35; living and working conditions for, 36, 38, 40, 65; migrant population and, 21–22, 33, 41; military trial for strikers and, 70–72, 229n103, 229n106; National Front and, 8, 51, 58–59, 226n36; national government's protection of private foreign-controlled industry and, 29–32, 38–39, 41, 48, 219n61; national government's protection of workers' rights and, 28, 38, 45; nationalism and, 28, 31, 37, 42; nationalization of, 43, 45, 47–48, 51; National Police security and, 33–34; oil production and, 30, 43, 56–57, 69, 218n50, 223n136; *paro cívico por la vida* and, 7; political jurisdictions and, 34; population of, 32, 33, 220n78; private foreign-controlled development and, 28–32, 29–32, 38–39, 41, 48, 218n42, 219n61; radical politics and, 9, 41–42, 51, 59; royalties and, 21–22, 39, 219n67; social activism and, 42, 207; social exclusion and, 34, 36; La Troco conflicts with, 28, 35–36; La Violencia and, 9, 47–48; women domestic workers protests and, 43–44. *See also* Barrancabermeja (Barranca); USO (Unión Sindical Obrera, or Unión Obrera; United Workers Union); *and specific oil companies*

Operación Anorí, 73, 110–111, 113

Oquist, Paul, 47

Organización Femenina Popular (OFP; Popular Women's Organization). *See* OFP (Organización Femenina Popular; Popular Women's Organization)

Organization of American States (OAS), 17, 84, 155, 165–166, 169, 233n18. *See also* Inter-American Commission on Human Rights; Inter-American Court of Human Rights

Ospina Pérez, Mariano, 45

paramilitarism: in Barranca, xv–xvi, 14, 138–140, 142, 152–153, 163–164, 175–177, 181–183, 189–191, 239n24; Catholic Church paramilitarism (*continued*)

and, 124–125, 240n47, 241n57; Colombian armed forces' link with, xv, 11–12, 14, 92–93, 130, 147–148, 151, 153–158, 164–167, 204, 234n50, 235n61, 235n67, 244nn2–3, 246nn32–33, 246n38, 248n66; counterinsurgency operations and, 12, 14; death threats and, 12, 130, 229n117, 253n48; definition of, 11–12, 153, 246n30; disappeared and, 103, 142, 177, 191, 212n4; elected officials and, 183; extortion and, 182–183; homicides and, 139–140, 213n15; human rights activism and, 11, 87–88, 147–148, 154–158, 183, 204, 235n67, 244nn2–3, 246nn32–33, 246n38, 252n31; human rights violations and, 11–12, 87, 120, 130, 175, 202; leftist politics and, 90, 164, 183; in Magdalena Medio, 8, 12, 82, 87–95, 140–141, 147–148, 153–154, 163, 200–201, 231n2, 233n27, 235n61; national government reports on, 92–93, 124–125; national government's link with, 11–12, 14, 130, 163, 214n28; National Police's link with, 130; peasants and, 11, 89, 92, 140–141; against popular leaders, 138–140; rural violence and, 8, 88–95, 155; scholarship on, 153; social activism and, 12, 14, 124, 183, 190, 252n31; unions and, 91, 166; UP and, 117–118, 125; La Violencia and, 12, 231n2; Vuelta Acuña massacre and, 82–83, 101–103

paramilitary groups: allegations against leftist guerrillas, 156–157; civic-popular movement repression by, 8; contraband and, 129, 175, 183; counterinsurgency operations and, 14; as death squads, 11–12, 89, 116–117, 172, 174–175; definition of, 11–12, 153, 246n30; drug traffickers and, 12, 14, 90, 175, 183; extortion and, 183; FARC allegations and, 156–157; FARC and, 251n22; informants for, 177–178, 189; leftist guerrillas armed conflict with, 177, 179, 181–183, 189–191, 246n30; local administration and, 183; May 16, 1998, massacre and, 181, 251n23; national government's clemency for, xvi, 129, 174–175, 186–187, 251n23; national government's

demobilization of, xvi, 12, 129, 130, 172, 174–175, 186–187, 250n102, 251n23; provincial/rural elites and, 14; state of siege and, 11; during La Violencia, 12, 174–175, 231n2, 250n3. *See also specific paramilitary groups*

Pardo Leal, Jaime, 125

paros cívicos (citizen-led general strikes): Catholic Church and, 66; coalitions and, 55, 66, 75; Colombian armed forces and, 98–100, 237n93; *comité de paro* and, 6, 95–97, 121; Communism and, 117–118; Coordinadora Popular de Barrancabermeja and, 96–101, 111–112; CREDHOS and, 141; during dirty war, 3–7, 10, 109, 121–126, 131, 141–142; history and description of, 5–7, 52–53, 122, 170–171, 193, 199; local elected officials' participation in, 55; May Day celebrations and, 99, 119–120; national government and, 79–80; oil workers' strike solidarity and, 80; *paro cívico nacional* and, 53, 78–80; *paro cívico por el agua* and, 75–77; *paro cívico por la vida* and, 3–4, 6–7, 121–123; *paro del nororiente* and, 7, 123–124, 131, 141–142; *paros armados* and, 125–126, 170–171, 190; political violence protests and, 122, 165–167, 169–170, 178–179, 184, 191; public services and, 53–56, 97–100; radical politics and, 120; state of siege during, 11, 55; statistics on, 4; unions and, 4, 55, 80, 98; UP and, 117–118, 117–119; USO and, 141; water supply and, 53, 55–56, 75–76, 99–100. *See also* civic-popular movement

Partido Comunista de Colombia (PCC; Communist Party of Colombia). *See* PCC (Partido Comunista de Colombia; Communist Party of Colombia)

Partido Socialista Revolucionario (PSR; Socialist Revolutionary Party), 37, 59

Pastoral Social: civic-popular movements and, 63, 65–66, 68, 170; coalitions and, 96; Coordinadora Popular de Barrancabermeja and, 97; CREDHOS and, 134; death threats and, 124, 170; Espacio and, 186, 253n40; exile of leaders in, 170;

FARC and, 63; guerrilla groups in context of autonomy of urban, 10, 109, 114; history of, xvi, 5, 10–11, 42; human rights' link with, 5, 10–11, 15, 17–19, 85, 103, 120, 160, 193–194, 203–205; inequalities link with political violence in urban, 18, 200–201; international reports and, 85–86; labor rights and, 10; leftist guerrillas and, 19; leftist politics and, 71–72; local administration participation and, 68; local elected officials' participation in, 4, 7, 108, 117, 166; National Front and, 8; national government repression of, 10, 42, 47, 54; oil workers and, 42, 207; paramilitarism and, 12, 14, 124, 183, 190, 252n31; *paro cívico* and, 5; political economy and, 5; political violence and, 6, 11, 14, 18, 102, 200–201; politics and, 51, 54, 71–72, 144; public meetings participation by, 148; regional approach and, 25, 52, 59–60, 198, 254n11; Rondón's murder response from, 3–4, 6; rural versus urban, 199–200; rural violence and, 83–84; scholarship on, 15, 214n30; social justice and, 5, 10, 14; urban, 5, 83–84, 131, 199–201; USO and, 69, 71, 170; Vuelta Acuña massacre and, 82–83. *See also* civic-popular movement

social exclusion: in Barranca, 95; lived experiences of, 14; oil industry and, 34, 36; Tropical Oil Company and, 34, 36

social-historical approach, 16–17

social justice: civic-popular movement and, 10, 14, 195–196; CREDHOS and, 185, 187; human rights in context of, 129, 185, 187–189, 203; national government and, 84, 89; peasants and, 89; political violence in context of, 148; social activism and, 5, 10, 14; USO and, 28, 69

social memory of human rights activism, xix, 15–16, 157, 175–176, 186–189, 192–193, 214n35, 253n43

Solano Sepúlveda, José, 62

Solón Wilches, José Pacífico, 25

Space of Magdalena Medio Human Rights Workers (Espacio; Espacio de Trabajadores y Trabajadoras de Derechos

Humanos del Magdalena Medio), 186, 253n40

Standard Oil of New Jersey (Jersey Standard), 28–32, 39–40, 47, 219n60, 219n61. *See also* Tropical Oil Company (La Troco)

state of siege (*estado de sitio*): paramilitary groups and, 11; during *paros cívicos*, 11; as permanent, 86; student strikes and, 50, 63–64, 77, 100, 224n4, 236n87; as term of use, 222n118; USO strikes and, 8, 11, 40, 79

state security forces. *See* Colombian armed forces

student activism, 50, 63–64, 77, 93, 100, 134, 224n4, 236n87. *See also* youth movements

Tate, Winifred, 10, 16–17, 149–150, 173, 191, 206

Taussig, Michael, 176

Tavera Sosa, René, 167

Texas Petroleum Company, 31, 57, 61

Thousand Days War, 22, 26, 28, 38, 41, 58, 198

Tirado Mejía, Álvaro, 129

Tolosa Pontón, Ángel, 89, 103, 131, 159, 187–188

Torres Giraldo, Ignacio, 39–40

Torres Restrepo, Camilo, 64–65, 68, 74, 122, 176, 227n78, 238n13, 240n47

trade unions (unions): coalitions and, xiv, 17, 63–64, 100, 103, 134, 186; counterinsurgency operations and, 72; history of, 8, 37–38, 42; homicides and, 195–196; human rights activism and, 15, 123, 134, 158; international support for, 160; leaders and activists in, 75, 81, 123, 126, 132–133, 136, 168; leftist politics and, 37–42, 221n113; national government and, 47–48, 57, 61, 68, 81, 107, 166; paramilitarism and, 91, 166; *paros cívicos* and, 4, 55, 80, 98; public services demands and, 100. *See also specific unions*

Tribunal Especial de Instrucción, 122–123

Tribunal Superior de Orden Público, 157

Trillos Novoa, Jaime, 70

La Troco (Tropical Oil Company). *See* Tropical Oil Company (La Troco)

Tropical Oil Company (La Troco): armed conflict and, 41, 48, 222n129; challenges for, 28, 30; collective bargaining with, 38, 199; Colombian armed forces security for, 38; De Mares Concession and, 28–30, 42–43, 47, 49, 54; history of, 29; inequalities and, 32–34; infrastructure for, 29–30; International Petroleum and, 30, 47; lived experiences for oil workers and, 32–35; living and working conditions protests against, 36, 38, 40; national government's protection of private foreign-controlled industry and, 29–32, 38–39, 41, 48, 219n61; national government's protection of worker's rights and, 28, 38, 45; nationalization of, 43, 45, 47–48; oil production and, 30, 43, 218n50, 223n136; oil workers' conflicts with, 28, 35–36; political jurisdictions and, 34; royalties from, 21–22, 39, 219n67; social exclusion and, 34, 36; women domestic workers protests and, 43–44; worker population for, 21–22, 27, 32, 33, 220n78. *See also* Standard Oil of New Jersey (Jersey Standard)

Tulio Torres, Marco, 185

Turbay Ayala, Julio César, 80, 85–86, 106–107, 129

UIS (Universidad Industrial de Santander; Industrial University of Santander), 63–65, 110, 227nn65–66

Umaña Luna, Eduardo, 122–123

Union Patriótica (UP; Patriotic Union). *See* UP (Union Patriótica; Patriotic Union)

unions (trade unions). *See* trade unions (unions)

Unión Sindical Obrera (USO; United Workers Union, or Unión Obrera). *See* oil workers and industry; USO (Unión Sindical Obrera, or Unión Obrera; United Workers Union)

United Nations (UN), 18, 84, 158–159, 205

UN Human Rights Commission, 85, 150–151

United States: Colombian armed forces funds and, xv, 151, 166, 172, 193, 211n5; guerrilla groups' conflation with drug traffickers by, 146, 151; homicide protests from, 166; human rights hearings in, 166, 248n74; imperialism and, 31, 219n61; Plan Colombia and, xv, 193, 211n5; UIS funding from, 227n66; War on Drugs sponsored by, 14, 146, 151

United States Agency for International Development (USAID), 54

Universidad Industrial de Santander (UIS; Industrial University of Santander), 63–65, 110, 227nn65–66

UP (Union Patriótica; Patriotic Union): coalitions and, 113; death threats and, 107; disappeared and, 117; elected officials and, 108, 117–119, 125, 164, 166, 239n32, 240n40; FAM and, 113; homicides and, 93, 125, 132, 144–145, 154, 164, 166, 188, 235n60; leftist politics and, 113; paramilitarism and, 117–118, 125; *paros cívicos* and, 117–119; student activism and, 93

urban activism, 5, 83–84, 131, 199–201. *See also* human rights activism; social activism/movements

urban elites, 16, 45–47, 50

urban land invasions, 5, 68, 77, 83–84, 132–133, 200

Uribe, María Elisa, 138–139

Uribe Vélez, Álvaro, 174, 183, 186, 214n28, 237n97

USAID (United States Agency for International Development), 54

USO (Unión Sindical Obrera, or Unión Obrera; United Workers Union): ban of, 59; collective agreements with, 57–59, 69, 79, 100; collective bargaining rights of, 6, 38, 57, 199, 207; Colombian armed forces security and, 38–40, 70; Communism and, 37, 57, 59; Conservatives and, 71; Coordinadora de Solidaridad and, 95–96; Coordinadora Popular de Barrancabermeja and, 97–98; CREDHOS and, 136; CSPP and, 69, 72, 78, 85; CSTC and, 59, 197; death threats and, 139, 180; Espacio and, 186, 253n40; history of, 38; homicides and, 138, 140, 170; human rights and, 7, 15, 18, 28, 153, 161; leaders and members of, 138, 140, 170, 171; leftist

Critical Human Rights

The Politics of Necessity: Community Organizing and Democracy in South Africa
Elke Zuern

www.ingramcontent.com/pod-product-compliance
Lightning Source LLC
Chambersburg PA
CBHW030639270326
41929CB00007B/137